Reading Homer

Reading Homer presents two highlights of the *Iliad*: Book 16, where Patroclus fights and dies, and Book 18, where Achilles grieves for him and is awarded new armour before he returns to battle. It enables students who have been learning Greek for perhaps a year to approach Homer for the first time, and to have the satisfaction of reading two whole books in the original language. Full and detailed help is given with vocabulary, accidence and syntax. Homeric forms are introduced and set alongside Attic ones, enabling students to consolidate their existing knowledge at the same time as extending it. The Introduction and notes enable students to see these two books in the context of the whole epic, and the epic itself in the context of early Greek society. They also encourage students to consider why the Greeks themselves regarded Homer as the master poet.

Stephen Anderson is a Lecturer in Classics at New College Oxford, having formerly been Head of Classics at Winchester College. He is the co-author of *Greek Unseen Translation* (2005) and *Writing Greek* (2010).

Keith Maclennan was Head of Classics at Rugby School. He published editions of Virgil's *Aeneid* Books 1, 4, 6 and 8 (2003–10), and co-authored another of Plautus' *Aulularia* (2016).

Naoko Yamagata is Senior Lecturer in Classical Studies at the Open University. She is the author of *Homeric Morality* (1994).

THE JOINT ASSOCIATION OF
CLASSICAL TEACHERS' GREEK COURSE

Reading Homer

Iliad Books 16 and 18

Stephen Anderson
Keith Maclennan
Naoko Yamagata

GENERAL EDITOR
John Taylor

CAMBRIDGE
UNIVERSITY PRESS

Shaftesbury Road, Cambridge CB2 8BS, United Kingdom

One Liberty Plaza, 20th Floor, New York, NY 10006, USA

477 Williamstown Road, Port Melbourne, VIC 3207, Australia

314–321, 3rd Floor, Plot 3, Splendor Forum, Jasola District Centre, New Delhi – 110025, India

103 Penang Road, #05–06/07, Visioncrest Commercial, Singapore 238467

Cambridge University Press is part of Cambridge University Press & Assessment, a department of the University of Cambridge.

We share the University's mission to contribute to society through the pursuit of education, learning and research at the highest international levels of excellence.

www.cambridge.org
Information on this title: www.cambridge.org/highereducation/isbn/9781107000933
DOI: 10.1017/9781139051545

First published 2023

Printed in the United Kingdom by TJ Books Limited, Padstow Cornwall

A catalogue record for this publication is available from the British Library.

ISBN 978-1-107-00093-3 Hardback
ISBN 978-0-521-17088-8 Paperback

In memoriam
WIKM et JHWM

Contents

Illustrations

Preface

Reading Homer presents two books of the *Iliad*, both high points in its story: 16 (the death of Patroclus) and 18 (the grief of Achilles and the award to him of new armour). The Introduction provides an account of the whole poem and its background. The Greek (Oxford text) is accompanied by full vocabulary, with notes on grammar and content. *Reading Homer* forms part of the JACT/Cambridge University Press *Reading Greek* series, but is designed to be accessible to those who have completed any beginners' course in Greek and are approaching Homer for the first time. Peter Jones, the original editor of the *Reading Greek* series, commissioned the book and has given valuable support and encouragement throughout. Naoko Yamagata (Senior Lecturer in Classical Studies at the Open University) produced first drafts of everything. Stephen Anderson (Lecturer in Classics at New College, Oxford) then worked on Book 16 and the Vocabulary, and the late Keith Maclennan (formerly Head of Classics at Rugby School) on Book 18 and the Introduction. John Taylor (one of the current series editors) is responsible for the final editing. He wishes to thank Edward Kendrick for working through the text and making valuable comments from a student's viewpoint. Thanks are also due to Michael Sharp and his colleagues at Cambridge University Press for their help and patience, and to Jane Burkowski for eagle-eyed copy-editing. The book is dedicated to the memory of Keith and of James Morwood: good friends, and good friends of Greek.

Abbreviations

abs.	absolute		m.	masculine
acc.	accusative		mid.	middle
act.	active		n.	neuter
adj.	adjective		nom.	nominative
adv.	adverb		oft.	often
aor.	aorist		opt.	optative
Att.	Attic		part.	participle
cf.	compare (Latin *confer*)		pass.	passive
comp.	comparative		perf.	perfect
conj.	conjunction		pl.	plural
dat.	dative		plup.	pluperfect
decl.	declension		prep.	preposition
f.	feminine		pres.	present
fut.	future		pron.	pronoun
gen.	genitive		rel.	relative
imper.	imperative		resp.	respect
impf.	imperfect		s.	singular
indec.	indeclinable		subj.	subjunctive
indic.	indicative		sup.	superlative
inf.	infinitive		tr.	translate(d), translation
intrans.	intransitive		trans.	transitive
irreg.	irregular		usu.	usually
lit.	literally		voc.	vocative

Notes for the Reader

The running vocabularies use the following conventions:

All words are glossed at first occurrence within each book (so readers can start with either), and can also be checked in the alphabetical Vocabulary.

A bracketed letter indicates an alternative spelling or a final vowel elided in the text.

Additional endings preceded by a hyphen replace the last syllable of the headword.

Nouns are given with nominative and genitive, and the definite article to indicate gender, e.g. κρήνη -ης, ἡ.

Adjectives are given with masculine, feminine (if different from masculine) and neuter, e.g. θερμός -ή -όν; adjectives whose masculine and neuter are third declension also have in brackets the genitive singular for those forms to show the stem, e.g. δακρυόεις -εσσα -εν (-εντος); adjectives with only one (masculine and/or feminine) nominative singular form are given with that and the genitive, e.g. γλαυκῶπις -ιδος (f. adj.).

Verbs are normally given in the first-person singular at first occurrence; forms likely to cause difficulty are thereafter quoted as in the text, with explanation and cross reference, e.g. βέβληται: 3 s. perf. pass. of βάλλω (cf. 24).

A default system operates, i.e. a verb is indicative and active unless otherwise specified.

Help with the identification of forms generally is given more fully in the early part of each book.

A colon after the headword indicates that an explanation rather than a translation immediately follows.

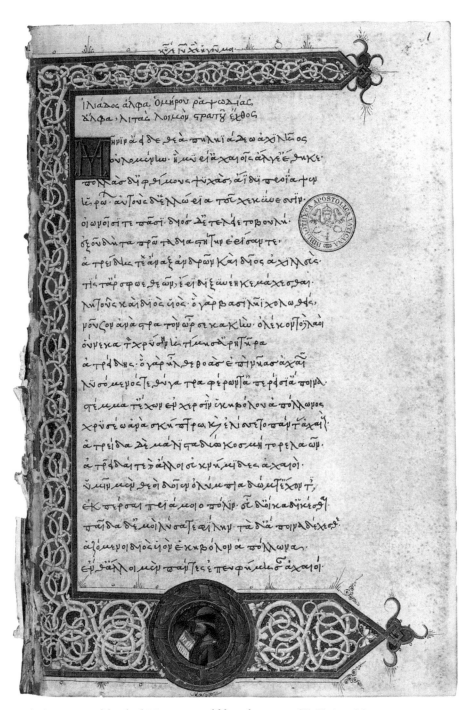

1 The beginning of the *Iliad*. Manuscript of fifteenth century CE. Vatican Museum.

Introduction

A.   Homer and the *Iliad*

The *Iliad* and *Odyssey* are the oldest works of European literature. Both were attributed by later Greeks to the poet Homer. But even for Greeks of the classical period Homer was a figure of legend. The historian Herodotus, who lived in the fifth century BCE, believed that Homer had lived 'no more than 400 years' before him (Herodotus 2.53), but there was general agreement that Homer's epics were composed earlier than any other surviving Greek poetry. However, we can say nothing for certain about Homer as a person. He does not mention himself in his poems, and there is no reference to any contemporary event. We cannot be sure that the *Iliad* and the *Odyssey* are works of the same poet. There are grounds for an argument that they are not, though the author of the *Odyssey* was evidently familiar with the *Iliad*. All we know for certain is that most later Greeks attributed both *Iliad* and *Odyssey* to a single individual whom they named 'Homer', along with a substantial collection of poems dedicated to individual gods (the *Homeric Hymns*, most of which are now thought to be later in date than the two epics).

We know that other epic poems were produced in the pre-classical era, though none survive except in small fragments, or as summaries or allusions preserved by later authors. Some of them were occasionally also attributed to Homer. There were epics dealing with the antecedents of the Trojan War, its course before the period covered by the *Iliad*, subsequent events leading up to the end of the war, the capture of Troy, and the later experiences of those who fought there. Still others dealt with mythological subjects not directly connected with Troy, such as the Theban legend. References within the *Iliad* and *Odyssey* show awareness of other legendary narratives. The conventional name for this whole cluster of lost poems is the 'Epic Cycle'.

'Iliad' means 'Troy-story', from 'Ilios' (more familiar as the latinised 'Ilium'), an alternative name for the city. Greek mythology locates Troy on the Asian side of the Dardanelles ('Hellespont'). During the reign of its king, Priam, a Greek army attacked Troy, and eventually captured the city after a siege of ten years. ('Greek' is a word coined many centuries after this legendary time; Homer variously describes these people as 'Achaeans', 'Argives' or 'Danaans'.) The war arose because Priam's son Paris offended Menelaus, King of Sparta, by carrying off his wife Helen. Menelaus appealed to his brother Agamemnon, the most powerful of the Achaean chieftains; Agamemnon raised an army that combined forces provided by other rulers who accepted his authority. The greatest of them was Achilles, son of Peleus king of Phthia in northern Greece. Achilles became most passionately engaged in the war when his companion Patroclus was killed by the Trojan hero Hector. In fury Achilles killed Hector. His own death followed shortly afterwards, but so did the capture of Troy.

The *Iliad* covers fifty days in the final year of the war, stopping short of these two last events. Most of the poem concentrates on the few days leading up to the death of Patroclus in Book 16, which is the turning point of the whole epic. In *Reading Homer* we concentrate on that and on the reaction of Achilles (Book 18), which sets in train the tragic sequel. The poem ends with Hector's funeral.

For Homer, the war took place in a distant but unspecified past. ('Distant' partly because the poet regularly speaks of men as being bigger and stronger in those days.) Many elements of this past time are consistent with what we know of the Greek lands in the late Bronze Age towards the end of the second millennium BCE. The traditional date of 1184 BCE calculated by ancient scholars for the Fall of Troy may not be wide of the mark. Homer's centres of 'political' importance are Mycenae, Sparta, Pylos, Argos, Crete. Archaeology has shown that there were flourishing palace-based societies at all these places in this period. Conversely, little attention is given in the epics to places such as Athens and Delphi which did not become important until the eighth century. Bronze (rather than iron) is the material still almost exclusively used for weapons and armour. Many of the artefacts referred to in Homer can be shown to have a Bronze Age origin. The names of several of the gods are found on clay tablets written in Linear B (an early form of Greek) from Bronze Age sites. In 1870 Heinrich Schliemann excavated a Bronze Age city on the shore of the Dardanelles whose location was consistent with Homeric Troy. It had been damaged and rebuilt several times, suggesting there were indeed Trojan wars, probably fought over access to the Black Sea for trade. The search for history in Homer is endlessly fascinating, but of limited help in evaluating the *Iliad* as literature.

Ignorance about the author and his times focuses attention on the work. What matters most about the *Iliad* is that it is a great story, a story of war and heroes: glory, futility, triumph, defeat, suffering, love, friendship. Its principal theme is anger, and 'anger' is the first word: μῆνιν ἄειδε, θεά ... 'Anger, goddess, sing to me of it ...'. It is the anger of Achilles, which, over the course of fifteen books, brings disaster to the Achaeans, then to Achilles himself, and finally to Priam and his city, whose fall is imminent at the end of the poem.

B.   The story of the *Iliad*

The *Iliad* begins towards the end of the tenth and last year of the Trojan War. Agamemnon, leader of the Achaeans, has received as a war-prize the daughter of a priest of Apollo. Her father offers to ransom her. Agamemnon, against the universal will of the Achaeans, rejects him and insults him too. Apollo now sends a plague on the Achaeans. The prophet Calchas is aware of the reason for this and is encouraged by Achilles to say so in public 'even if you mention Agamemnon, who now claims to be far the best of the Achaeans' (1.90–1). Agamemnon, enraged, blames Achilles. He will concede in sending the girl back to her father, but he will take Achilles' prize-girl in compensation. Achilles bows to Agamemnon's authority and allows him to take his girl, but from now on will take no part in the fighting.

The conflict is between Agamemnon's power, military and political, and that of Achilles, physical and charismatic. It is also a conflict between generations, the older man with superior authority and the younger man who bears the brunt of the actual fighting. At the same time, it is not merely a quarrel at the human level. Achilles enlists the help of his mother, the sea-goddess Thetis. She goes on his behalf to Olympus and secures from Zeus a promise to support the Trojans until Agamemnon shows Achilles due respect.

Achilles now withdraws from the fighting. For seven books the theme of his anger remains in the background. On the one hand this long delay provides for the painfully slow working out of Zeus's promise. On the other it allows the poet to develop the second, unstated, theme of the poem. The *Iliad* is not only the story of Achilles' anger. It is the story of the whole ten-year Trojan War, compressed into the poem's time span of a few weeks. Book 2 lists the forces available to each side. In Book 3 we are presented with the two individuals whose dispute has involved all these forces. Paris, prince of Troy, has seduced Helen, wife of Menelaus, king of Sparta and brother of Agamemnon. A truce is declared while Paris and Menelaus fight a duel, with Helen as prize for the winner. The arrangement is implausible in the tenth year of fighting, but it serves as a convincing, compressed re-enactment of the start of the war. The duel is aborted when Aphrodite intervenes on behalf of her favourite, Paris, thus focusing our attention on the two characters most responsible for the conflict, one divine, the other human (see Section C (vii) below).

For the purposes of the *Iliad*, then, the war proper starts at the beginning of Book 4. Already in Book 3 the process has begun whereby we are gradually and with great care and variety introduced to the principal characters, both on the Trojan and on the Achaean side. Books 4–6 make it clear that the Achaeans are superior fighters: in particular the absence of Achilles is compensated by the presence of Diomedes, who dominates the battles throughout Book 5 and for much of 6, even wounding two gods supporting the Trojans, Aphrodite and Ares. (This sort of triumphant progress by a hero is given the name *aristeia*.) Achaean success provides the opportunity for an interlude inside the Trojan walls. Hector leaves the fighting in order to get his mother to make an (unsuccessful) offering to Athena and win her over; while in the city he has his famous, and last, conversation with his wife Andromache.

In Books 7 and 8, Zeus's promise to Thetis begins to be fulfilled. Limited Trojan success in 7 prompts the Achaeans to build a defensive wall and ditch around their camp. In 8 they are driven back to the ships, and the book concludes with the Trojans camped outside the Greek fortifications, their fires in the darkness like the stars of heaven. Now (Book 9) there is an appeal to Achilles: 'Come back to the fight and save us.' It comes not directly from Agamemnon but from Odysseus, the arch-persuader, Phoenix, an old member of Achilles' household, and Ajax, the greatest of the Achaeans after Achilles himself. Totally resistant at first, Achilles concludes by declaring that he will not return to the fight until the Trojan attack reaches his own ships.

Book 10 is a night-time interlude. Odysseus and Diomedes undertake a spying mission into the Trojan camp; in the dark they encounter a Trojan spy on a corresponding errand. He reveals the location of the newly arrived Thracian prince Rhesus. The Achaean pair kill Rhesus and his companions and return to camp with his horses.

Book 11 sees the Achaeans fighting successfully until several of the heroes, major and minor, are wounded. The Achaeans fall back to the wall. Now Achilles tells Patroclus to enquire about one of the wounded. Patroclus meets the old king Nestor, who makes the fatal suggestion that Achilles should lend Patroclus his armour so that Patroclus, disguised, can frighten the Trojans away from the ships. For four long books (12–15) this suggestion is held in abeyance. During this time the Achaeans rally, aided by Poseidon and by Hera, who diverts Zeus's attention into an afternoon of lovemaking high on Mount Ida. During this time Hector is stunned by a great stone cast by Ajax, and temporarily disabled. When Zeus wakes, he restores Hector, and by the end of Book 15 the Trojans are on the point of setting fire to the ships. Only at this point (Book 16) does Patroclus get back to Achilles and persuade him to do as Nestor has suggested. Achilles orders Patroclus to do only what the situation requires and to come back to his camp as soon as the Trojans are driven off. Patroclus is carried away by his own success. He kills the Trojan hero Sarpedon, son of Zeus, but is then himself killed in an encounter with Hector and the god Apollo.

What will happen when the news reaches Achilles? This is delayed for the whole of Book 17, an agonising description of the battle for Patroclus' body (Hector has taken possession of the arms). At last, at the beginning of Book 18, young Antilochus reaches Achilles' camp and tells him. Achilles' overwhelming grief reaches his mother in the depths of the sea. She visits him; he tells her his one wish is to take revenge on Hector; she tells him that his own death will follow Hector's immediately. Now Achilles, unarmed, inspired by Hera and Athena, stands on the edge of the Achaeans' defensive ditch and utters a mighty battle cry. The Trojan advance is halted. Night falls, and the Trojans discuss whether to remain camped out in the plain. As Achilles has made his death certain by resolving to kill Hector, so Hector now makes his own death certain by persuading the Trojans to stay where they are and face Achilles in the morning. But for the moment there is a pause. Achilles' arms are in Hector's possession. Thetis will visit the smith-god Hephaestus on Olympus to have new ones made. The rest of Book 18 sees Thetis kindly received by Hephaestus and the arms, above all the shield, made and described.

Books 19–21 form a long prelude to the contest of Achilles and Hector. First, Agamemnon and Achilles are formally reconciled. Then (Book 20) Achilles goes into battle. To begin with he has a long and inconclusive encounter with Aeneas (who is rescued by Poseidon). His *aristeia* proceeds with the killing of a large number of lesser Trojans, and then (Book 21) he fights, first, two of the greater Trojan heroes, and then the river-god himself of Troy, the Scamander. Now he turns his attention to Hector, to be delayed by Apollo, who disguises himself as the Trojan Agenor and lures Achilles into chasing him far over the plain, giving the Trojans time to reach the city.

But Hector (Book 22) knows that he has brought the Trojans to this pass by his decision to spend the night on the plain. Shame forces him to await Achilles outside the gate. Then at the last minute he turns and runs away – until he is deceived by Athena into turning and facing Achilles. The duel is short. Hector dies. His body is dragged behind Achilles' chariot to the Achaean camp while the Trojans on the walls lament.

Book 23 deals with the funeral of Patroclus and the games held by Achilles in his honour. The Achaean heroes appear for the last time, now engaged in the activities of peace. But Achilles (Book 24), his rage unabated, continues to maltreat Hector's body, to the displeasure of the gods. Thetis is sent to persuade Achilles to accept a ransom and give the body up for burial. King Priam visits Achilles in the dead of night, and there is an intensely moving scene where the two of them recognise each other's humanity and grief. Priam recovers his son's body and the epic ends with Hector's funeral.

C.   Reading Homer

(i)   *Repetitions and oral theory*

Any reader of Homer will soon notice repeated expressions such as 'swift-foot-ed Achilles' or 'winged words'. Sometimes a whole line, such as 'Then in turn wind-footed swift Iris spoke to him' (e.g. *Iliad* 18.183 = 196) is repeated. These re-peated expressions are called 'formulae' (singular: 'formula') and regularly recurring adjectives such as 'swift-footed' for Achilles are called 'epithets'. The use of epithets and formulae in Homer has been much discussed, especially since the 1930s when Milman Parry proposed that these repeated expressions are evidence for the oral origin of Homeric epic poetry: the poet composed without writing but helped by the building blocks of formulaic expressions.[1] He demonstrated that there is an exten-sive system of formulae in Homeric verse, each designed to fit a particular place in a line of epic verse (see Section E below), helping the poet to maintain momentum in composing as he performs. Parry and his pupil Albert Lord backed up this theory by studying the practice of living singer-composers in the Balkans, drawing parallels in the use of formulaic expressions between Homer and the poetry of the southern Slavs.[2] They also claimed that the extensive system of formulae found in Homer can-not have been developed single-handedly by one poet, but will have resulted from many generations of singers expanding and handing down the stock phrases and techniques. If the claims of the Parry–Lord theory are accepted, Homer 'sang' rather than 'wrote' his poems.

---

1 His groundbreaking studies are published in A. Parry, ed. (1971) *The Making of Homeric Verse: The Collected Papers of Milman Parry*, Oxford: Oxford University Press.

2 This comparative study is explained in A. B. Lord (1960, 2nd ed. 2000) *The Singer of Tales*, Cambridge, MA: Harvard University Press.

But if Homer only sang, how can so massive and well-structured a work as the *Iliad* have survived the death of its author? There were organised recitations of the whole *Iliad* and *Odyssey* at Athens from at least the sixth century BCE, indicating that written texts existed by this date. It is plausible (though unprovable) that they go back to the lifetime of the poet, usually put in the second half of the eighth century. (The *Odyssey* was seen by one ancient critic as the work of Homer's old age; if there were two poets, the *Odyssey* was perhaps composed a generation after the *Iliad* by a son, apprentice or admirer.) The Bronze Age Linear B script was as far as we know used only for palace records, and died out in the ensuing Dark Age. The Greek alphabet in roughly the form we know it seems to have been introduced in the early eighth century, adapted from Phoenician, which Greeks will have encountered in a new era of expansion and overseas trade. The new availability of writing may have inspired an exceptionally talented poet, trained as an oral bard, to conceive a work of unprecedented scale and sophistication, which he presumably worked on for many years, either writing it down himself or more plausibly dictating it to a scribe. On this view, the *Odyssey* then emulated the *Iliad*, making both epics the untypical and monumental end products of a vast and fluid oral tradition.

Written texts certainly did in due course circulate widely, but the epics remained oral poems in the important sense that most Greeks will have encountered them in performance, by professional reciters known as 'rhapsodes'. Written texts could themselves vary quite considerably, and it was the work of the scholars at the great Library in Alexandria in the third and second centuries BCE to establish a standard version. They are probably also responsible for the division of the *Iliad* (and likewise the *Odyssey*) into twenty-four books, traditionally designated by letters of the Greek alphabet (so Book 16 is Π and Book 18 is Σ). Each book would occupy a single scroll. Book divisions sometimes coincide with natural breaks in the narrative, sometimes not.

(ii)   *Themes*

Repetitions are not confined to formulaic phrases and recurring lines. There are many stock themes, often following similar patterns and containing repeated expressions: the arming of a hero, sacrifice, a meal, bathing or the arrival of a visitor. The arming of Patroclus at 16.130–44 can be compared to that of Agamemnon at 11.15–46. The arrival of Thetis to Hephaestus at 18.369–90 can be compared to that of Agamemnon's representatives to Achilles at 9.185–200. Accounts of combat between individuals tend to start from a formulaic base (e.g. A throws a spear at B and misses, B retaliates but also misses, then A kills B with a sword), but this is frequently elaborated or varied.[3] The poet can thus compose larger building blocks of his story, whilst also preventing the description of battles from becoming monotonous. Whole sequences of events can follow a common pattern. Book 16 and Book 18 start in a similar way,

---

3   Cf. B. Fenik (1968) *Typical Battle Scenes in the Iliad* (*Hermes* Einzelschriften 21), Wiesbaden: F. Steiner.

with bad news brought to Achilles, followed by his reaction to it. On a still larger scale, the narrative of the death of Patroclus in Book 16 and that of the death of Hector in Book 22 develop in parallel ways. Important advice (from Achilles to Patroclus, from Polydamas to Hector) is ignored. The victim is decisively weakened by a god (Patroclus by Apollo, Hector by Athena). The victor inflicts a fatal injury and the victim falls to the ground. The victor makes a speech of triumph, starting a dialogue that ends with the last words of the victim, warning that the victor's death will soon follow. The actual deaths are described in identical words (16.855–7 = 22.361–3). Hector rejects the prophecy of his own death; Achilles accepts it.

(iii)   *Foreshadowing*

One death foreshadows another, and all the deaths within the poem foreshadow the big one beyond its end. Throughout the *Iliad* the poet suggests how the story will develop, sometimes in clear terms, sometimes by allusion. Perhaps the most provocative is 1.5, 'and Zeus's plan was accomplished'. Is this plan what he agrees with Thetis later in the book, that he will allow the Trojans to succeed until Agamemnon is forced to acknowledge his offence against Achilles? Is it also that this will lead to the death of Patroclus, then to that of Hector and to the fall of Troy? Does it imply a dark view of the nature of the gods, delighting in human misery? The death of Achilles is often foretold, in terms which become more specific as the event comes closer. At 1.352 he is 'born to live only a short while'. At 9.412–13 he can go home and live in safety, but his death is inevitable if he stays at Troy. At 18.96, he is told his death will follow immediately upon Hector's. More allusively, the scene at 18.35–51 where Thetis brings the sea-nymphs to Achilles' camp to mourn Patroclus' death seems to foreshadow another scene (*Odyssey* 24.47–9) where the same company assembles to mourn Achilles' own death. The structure of Book 16 is shaped by the poet's comment when Patroclus asks to be sent out as a substitute Achilles: 'Poor fool! He was asking for his own death' (16.46–7). Allusively, the death of the hero Epeigeus (16.570–5) may look forward to Patroclus' death. Epeigeus, like Patroclus, is 'best of the Myrmidons', and, like Patroclus, he has sought refuge among them after killing a man in his home country.

(iv)   *Speeches*

Achilles' tutor Phoenix was charged by his father Peleus to make his son 'a speaker of words' as well as 'a doer of deeds' (9.443). Speeches occupy about 45 per cent of the *Iliad*. Achilles himself speaks almost 1,000 lines, his strong emotions often expressed in strong and unusual language. Characters evaluate events and each other in their speeches. We in turn evaluate them by what they say: the poet rarely steers us by commenting directly. Speeches within a single book can show a remarkable variety of style and effect.

In Book 16 speeches show us the relationship of Achilles and Patroclus. We have Achilles encouraging the Myrmidons and praying in vain to Zeus. Sarpedon encourages the Lycian allies of Troy and is himself the subject of a tense dialogue between Zeus and Hera. Dying at the hands of Patroclus, he urges on Glaucus, who in turn urges on Hector. Finally comes the exchange referred to above between Hector and the dying Patroclus.

Book 18 starts with an anxious monologue by Achilles. After Antilochus gives him the news, we have Thetis in conversation with the Nereids and with Achilles, then Iris (sent by Hera) with Achilles. The disagreement between Polydamas and Hector (the former impressively persuasive, though unsuccessful) returns us to the human battlefield. Achilles remorsefully addresses the Myrmidons and the dead Patroclus. Hera's gloating to Zeus about her success in bringing Achilles back into action is followed by the happier conversation of Thetis with Hephaestus and his hospitable wife. Homer presents the whole range of human and divine life in speech. This enabled the *Iliad* to provide a model for the later genre of tragic drama. It is also one reason why the epic has lent itself well to dramatisation for radio.

(v)   Similes and descriptions

Homer's similes are famous and frequent: 'Just as … a spring of dark water' (Patroclus' tears, 16.3); '… a little girl begging her mother to pick her up' (Achilles' gently mocking description of weeping Patroclus, 16.7); '… flies gathered round milk-pails' (of warriors fighting over Sarpedon's corpse, 16.641–3). They may consist of a couple of words (Thetis 'like a hawk', 18.616) or occupy a dozen lines. They may focus our attention on particular points of the scene described, or they may withdraw our attention from it on to something extraneous, a sort of relief from tension. The number of similes varies greatly from section to section of the poem: there are twenty-one in Book 16, only six of any substance in Book 18. The Myrmidons going out to battle qualify for three in quick succession (16.156–63, 212–13, 259–65): a means of underlining the structural importance as well as the vividness of this event. For any simile, the points of contact between it and the narrative from which it springs may be complex: they repay careful analysis.

Another method of varying the narrative consists of protracted descriptions. Such an extensive description is called *ekphrasis*. The description of the shield of Achilles being made by Hephaestus in *Iliad* 18.478–608 is the most extensive example in the poem. Agamemnon's shield is described (splendidly but briefly) at 11.32–40; the huge difference in length between the two descriptions draws attention to the relative importance of the characters.

(vi)   Heroic values

Homeric heroes are concerned above all with defending their honour (*timē*) and winning glory (*kudos* or *kleos*). Achilles is dishonoured when Agamemnon takes away the girl who is his prize (*geras*) and the outward token of his *timē* (a word that significantly also means 'price'). The behaviour of heroes is determined by fear of disgrace and (still worse) ridicule: this is in anthropological terms a 'shame culture' (in contrast to a 'guilt culture', where behaviour is determined by an internalised moral code —though such a stark dichotomy does less than justice to Homer). It is intensely competitive and individualistic. Excellence is primarily measured by prowess on the battlefield, though (as we have seen) wise words also rank very high. Revenge is accepted as natural. Achilles' fixation may be extreme, but it is never suggested that he is wrong to feel himself wronged by Agamemnon. 'Win great honour and glory for me', he instructs Patroclus (16.84), and Patroclus duly tells the Myrmidons they are to win back what Agamemnon has taken away (16.270–4).

Both sides in the war subscribe to the same values, just as they worship the same gods and (by literary convention) speak the same language. Sarpedon encourages his Lycians by appealing to their sense of shame (16.422), and one of the fullest statements of heroic values in the poem is his speech to his cousin and deputy Glaucus at 12.310–28 (see also (vii) below). The sense there of *noblesse oblige* (heroes must justify their privileges) reminds us that this is the code of a warrior elite, but also shows that considerations of social responsibility and justice have a place in the Homeric world.

Sarpedon before his killing by Patroclus is honoured with a shower of blood-stained raindrops from his father Zeus (16.459), and after it with miraculous transportation of his body to Lycia for burial by his kinsmen (16.676–83). He thus avoids in an especially privileged way what every hero dreads: to be denied proper burial, his body left as prey for dogs and carrion birds (1.4–5 and many other passages). Being unburied is a physical expression of being forgotten. Heroes seek recognition from their comrades, but they aspire also to what Achilles was offered by Thetis if he stayed and fought at Troy, a *kleos* that is imperishable (9.413). The poet was perhaps not unaware that it lay in his own gift to confer this.

(vii)   Gods

Gods are vividly present throughout the *Iliad*. They are important to the epic in a number of ways, and it is hard to say that one is more important than another.

Their first three appearances are frightening. Zeus's will, that ambiguous phrase (see (iii) above), is mentioned in line 5 of Book 1. In 43 Apollo, enraged, comes like night upon the Achaeans and inflicts a plague on them. In 194 Athena, her eyes terrifyingly aflame, seizes Achilles by the hair as he is about to strike Agamemnon. But then at the end of Book 1 there is a scene of total contrast. It is on Olympus, at a gathering of the gods. Achilles' mother Thetis wheedles Zeus into agreeing to her request that he support her son in his dispute with Agamemnon. Zeus is, with reason, anxious that he may be in trouble with Hera if she spots him in private conversation with Thetis. A domestic dispute develops, which is resolved by Hephaestus bustling round and serving drinks to everyone.

One function of the gods then seems to be as a foil to human existence. The deadly seriousness of the dispute at the beginning of Book 1 is set against the lightheartedness of that at the end. The gods 'live easily'. And being immortal, they are a foil in another sense, as appears in Book 12 when Sarpedon makes moving use of this point in his speech to Glaucus: 'If we were immortal, I would not trouble to fight; but as it is, death surrounds us on all sides: on with us then, and let us see whether we yield the glory to another or he to us' (12.322–8). A central idea in the *Iliad* is that mortality gives to human life a seriousness, urgency and potential for tragedy outside the experience of the gods. War intensifies and clarifies this awareness. Achilles' excellence lies in that he knows his own death will follow the success of his revenge, and yet he goes through with it.

There is a hierarchy of gods, and they are variously well- or ill-disposed towards the Trojans. At the head is Zeus, whose power is greater than that of all the rest put together. While not overtly hostile to Troy, he knows that Troy is fated to fall. Of the other gods, Hera, Athena, Poseidon and Hephaestus are hostile to the Trojans, while Apollo, Aphrodite, Ares and Artemis (who scarcely appears) support them. Hera and Athena are the most active and virulent in their hatred. This arose from the famous occasion when Paris, invited to name the most beautiful of the three goddesses Hera, Athena and Aphrodite, chose Aphrodite: the 'judgement of Paris', for which Paris was rewarded by the right to possess Helen, though this was the cause of the war. But apart from a passing reference in Book 24 the *Iliad* ignores the judgement of Paris: the hatred matters more than the reason for it. Hera demonstrates this when, rather than make any allowances for Troy, she offers to let Zeus destroy all her own favoured cities, Argos, Sparta and Mycenae (4.51–3). Of the pro-Trojan gods, only Apollo is treated with consistent respect: all the others are at one time or another humiliated either by a mortal or a fellow god.

Gods are ever present in human motivation, giving a man courage, strength or speed, or filling him with terror. Normally, for a hero to receive help from a god is a sign of the hero's excellence rather than his weakness. Occasionally the opposite point can be made: Patroclus belittles Hector's triumph over him by attributing his success to Apollo (16.849–50).

Of one idea there is little mention: that the gods are concerned with morality and what is right. Menelaus at 13.625 appeals to Zeus as the 'god of hosts and guests' (ξεί-νιος) who should punish the Trojans because Paris betrayed his host. At 16.385–8 (in a simile) Zeus sends torrential rain to punish men for giving crooked judgements. In Book 24 the gods 'pity' Hector (23) and Apollo condemns Achilles as 'shameless' (44). But these instances are rare and exceptional. For the most part, those whom the gods of the *Iliad* favour are their children or enemies of their enemies. The *Odyssey* (with its hero's recurrent question about unknown people 'Are they god-fearing and friendly to strangers?') seems to reflect a different world view.

D.   Homer's language

Homer's Greek is a mixture of different dialects, which makes it likely that it is an artificial language devised (by generations of oral poets) for the purpose of epic verse-making. The basic dialect is Ionic, spoken on the eastern coast of the Aegean (modern Turkey), with a significant admixture of Aeolic, spoken in the northern region of this same coast. There are also elements of other dialects. This gives a unique variety of vocabulary which the poet can use to suit particular contexts and metrical positions. Individual words frequently exist in different forms (e.g. with a single or double consonant, or with endings of different declensions), again for metrical flexibility. Linguistic features also enable us to posit the eighth century BCE as the likely time for the composition of the poems.

Main features of Homeric dialect against their Attic equivalent (i.e. the Greek written by most major authors of the classical period):

1. The augment is often omitted: λάβε = ἔλαβε; πίπτε = ἔπιπτε
2. Nominative singular: Att. -ᾱ appears as -η: χώρη = χώρα
3. Genitive singular in -οιο (2nd decl.): πολέμοιο = πολέμου; also in -ᾱο/εω (1st decl. m.): Πηληϊάδαο, Πηληϊάδεω = Πηληϊάδου
4. Dative plural:
   1st decl. Att. -αις appears as -ῇς or -ῇσι: πύλῃς or πύλῃσι = πύλαις; τῇς or τῇσι = ταῖς
   2nd decl. words can end -οισι: ἵπποισι = ἵπποις
   3rd decl. words can end -σσι or -εσσι: ποσσί = ποσί; ἄνδρεσσι = ἀνδράσι
5. Definite article (ὁ ἡ τό):
   (a) most commonly used as a personal or demonstrative pronoun 'he', 'she', 'it', 'they', 'these men' etc.
   (b) οἱ and αἱ appear also as τοί and ταί
   (c) forms identical with the definite article are used as the relative pronoun, though the masculine nominative singular of the relative pronoun is ὅς as in Attic
6. Use of οἱ to mean 'to him/her' and τοι to mean 'to you' (s.)
7. Active infinitives often end in -μεν, -μεναι, -εναι: ἔμμεν, ἔμεναι, ἔμμεναι all = εἶναι
8. κε (κ᾽, κεν) is very often used in place of ἄν
9. Tmesis (lit. 'cutting') of a compound verb, where the prefix is separated from the verb to which it is joined in Att., e.g. ἐν δ᾽ ἔπεσον = ἐνέπεσον δέ … (16.276).

Two more general characteristics of Homeric Greek should also be noted: prepositions are used very flexibly (so e.g. κατά + acc. needs to be translated in several different ways, according to context); and verbs can be used in middle forms with the same meaning as the active (often for metrical convenience).

Further details of Homeric Greek are explained when met in the text.

E.   Metre

Homeric epic is composed in a verse form called 'hexameter' (literally 'six measures'). Each line consists of six 'feet'. Each foot is a cluster of syllables, forming either a 'dactyl' (one long syllable plus two short ones, represented as – ⏑ ⏑) or a 'spondee' (two long syllables, – –), one long thought of as equivalent to two shorts; except that the final foot of the line can be either a spondee or a 'trochee' (one long plus one short, – ⏑).[4]

The other feet can be either dactyls or spondees, though the fifth is most often a dactyl. The pattern of the line (with vertical lines showing the foot divisions) is therefore:

1	2	3	4	5	6	
– ⏑ ⏑	– ⏑ ⏑	– ⏑ ⏑	– ⏑ ⏑	– ⏑ ⏑	– x	(x indicating a syllable
– –	– –	– –	– –	– –	– –	that can be long or short)

To read out a line correctly, you need to establish whether each syllable is long or short (the criterion is length or 'quantity', rather than stress, but in practice more weight is put on the long syllables). This process is called 'scansion', and the way a line scans is shown by writing the appropriate symbols above it. The first line of Book 18 scans as follows:

$$- \quad -|- \quad - \ |- \ \cup \ \cup|- \quad \cup \cup \ |- \ \cup \cup|-x$$
Ὣς οἱ μὲν μάρναντο δέμας πυρὸς αἰθομένοιο

Each syllable normally contains one vowel or diphthong (two vowels pronounced together, e.g. αυ). For scansion purposes it consists of the vowel or diphthong plus following consonant(s).

Some practical rules for identifying the length of a syllable:

1. A long vowel (η, ω) or diphthong (e.g. αυ, ει, οι) naturally creates a long syllable.
2. A short vowel (ε, ο) creates a short syllable if followed by a single consonant.
3. The other three vowels (α, ι, υ) might be long or short, so cannot in themselves be used to determine syllable length.
4. Any vowel, even if itself short, if followed by two consonants (not necessarily in the same word, e.g. μὲν περί) normally creates a long syllable (note that ζ, ξ and ψ count as double consonants).
5. Short syllables always come in pairs, except at the end of a line.
6. A short vowel at the end of one word followed by a vowel at the beginning of the next is normally 'elided' (i.e. 'struck off'), indicated by an apostrophe in the text, and ignored for scansion purposes.

A hexameter line is usually divided into two by a 'caesura' (Latin for 'cutting'): in effect a breathing space, at the end of a word but not at the end of a foot, coming typically within the third or fourth foot. It is indicated by two oblique lines (//):

4 The types of foot get their names as follows:
    Dactyl from δάκτυλος (finger): one long bone and two short;
    Spondee from σπονδή (solemn drink-offering): it sounds like the accompanying chant;
    Trochee from τρέχω (I run): a series of them (not in a hexameter) has a fast forward momentum.

‒ ‒|‒ ‒ |‒ ◡//◡|‒   ◡ ◡ |‒ ◡ ◡|‒x
Ὣς οἱ μὲν μάρναντο δέμας πυρὸς αἰθομένοιο

The guide above will enable you to scan most lines. But there are many exceptions to the rules given (many of them 'special licences' to make the poet's job easier). These are explained in the notes, each at its first occurrence.

Select Bibliography

Editions and commentaries

Brügger, C. (2018) *Homer's Iliad: The Basel Commentary: Book XVI*, Boston and Berlin: De Gruyter.

Coray, M. (2018) *Homer's Iliad: The Basel Commentary: Book XVIII*, Boston and Berlin: De Gruyter.

Edwards, M. W. (1991) *The Iliad: A Commentary. Volume V: Books 17–20*, Cambridge: Cambridge University Press.

Janko, R. (1992) *The Iliad: A Commentary. Volume IV: Books 13–16*, Cambridge: Cambridge University Press.

Jones, P. (2003) *Homer's Iliad: A Commentary on Three Translations*, London: Bristol Classical Press.

Murray, A. T., revised Wyatt, W. F. (1999) *Homer, Iliad Books 13–24*, Cambridge, MA: Loeb Classical Library, Harvard University Press.

Postlethwaite, N. (2000) *Homer's Iliad: A Commentary on the Translation of Richmond Lattimore*, Exeter: University of Exeter Press.

Rutherford, R. B. (2019) *Homer: Iliad Book XVIII*, Cambridge: Cambridge University Press.

Willcock, M. M. (1976) *A Companion to the Iliad Based on the Translation by Richmond Lattimore*, Chicago and London: University of Chicago Press.

Willcock, M. M. (1984) *The Iliad of Homer, Books XIII–XXIV*, London: St Martin's Press.

General books on Homer and the *Iliad*

Allan, W. (2012) *Homer: The Iliad*, London: Bristol Classical Press.

Barker, E. and Christensen, J. (2013) *Homer: A Beginner's Guide*, London: Oneworld Publications.

Cairns, D. L., ed. (2001) *Oxford Readings in Homer's Iliad*, Oxford: Oxford University Press.

Edwards, M. W. (1987) *Homer: Poet of the Iliad*, Baltimore and London: Johns Hopkins University Press.

Finkelberg, M., ed. (2011) *The Homer Encyclopedia*, 3 vols, Chichester: Wiley-Blackwell.

Fowler, R., ed. (2004) *The Cambridge Companion to Homer*, Cambridge: Cambridge University Press.

Griffin, J. (2001) *Homer*, 2nd ed., Cambridge: Cambridge University Press.

Morris, I. and Powell, B., eds. (1997) *A New Companion to Homer*, Leiden: Brill.

Silk, M. (2004) *Homer: The Iliad*, 2nd ed., Cambridge: Cambridge University Press.

Iliad Book 16

Iliad Book 16 (ancient title Πατρόκλεια: Patroclus fights and dies)

Patroclus, who has earlier been sent to consult Nestor, returns to Achilles' hut and urges him to help the hard-pressed Achaeans, either by returning to the battlefield himself, or by sending him, Patroclus, as a substitute. Achilles agrees to the second proposal, and Patroclus leads the Myrmidons out to battle. Initially he has great success, but his luck turns and he is eventually killed by Hector.

2. Achilles. Red-figure amphora (detail), c.445 BCE. Gregorian Etruscan Museum, Rome.

Ὣς οἱ μὲν περὶ νηὸς ἐϋσσέλμοιο μάχοντο·
Πάτροκλος δ' Ἀχιλῆϊ παρίστατο, ποιμένι λαῶν,
δάκρυα θερμὰ χέων ὥς τε κρήνη μελάνυδρος,
ἥ τε κατ' αἰγίλιπος πέτρης δνοφερὸν χέει ὕδωρ.

1–19: Patroclus returns to Achilles' hut in tears. Achilles asks what is troubling him.

1 ὥς (accented) so, thus (= Att. οὕτως)

οἱ they, these men. The article (ὁ ἡ τό) in Homer usu. has its original role as a personal or demonstrative pronoun. It refers here to the Achaeans led by Ajax who at the end of Book 15 were fighting in defence of the ship that had brought Protesilaus to Troy. Protesilaus was the first Greek killed in the war, and his is the first ship to be set on fire.

μέν: sets up a contrast with δέ (2)

περί (+ gen.) around

νηῦς νηός, ἡ ship (= Att. ναῦς νεώς)

ἐϋσσέλμος -ον well-decked. Note that -οιο is an alternative gen. ending, frequent in Homer, for 2nd decl. genitives in -ου.

μάχομαι I fight; μάχοντο is 3 pl. impf. with the augment omitted, as oft. in Homer.

2 Πάτροκλος -ου/οιο, ὁ Patroclus

δ(έ) and, but; a short vowel at the end of a word is normally elided when the next word starts with a vowel. See Introduction Section E for metre and scansion.

Ἀχιλ(λ)εύς -ῆος, ὁ Achilles; Ἀχιλῆϊ is dat., the diaeresis (two dots) above the last letter indicating that it is pronounced separately. Alternative spellings with single or double consonant give the poet greater metrical flexibility by allowing short or long syllable.

παρίσταμαι I go and stand beside (+ dat.); παρίστατο is 3 s. impf.

ποιμήν -ένος, ὁ shepherd

λαός -οῦ, ὁ people, army (= Att. λεώς -ῶ); usu. pl. with collective s. sense

3 δάκρυ (no gen. s.), τό tear

θερμός -ή -όν warm, hot. Tears are hot because freshly welling up (not as a

symbol of anger). They contrast here with the cold waterfall. Homeric heroes regularly express emotion by weeping.

χέω I pour, (here) shed; χέων is pres. part. (m. nom. s.)

ὥς as, like (here introducing simile); usu. unaccented ὡς in this sense (cf. on 1) but here acquires an accent because the next word (τε) is an unaccented 'enclitic' (lit. 'leaning on'), i.e. a short unemphatic word joined closely in pronunciation to the one before it.

τε: the 'generalising' τε, oft. used in similes; usu. redundant in tr. but implies 'as regularly happens', 'as everyone knows'. Further examples at 4, 8, 9 and many more.

κρήνη -ης, ἡ spring

μελάνυδρος -ον of dark (lit. black) water. The word suggests something deep and cold, reflecting Patroclus' dark mood.

4 ὅς ἥ ὅ (rel. pron.) who, which

κατ(ά) (+ gen.) down from

αἰγίλιψ -ιπος (f. adj.) sheer; lit. perhaps 'goat-left', i.e. too steep even for them

πέτρη -ης, ἡ rock, cliff (= Att. πέτρα -ας)

δνοφερός -ή -όν dark, murky

ὕδωρ -ατος, τό water. In scanning χέει ὕδωρ note that -ει is short (a long vowel or diphthong ending a word in Homer oft. undergoes 'correption' ('shortening') when the next word starts with a vowel) and also that υ in ὕδωρ (normally short) is made long for the metre (as oft. in Homer, especially in the last foot).

τὸν δὲ ἰδὼν ᾤκτιρε ποδάρκης δῖος Ἀχιλλεύς,   5
καί μιν φωνήσας ἔπεα πτερόεντα προσηύδα·
"τίπτε δεδάκρυσαι, Πατρόκλεες, ἠΰτε κούρη
νηπίη, ἥ θ' ἅμα μητρὶ θέουσ' ἀνελέσθαι ἀνώγει,
εἰανοῦ ἁπτομένη, καί τ' ἐσσυμένην κατερύκει,
δακρυόεσσα δέ μιν ποτιδέρκεται, ὄφρ' ἀνέληται·   10
τῇ ἴκελος, Πάτροκλε, τέρεν κατὰ δάκρυον εἴβεις.
ἠέ τι Μυρμιδόνεσσι πιφαύσκεαι, ἢ ἐμοὶ αὐτῷ,
ἦέ τιν' ἀγγελίην Φθίης ἐξ ἔκλυες οἶος;
ζώειν μὰν ἔτι φασὶ Μενοίτιον, Ἄκτορος υἱόν,
ζώει δ' Αἰακίδης Πηλεὺς μετὰ Μυρμιδόνεσσι,   15
τῶν κε μάλ' ἀμφοτέρων ἀκαχοίμεθα τεθνηώτων.

5 τόν him; m. acc. s. of article, again as personal pron.
    ἰδών: aor. part. (m. nom. s.) of ὁράω I see. There is no elision of δέ because ἰδών originally began with the obsolete consonant digamma (ϝ = w). Further examples at 11, 19, 41 and many more.
    οἰκτείρω I pity; ᾤκτιρε is 3 s. aor.
    ποδάρκης -ες swift-footed; a standard epithet of Achilles, evoking one of his defining characteristics. He is 'swift-footed' even when not running.
    δῖος -α -ον noble, glorious, godlike

6 καί and
    μιν him, her, it (acc. s. personal pron., = αὐτόν -ήν -ό), here 'him'
    φωνέω I speak; φωνήσας is aor. part. (m. nom. s.)
    ἔπος -εος, τό word; ἔπεα is acc. pl.
    πτερόεις -εσσα -εν (-εντος) winged (words are so called in this formulaic phrase because they fly from speaker to hearer)
    προσαυδάω I speak to, address; προσηύδα is 3 s. impf., here with double acc. 'he addressed winged words to him'

7-11: Achilles likens Patroclus to a little girl, by implication comparing himself with her mother. It is interesting to ask how this imagery affects our perception of their relationship, and of the character of Achilles. His words combine affection and irony.

7 τίπτε why ever? ('syncopated' i.e. telescoped form of τί ποτε)
    δακρύω I weep, pass. I am bathed in tears; δεδάκρυσαι is 2 s. perf. pass.
    Πατρόκλεες: voc. of Πατροκλῆς -ῆος, 3rd decl. form of the name Patroclus (cf. 2); alternative forms such as this further increase metrical flexibility.
    ἠΰτε just like, as when (introducing simile). Similes are common in the narrative of the *Iliad*; they are comparatively rare in direct speech, but Achilles utters more than any other character.
    κούρη -ης, ἡ girl (= Att. κόρη). Children and their behaviour oft. feature in Homeric similes. Here the child's close

dependency on her mother suggests a similar relationship between Patroclus and Achilles.

8 νήπιος -η -ον (here) young, helpless; emphasised by enjambment (syntactical continuity over line end)
    θ' = τε (before vowel with rough breathing); again generalising here
    ἅμα (+ dat.) along with
    μήτηρ μητρός, ἡ mother
    θέω I run; θέουσ(α) is pres. part. (f. nom. s.)
    ἀναιρέομαι I pick up, take in my arms; ἀνελέσθαι is aor. inf.
    ἄνωγα (perf. with pres. sense) I order, (here) urge; ἀνώγει is 3 s. past but tr.

as pres. and understand 'her' (i.e. the mother) as object

9 ἑανός/εἱανός -οῦ, ὁ dress; the first syllable is lengthened here for the metre.

ἅπτομαι I touch, cling to (+ gen.); ἁπτομένη is pres. part. (f. nom. s.)

σεύομαι I am in a hurry; ἐσσυμένην is perf. part. (f. acc. s.) agreeing with understood 'her', again the girl's mother

κατερύκω I hold back, hinder

10 δακρυόεις -εσσα -εν (-εντος) weeping, in tears

μιν (here) her (cf. 6)

ποτιδέρκομαι I look at (= Att. προσδέρκομαι)

ὄφρα (+ subj.) so that (introducing purpose clause), or perhaps here 'until'

ἀνέληται: 3 s. aor. subj. of ἀναιρέομαι (cf. 8)

11 τῇ her (dat.); again article as personal pron. τῇ is not shortened by correption (cf. on 4) even though the next word begins with a vowel. This (or the non-elision of a short final vowel) is called 'hiatus' ('gap'), oft. (as here) explained by a lost digamma (cf. on 5).

ἴκελος -η -ον like, resembling (+ dat.); the word originally began with digamma

τέρην -εινα -εν tender, soft

κατείβω I shed; in κατὰ … εἴβεις (2 s. pres.) the two parts of the compound verb are separated by 'tmesis' ('cutting'), though this is strictly a misnomer, as in Homer's time they had not yet fully coalesced

δάκρυον -ου, τό tear; 2nd decl. form of δάκρυ (cf. 3)

12–19: Achilles affectionately teases Patroclus, asking if he has had some bad news from home; he then reveals that he knows perfectly well what the trouble is, i.e. the slaughter of the Achaeans by the ships. He wisely says nothing of his own private arrangement with Zeus, via his mother, that this should be the case.

12 ἠέ … ἦέ (13) … ἦε (17): three questions, 'is it that … or is it that … or perhaps?' (all = Att. ἤ)

τις τι (τινός) someone, something, some

Μυρμιδόνες -ων, οἱ Myrmidons; Μυρμιδόνεσσι is Homeric dat. pl. The Myrmidons are Achilles' people, from Phthia in Thessaly, a region of north-eastern Greece.

πιφαύσκομαι I declare, make known, reveal; πιφαύσκεαι is 2 s. pres.

ἤ or (here introducing an alternative within the first question)

ἐμοί to me; dat. of ἐγώ I

αὐτός -ή -ό self (emphatic pron.), here 'myself'

13 ἀγγελίη -ης, ἡ message, news (= Att. ἀγγελία -ας)

Φθίη -ης, ἡ Phthia (= Att. Φθία -ας)

ἐξ (+ gen.) out of, from (= ἐκ before vowel); accented when used as postposition, i.e. coming after its noun

κλύω I hear; ἔκλυες is 2 s. aor.

οἶος -η -ον alone

14 ζώω I live (= Att. ζάω)

μάν (here) but, yet (= Att. μήν)

ἔτι (adv.) still

φημί I say, think; φασί is 3 pl. pres. (understanding 'people' as subject), introducing indirect statement with acc. + inf.

Μενοίτιος -ου, ὁ Menoetius, father of Patroclus

Ἄκτωρ -ορος, ὁ Actor, father of Menoetius

υἱός -οῦ/έος, ὁ son

15 Αἰακίδης -αο/εω, ὁ son of Aeacus (who is grandfather of Achilles)

Πηλεύς -ῆος/έος, ὁ Peleus, father of Achilles. The hero constantly brings him to mind, fearing that he might have died.

μετά (+ dat.) among

16 τῶν for whom (m. gen. pl. of article here as rel. pron.; gen. of cause)

κε: particle indicating potential or conditional action, κεν before a vowel or elided κ' (= Att. ἄν; Homer uses both, but more often κε); here + opt. 'would'

μάλ(α) (adv.) very, much

ἀμφότεροι -αι -α both

ἄχομαι I am distressed; ἀκαχοίμεθα is 1 pl. aor. opt. in 'reduplicated' form (i.e. with first consonant sound repeated)

θνήσκω I die; τεθνηώτων is perf. part. (m. gen. pl.), here in gen. abs. with conditional force 'if they were dead'

ἦε σύ γ’ Ἀργείων ὀλοφύρεαι, ὡς ὀλέκονται
νηυσὶν ἔπι γλαφυρῇσιν ὑπερβασίης ἕνεκα σφῆς;
ἐξαύδα, μὴ κεῦθε νόῳ, ἵνα εἴδομεν ἄμφω."
    Τὸν δὲ βαρὺ στενάχων προσέφης, Πατρόκλεες ἱππεῦ·   20
"ὦ Ἀχιλεῦ, Πηλῆος υἱέ, μέγα φέρτατ’ Ἀχαιῶν,
μὴ νεμέσα· τοῖον γὰρ ἄχος βεβίηκεν Ἀχαιούς.
οἱ μὲν γὰρ δὴ πάντες, ὅσοι πάρος ἦσαν ἄριστοι,
ἐν νηυσὶν κέαται βεβλημένοι οὐτάμενοί τε.
βέβληται μὲν ὁ Τυδεΐδης κρατερὸς Διομήδης,   25
οὔτασται δ’ Ὀδυσεὺς δουρικλυτὸς ἠδ’ Ἀγαμέμνων,
βέβληται δὲ καὶ Εὐρύπυλος κατὰ μηρὸν ὀϊστῷ.
τοὺς μέν τ’ ἰητροὶ πολυφάρμακοι ἀμφιπένονται,
ἕλκε’ ἀκειόμενοι· σὺ δ’ ἀμήχανος ἔπλευ, Ἀχιλλεῦ.

17 σύ you (s.)
    γ(ε) at least, at any rate
    Ἀργεῖοι -ων, οἱ Argives, i.e. Greeks. Named
        from the city of Argos in the Pelopon-
        nese (cf. 26) but used as a general term
        for all those fighting against the Trojans
        and their allies, synonymous with
        'Achaeans' (cf. 21).
    ὀλοφύρομαι I lament, mourn, feel sympa-
        thy for (+ gen.); ὀλοφύρεαι is 2 s. pres.
    ὡς how (introducing indirect question or
        exclamation)
    ὀλέκω I destroy; mid. I perish
18 νηυσίν: dat. pl. of νηῦς (cf. 1)
    ἐπί (+ dat.) by, beside; when a two-syllable
        prep. is used as postposition (cf. on 13),
        the accent moves back from the second
        syllable to the first, so here ἔπι
    γλαφυρός -ή -όν hollow; note that the
        ending -ῃσ(ι) is the norm in Homer for
        1st decl. dat pl. (= Att. -αις)

ὑπερβασίη -ης, ἡ transgression,
    presumptuousness (= Att. ὑπερβασία
    -ας). This of course is Achilles' view of
    the matter.
ἕνεκα because of (with preceding gen.)
σφός -ή -όν their, their own
19 ἐξαυδάω I speak out; ἐξαύδα is 2 s. imper.
    μή (+ imper.) don't … !
    κεύθω I hide, cover; κεῦθε is 2 s. imper.
        with 'it' understood as object
    νόος -ου, ὁ mind; here 'local' dat. 'in your
        mind'
    ἵνα (+ subj.) so that (introducing purpose
        clause)
    οἶδα (perf. with pres. sense) I know;
        εἴδομεν is 1 pl. subj. (= Att. εἰδῶμεν); the
        word originally began with digamma
        (cf. on 5), hence preceding hiatus (cf.
        on 11). Note that subj. forms in Homer
        oft. have a short vowel in the ending.
    ἄμφω both; used as nom. (as here) or acc.

20–47: Patroclus appeals to Achilles to help the Achaeans.

20 βαρύς -εῖα -ύ heavy; n. here as adv.
    'heavily'
    στενάχω I groan
    πρόσφημι I speak to, address; προσέφης
        is 2 s. impf. The poet himself here
        addresses Patroclus directly ('apos-
        trophe'), with 2 s. verb and voc. This
        has an emotive effect, denoting strong
        personal sympathy. Patroclus is so
        addressed eight times in Book 16 (and

nowhere else), the pathos increasing as
    his tragedy unfolds.
ἱππεύς -ῆος, ὁ horseman; used as an hon-
    orific epithet of Patroclus
21 ὦ O! (interjection with voc.)
    υἱέ: voc. of υἱός (cf. 14); scanned short-
        long. The first syllable is short perhaps
        because the poet thinks of the word as
        ὑέ; the second is long by special licence
        ('honorary long') because it comes at

the beginning of its foot and before
a 'liquid' consonant – λ, μ, ν, ρ, (ϝ).
Further examples at 237, 358, 375, and
many others.

μέγας μεγάλη μέγα big, great; n. as adv.
with sup. 'by far …'

φέρτατος -η -ον strongest, mightiest

Ἀχαιοί -ῶν, οἱ Achaeans. The regular term
in Homer for Greeks: Ἕλληνες (the
usual term in classical Greek) occurs
only once in the *Iliad*, at 2.684, for inhabitants of Hellas, a then insignificant
region of north-west Greece. Achaea
was a region of the more important
Peloponnese in southern Greece (cf. 17
and 39).

22 νεμεσάω I am angry; νεμέσα is 2 s. imper.
Patroclus is afraid that Achilles may be
angry at his pity for the Achaeans.

τοῖος -η -ον such

γάρ for

ἄχος -εος, τό grief. The first two letters
of the word pick up Ἀχιλεῦ and Ἀχαιῶν
in 21, and Ἀχαιούς in 22. The Greeks

thought of 'Achi-lles' bringing ἄχος to
the Greek λαός (cf. 2).

βιάω I overwhelm; βεβίηκε is 3 s. perf.

23 δή indeed

πᾶς πᾶσα πᾶν (παντ-) all

ὅσοι -αι -α as many as, (all) those who

πάρος (adv.) before, formerly

εἰμί I am; ἦσαν is 3 pl. impf.

ἄριστος -η -ον best

24 ἐν (+ dat.): here 'among' rather than 'in'

κεῖμαι I lie; κέαται is 3 pl. pres. (= Att.
κεῖνται)

βάλλω I throw, hit, strike; βεβλημένοι is
perf. pass. part. (m. nom. pl.)

οὐτάω I stab, wound; οὐτάμενοι is perf.
pass. part. (m. nom. pl.)

τε and (tr. before the word it follows);
βεβλημένοι οὐτάμενοί τε 'struck and
wounded': βάλλω is used of striking
with a missile, οὐτάω of wounding with
a weapon held in the hand. In the three
following lines Diomedes and Eurypylus
have been struck by arrows, Odysseus
and Agamemnon wounded by spears.

*25–7: The fact that three such important heroes as Diomedes, Odysseus and
Agamemnon are wounded highlights the seriousness of the Achaeans' plight.
Eurypylus was leader of a contingent from Thessaly (2.734–7), a minor hero in the
Iliad. Patroclus had helped him back to his hut and removed the arrow from his
thigh, after he had received the wound here referred to (11.575–84 and 804–48).*

25 βέβληται: 3 s. perf. pass. of βάλλω (cf. 24)

Τυδεΐδης -αο/εω, ὁ son of Tydeus

κρατερός -ή -όν strong, mighty

Διομήδης -εος, ὁ Diomedes, one of the
chief Achaean warriors. He brought a
contingent of eighty ships from Argos
and Tiryns (2.559–68) and has been
prominent in the action during the
absence of Achilles.

26 οὔτασται: 3 s. perf. pass. of οὐτάω (cf.
24); s. with the first of two subjects but
understood again with the second, as
oft.

Ὀδυσ(σ)εύς -ῆος, ὁ Odysseus, king of
Ithaca, famed for his cunning, and hero
of the *Odyssey*; again note the variant
for metrical flexibility (cf. on 2)

δουρικλυτός -όν renowned for the spear

ἠδ(έ) and

Ἀγαμέμνων -ονος, ὁ Agamemnon, king of
Argos and overall leader of the Achaean
expedition against Troy

27 Εὐρύπυλος -ου, ὁ Eurypylus

κατά (+ acc.) in

μηρός -οῦ, ὁ thigh

ὀϊστός -οῦ, ὁ arrow

28 τ(ε): again generalising

ἰητρός -οῦ, ὁ doctor (= Att. ἰατρός)

πολυφάρμακος -ον skilled in many drugs

ἀμφιπένομαι I am busied about, take care
of

29 ἕλκος -εος, τό wound; ἕλκε(α) is acc. pl.

ἀκέομαι I heal; ἀκειόμενοι is pres. part. (m.
nom. pl.), again with lengthened syllable (to avoid a run of short ones)

ἀμήχανος -ον impossible (to deal with)

πέλομαι I am, become; ἔπλευ is 2 s. aor.
with pres. sense

μὴ ἐμέ γ᾽ οὖν οὖτός γε λάβοι χόλος, ὃν σὺ φυλάσσεις,   30
αἰναρέτη· τί σευ ἄλλος ὀνήσεται ὀψίγονός περ,
αἴ κε μὴ Ἀργείοισιν ἀεικέα λοιγὸν ἀμύνῃς;
νηλεές, οὐκ ἄρα σοί γε πατὴρ ἦν ἱππότα Πηλεύς,
οὐδὲ Θέτις μήτηρ· γλαυκὴ δέ σε τίκτε θάλασσα   35
πέτραι τ᾽ ἠλίβατοι, ὅτι τοι νόος ἐστὶν ἀπηνής.
εἰ δέ τινα φρεσὶ σῇσι θεοπροπίην ἀλεείνεις
καί τινά τοι πὰρ Ζηνὸς ἐπέφραδε πότνια μήτηρ,
ἀλλ᾽ ἐμέ περ πρόες ὦχ᾽, ἅμα δ᾽ ἄλλον λαὸν ὄπασσον
Μυρμιδόνων, ἤν πού τι φόως Δαναοῖσι γένωμαι.   40
δὸς δέ μοι ὤμοιιν τὰ σὰ τεύχεα θωρηχθῆναι,
αἴ κ᾽ ἐμὲ σοὶ ἴσκοντες ἀπόσχωνται πολέμοιο
Τρῶες, ἀναπνεύσωσι δ᾽ ἀρήϊοι υἷες Ἀχαιῶν

30 μή (+ opt.) may ... not ... (in negative wish)
  ἐμέ: acc. of ἐγώ (cf. 12)
  οὖν therefore, then
  οὗτος αὕτη τοῦτο this
  γε at least, at any rate (usu. emphasises preceding word)
  λαμβάνω I take; λάβοι is 3 s. aor. opt.
  χόλος -ου, ὁ anger
  φυλάσσω I guard, (here) I harbour, cherish
31 αἰναρέτης -αο/εω (m. adj.) of harmful valour; αἰναρέτη is voc. s. 'you whose valour causes harm'
  τίς τί (τίνος) who? what?; n. here as adv. 'in what way?'
  σευ: Homeric gen. of σύ (cf. 17; = Att. σου); gen. here 'from you'

ἄλλος -η -ο other; here 'another man'
ὀνίνημι I benefit (someone), mid. I benefit from (+ gen.); ὀνήσεται is 3 s. fut. mid.
ὀψίγονος -ον born in a later age, of a future generation
περ: enclitic particle emphasising the preceding word and oft. suggesting 'even' or 'although'
32 αἴ κε (+ subj.) if (in fut. open condition; = Att. ἐάν)
  Ἀργείοισιν: dat. of Ἀργεῖοι (cf. 17); note Homeric ending -οισι with movable ν added before vowel (= Att. Ἀργείοις)
  ἀεικής -ές unseemly, disgraceful; ἀεικέα is m. acc. s.
  λοιγός -οῦ, ὁ ruin, death
  ἀμύνω I ward off X (acc.) from Y (dat.)

33–5: Achilles' utter lack of pity leads Patroclus to declare that he is of no human parentage, but rather the child of rocks and the sea, naturally harsh and unfeeling elements.

33 νηλεής -ές pitiless, merciless; νηλεές here is m. voc. s. 'pitiless man'. Achilles is the only person so described in Homer – apart from the Cyclops (*Odyssey* 9.272 and 368).
  οὐ/οὐκ/οὐχ not; οὐκ before vowel with smooth breathing, οὐχ before vowel with rough breathing
  ἄρα then, in that case (ἄρα is oft. hard to translate, but typically expresses a consequence); οὐκ ἄρα ... ἦν 'clearly wasn't'

πατήρ πατρός, ὁ father
ἦν: 3 s. impf. of εἰμί (cf. 23)
ἱππότα -εω, ὁ horseman
34 οὐδέ and not, nor
  Θέτις -ιδος, ἡ Thetis, a sea-goddess and Achilles' mother. Both Zeus and his brother Poseidon had wished to possess her, but there existed a prophecy that Thetis' son would be greater than his father, so Zeus forced her to marry the

mortal Peleus. Their son was indeed greater than his father.

γλαυκός -ή -όν grey

σε: acc. of σύ (cf. 17)

τίκτω I give birth to; τίκτε is 3 s. impf.

θάλασσα -ης, ή sea

35 ἠλίβατος -ον lofty, sheer

ὅτι because

τοι = σοι; dat. of σύ (cf. 17) in unaccented enclitic form, here possessive 'to you there is' i.e. 'you have'

ἀπηνής -ές unfeeling, harsh

36–45: These lines repeat almost verbatim 11.794–803 where Nestor first suggests to Patroclus that he should lead the Myrmidons into battle wearing Achilles' armour. Perhaps Patroclus does not reveal that the proposal is really Nestor's for fear that Achilles might reject any proposal coming from the Achaeans.

36 εἰ if

τις τι (τιν-) some, any

φρήν φρενός, ή mind, heart, soul (location of emotions and mental processes); here pl. for s. (as oft.)

σός σή σόν your, of you (s.); σῇσι is f. dat. pl. (= Att. σαῖς; cf. on 18)

θεοπροπίη -ης, ή prophecy, divine pronouncement (= Att. θεοπροπία -ας). Even though Achilles denies it a few lines later, this probably alludes to his statement at (9.410–16) about Thetis offering him a choice of lives: short and glorious, or long and obscure.

ἀλεείνω I shun, avoid

37 πάρ = παρά (+ gen.) from

Ζεύς Ζηνός/Διός, ὁ Zeus

φράζω I tell, declare; ἐπέφραδε is reduplicated 3 s. aor.

πότνια, ή (noun or f. adj.) lady; respectful title for a woman or goddess

38 ἀλλ(ά) but; ἀλλὰ … περ but at least. Patroclus is in a difficult position: he wants to help the Achaeans, but doesn't want to compromise Achilles' stand against Agamemnon.

προΐημι I send out; πρόες is 2 s. imper.

ὦκα (adv.) quickly; here elided and aspirated form ὦχ' (before vowel with rough breathing)

ἅμα (as adv.) at the same time

ἄλλος -η -ο (here) the rest of

ὀπάζω I make to follow; ὄπασσον is 2 s. aor. imper.

39 ἤν πού τι (+ subj.) in the hope that somehow (= Att. ἐάν …)

φόως/φάος φάεος, τό light (= Att. φῶς φωτός); here '(a light of) deliverance'

Δαναοί -ῶν, οἱ Danaans, i.e. Greeks; again note Homeric dat. pl. ending -οισι. In origin probably a people inhabiting the region of Argos (cf. 17 and 26), but used (like 'Argives') as a general term for the Greeks fighting at Troy, and again synonymous with 'Achaeans' (cf. 21).

γίγνομαι I become, (here) I prove; γένωμαι is 1 s. aor. subj.

40 δίδωμι I give, (here) I grant; δός is 2 s. aor. imper.

μοι: dat. of ἐγώ (cf. 12)

ὦμος -ου, ὁ shoulder; ὤμοιιν is dat. dual, here local 'on my (two) shoulders'

τεύχεα -ων, τά armour

θωρήσσω I arm (lit. with a breastplate), mid. and pass. I arm myself; θωρηχθῆναι is aor. pass. inf., here expressing purpose

41 αἴ κ(ε) (+ subj.) to see if

ἴσκω I liken X (acc.) to Y (dat.), i.e. take X for Y; the word originally began with digamma (cf. on 5)

ἀπέχομαι I hold off from (+ gen.); ἀπόσχωνται is 3 pl. aor. subj.

πόλεμος -ου/οιο, ὁ war, warfare, the fighting; note again the Homeric gen. s. ending

42 Τρῶες -ων, οἱ Trojans

ἀναπνέω I breathe again, rest myself; ἀναπνεύσωσι is 3 pl. aor. subj.

ἀρήϊος (-η) -ον warlike

υἷες: 3rd decl. form nom. pl. of υἱός (cf. 14); 'sons of the Achaeans' is a formulaic phrase just meaning 'Achaeans' (cf. biblical 'sons of Israel')

τειρόμενοι· ὀλίγη δέ τ᾽ ἀνάπνευσις πολέμοιο.
ῥεῖα δέ κ᾽ ἀκμῆτες κεκμηότας ἄνδρας ἀϋτῇ
ὤσαιμεν προτὶ ἄστυ νεῶν ἄπο καὶ κλισιάων."   45
    Ὣς φάτο λισσόμενος μέγα νήπιος· ἦ γὰρ ἔμελλεν
οἷ αὐτῷ θάνατόν τε κακὸν καὶ κῆρα λιτέσθαι.
τὸν δὲ μέγ᾽ ὀχθήσας προσέφη πόδας ὠκὺς Ἀχιλλεύς·
"ὤ μοι, διογενὲς Πατρόκλεες, οἷον ἔειπες·
οὔτε θεοπροπίης ἐμπάζομαι, ἥν τινα οἶδα,   50
οὔτέ τί μοι πὰρ Ζηνὸς ἐπέφραδε πότνια μήτηρ·
ἀλλὰ τόδ᾽ αἰνὸν ἄχος κραδίην καὶ θυμὸν ἱκάνει,
ὁππότε δὴ τὸν ὁμοῖον ἀνὴρ ἐθέλησιν ἀμέρσαι
καὶ γέρας ἂψ ἀφελέσθαι, ὅ τε κράτεϊ προβεβήκῃ·
αἰνὸν ἄχος τό μοί ἐστιν, ἐπεὶ πάθον ἄλγεα θυμῷ.   55
κούρην ἣν ἄρα μοι γέρας ἔξελον υἷες Ἀχαιῶν,

43 τείρω I wear out, exhaust; τειρόμενοι is
    pres. pass. part. (m. nom. pl.)
ὀλίγος -η -ον little, small
τ(ε): generalising in a proverbial statement
    'any respite in war is little', implying 'but
    valuable'
ἀνάπνευσις -εως, ἡ respite in, rest from (+
    gen.)
44 ῥεῖα (adv.) easily
ἀκμής -ῆτος unwearied
κάμνω I grow tired; κεκμηότας is perf.
    part. (m. acc. pl.). Note the powerful
    antithesis between juxtaposed ἀκμῆτες
    and κεκμηότας.
ἀνήρ ἀνδρός/ἀνέρος, ὁ man
ἀϋτή -ῆς, ἡ battle (properly 'battle cry'
    but regularly used to refer to the battle
    itself); dat. here with κεκμηότας ἄν-
    δρας 'men wearied with battle'
45 ὠθέω I push, drive; ὤσαιμεν is 1 pl. aor.
    opt., again potential with κ(ε) (cf. 16)
    'we would easily ...'
προτί = πρός (+ acc.) to
ἄστυ -εος, το city, town; the word original-
    ly began with digamma

ἀπό (+ gen.) (away) from; ἄπο here ac-
    cented as postposition (cf. on 18)
κλισίη -ης, ἡ hut (= Att. κλισία -ας)
46 φάτο: 3 s. impf. mid. of φημί (cf. 14)
λίσσομαι I beseech, pray
μέγα greatly; n. of μέγας (cf. 21) as adv.
νήπιος (here) senseless, foolish (the usu.
    sense in Homer; cf. 8); tr. phrase 'great
    fool that he was'
ἦ indeed, truly
μέλλω I am about to, (here) fated to
    (+ inf.). Homer as narrator rarely
    comments on the action, making it the
    more starkly significant when he does.
    Patroclus' impending death is constant-
    ly foreseen in this book, especially from
    647 onwards.
47 οἷ: dat. of personal pron. ἕ (acc.) οὗ
    (gen.) οἷ (dat.) him, her, it; οἷ αὐτῷ 'for
    himself'
θάνατος -ου/οιο, ὁ death
κακός -ή -όν bad, evil, cruel
κήρ κηρός, ἡ fate, death
λιτέσθαι: aor. inf. of λίσσομαι (cf. 46), here
    trans. 'to pray for'

48–100: Achilles replies, first recounting his grievance against Agamemnon (49–63), then giving Patroclus permission to enter the battle (64–82), but warning him not to press on to the city after driving back the Trojans from the ships (83–100).

48 ὀχθέω I am disturbed, angered; ὀχθήσας is
aor. part. (m. nom. s.)

προσέφη: 3 s. impf. of πρόσφημι (cf. 20)

πούς ποδός, ὁ foot

ὠκύς -εῖα/έα -ύ swift; acc. πόδας limits the
application of the adj. (lit. 'swift with respect to his feet') i.e. 'swift-footed' (this

is called 'accusative of respect'). This
formulaic phrase is a frequent epithet
for Achilles and unique to him, though
synonymous variants are sometimes
used of others (e.g. Antilochus as πόδας
ταχύς at 18.2, Iris as πόδας ὠκέα at
18.202).

49–63: Achilles explains his continuing absence from battle. He is in fact still fixated by the same issues which caused him to withdraw from the fighting in the first place, i.e. Agamemnon's dishonouring him by seizing his prize, Briseis.

49 ὤ μοι alas! ah me!

διογενής -ές Zeus-born; διογενές is voc.

οἷος -η -ον such; here exclamatory 'what a
thing …!'

ἔειπες = εἶπες, 2 s. aor. of λέγω I say.
This earlier, uncontracted form (here
convenient for the metre) originally had
digamma between the first two vowels.

50 οὔτε … οὔτε (51) neither … nor

ἐμπάζομαι I care about (+ gen.)

ὅστις ἥτις ὅ τι who(ever), which(ever);
ἥν τινα is f. acc. s.; οὔτε … οἶδα lit. 'I
neither care about an oracle, whichever
one I know of' i.e. 'I neither care about
any oracle that I know of'. Achilles here
rejects the suggestion made by Patroclus at 36.

51 τι anything; usu. unaccented in this
sense but here accented because the
next word is an enclitic (cf. on 3).
Note the similarity of this line to 37,
exemplifying the closeness with which
points raised are answered in Homeric
conversation (the near-repetition also
aiding the process of composition).

52 ὅδε ἥδε τόδε this

αἰνός -ή -όν dreadful

κραδίη -ης, ἡ heart (= Att. καρδία -ας)

θυμός -οῦ, ὁ mind, heart, soul (location of
emotions and mental processes); here

virtually synonymous with κραδίη (and
also with φρήν, cf. 36)

ἱκάνω I come upon

53 ὁπ(π)ότε (+ subj.) whenever

ὁμοῖος -η -ον similar, equal; τὸν ὁμοῖον 'one
who is his equal'

ἐθέλω I wish; ἐθέλησιν is 3 s. pres. subj., here
'indefinite', expressing a generalisation

ἀμέρδω I deprive, rob; ἀμέρσαι is aor. inf.

54 γέρας -αος, τό prize, privilege, gift of honour

ἄψ (adv.) back

ἀφαιρέω I take away; ἀφελέσθαι is aor. mid.
inf.

ὅ τε = ὅστις (cf. 50), referring back to ἀνήρ
(53)

κράτος -εος, τό strength, power

προβαίνω I go forward, (here) am superi-
or; προβέβηκη is 3 s. perf. subj.

55 τό that (article as demonstrative pron.)

ἐπεί because, since

πάσχω I suffer; πάθον is unaugmented 1
s. aor.

ἄλγος -εος, τό pain, sorrow, pl. troubles

56 κούρην (cf. 7): i.e. Briseis, Achilles' prize of
honour after his sacking of Lyrnessus, a
city south-east of Troy (2.690–1)

ἄρα (here) as is well known

ἐξαιρέω I select, choose; ἔξελον is 3 pl. aor.,
and here implies 'from the war booty'

δουρὶ δ' ἐμῷ κτεάτισσα, πόλιν εὐτείχεα πέρσας,
τὴν ἂψ ἐκ χειρῶν ἕλετο κρείων Ἀγαμέμνων
Ἀτρεΐδης ὡς εἴ τιν' ἀτίμητον μετανάστην.
ἀλλὰ τὰ μὲν προτετύχθαι ἐάσομεν· οὐδ' ἄρα πως ἦν   60
ἀσπερχὲς κεχολῶσθαι ἐνὶ φρεσίν· ἤτοι ἔφην γε
οὐ πρὶν μηνιθμὸν καταπαυσέμεν, ἀλλ' ὁπότ' ἂν δὴ
νῆας ἐμὰς ἀφίκηται ἀϋτή τε πτόλεμός τε.
τύνη δ' ὤμοιιν μὲν ἐμὰ κλυτὰ τεύχεα δῦθι,
ἄρχε δὲ Μυρμιδόνεσσι φιλοπτολέμοισι μάχεσθαι,   65
εἰ δὴ κυάνεον Τρώων νέφος ἀμφιβέβηκε
νηυσὶν ἐπικρατέως, οἱ δὲ ῥηγμῖνι θαλάσσης
κεκλίαται, χώρης ὀλίγην ἔτι μοῖραν ἔχοντες,
Ἀργεῖοι· Τρώων δὲ πόλις ἐπὶ πᾶσα βέβηκε
θάρσυνος· οὐ γὰρ ἐμῆς κόρυθος λεύσσουσι μέτωπον   70
ἐγγύθι λαμπομένης· τάχα κεν φεύγοντες ἐναύλους
πλήσειαν νεκύων, εἴ μοι κρείων Ἀγαμέμνων
ἤπια εἰδείη· νῦν δὲ στρατὸν ἀμφιμάχονται.
οὐ γὰρ Τυδεΐδεω Διομήδεος ἐν παλάμῃσι
μαίνεται ἐγχείη Δαναῶν ἀπὸ λοιγὸν ἀμῦναι·   75

57 δόρυ -ατος, τό spear; δουρί is an alternative dat. s.

ἐμός -ή -όν my

κτεατίζω I obtain, win; κτεάτισσα is 1 s. aor.

πόλις -ιος/ηος, ἡ city (= Att. πόλις -εως); the ι of πόλιν, normally short, has to be scanned long, as with πόλις in 69. Other anomalous long iotas appear in 322 and 560.

εὐτειχής -ές well-walled; εὐτείχεα is acc. s.

πέρθω I sack; πέρσας is aor. part. (m. nom. s.)

58 τήν her (article as personal pron.), picking up κούρην (56)

χείρ χειρός, ἡ hand

αἱρέω I take, seize; ἕλετο is 3 s. aor. mid. 'took for himself'

κρείων -οντος, ὁ lord, ruler

59 Ἀτρεΐδης -αο/εω, ὁ son of Atreus

ὡς εἰ as if

ἀτίμητος -ον dishonoured, without rights

μετανάστης -αο/εω, ὁ migrant, refugee; acc. agreeing with με understood in previous clause in double acc. construc-

tion (common with verbs of taking away) 'has taken her back (from me), as if I were some migrant without rights'. Such a person would be socially very vulnerable.

60 τὰ μέν these things (article as demonstrative pron.)

προτεύχω I do beforehand; προτετύχθαι is perf. pass. inf., lit. 'to have been done beforehand', i.e. 'to be over and done with' (cf. 18.112)

ἐάω I allow, leave (something) be; ἐάσομεν is 1 pl. aor. subj., here 'jussive' ('let us …') and again with short vowel (= Att. ἐάσωμεν; cf. on 19). The pl. associates Achilles with all who have similar feelings.

πως (adv.) somehow; οὐδ' ἄρα πως 'in no way then … '

ἦν (here) it was possible (= ἐξῆν)

61 ἀσπερχές (adv.) unceasingly

χολόομαι I am angry; κεχολῶσθαι is perf. inf.

ἐνί = ἐν

ἤτοι though to be sure

ἔφην: 1 s. impf. of φημί (cf. 14), here 'I thought'; again introducing indirect statement, with nom. (understood) + inf.

62 πρίν (adv.) before, sooner
μηνιθμός -οῦ, ὁ wrath
καταπαύω I put an end to; καταπαυσέμεν is fut. inf.
ἀλλ᾽ ὁπότ᾽ ἄν (+ subj.) but only when, except when

63 ἀφικνέομαι I reach, arrive (at); ἀφίκηται is 3 s. aor. subj. (s. because the two following nouns form a single concept)
τε ... τε both ... and
πτόλεμος = πόλεμος -ου/οιο, ὁ war, fighting; πτ- for π- is another common type of variant spelling (cf. on 2), again for metrical flexibility (πτ- allows short vowel ending preceding word to create a long syllable)

64–82: Patroclus is given permission to lead the Myrmidons into battle wearing Achilles' armour.

64 τύνη = σύ (cf. 17)
κλυτός -η -ον famous, glorious
δύ(ν)ω I put on (clothes etc.); δῦθι is 2 s. aor. imper.

65 ἄρχω I lead (+ dat.); ἄρχε is 2 s. imper.
φιλοπτόλεμος -ον war-loving (= Att. φιλοπόλεμος -ον); again note Homeric dat. pl. ending -οισι
μάχεσθαι: inf. expressing purpose after ἄρχε

66 κυάνεος -η -ον dark
νέφος -εος, τό cloud. These words paint a threatening picture, as if a storm is about to envelop the Achaean ships.
ἀμφιβαίνω I surround; ἀμφιβέβηκε is 3 s. perf.

67 ἐπικρατέως (adv.) mightily, victoriously
οἱ δέ: pron. redundant in tr., anticipating postponed subject Ἀργεῖοι (69); cf. Yorkshire idiom 'it's a nice town, is Harrogate'
ῥηγμίς -ῖνος, ἡ shore

68 κλίνω I lean; κεκλίαται is 3 pl. perf. pass (= Att. κεκλιμένοι εἰσί), lit. 'have been leant against', i.e. 'are right up against' (+ dat.)
χώρη -ης, ἡ land (= Att. χώρα -ας)
μοῖρα -ης, ἡ portion, space; χώρης ὀλίγην ... μοῖραν 'just a little space of land'
ἔχω I have, hold; ἔχοντες is pres. part. (m. nom. pl.)

69 ἐπιβαίνω I come (out) against; ἐπί ... βέβηκε is tmesis of 3 s. perf. with 'them' understood as object

70 θάρσυνος -ον full of confidence; again note enjambment, here (as oft.) ending a sense unit

κόρυς -υθος, ἡ helmet
λεύσσω I see
μέτωπον -ου, τό forehead, brow; (here) front (of helmet)

71 ἐγγύθι (adv.) near at hand
λάμπω I shine; λαμπομένης is pres. mid. part. (f. gen. s.) with same sense as act.
τάχα (adv.) quickly, (here) soon
κεν = κε (cf. 16)
φεύγω I run away, flee; φεύγοντες is pres. part. (m. nom. pl.)
ἔναυλος -ου, ὁ watercourse, channel

72 πίμπλημι I fill X (acc.) with Y (gen.); πλήσειαν is 3 pl. aor. opt. 'would fill' in fut. 'less likely' condition
νέκυς -υος, ὁ dead body, corpse

73 ἤπιος -η -ον kind, mild
εἰδείη: 3 s. opt. of οἶδα (cf. 19); ἤπια εἰδείη lit. 'were to know kind things', i.e. 'be well disposed'
νῦν (adv.) now
στρατός -οῦ, ὁ army, camp (usu. sense in the Iliad). Here the Greek camp: the Trojans have become unprecedentedly daring.
ἀμφιμάχομαι I fight around (+ acc.)

74 Τυδεΐδεω: gen. s. (cf. 25)
παλάμη -ης, ἡ palm, hand; παλάμῃσι is dat. pl. (cf. on 18)

75 μαίνομαι I rage, rave
ἐγχείη -ης, ἡ spear
ἀπαμύνω I ward off X (acc.) from Y (gen.); ἀπὸ ... ἀμῦναι is tmesis of aor. inf., here expressing purpose 'so as to ward off'

οὐδέ πω Ἀτρεΐδεω ὀπὸς ἔκλυον αὐδήσαντος
ἐχθρῆς ἐκ κεφαλῆς· ἀλλ' Ἕκτορος ἀνδροφόνοιο
Τρωσὶ κελεύοντος περιάγνυται, οἱ δ' ἀλαλητῷ
πᾶν πεδίον κατέχουσι, μάχῃ νικῶντες Ἀχαιούς.
ἀλλὰ καὶ ὧς, Πάτροκλε, νεῶν ἀπὸ λοιγὸν ἀμύνων   80
ἔμπεσ' ἐπικρατέως, μὴ δὴ πυρὸς αἰθομένοιο
νῆας ἐνιπρήσωσι, φίλον δ' ἀπὸ νόστον ἕλωνται.
πείθεο δ' ὥς τοι ἐγὼ μύθου τέλος ἐν φρεσὶ θείω,
ὡς ἄν μοι τιμὴν μεγάλην καὶ κῦδος ἄρηαι
πρὸς πάντων Δαναῶν, ἀτὰρ οἱ περικαλλέα κούρην   85
ἂψ ἀπονάσσωσιν, ποτὶ δ' ἀγλαὰ δῶρα πόρωσιν.
ἐκ νηῶν ἐλάσας ἰέναι πάλιν· εἰ δέ κεν αὖ τοι
δώῃ κῦδος ἀρέσθαι ἐρίγδουπος πόσις Ἥρης,
μὴ σύ γ' ἄνευθεν ἐμεῖο λιλαίεσθαι πολεμίζειν
Τρωσὶ φιλοπτολέμοισιν· ἀτιμότερον δέ με θήσεις·   90
μηδ' ἐπαγαλλόμενος πολέμῳ καὶ δηϊοτῆτι,
Τρῶας ἐναιρόμενος, προτὶ Ἴλιον ἡγεμονεύειν,
μή τις ἀπ' Οὐλύμποιο θεῶν αἰειγενετάων
ἐμβήῃ· μάλα τούς γε φιλεῖ ἑκάεργος Ἀπόλλων·

76 πω (adv.) yet
  ὄψ ὀπός, ἡ voice
  ἔκλυον: 1 s. impf. of κλύω (cf. 13) here +
    gen. (as oft.)
  αὐδάω I speak, shout; αὐδήσαντος is aor.
    part. (m. gen. s.)
77 ἐχθρός -ή -όν hateful; emphatically first
    word in the line. Achilles cannot hold
    back his hatred for Agamemnon.
  κεφαλή -ῆς, ἡ head
  Ἕκτωρ -ορος, ὁ Hector; understand ὄψ
    with Ἕκτορος
  ἀνδροφόνος -ον man-slaying; a standard
    epithet of Hector
78 κελεύω I order, give orders to (here + dat.,
    as oft. in Homer)
  περιάγνυμι I break around; περιάγνυται is
    3 s. pass., here 'reverberates all around'
  οἱ δ(έ) and they, i.e. the Trojans; again
    article as personal pron.
  ἀλαλητός -οῦ, ὁ war cry; note the onomat-
    opoeia
79 πεδίον -ου, τό plain
  κατέχω (here) I fill X (acc.) with Y (dat.)

μάχη -ης, ἡ battle
νικάω I defeat; νικῶντες is pres. part. (m.
  nom. pl.)
80 καὶ ὧς even so. Achilles acknowledges here
    that the conditions for his own return
    to the fighting have not yet been fully
    met.
  ἀπὸ … ἀμύνων: tmesis of pres. part. (m.
    nom. s.) of ἀπαμύνω (cf. 75)
81 ἐμπίπτω I fall upon; ἔμπεσ(ε) is 2 s. aor.
    imper. with 'them' (i.e. the Trojans)
    understood as object
  μή (+ subj.) lest, so that … not (introduc-
    ing negative purpose clause)
  πῦρ πυρός, τό fire; gen. of material 'with
    … fire'
  αἴθω I set ablaze; αἰθομένοιο is pres. pass.
    part. (n. gen. s.) 'blazing'
82 ἐμπίμπρημι I burn; ἐνιπρήσωσι is 3 pl. aor.
    subj.
  φίλος -η -ον dear
  νόστος -ου, ὁ homecoming
  ἀπὸ … ἕλωνται: tmesis of ἀφέλωνται, 3 pl.
    aor. subj. mid. of ἀφαιρέω (cf. 54)

83–96: Achilles warns Patroclus not to exceed his orders in case he outshines his leader, or runs into danger himself.

83 πείθομαι I listen, obey; πείθεο is 2 s. aor. imper. (= πείθου)
ὥς (adv.) as; accented because of enclitic τοι (cf. on 3)
τοι = σοι: dat. here possessive 'in your mind'
μῦθος -ου, ὁ word, speech, (here) instructions
τέλος -εος, τό end, (here) purpose
τίθημι I put, place; θείω is 1 s. aor. subj., here 'prospective' (i.e. like fut.)

84 ὡς ἄν (+ subj.) so that, in order that (introducing purpose clause)
τιμή -ῆς, ἡ honour
κῦδος -εος, τό glory
ἄρνυμαι I win, earn; ἄρηαι is 2 s. aor. subj.

85 πρός (+ gen.) from
πάντων: i.e. including Agamemnon
ἀτάρ but, (here) and in turn
οἱ they, i.e. the Achaeans; again article as personal pron.
περικαλλής -ές very beautiful

86 ἀποναίω I send back; ἀπονάσσωσιν is 3 pl. aor. subj.
ποτί = πρός (as adv.) in addition
ἀγλαός -ή -όν splendid, shining
δῶρον -ου, τό gift
ἔπορον (aor. only) I gave, provided; πόρωσι is 3 pl. subj. (with pres. sense). Achilles seems here to forget that he has already been offered exactly such compensation. Perhaps, as in the Meleager incident (9.597–9), the offer has been withdrawn after Achilles' refusal, but in a new frame of mind he is having second thoughts; τιμή and κῦδος still mean everything to him.

87 ἐλαύνω I drive; ἐλάσας is aor. part. (m. nom. s.) with object 'them' (i.e. the Trojans) understood
εἶμι I go, come; ἰέναι is inf., here used as imper. (likewise the infs. in 89, 92, 95 and 96)
πάλιν (adv.) back
εἰ ... κεν (+ subj.) if (in fut. open condition; = Att. ἐάν)
αὖ (adv.) in (your) turn
τοι = σοι

88 δώῃ: 3 s. aor. subj. of δίδωμι (cf. 40)
ἀρέσθαι: aor. inf. of ἄρνυμαι (cf. 84)
ἐρίγδουπος -ον loud-thundering
πόσις -ιος, ὁ husband
Ἥρη -ης, ἡ Hera (= Att. Ἥρα -ας). The 'loud-thundering husband of Hera' is of course Zeus.

89 μή (+ inf.) (here) do not ...!
ἄνευθεν (+ gen.) apart from
ἐμεῖο: Homeric gen. of ἐγώ (= ἐμοῦ; cf. 12)
λιλαίομαι I desire, am eager; inf. λιλαίεσθαι here as imper.
πολεμίζω I fight, make war against (+ dat.)

90 ἄτιμος -ον dishonoured; ἀτιμότερον is comp. (m. acc. s.), implying 'you will remove any chance of me getting my τιμή back'
δέ: here explanatory 'for'
θήσεις: 2 s. fut. of τίθημι (cf. 83), here 'you will make'

91 μηδ(έ) (here) and don't; with inf. ἡγεμονεύειν (92), continuing the commands
ἐπαγάλλομαι I exult in (+ dat.); ἐπαγαλλόμενος is pres. part. (m. nom. s.)
δηϊοτής -ῆτος, ἡ combat

92 ἐναίρομαι I kill (in battle); ἐναιρόμενος is pres. part. (m. nom. s.)
Ἴλιος -ου, ἡ or Ἴλιον -ου, τό Ilium, another name for Troy
ἡγεμονεύω I lead the way

93 μή (+ subj.) (here) in case, for fear that
Ὄλυμπος/Οὔλυμπος -ου/οιο, ὁ Mount Olympus, home of the gods; first syllable oft. lengthened for the metre
θεός -οῦ, ὁ god
αἰειγενέτης -αο/εω (m. adj.) immortal (= Att. ἀειγενέτης -ου)

94 ἐμβαίνω I step into; ἐμβήῃ is 3 s. aor. subj. 'enter the fighting'. This is exactly what does happen later when Patroclus disobeys his instructions.
τούς them, i.e the Trojans
φιλέω I love
ἑκάεργος -ον far-working, far-shooting
Ἀπόλλων -ωνος, ὁ Apollo

ἀλλὰ πάλιν τρωπᾶσθαι, ἐπὴν φάος ἐν νήεσσι   95
θήῃς, τοὺς δ᾽ ἔτ᾽ ἐᾶν πεδίον κάτα δηριάασθαι.
αἲ γάρ, Ζεῦ τε πάτερ καὶ Ἀθηναίη καὶ Ἄπολλον,
μήτε τις οὖν Τρώων θάνατον φύγοι, ὅσσοι ἔασι,
μήτε τις Ἀργείων, νῶϊν δ᾽ ἐκδῦμεν ὄλεθρον,
ὄφρ᾽ οἶοι Τροίης ἱερὰ κρήδεμνα λύωμεν."   100
    Ὣς οἱ μὲν τοιαῦτα πρὸς ἀλλήλους ἀγόρευον,
Αἴας δ᾽ οὐκέτ᾽ ἔμιμνε· βιάζετο γὰρ βελέεσσι·
δάμνα μιν Ζηνός τε νόος καὶ Τρῶες ἀγαυοὶ
βάλλοντες· δεινὴν δὲ περὶ κροτάφοισι φαεινὴ
πήληξ βαλλομένη καναχὴν ἔχε, βάλλετο δ᾽ αἰεὶ   105

3. Achilles tending the wounded Patroclus. Attic red-figure kylix, c.500 BCE.
Altes Museum, Berlin.

95 τρωπάω I turn, change; τρωπᾶσθαι is mid. inf. (again as imper.) 'turn' (intrans.)
ἐπήν (+ subj.) when, whenever (= ἐπεί + ἄν)
φάος (here again) light of deliverance (cf. 39)
νήεσσι: dat. pl. of νηῦς (cf. 1)

96 θήῃς: 2 s. aor. subj. of τίθημι (cf. 83)
τούς (here) the rest
ἐᾶν: pres. inf. of ἐάω (cf. 60), again as imper.
κάτα: accented as postposition (cf. on 18)
δηριάομαι I fight; δηριάασθαι is inf.

97–100: Achilles' prayer to the gods shows clearly both his close affection for Patroclus and his hostility, not only to the Trojans, but also to the rest of the Achaeans who have so humiliated him.

97 αἲ γάρ (+ opt.) would that …! (introducing a wish; oft., as here, one that cannot be fulfilled; = Att. εἰ γάρ)
Ζεῦ: voc. of Ζεύς (cf. 37)
Ἀθηναίη -ης, ἡ Athena (= Att. Ἀθηνᾶ -ᾶς)
Ἄπολλον: voc. of Ἀπόλλων (cf. 94)
98 μήτε … μήτε (99) neither … nor
ὅσσοι = ὅσοι (cf. 23)
ἔασι: 3 pl. pres. of εἰμί (cf. 23; = Att. εἰσί)
99 νῶϊν we two (nom. dual; = Att. νῷν)
ἐκδύ(ν)ω I get out from, escape; ἐκδῦμεν is 1 pl. opt. (with υι contracted)

ὄλεθρος -ου, ὁ destruction. Note the irony, as both Patroclus and Achilles will be dead before Troy falls.
100 ὄφρα (+ subj.) so that (introducing purpose clause)
Τροίη -ης, ἡ Troy (= Att. Τροία -ας)
ἱερός -ή -όν sacred, holy
κρήδεμνον -ου, τό headband, diadem; pl. battlements (forming similar shape)
λύω I loose, undo. The breaching of the citadel's ring of walls is likened to the violent removal of a woman's headdress; there is almost a hint of rape here.

101–29: Ajax, still fighting by Protesilaus' ship, grows tired; and with an appeal to the Muses, the poet tells how Hector forces him to retire and fire is thrown on the ship. Achilles urges Patroclus on.

101 τοιοῦτος τοιαύτη τοιοῦτο(ν) such
πρός (+ acc.) to
ἀλλήλους -ας -α (no nom.) each other, one another
ἀγορεύω I speak; ἀγόρευον is 3 pl. impf.
102 Αἴας -αντος, ὁ Ajax
οὐκέτ(ι) (adv.) no longer
μίμνω = μένω I remain, wait, (here) I hold my ground; ἔμιμνε is 3 s. impf.
βιάζω I press hard, overpower; βιάζετο is 3 s. impf. pass.
βέλος -εος, τό missile; βελέεσσι is dat. pl.
103 δαμνάω I subdue, overcome; δάμνα is 3 s. impf. (with νόος as subject; 3 pl. understood with Τρῶες: cf. on 26). Ajax is subdued by forces both human and divine, a good example of so-called 'double determination'.
τε … καί both … and
ἀγαυός -ή -όν lordly, illustrious

104 βάλλοντες: pres. part. (m. nom. pl.) of βάλλω (cf. 24) 'throwing', with 'missiles' understood as object. Note the emphatic repetition of the verb in this line and the next.
δεινός -ή -όν terrible, terrifying
περί (+ dat.) around
κρόταφος -ου, ὁ temple (of the head)
φαεινός -ή -όν bright, shining
105 πήληξ -ηκος, ἡ helmet
βαλλομένη: pres. pass. part. (f. nom. s.) of βάλλω 'as it was struck'
καναχή -ῆς, ἡ ringing sound
ἔχε: 3 s. impf. of ἔχω (cf. 68); δεινὴν … καναχὴν ἔχε 'made (lit. had) a terrible ringing'
βάλλετο: unaugmented 3 s. impf. pass. of βάλλω
αἰεί (adv.) always, constantly, ever (= Att. ἀεί)

κὰπ φάλαρ᾽ εὐποίηθ᾽· ὁ δ᾽ ἀριστερὸν ὦμον ἔκαμνεν,
ἔμπεδον αἰὲν ἔχων σάκος αἰόλον· οὐδ᾽ ἐδύναντο
ἀμφ᾽ αὐτῷ πελεμίξαι ἐρείδοντες βελέεσσιν.
αἰεὶ δ᾽ ἀργαλέῳ ἔχετ᾽ ἄσθματι, κὰδ δέ οἱ ἱδρὼς
πάντοθεν ἐκ μελέων πολὺς ἔρρεεν, οὐδέ πη εἶχεν   110
ἀμπνεῦσαι· πάντη δὲ κακὸν κακῷ ἐστήρικτο.

  Ἔσπετε νῦν μοι, Μοῦσαι Ὀλύμπια δώματ᾽ ἔχουσαι,
ὅππως δὴ πρῶτον πῦρ ἔμπεσε νηυσὶν Ἀχαιῶν.

  Ἕκτωρ Αἴαντος δόρυ μείλινον ἄγχι παραστὰς
πλῆξ᾽ ἄορι μεγάλῳ, αἰχμῆς παρὰ καυλὸν ὄπισθεν,   115
ἀντικρὺ δ᾽ ἀπάραξε· τὸ μὲν Τελαμώνιος Αἴας
πῆλ᾽ αὔτως ἐν χειρὶ κόλον δόρυ, τῆλε δ᾽ ἀπ᾽ αὐτοῦ
αἰχμὴ χαλκείη χαμάδις βόμβησε πεσοῦσα.
γνῶ δ᾽ Αἴας κατὰ θυμὸν ἀμύμονα, ῥίγησέν τε,
ἔργα θεῶν, ὅ ῥα πάγχυ μάχης ἐπὶ μήδεα κεῖρε   120
Ζεὺς ὑψιβρεμέτης, Τρώεσσι δὲ βούλετο νίκην·
χάζετο δ᾽ ἐκ βελέων. τοὶ δ᾽ ἔμβαλον ἀκάματον πῦρ
νηΐ θοῇ· τῆς δ᾽ αἶψα κατ᾽ ἀσβέστη κέχυτο φλόξ.

106 κὰπ = κατά
  φάλαρα -ων, τά metal plates
  εὐποίητος -ον well-made
  ὁ δ(έ) and he, i.e. Ajax
  ἀριστερός -ή -όν left, on the left; ἀρι-
    στερὸν ὦμον is acc. of resp. 'in the left
    shoulder'
107 ἔμπεδος -ον firm, steady
  αἰέν = αἰεί
  σάκος -εος, τό shield; this great, tow-
    er-like shield is Ajax's trademark,
    memorably visualised at 7.219–23
  αἰόλος -η -ον glittering, flashing
  δύναμαι I am able; ἐδύναντο is 3 pl.
    impf. with 'the Trojans' understood as
    subject
108 ἀμφ(ί) (+ dat.) around
  αὐτόν -ήν -ό him, her, it (personal pron.,
    not used in nom.)
  πελεμίζω I shake; πελεμίξαι is aor. inf.
    '(nor were they able) to shake (the
    shield) around him', i.e. 'they couldn't
    knock it away from him'
  ἐρείδω I press hard, i.e. hit repeatedly;
    ἐρείδοντες is pres. part. (m. nom. pl.)

109 ἀργαλέος -η -ον difficult, painful
  ἔχετο: 3 s. impf. pass. of ἔχω (cf. 68; =
    εἴχετο) 'he was gripped'
  ἄσθμα -ατος, τό panting
  καταρρέω I flow down; κὰδ ... ἔρρεεν
    (110) is tmesis of 3 s. impf. (κάδ =
    κατά before δ)
  οἱ his (possessive dat., lit. to/for him
    = αὐτῷ); the personal pron. (cf. 47)
    is oft. used in unaccented enclitic
    forms ἑ οὑ οἱ when non-reflexive (cf.
    on 3)
  ἱδρώς -ῶτος, ὁ sweat
110 πάντοθεν (adv.) on every side, all
    around
  μέλος -εος, τό limb; οἱ ... ἐκ μελέων 'from
    his limbs'
  πολύς πολλή πολύ much, pl. many
  πη (adv.) in any way
  ἔχω (here) I am able (+ inf.)
111 ἀμπνεῦσαι: aor. inf. ἀναπνέω (cf. 42)
  πάντη (adv.) on all sides
  στηρίζω I set firmly; ἐστήρικτο is 3 s.
    plup. pass., lit. 'had been set firmly',
    i.e. 'was piled upon'

112–13: *The poet appeals to the Muses, omniscient as they are, for information of which he himself is ignorant.*

112 ἐνέπω I tell, relate; ἔσπετε is 2 pl. aor.
  imper.
  μοῦσα -ης, ἡ Muse (goddess of poetic
  inspiration)
  Ὀλύμπιος -ον Olympian, on Mount
  Olympus

δῶμα -ατος, τό home
113 ὅπ(π)ως (adv.) how
  πρῶτον (adv.) (at) first
  ἔμπεσε: 3 s. aor. of ἐμπίπτω (cf. 81)

114–29: *When his spear is broken by Hector, Ajax withdraws from the fighting. Achilles encourages Patroclus.*

114 μείλινος -η -ον made of ash, ashen (= Att.
  μέλινος)
  ἄγχι (adv.) nearby
  παραστάς: aor. part. (m. nom.
    s.) of παρίσταμαι (cf. 2), here
    'approaching'
115 πλήσσω I strike; πλῆξ(ε) is 3 s. aor.
  ἄορ ἄορος, τό sword
  αἰχμή -ῆς, ἡ spear-point
  παρά (+ acc.) close by
  καυλός -οῦ, ὁ socket, i.e. where the
    spear's wooden shaft connects with its
    bronze tip
  ὄπισθεν (+ gen.) behind; αἰχμῆς … ὄπι-
    σθεν 'behind the point'
116 ἀντικρύ (adv.) completely
  ἀπαράσσω I strike off; ἀπάραξε is 3 s.
    aor. with 'the point' understood as
    object
  τό: pron. redundant in tr., anticipating
    κόλον δόρυ as object of πῆλ(ε) (117)
  Τελαμώνιος -ον of Telamon, (here) son of
    Telamon
117 πάλλω I brandish, shake; πῆλε is 3 s. aor.
  αὔτως (adv.) just as it was, i.e. uselessly
  κόλος -ον broken off, without its point. A
    perfect cinematic image: Ajax briefly
    wields his weapon without realising
    that its point, sliced off, is whirling
    through the air to clang on to the
    ground.
  τῆλε (adv.) far. The striking assonance
    with πῆλε perhaps evokes the two
    parts of the spear.
118 χάλκειος -η -ον (made of) bronze
  χαμάδις (adv.) to the ground
  βομβέω I clang; βόμβησε is 3 s. aor.

πίπτω I fall; πεσοῦσα is aor. part. (f.
  nom. s.); tr. phrase 'fell with a clang'
119 γιγνώσκω I get to know, realise; γνῶ is 3
  s. aor.
  ἀμύμων -ονος blameless, excellent
  ῥιγέω I shudder (at); ῥίγησεν is 3 s. aor.
120 ἔργον -ου, τό work, deed
  ὅ ῥα that after all (= ὅτι ἄρα); ῥα is an
    enclitic form of ἄρα (cf. 33)
  πάγχυ (adv.) entirely (= Att. πάνυ)
  ἐπικείρω I mow down, (here) I thwart;
    ἐπὶ … κεῖρε is tmesis of 3 s. impf.
  μῆδος -εος, τό plan, counsel; μάχης μήδεα
    'their battle plans'
121 ὑψιβρεμέτης -αο/εω (m. adj.) high-
    thundering
  βούλομαι I want, wish (for); βούλετο is 3
    s. impf.
  νίκη -ης, ἡ victory
122 χάζομαι I draw back, give way; χάζετο
    is 3 s. impf. Even heroes can take the
    hint when they sense the intervention
    of a god.
  τοί = οἱ they, i.e. the Trojans; note that
    m. and f. nom. pl. forms of the article/
    pron. oft. have initial τ in Homer
  ἐμβάλλω I throw on; ἔμβαλον is 3 pl. aor.
  ἀκάματος -ον untiring, inexhaustible
123 θοός -ή -όν swift. The 'swift ship' is that of
    Protesilaus (cf. on 1).
  τῆς it, i.e. the ship
  αἶψα (adv.) at once
  ἄσβεστος -ον inextinguishable
  καταχέω I pour over (+ gen.); κατ(ὰ) …
    κέχυτο is tmesis of 3 s. plup. pass. 'over
    it streamed' (lit. 'had been poured')
  φλόξ φλογός, ἡ flame

ὣς τὴν μὲν πρύμνην πῦρ ἄμφεπεν· αὐτὰρ Ἀχιλλεὺς
μηρὼ πληξάμενος Πατροκλῆα προσέειπεν·   125
"ὄρσεο, διογενὲς Πατρόκλεες, ἱπποκέλευθε·
λεύσσω δὴ παρὰ νηυσὶ πυρὸς δηΐοιο ἰωήν·
μὴ δὴ νῆας ἕλωσι καὶ οὐκέτι φυκτὰ πέλωνται·
δύσεο τεύχεα θᾶσσον, ἐγὼ δέ κε λαὸν ἀγείρω."
      Ὣς φάτο, Πάτροκλος δὲ κορύσσετο νώροπι χαλκῷ.   130
κνημῖδας μὲν πρῶτα περὶ κνήμῃσιν ἔθηκε
καλάς, ἀργυρέοισιν ἐπισφυρίοις ἀραρυίας·
δεύτερον αὖ θώρηκα περὶ στήθεσσιν ἔδυνε
ποικίλον ἀστερόεντα ποδώκεος Αἰακίδαο.
ἀμφὶ δ' ἄρ' ὤμοισιν βάλετο ξίφος ἀργυρόηλον   135
χάλκεον, αὐτὰρ ἔπειτα σάκος μέγα τε στιβαρόν τε·
κρατὶ δ' ἐπ' ἰφθίμῳ κυνέην εὔτυκτον ἔθηκεν
ἵππουριν· δεινὸν δὲ λόφος καθύπερθεν ἔνευεν.
εἵλετο δ' ἄλκιμα δοῦρε, τά οἱ παλάμηφιν ἀρήρει.
ἔγχος δ' οὐχ ἕλετ' οἶον ἀμύμονος Αἰακίδαο,   140
βριθὺ μέγα στιβαρόν· τὸ μὲν οὐ δύνατ' ἄλλος Ἀχαιῶν
πάλλειν, ἀλλά μιν οἶος ἐπίστατο πῆλαι Ἀχιλλεύς,

124 πρύμνη -ης, ἡ stern (of a ship). The prows of the Achaean ships are pointing towards the water, for a quick getaway if needed.

ἀμφέπω I envelop; ἄμφεπεν is 3 s. impf.

αὐτάρ (conj.) but

125 μηρώ: acc. dual of μηρός (cf. 27). Thigh-slapping in Homer indicates emotional stress.

προσέειπον (aor.) I spoke to, addressed

126 ὄρνυμαι I get up, set out; ὄρσεο is 2 s. aor. imper.

ἱπποκέλευθος -ον horse-driving; (as noun) charioteer

127 παρά (+ dat.) beside, by

δήϊος (-η) -ον hostile, (of fire) destructive (= Att. δάϊος -α -ον)

ἰωή -ῆς, ἡ blaze; hiatus (cf. 11) precedes ἰωήν (as it usu. does with this noun in Homer)

128 μή: used as at 93

ἕλωσι: 3 pl. aor. subj. of αἱρέω (cf. 58) with 'the Trojans' understood as subject

φυκτά -ῶν, τά means of escape. If the Trojans take the ships, escape becomes impossible for the Achaeans.

πέλωνται: 3 pl. subj. of πέλομαι (cf. 29). Homer does not consistently observe the rule that n. pl. subject takes s. verb.

129 δύσεο: 2 s. aor. mid. imper. of δύ(ν)ω (cf. 64)

τεύχεα: i.e. 'my armour'

θᾶσσον (more) quickly, immediately; comp. adv. from ταχύς quick, swift

ἀγείρω I gather; here 1 s. subj. + κε, prospective (cf. on 83) 'I will gather'

130–277: Patroclus puts on Achilles' armour and the charioteer Automedon harnesses the divine horses. Achilles meanwhile encourages the men, and, returning to his hut, prays that Patroclus will both drive back the Trojans and return safely to the ships. Patroclus then leads the Myrmidons out to battle. These lengthy preliminaries whet our appetite for the fighting when it eventually comes.

130–9: Elaborate arming scenes like this are set pieces in Homeric poetry, shining a spotlight on the ἀριστεία *(brilliant feat of arms) of one particular hero. Here Patroclus'* ἀριστεία *is also, ironically, his final moment of glory.*

130 κορύσσω I arm; κορύσσετο is 3 s. impf.
  'armed himself'
  νῶροψ -οπος (m. adj.) shining
  χαλκός -οῦ, ὁ bronze
131 κνημίς -ῖδος, ἡ greave, shin guard
  πρῶτα (adv.) first
  κνήμη -ης, ἡ shin, leg
  ἔθηκε: 3 s. aor. of τίθημι (cf. 83)
132 κᾱλός -ή -όν beautiful, fine (long α in
  Homer, short in Att.)
  ἀργύρεος -η -ον (made of) silver (= Att.
  ἀργυροῦς -ᾶ -οῦν)
  ἐπισφύριον -ου, τό ankle protector
  ἀραρίσκω I fit; ἀραρυίας is perf. part. (f.
  acc. pl.) with pass. sense 'fitted with'
  (+ dat.)
133 δεύτερον αὖ (adv.) second, next
  θώρηξ -ηκος, ὁ breastplate, corselet (=
  Att. θώραξ -ακος)
  στῆθος -εος, τό breast, chest; here pl. for
  s. (as oft.)
134 ποικίλος -η -ον (here) skilfully made
  ἀστερόεις -εσσα -εν (-εντος) shining like
  a star
  ποδώκης -ες swift-footed
  Αἰακίδης -αο/εω, ὁ son or (as here) descendant of Aeacus (cf. on 15)

135 ἀμφιβάλλω I put X (acc.) around/over Y
  (dat.); ἀμφὶ … βάλετο is tmesis of 3 s.
  aor. mid.
  ξίφος -εος, τό sword
  ἀργυρόηλος -ον silver-studded
136 χάλκεος -ον (made of) bronze (= χάλκειος -η -ον, cf. 118)
  αὐτὰρ ἔπειτα (adv.) and then, next
  στιβαρός -ή -όν firm, strong
137 κάρη κρατός, τό head
  ἐπ(ί) (+ dat.) (here) on
  ἴφθιμος -η -ον strong
  κυνέη -ης, ἡ helmet, cap (= Att. κυνῆ -ῆς)
  εὔτυκτος -ον well-made
138 ἵππουρις -ιδος (f. adj.) with horse-hair
  crest
  δεινόν: n. as adv. (cf. 104)
  λόφος -ου, ὁ crest, plume
  καθύπερθεν (adv.) (from) above
  νεύω I nod
139 εἵλετο: 3 s. aor. mid. of αἱρέω (cf. 58)
  ἄλκιμος -ον strong, stout
  δοῦρε: acc. dual of δόρυ (cf. 57) 'two
  spears'
  οἱ his (possessive dat., cf. 109)
  παλάμηφιν: dat. pl. of παλάμη (cf. 74)
  ἀρήρει: 3 s. plup. of ἀραρίσκω (cf. 132);
  τά … ἀρήρει 'which fitted his grasp'

140–4: Patroclus doesn't take Achilles' spear, a poignant reminder of his relative weakness.

140 ἔγχος -εος, τό spear; ἔγχος … οἶον 'but
  the spear alone … he did not take'
141 βριθύς -εῖα -ύ heavy
  τὸ μέν it
  δύνατ(ο): unaugmented 3 s. impf. of
  δύναμαι (cf. 107)

142 μιν (here) it (cf. 6)
  ἐπίσταμαι I know how to (+ inf.); ἐπίστατο is 3 s. impf.
  πῆλαι: aor. inf. of πάλλω (cf. 117). The
  play on words with Πηλιάδα and Πηλίου in the next two lines is deliberate.

Πηλιάδα μελίην, τὴν πατρὶ φίλῳ πόρε Χείρων
Πηλίου ἐκ κορυφῆς, φόνον ἔμμεναι ἡρώεσσιν.
ἵππους δ' Αὐτομέδοντα θοῶς ζευγνῦμεν ἄνωγε,   145
τὸν μετ' Ἀχιλλῆα ῥηξήνορα τῖε μάλιστα,
πιστότατος δέ οἱ ἔσκε μάχῃ ἔνι μεῖναι ὁμοκλήν.
τῷ δὲ καὶ Αὐτομέδων ὕπαγε ζυγὸν ὠκέας ἵππους,
Ξάνθον καὶ Βαλίον, τὼ ἅμα πνοιῇσι πετέσθην,
τοὺς ἔτεκε Ζεφύρῳ ἀνέμῳ Ἅρπυια Ποδάργη,   150
βοσκομένη λειμῶνι παρὰ ῥόον Ὠκεανοῖο.
ἐν δὲ παρηορίῃσιν ἀμύμονα Πήδασον ἵει,
τόν ῥά ποτ' Ἠετίωνος ἑλὼν πόλιν ἤγαγ' Ἀχιλλεύς,
ὃς καὶ θνητὸς ἐὼν ἕπεθ' ἵπποις ἀθανάτοισι.

Μυρμιδόνας δ' ἄρ' ἐποιχόμενος θώρηξεν Ἀχιλλεὺς   155
πάντας ἀνὰ κλισίας σὺν τεύχεσιν· οἱ δὲ λύκοι ὣς
ὠμοφάγοι, τοῖσίν τε περὶ φρεσὶν ἄσπετος ἀλκή,
οἵ τ' ἔλαφον κεραὸν μέγαν οὔρεσι δῃώσαντες
δάπτουσιν· πᾶσιν δὲ παρήϊον αἵματι φοινόν·

143 Πηλιάς -άδος Pelian, from Mount Pelion
μελίη -ης, ἡ ash spear (= Att. μελία -ας)
πόρε: unaugmented 3 s. of ἔπορον (cf. 86)
Χείρων -ωνος, ὁ Chiron, a centaur (with body of a horse, torso and head of a man) but an untypically civilised one. He lived in a cave on Mount Pelion and had a role in the education of several heroes, notably Peleus, Achilles and Jason.

144 Πήλιον -ου, τό Pelion, a mountain in Thessaly. Note further wordplay here with Πηλεύς, Achilles' father and first recipient of the spear.
κορυφή -ῆς, ἡ summit
φόνος -ου, ὁ slaughter, means of slaughter
ἔμμεναι: pres. inf. of εἰμί (= εἶναι), here expressing purpose
ἥρως -ωος, ὁ hero; ἡρώεσσιν is dat. pl.

145–54: The charioteer Automedon harnesses Achilles' horses.

145 ἵππος -ου, ὁ horse
Αὐτομέδων -οντος, ὁ Automedon, Achilles' charioteer
θοῶς (adv. from θοός, cf. 123) swiftly
ζεύγνυμι I yoke together; ζευγνῦμεν is pres. inf.
ἄνωγε: 3 s. of ἄνωγα (cf. 8); the subject is Patroclus
146 μετ(ά) (+ acc.) after
ῥηξήνωρ -ορος (m. adj.) breaking through ranks (leading to a rout); (epithet of Achilles) 'breaker of ranks'
τίω I honour, value
μάλιστα (adv.) most, especially (sup. of μάλα, cf. 16)

147 πιστός -ή -όν trusty, faithful; πιστότατος is sup. (m. nom. s.)
οἱ to him (cf. 47 and 109)
ἔσκε: 3 s. impf. of εἰμί (= ἦν); the subject is Automedon. This is an 'iterative' form of the impf. (identified by -σκ-) to indicate regular or repeated action, here implying 'was always'.
μένω I wait for; μεῖναι is aor. inf., here explanatory after πιστότατος 'most faithful to him in waiting for his call in battle'. Heroes went into battle by chariot, and dismounted to fight. It was the charioteer's job to stay close at hand and respond at once when summoned.

ἔνι = ἐν; accented as postposition (cf. on 18)

ὁμοκλή -ῆς, ἡ call

148 τῷ δὲ καί and for him, i.e. Patroclus

ὑπάγω I lead X (acc.) under Y (also acc.)

ζυγόν -οῦ, τό yoke

149 Ξάνθος -ου, ὁ Xanthus ('Bay')

Βαλίος -ου, ὁ Balius ('Dapple'). They are Achilles' two immortal horses.

τώ the two of whom (nom. dual of article here as rel. pron.)

ἅμα (cf. 8): here implying 'as fast as'

πνοιή -ῆς, ἡ breath, (here) blast of wind (= Att. πνοή -ῆς)

πέτομαι I fly; πετέσθην is dual impf.

150 ἔτεκε: 3 s. aor. of τίκτω (cf. 34)

Ζέφυρος -ου, ὁ Zephyrus, the west wind

ἄνεμος -ου, ὁ wind

Ἅρπυια -ας, ἡ Harpy. In later tradition a monstrous bird, but in Homer no more than the personified force of a storm, a fitting mother for a pair of swift horses.

Ποδάργη -ης, ἡ Podarge (probably 'White Foot')

151 βόσκομαι I feed, graze

λειμών -ῶνος, ὁ meadow; dat. here local 'in a meadow'

ῥόος -ου, ὁ stream

Ὠκεανός -οῦ/οῖο, ὁ Oceanus, the mighty river believed to surround the whole (flat) earth

152 παρηορίαι -ῶν, αἱ side-traces. These were reins by which a third horse was attached as a reserve beside the regular pair yoked to a chariot, in case one of them was put out of action, but trace-horses are rarely mentioned in the *Iliad*, and the function of the mortal Pedasus may be just to provide a victim for Sarpedon's spear (466–9).

Πήδασος -ου, ὁ Pedasus ('Leaper')

ἵημι I send, (here) I place; ἵει is 3 s. impf.

153 ποτ(έ) (adv.) once

Ἠετίων -ωνος, ὁ Eëtion, king of Thebe (a city just south of Troy) and father of Andromache (6.395)

ἑλών: aor. part. (m. nom. s.) of αἱρέω (cf. 58)

ἄγω I lead, (here) carry off (by force); ἤγαγε is 3 s. aor. Pedasus was war booty, a high mark of esteem, since Achilles took only the best.

154 ὅς: rel. pron. referring back to Πήδασον in 152

καί (here) although (= Att. καίπερ)

θνητός -ή -όν mortal

ἐών: pres. part. (m. nom. s.) of εἰμί (= ὤν)

ἕπομαι I follow, (here) I keep pace with (+ dat.); ἕπεθ' (= ἕπετο) is 3 s. impf.

ἀθάνατος (-η) -ον immortal. Pedasus' mortality is consciously contrasted with the immortality of Xanthus and Balius.

155–67: Achilles arms the Myrmidons, who are likened to ravening wolves: just as the wolves go forth in a pack, so the Myrmidons array themselves around Patroclus.

155 ἐποίχομαι I go to and fro, walk back and forth; tr. ἐποιχόμενος with ἀνὰ κλισίας (156), and πάντας with Μυρμιδόνας

θώρηξεν: 3 s. aor. of θωρήσσω (cf. 40)

156 ἀνά (+ acc.) throughout, among

σύν (+ dat.) with, (here) in

οἱ δέ and they; understand 'rushed forth', anticipating ῥώοντ(ο) in 166

λύκος -ου, ὁ wolf

157 ὠμοφάγος -ον ravening (lit. eating raw flesh)

τοῖσιν: possessive dat. with 'is' understood, so 'in whose hearts is'

περί (+ dat.) (here) in

ἄσπετος -ον unspeakable

ἀλκή -ῆς, ἡ fighting spirit

158 ἔλαφος -ου/οιο, ὁ stag

κεραός -οῦ (m. adj.) horned

ὄρος -εος, τό mountain; Homeric dat. pl. οὔρεσι here local 'in the mountains'

δηόω/δηϊόω I cut down, kill; δηώσαντες is aor. part. (m. nom. pl.)

159 δάπτω I devour

παρήϊον -ου, τό cheek

αἷμα -ατος, τό blood

φοινός -ή -όν red

καί τ' ἀγεληδὸν ἴασιν ἀπὸ κρήνης μελανύδρου   160
λάψοντες γλώσσησιν ἀραιῇσιν μέλαν ὕδωρ
ἄκρον, ἐρευγόμενοι φόνον αἵματος· ἐν δέ τε θυμὸς
στήθεσιν ἄτρομός ἐστι, περιστένεται δέ τε γαστήρ·
τοῖοι Μυρμιδόνων ἡγήτορες ἠδὲ μέδοντες
ἀμφ' ἀγαθὸν θεράποντα ποδώκεος Αἰακίδαο   165
ῥώοντ'· ἐν δ' ἄρα τοῖσιν ἀρήϊος ἵστατ' Ἀχιλλεύς,
ὀτρύνων ἵππους τε καὶ ἀνέρας ἀσπιδιώτας.

   Πεντήκοντ' ἦσαν νῆες θοαί, ᾗσιν Ἀχιλλεὺς
ἐς Τροίην ἡγεῖτο Διῒ φίλος· ἐν δὲ ἑκάστῃ
πεντήκοντ' ἔσαν ἄνδρες ἐπὶ κληῖσιν ἑταῖροι·   170
πέντε δ' ἄρ' ἡγεμόνας ποιήσατο τοῖς ἐπεποίθει
σημαίνειν· αὐτὸς δὲ μέγα κρατέων ἤνασσε.
τῆς μὲν ἰῆς στιχὸς ἦρχε Μενέσθιος αἰολοθώρηξ,
υἱὸς Σπερχειοῖο, διιπετέος ποταμοῖο·
ὃν τέκε Πηλῆος θυγάτηρ, καλὴ Πολυδώρη,   175
Σπερχειῷ ἀκάμαντι, γυνὴ θεῷ εὐνηθεῖσα,
αὐτὰρ ἐπίκλησιν Βώρῳ, Περιήρεος υἷι,
ὅς ῥ' ἀναφανδὸν ὄπυιε, πορὼν ἀπερείσια ἕδνα.
τῆς δ' ἑτέρης Εὔδωρος ἀρήϊος ἡγεμόνευε,
παρθένιος, τὸν τίκτε χορῷ καλὴ Πολυμήλη,   180
Φύλαντος θυγάτηρ· τῆς δὲ κρατὺς Ἀργειφόντης
ἠράσατ', ὀφθαλμοῖσιν ἰδὼν μετὰ μελπομένῃσιν

160 ἀγεληδόν (adv.) in a pack
   ἴασιν they go; 3 pl. pres. of εἶμι (I go, cf.
      87)
   κρήνης μελανύδρου: cf. 3
161 λάπτω I lap up, drink; λάψοντες is fut.
      part. (m. nom. pl.)
   γλῶσσα -ης, ἡ tongue
   ἀραιός -ή -όν slender
   μέλας μέλαινα μέλαν black, dark
162 ἄκρος -η -ον top part of; μέλαν ὕδωρ
      ἄκρον 'the surface of the dark water'
   ἐρεύγομαι I belch forth
   φόνος -ου, ὁ (here) gore, clotted blood
      (cf. 144); φόνον αἵματος 'gore (consist-
      ing) of blood', i.e. 'bloody gore'
163 ἄτρομος -ον fearless
   περιστένω I cram full
   γαστήρ -έρος/ρός, ὁ belly

164 τοῖος -η -ον (here) like this (cf. 22). The
      Myrmidons rush forth like wolves;
      and just as the wolves in the simile end
      up satisfied, so will the Myrmidons
      shortly satisfy their hunger for blood.
   ἡγήτωρ -ορος, ὁ leader
   μέδων -οντος, ὁ ruler
165 ἀμφί (+ acc.) around
   ἀγαθός -ή -όν good, brave
   θεράπων -οντος, ὁ aide, battle companion
166 ῥώομαι I move quickly, rush forth
   ἐν (+ dat.) among; here with τοῖσιν
      'among them'
   ἵσταμαι I stand; ἵστατ(ο) is 3 s. impf.
167 ὀτρύνω I rouse, urge on
   ἀνέρας = ἄνδρας
   ἀσπιδιώτης -αο/εω (m. adj.) shield-
      bearing

168–97: The poet now underlines the importance of the coming attack, and builds up tension before it, by providing a catalogue of the Myrmidons. There are fifty ships of fifty men each, and the whole force is divided into five battalions, each with its own commander. It is notable that none of these plays any further part in the coming battle.

168 πεντήκοντ(α) fifty
ᾗσιν: f. dat. pl. of rel. pron.

169 ἐς = εἰς (+ acc.) to, into
ἡγέομαι I lead (+ dat.)
ἕκαστος -η -ον each

170 ἔσαν = ἦσαν
ἐπί (+ dat.) (here) at
κληΐς -ῗδος, ἡ (here) oar lock (technical
term 'thole pin', a wooden pin used
with rope or leather strap to hold oar
in place; = Att. κλείς κλειδός)
ἑταῖρος -ου, ὁ companion, comrade

171 πέντε five
ἡγεμών -όνος, ὁ leader
ποιέομαι (here) I appoint; ποιήσατο is
3 s. aor. but tr. here as plup. 'he had
appointed'
πέποιθα (perf. with pres. sense) I trust (+
dat.); ἐπεποίθει is 3 s. plup. with impf.
sense 'he trusted'

172 σημαίνω I command, give orders
κρατέω I have power; μέγα κρατέων
'with great power'
ἀνάσσω I rule, am lord; ἤνασσε is 3 s.
impf. 'was commander-in-chief'

173 τῆς: note how repetition at 179, 193 and
196 (though not 197) itemises the list
ἰῆς = μιᾶς, f. gen. of εἷς one, here implying
'first' (in list)
στιχός (only gen. in s.), τῆς (here) line
of ships
ἦρχε: 3 s. impf. of ἄρχω, here + gen. (cf.
65)
Μενέσθιος -ου, ὁ Menesthius, a Myrmidon leader
αἰολοθώρηξ -ηκος (m. adj.) of the glittering breastplate

174 Σπερχειός -οῦ/οῖο, ὁ Spercheius, a river
in Thessaly
διιπετής -ές fallen from Zeus, (here) fed
by rain from Zeus
ποταμός -οῦ/οῖο, ὁ river

175 τέκε: unaugmented 3 s. aor. of τίκτω (cf.
34)
θυγάτηρ -έρος/ρός, ἡ daughter

Πολυδώρη -ης, ἡ Polydora. As a daughter
of Peleus by a human wife, she was
Achilles' half-sister (making Menesthius Achilles' nephew).

176 ἀκάμας -αντος (m. adj.) untiring
γυνή γυναικός, ἡ woman
εὐνάομαι I sleep with (+ dat.); εὐνηθεῖσα
is aor. part. (f. nom. s.)

177 ἐπίκλησις -εως, ἡ name; acc. here as adv.
'nominally'
Βῶρος -ου, ὁ Borus, husband of Polydora
Περιήρης -εος, ὁ Perieres, father of Borus

178 ἀναφανδόν (adv.) openly, publicly
ὀπυίω I have as wife, am married to;
ὄπυιε is 3 s. impf.
ἔπορον (aor.) I gave, provided (cf. 86);
πορών is part. (m. nom. s.), here with
pres. sense
ἀπερείσιος -ον unlimited, boundless
ἕδνα -ων, τά bridal gifts

179 ἕτερος -η -ον the other (of two), (here)
second; picking up from 173
Εὔδωρος -ου, ὁ Eudorus, a Myrmidon
leader
ἡγεμονεύω I am leader of (+ gen.)

180 παρθένιος -ου, ὁ child of an unmarried
mother. Eudorus, like Menesthius above,
has a human mother and divine father.
χορός -οῦ, ὁ dancing-floor, dance; χορῷ
καλή 'beautiful in the dance'
Πολυμήλη -ης, ἡ Polymele

181 Φύλας -αντος, ὁ Phylas
κρατύς (m. nom. s.) = κρατερός (cf. 25)
Ἀργειφόντης -αο/εω, ὁ Argeiphontes; traditional title of Hermes of uncertain
meaning, but oft. tr. 'killer of Argus' (a
monster)

182 ἐράομαι I fall in love with (+ gen.);
ἠράσατο is 3 s. aor. Ancient gods had
a weakness for mortals in affairs of the
heart, and it was oft. love at first sight.
ὀφθαλμός -οῦ, ὁ eye
μέλπομαι I celebrate with dance and
song; μελπομένῃσιν is pres. part. (f.
dat. pl.), here 'girls dancing'

ἐν χορῷ Ἀρτέμιδος χρυσηλακάτου κελαδεινῆς.
αὐτίκα δ᾽ εἰς ὑπερῷ᾽ ἀναβὰς παρελέξατο λάθρη
Ἑρμείας ἀκάκητα, πόρεν δέ οἱ ἀγλαὸν υἱὸν   185
Εὔδωρον, πέρι μὲν θείειν ταχὺν ἠδὲ μαχητήν.
αὐτὰρ ἐπεὶ δὴ τόν γε μογοστόκος Εἰλείθυια
ἐξάγαγε πρὸ φόωσδε καὶ ἠελίου ἴδεν αὐγάς,
τὴν μὲν Ἐχεκλῆος κρατερὸν μένος Ἀκτορίδαο
ἠγάγετο πρὸς δώματ᾽, ἐπεὶ πόρε μυρία ἕδνα,   190
τὸν δ᾽ ὁ γέρων Φύλας εὖ ἔτρεφεν ἠδ᾽ ἀτίταλλεν,
ἀμφαγαπαζόμενος ὡς εἴ θ᾽ ἑὸν υἱὸν ἐόντα.
τῆς δὲ τρίτης Πείσανδρος ἀρήϊος ἡγεμόνευε
Μαιμαλίδης, ὃς πᾶσι μετέπρεπε Μυρμιδόνεσσιν
ἔγχεϊ μάρνασθαι μετὰ Πηλεΐωνος ἑταῖρον.   195
τῆς δὲ τετάρτης ἦρχε γέρων ἱππηλάτα Φοῖνιξ,
πέμπτης δ᾽ Ἀλκιμέδων, Λαέρκεος υἱὸς ἀμύμων.
αὐτὰρ ἐπεὶ δὴ πάντας ἅμ᾽ ἡγεμόνεσσιν Ἀχιλλεὺς
στῆσεν ἐῢ κρίνας, κρατερὸν δ᾽ ἐπὶ μῦθον ἔτελλε·
"Μυρμιδόνες, μή τίς μοι ἀπειλάων λελαθέσθω,   200
ἃς ἐπὶ νηυσὶ θοῇσιν ἀπειλεῖτε Τρώεσσι
πάνθ᾽ ὑπὸ μηνιθμόν, καί μ᾽ ἠτιάασθε ἕκαστος·
'σχέτλιε Πηλέος υἱέ, χόλῳ ἄρα σ᾽ ἔτρεφε μήτηρ,
νηλεές, ὃς παρὰ νηυσὶν ἔχεις ἀέκοντας ἑταίρους·
οἴκαδέ περ σὺν νηυσὶ νεώμεθα ποντοπόροισιν   205

183 Ἄρτεμις -ιδος, ἡ Artemis
   χρυσηλάκατος -ον of the golden arrow
      (or distaff)
   κελαδεινός -ή -όν sounding, echoing; here
      perhaps '(goddess) of the echoing
      hunt' (or 'dance')
184 αὐτίκα (adv.) at once, straight away
   ὑπερῷον -ου, τό upper room; here pl.
      for s.
   ἀναβαίνω I go up; ἀναβάς is aor. part. (m.
      nom. s.)
   παραλέγομαι I lie with; παρελέξατο is 3 s.
      aor. with dat. 'her' understood
   λάθρη (adv.) secretly (= Att. λάθρα)
185 Ἑρμείας -αο/εω, ὁ Hermes (= Att. Ἑρμῆς
      -ου)
   ἀκάκητα -αο/εω (m. adj.) the deliverer
      (epithet of Hermes)
   πόρεν: unaugmented 3 s. of ἔπορον (cf.
      178)
   ἀγλαόν: cf. 86

186 πέρι (here as adv.) exceedingly
   θείω I run (= θέω); πέρι μὲν θείειν τα-
      χύν lit. 'exceedingly swift to run', i.e.
      'an outstanding runner'; the inf. is
      explanatory
   μαχητής -ᾶο/έω, ὁ fighter
187 τόν him
   μογοστόκος -ον producer of labour
      pains
   Εἰλείθυια -ας, ἡ Eilithyia, goddess of
      childbirth
188 ἐξάγω I bring (out); ἐξάγαγε is 3 s. aor.
   πρό (here as adv.) forth
   φόωσδε to the light (cf. 39)
   ἠέλιος -ου/οιο, ὁ sun (= Att. ἥλιος -ου)
   ἴδεν: 3. s. aor. of ὁράω (cf. 5) (= εἶδεν)
   αὐγή -ῆς, ἡ beam
189 τὴν μέν her
   Ἐχεκλῆς -ῆος, ὁ Echecles
   μένος -εος, τό might; Ἐχεκλῆος κρα-
      τερὸν μένος lit. 'the strong might of

Echecles', i.e. 'the strong and mighty
Echecles'

Ἀκτορίδης -αο/εω, ὁ son of Actor

190 ἠγάγετο: 3 s. aor. mid. of ἄγω (cf. 153),
here 'took as wife' (as oft.)

μυρίοι -αι -α countless

191 τὸν δ(έ) but him, i.e. Eudorus (picking
up τὴν μέν, 189)

γέρων -οντος, ὁ old man

εὖ (adv.) well

τρέφω I bring up, rear

ἀτιτάλλω I cherish

192 ἀμφαγαπάζω I love dearly

ὡς εἰ: cf. 59; here + part.

ἑός ἑή ἑόν his (own), her (own);
third-person possessive pron./adj.,
usu. reflexive, also in the form ὅς ἥ ὅν
(distinguish from rel. ὅς ἥ ὅ)

ἐόντα = ὄντα

193 τρίτος -η -ον third, i.e. the third line of
ships (similarly 196 and 197)

Πείσανδρος -ου, ὁ Pisander, a Myrmidon
leader

194 Μαιμαλίδης -αο/εω, ὁ son of Maemalus

μεταπρέπω I am conspicuous among
(+ dat.)

195 μάρναμαι I fight; inf. μάρνασθαι here
explanatory 'in fighting'.

Πηλεΐων -ωνος, ὁ son of Peleus. The
'comrade of the son of Peleus' is of
course Patroclus.

196 τέταρτος -η -ον fourth

ἱππηλάτα -εω, ὁ horseman, charioteer

Φοῖνιξ -ικος, ὁ Phoenix, friend and tutor
of Achilles; he plays a major role in
the embassy to Achilles in Book 9

197 πέμπτος -η -ον fifth

Ἀλκιμέδων -οντος, ὁ Alcimedon, a Myrmidon leader

Λαέρκης -εος, ὁ Laerces, a Myrmidon.
The amount of detail becomes less
towards the end of the list: the poet
knows when to stop.

*198–220: Achilles encourages the troops with a self-confident speech that shows just
how relaxed he is about the effect his anger has had on his men. The Myrmidons
then, eager for battle, array themselves in their ranks.*

199 ἵστημι I make to stand, (here) I set in
order; στῆσεν is 3 s. aor.

ἐΰ = εὖ

κρίνω I divide, organise; κρίνας is aor.
part. (m. nom. s.)

δέ: here 'apodotic', i.e. simply indicates
the beginning of the main clause
(redundant in tr.)

ἐπιτέλλω I lay (an instruction) on; ἐπὶ ...
ἔτελλε is tmesis of 3 s. impf.; tr. phrase
'he laid a stern instruction on them'

200 ἀπειλή -ῆς, ἡ threat

λανθάνομαι I forget (+ gen.); λελαθέσθω
is reduplicated 3 s. aor. mid. imper.
'let me have no one forgetting'; μοι is
'ethic' dat. ('of feeling'), expressing the
involvement of the speaker, though
the nuance is oft. hard to tr.

201 ἀπειλέω I threaten, make (threats)
against (+ dat.); ἀπειλεῖτε is unaugmented 2 pl. impf. (indistinguishable
from pres.). Tautology (lit. 'the threats
you threatened') gives emphasis.

202 ὑπό (+ acc.) (here) throughout the time
of

μηνιθμόν: cf. 62

αἰτιάομαι I accuse; ἠτιάασθε is 2 pl.
impf.; tr. phrase 'and you accused me,
each one of you'

203 σχέτλιος -η -ον cruel, hard

χόλος -ου, ὁ (here) bile, gall (here as
opposed to mother's milk)

ἄρα then, as it turns out

204 νηλεές: cf. 33

ἔχω (here) I hold back

ἀέκων -ουσα -ον (-οντος) (adj. tr. as
adv.) unwillingly, unintentionally
(= Att. ἄκων)

205 οἴκαδε (adv.) home, homewards

νέομαι I go; νεώμεθα is 1 pl. pres. subj.,
here jussive. Going home is what
Achilles had threatened to do as a
result of Agamemnon's insult. The
Myrmidons clearly taunted him with
it.

ποντοπόρος -ον seafaring

αὖτις, ἐπεί ῥά τοι ὧδε κακὸς χόλος ἔμπεσε θυμῷ.'
ταῦτά μ' ἀγειρόμενοι θάμ' ἐβάζετε· νῦν δὲ πέφανται
φυλόπιδος μέγα ἔργον, ἕης τὸ πρίν γ' ἐράασθε.
ἔνθά τις ἄλκιμον ἦτορ ἔχων Τρώεσσι μαχέσθω."

   Ὣς εἰπὼν ὄτρυνε μένος καὶ θυμὸν ἑκάστου.   210
μᾶλλον δὲ στίχες ἄρθεν, ἐπεὶ βασιλῆος ἄκουσαν.
ὡς δ' ὅτε τοῖχον ἀνὴρ ἀράρῃ πυκινοῖσι λίθοισι
δώματος ὑψηλοῖο, βίας ἀνέμων ἀλεείνων,
ὣς ἄραρον κόρυθές τε καὶ ἀσπίδες ὀμφαλόεσσαι.
ἀσπὶς ἄρ' ἀσπίδ' ἔρειδε, κόρυς κόρυν, ἀνέρα δ' ἀνήρ·   215
ψαῦον δ' ἱππόκομοι κόρυθες λαμπροῖσι φάλοισι
νευόντων, ὡς πυκνοὶ ἐφέστασαν ἀλλήλοισι.
πάντων δὲ προπάροιθε δύ' ἀνέρε θωρήσσοντο,
Πάτροκλός τε καὶ Αὐτομέδων, ἕνα θυμὸν ἔχοντες,
πρόσθεν Μυρμιδόνων πολεμιζέμεν. αὐτὰρ Ἀχιλλεὺς   220
βῆ ῥ' ἴμεν ἐς κλισίην, χηλοῦ δ' ἀπὸ πῶμ' ἀνέῳγε
καλῆς δαιδαλέης, τήν οἱ Θέτις ἀργυρόπεζα
θῆκ' ἐπὶ νηὸς ἄγεσθαι, ἐῢ πλήσασα χιτώνων
χλαινάων τ' ἀνεμοσκεπέων οὔλων τε ταπήτων.
ἔνθα δέ οἱ δέπας ἔσκε τετυγμένον, οὐδέ τις ἄλλος   225
οὔτ' ἀνδρῶν πίνεσκεν ἀπ' αὐτοῦ αἴθοπα οἶνον,
οὔτε τεῳ σπένδεσκε θεῶν, ὅτε μὴ Διὶ πατρί.
τό ῥα τότ' ἐκ χηλοῖο λαβὼν ἐκάθηρε θεείῳ

---

206 αὖτις (adv.) once again
  τοι = σοι: here possessive dat. 'your'
  ὧδε (adv.) so, in this way
  ἔμπεσε: 3 s. aor. of ἐμπίπτω (cf. 81), here + dat. (θυμῷ), as oft.

207 μ' = με
  ἀγειρόμενοι: mid. part. (m. nom. pl.) of ἀγείρω (cf. 129)
  θάμ(α) (adv.) often. Clearly the Myrmidons kept on pestering Achilles.
  βάζω I say X (acc.) about Y (also acc.)
  φαίνομαι I appear; πέφανται is 3 s. perf.

208 φύλοπις -ιδος, ἡ combat
  ἕης = ἧς, f. gen. s. of rel. pron.
  τὸ πρίν = πρίν (adv.) (here) previously (cf. 62)
  ἐράασθε: 2 pl. impf. of ἐράομαι (cf. 182)

209 ἔνθα (adv.) so then
  τις (here) each one
  ἄλκιμος -ον (here) brave, valiant (cf. 139)
  ἦτορ (nom. and acc. only), τό heart

μαχέσθω: 3 s. imper. of μάχομαι (cf. 1).
  Achilles ends his speech by throwing down the gauntlet to the Myrmidons to show what they can do without him.

210 εἰπών: aor. part. (m. nom. s.) of λέγω (cf. 49)

211 μᾶλλον (adv.) more, (here) more tightly
  ἄρθεν: 3 pl. aor. pass. of ἀραρίσκω (cf. 132) here 'were joined together'
  βασιλεύς -ῆος, ὁ king (but oft. to be understood as a local lord or chieftain)
  ἀκούω I hear (+ gen. of person)

212 ὡς δ' ὅτε and just as when
  τοῖχος -ου, ὁ wall
  ἀράρῃ: 3 s. aor. subj. of ἀραρίσκω (cf. 132), here 'builds'
  πυκ(ι)νός -ή -όν (here) close-set
  λίθος -ου, ὁ stone

213 ὑψηλός -ή -όν high
  βίη -ης, ἡ force, violence, (pl. here) blasts (= Att. βία -ας)

ἀλεείνων: pres. part. (m. nom. s.) of ἀλε-
εἴνω (cf. 36) here 'conative', i.e. 'trying
to ward off'

214 ἄραρον: 3 pl. aor. of ἀραρίσκω (cf. 132),
here intrans. 'so their helmets ... fitted
together'
ἀσπίς -ίδος, ἡ shield
ὀμφαλόεις -εσσα -εν (-εντος) bossed, with
a central boss

215 ἐρείδω I press upon, bump into

216 ψαύω I touch
ἱππόκομος -ον with horse-hair crest
λαμπρός -ή -όν gleaming, shining
φάλος -ου, ὁ metal plate (reinforcing
leather helmet)

217 νευόντων: pres. part. (m. gen. pl.) of νεύω
(cf. 138), here '(helmets) of the men
moving their heads'

πυκνοί (here) close (cf. 212)
ἐφίσταμαι I stand by (+ dat.); ἐφέστασαν
is 3 pl. plup. It has been suggested that
this tight-packed formation hints at
the phalanx of a seventh-century BCE
hoplite army. In Homer battle is usu. a
much looser affair.

218 προπάροιθε in front of (+ gen.)
δύ(ο) two
ἀνέρε: Homeric nom. dual of ἀνήρ (cf. 44)
θωρήσσοντο: 3 pl. impf. of θωρήσσω
(cf. 40); perhaps here (since they are
already armed) referring to mental
state, i.e. 'readied themselves'

219 εἷς μία ἕν (ἑνός) one

220 πρόσθε(ν) (+ gen.) in front of
πολεμιζέμεν: pres. inf. of πολεμίζω (cf.
89), here expressing purpose 'to fight'

221–48: Achilles makes preparations and prays to Zeus that Patroclus may have success in battle and then return safely. It is ironic that this prayer is offered to a god now committed to helping the Trojans and bringing about Patroclus' death. The passage provides a quiet moment in contrast with the noisy preparations of the Myrmidons beforehand and their march into battle afterwards.

221 βαίνω I go; βῆ is 3 s. aor.
ἴμεν: Homeric inf. of εἶμι (I go, cf. 87); tr.
phrase 'made his way'
χηλός -οῦ/οῖο, ἡ chest, box
ἀπό: with χηλοῦ
πῶμα -ατος, τό lid
ἀνοίγω I open; ἀνέῳγε is 3 s. impf.

222 δαιδάλεος -η -ον skilfully made
ἀργυρόπεζα -ης (f. adj.) silver-
footed

223 θῆκ(ε): 3 s. aor. of τίθημι (cf. 83)
ἐπί (+ gen.) on, on board
ἄγομαι I take with me; οἱ ... ἄγεσθαι 'for
him to take with him'. Thetis had
lovingly packed warm garments for
Achilles, suggesting a touchingly close
relationship with her son (but perhaps
also fussiness).
πλήσασα: aor. part. (f. nom. s.) of
πίμπλημι (cf. 72)
χιτών -ῶνος, ὁ tunic

224 χλαῖνα -ης, ἡ cloak
ἀνεμοσκεπής -ές to keep the wind out
οὖλος -η -ον woolly
ταπής -ῆτος, ὁ rug

225 ἔνθα there, i.e. in the chest

οἱ ... ἔσκε (cf. 147): lit. 'there was to him'
(possessive dat.), i.e. 'he had' (cf. 35)
δέπας -αος, τό cup. This is another
personal item from Thetis, suggesting
further a close relationship between
Achilles and Zeus (cf. 227).
τεύχω I make; τετυγμένον is perf. pass.
part. (n. nom. s.) 'well-made'

226 πίνω I drink; πίνεσκεν is 3 s. impf. iterative (cf. on 147)
αἴθοψ -οπος (m. adj.) sparkling
οἶνος -ου, ὁ wine

227 τεῳ = τινί, dat. of τις (cf. 36)
σπένδω I pour a libation; σπένδεσκε is
again 3 s. impf. iterative
ὅτε μή except
Διί: dat. of Ζεύς (cf. 37)

228 τό it
τότε (adv.) then
λαβών: aor. part. (m. nom. s.) of λαμβάνω (cf. 30)
καθαίρω I clean, cleanse; ἐκάθηρε is 3 s. aor.
θέειον -ου, τό sulphur (= Att. θεῖον -ου); a
disinfectant, regularly used for clean-
ing. The Greeks connected it with θεός
(Plutarch, Moralia 665c).

πρῶτον, ἔπειτα δ᾽ ἔνιψ᾽ ὕδατος καλῇσι ῥοῇσι,
νίψατο δ᾽ αὐτὸς χεῖρας, ἀφύσσατο δ᾽ αἴθοπα οἶνον.   230
εὔχετ᾽ ἔπειτα στὰς μέσῳ ἕρκεϊ, λεῖβε δὲ οἶνον
οὐρανὸν εἰσανιδών· Δία δ᾽ οὐ λάθε τερπικέραυνον·
"Ζεῦ ἄνα, Δωδωναῖε, Πελασγικέ, τηλόθι ναίων,
Δωδώνης μεδέων δυσχειμέρου· ἀμφὶ δὲ Σελλοὶ
σοὶ ναίουσ᾽ ὑποφῆται ἀνιπτόποδες χαμαιεῦναι.   235
ἠμὲν δή ποτ᾽ ἐμὸν ἔπος ἔκλυες εὐξαμένοιο,
τίμησας μὲν ἐμέ, μέγα δ᾽ ἴψαο λαὸν Ἀχαιῶν,
ἠδ᾽ ἔτι καὶ νῦν μοι τόδ᾽ ἐπικρήηνον ἐέλδωρ·
αὐτὸς μὲν γὰρ ἐγὼ μενέω νηῶν ἐν ἀγῶνι,
ἀλλ᾽ ἕταρον πέμπω πολέσιν μετὰ Μυρμιδόνεσσι   240
μάρνασθαι· τῷ κῦδος ἅμα πρόες, εὐρύοπα Ζεῦ,
θάρσυνον δέ οἱ ἦτορ ἐνὶ φρεσίν, ὄφρα καὶ Ἕκτωρ
εἴσεται ἦ ῥα καὶ οἶος ἐπίστηται πολεμίζειν
ἡμέτερος θεράπων, ἦ οἱ τότε χεῖρες ἄαπτοι
μαίνονθ᾽, ὁππότ᾽ ἐγώ περ ἴω μετὰ μῶλον Ἄρηος.   245
αὐτὰρ ἐπεί κ᾽ ἀπὸ ναῦφι μάχην ἐνοπήν τε δίηται,
ἀσκηθής μοι ἔπειτα θοὰς ἐπὶ νῆας ἵκοιτο
τεύχεσί τε ξὺν πᾶσι καὶ ἀγχεμάχοις ἑτάροισιν."
     Ὣς ἔφατ᾽ εὐχόμενος, τοῦ δ᾽ ἔκλυε μητίετα Ζεύς.
τῷ δ᾽ ἕτερον μὲν ἔδωκε πατήρ, ἕτερον δ᾽ ἀνένευσε·   250
νηῶν μέν οἱ ἀπώσασθαι πόλεμόν τε μάχην τε
δῶκε, σόον δ᾽ ἀνένευσε μάχης ἐξ ἀπονέεσθαι.

---

229 νίζω I wash; ἔνιψ(ε) is 3 s. aor.
ῥοή -ῆς, ἡ stream
230 νίψατο: 3 s. aor mid. of νίζω; χεῖρας is
acc. of resp. (lit. 'washed himself as
to his hands') i.e. 'washed his hands'.
It was important to be physically
(and therefore ritually) clean before
approaching the gods.
ἀφύσσω I draw, draw off (liquid from a
cask); ἀφύσσατο is 3 s. aor. mid.
231 εὔχομαι I pray
στάς standing; aor. part. (m. nom. s.) of
ἵσταμαι (cf. 166)
μέσ(σ)ος -η -ον middle (part of)
ἕρκος -εος, τό enclosure, courtyard
λείβω I pour
232 οὐρανός -οῦ, ὁ sky, heaven
εἰσανιδών looking up into; aor. part. (m.
nom. s.) found only in this form

λανθάνω I escape the notice of (+ acc.);
λάθε is 3 s. aor.
τερπικέραυνος -ον delighting in
thunder
233 ἄναξ -ακτος, ὁ lord, master; ἄνα is voc. s.
Δωδωναῖος -η -ον of Dodona. Before
the rise of Delphi in the eighth
century BCE, the oracle of Zeus at
Dodona in northern Greece was the
main oracular centre in the Hellenic
world.
Πελασγικός -ή -όν Pelasgian. The Greeks
used the term to refer to the original
pre-Greek inhabitants of Greece and
the Aegean area.
τηλόθι (adv.) far away
ναίω I live, dwell
234 Δωδώνη -ης, ἡ Dodona
μεδέων = μέδων (cf. 164)

δυσχείμερος -ον wintry

ἀμφί (as adv.) round about

Σελλοί -ῶν, οἱ the Selli, priests of Zeus at Dodona

235 σοί: here m. nom. pl. of σός (cf. 36)

ὑποφῆτης -αο/εω, ὁ interpreter

ἀνιπτόπους -ουν (-ποδος) with un-washed feet. In this ancient and mysterious cult Zeus communicated through the rustling of the leaves of a sacred oak, which the priests inter-preted. Their feet were perhaps bare and unwashed to remain in contact with the earth from which it grew.

χαμαιεῦναι (m. pl. adj.) sleeping on the ground

236 ἠμὲν … ἠδέ (238) both … and, but tr. most neatly here 'just as … so'

εὐξαμένοιο: aor. part. (m. gen. s.) of εὔχομαι (cf. 231); here understand ἐμοῦ 'when I prayed'

237 τιμάω I honour; τίμησας is unaugmented 2 s. aor. (distinguished by accent from aor. part.)

ἵπτομαι I strike, chastise; ἵψαο is 2 s. aor. mid.

238 ἔτι καὶ νῦν this time too

τόδε this, i.e. 'the following'

ἐπικραίνω I fulfil, accomplish; ἐπικρήη-νον is 2 s. aor. imper.

ἐέλδωρ (nom. and acc. only), τό desire, wish

239 μενέω: 1 s. fut. (uncontracted) of μένω (cf. 102)

ἀγών -ῶνος, ὁ (here) assembly place

240 ἕταρος = ἑταῖρος (cf. 170)

πέμπω I send

πολέσιν = πολλοῖς

μετά (+ dat.) (here) with

241 μάρνασθαι: inf. of μάρναμαι (cf. 195), here expressing purpose

τῷ: with ἅμα 'with him'

πρόες: 2 s. aor. imper. of προΐημι (cf. 38)

εὐρύοπα -αο/εω (m. adj.) far-seeing (epithet of Zeus)

242 θαρσύνω I make bold (= Att. θαρρύνω); θάρσυνον is 2 s. aor. imper.

οἱ: possessive dat. (cf. 109)

καὶ Ἕκτωρ Hector too

243 εἴσεται: 3 s. fut. of οἶδα (cf. 19), here in a purpose clause after ὄφρα (242)

ἤ … ἤ (244) whether … or (introducing alternative indirect questions)

244 ἡμέτερος -η -ον our

τότε only then; taken up by ὁππότ(ε) (245)

ἄαπτος -ον unapproachable, invincible

245 μαίνονθ' = μαίνονται (cf. 75)

ἐγώ περ I myself also

ἴω: 1 s. pres. subj. of εἶμι (I go); indefinite with ὁππότ(ε)

μετά (+ acc.) among, into the midst of

μῶλος -ου, ὁ toil, struggle

Ἄρης -ηος, ὁ Ares, god of war, and so 'warfare'

246 ναῦφι: gen. pl. of νηῦς (cf. 1)

ἐνοπή -ῆς, ἡ din of battle

δίομαι I drive away; δίηται is 3 s. subj., indefinite with ἐπεί κ(ε)

247 ἀσκηθής -ές unscathed

ἐπί (+ acc.) to

ἱκνέομαι I arrive (at), reach; ἵκοιτο is 3 s. aor. opt., here expressing a wish 'unscathed then may he come back for me (ethic dat., cf. 200) to the swift ships'

248 ξύν = σύν (cf. 156)

ἀγχέμαχος -ον fighting hand-to-hand

249–56: Zeus hears Achilles' prayer but grants only part of his request. Tragic tension is increased by the poet's narrative intervention at 250–2 (cf. 46–7).

249 ἔφατ(ο): 3 s. aor. mid. of φημί (cf. 14)

τοῦ him, i.e. Achilles; likewise τῷ (250)

μητίετα (nom. only) ὁ counsellor

250 ἕτερον … ἕτερον the one (wish) … the other

ἔδωκε/δῶκε (252): 3 s. aor. of δίδωμι (cf. 40)

ἀνανεύω I deny, refuse

251 οἱ to him (i.e. Patroclus), with δῶκε 'he granted' in 252

ἀπωθέω I push away, drive away; ἀπώ-σασθαι is aor. mid. inf.

252 σόος -η -ον safe (= Att. σῶος -α -ον)

ἀπονέομαι I return; σόον … ἀπονέεσθαι 'that he should return safe'

ἦτοι ὁ μὲν σπείσας τε καὶ εὐξάμενος Διὶ πατρὶ
ἂψ κλισίην εἰσῆλθε, δέπας δ᾽ ἀπέθηκ᾽ ἐνὶ χηλῷ,
στῆ δὲ πάροιθ᾽ ἐλθὼν κλισίης, ἔτι δ᾽ ἤθελε θυμῷ   255
εἰσιδέειν Τρώων καὶ Ἀχαιῶν φύλοπιν αἰνήν.

Οἱ δ᾽ ἅμα Πατρόκλῳ μεγαλήτορι θωρηχθέντες
ἔστιχον, ὄφρ᾽ ἐν Τρωσὶ μέγα φρονέοντες ὄρουσαν.
αὐτίκα δὲ σφήκεσσιν ἐοικότες ἐξεχέοντο
εἰνοδίοις, οὓς παῖδες ἐριδμαίνωσιν ἔθοντες,   260
αἰεὶ κερτομέοντες, ὁδῷ ἔπι οἰκί᾽ ἔχοντας,
νηπίαχοι· ξυνὸν δὲ κακὸν πολέεσσι τιθεῖσι.
τοὺς δ᾽ εἴ περ παρά τίς τε κιὼν ἄνθρωπος ὁδίτης
κινήσῃ ἀέκων, οἱ δ᾽ ἄλκιμον ἦτορ ἔχοντες
πρόσσω πᾶς πέτεται καὶ ἀμύνει οἷσι τέκεσσι.   265
τῶν τότε Μυρμιδόνες κραδίην καὶ θυμὸν ἔχοντες
ἐκ νηῶν ἐχέοντο· βοὴ δ᾽ ἄσβεστος ὀρώρει.
Πάτροκλος δ᾽ ἑτάροισιν ἐκέκλετο μακρὸν ἀΰσας·
"Μυρμιδόνες, ἕταροι Πηληϊάδεω Ἀχιλῆος,
ἀνέρες ἔστε, φίλοι, μνήσασθε δὲ θούριδος ἀλκῆς,   270
ὡς ἂν Πηλεΐδην τιμήσομεν, ὃς μέγ᾽ ἄριστος
Ἀργείων παρὰ νηυσὶ καὶ ἀγχέμαχοι θεράποντες,
γνῷ δὲ καὶ Ἀτρεΐδης εὐρὺ κρείων Ἀγαμέμνων
ἣν ἄτην, ὅ τ᾽ ἄριστον Ἀχαιῶν οὐδὲν ἔτεισεν."

Ὣς εἰπὼν ὄτρυνε μένος καὶ θυμὸν ἑκάστου,   275
ἐν δὲ πέσον Τρώεσσιν ἀολλέες· ἀμφὶ δὲ νῆες

---

253 ἦτοι ὁ μέν then he, i.e. Achilles
  σπείσας: aor. part. (m. nom. s.) of σπέν-
      δω (cf. 227)
254 εἰσέρχομαι I go into; εἰσῆλθε is 3 s. aor.
  ἀποτίθημι I put away; ἀπέθηκ(ε) is 3 s.
      aor.
255 στῆ he stood; 3 s. aor. of ἵσταμαι (cf.
      166)
  πάροιθ(ε) (+ gen.) in front of
  ἔρχομαι I go, come; ἐλθών is aor. part.
      (m. nom. s.)

256 εἰσιδέειν: Homeric aor. inf. of εἰσοράω I
      look at
  φύλοπιν: acc. s. of φύλοπις (cf. 208), al-
      ternative to φυλόπιδα. Homer reports
      what people do and say, but only rare-
      ly goes into detail about their reasons.
      Here he does answer the question
      'why?' about Achilles' move out from
      his hut; but that immediately begs a
      second question: why does he want to
      watch the fighting?

257–77: The Myrmidons march out to battle and attack the Trojans like angry wasps. They are encouraged by Patroclus.

257 μεγαλήτωρ -ορος (m. adj.) great-
      hearted
  θωρηχθέντες: aor. pass. part. (m. nom.
      pl.) of θωρήσσω (cf. 40)

258 στείχω I march (out); ἔστιχον is 3 pl. aor.
  ὄφρ(α) (here) until
  φρονέω I think; μέγα φρονέοντες lit.
      'thinking big', i.e. 'proudly'

ὀρούω I rush forth, dart forward; ὄρουσαν is 3 pl. aor.

259 σφής σφηκός, ὁ wasp
ἔοικα (perf. with pres. sense) I am like (+
dat.); ἐοικότες is part. (m. nom. pl.)
ἐκχέω I pour out; ἐξεχέοντο is 3 pl. impf.
mid./pass. 'they poured out'

260 εἰνόδιος -η -ον by the roadside
παῖς παιδός, ὁ boy
ἐριδμαίνω I irritate; ἐριδμαίνωσιν is
3 pl. pres. subj., here generalising
(as oft. with subordinate clauses in
similes)
ἔθων -οντος (m. part.) (doing something)
habitually, typically

261 κερτομέω I torment, provoke
ὁδός -οῦ, ἡ road, path
οἰκία -ων, τά dwellings; ὁδῷ …
ἔχοντας lit. 'having their dwellings
on the road', i.e. 'in their nests by the
wayside'. Homer's wasps, just like
people, have dwellings and protect
their children. Similes typically
ascribe human qualities to animals.

262 νηπίαχος = νήπιος (cf. 46); here 'little
fools that they are'
ξυνός -ή -όν common, shared
δέ (here) for (explaining the comment
just made)
πολέεσσι = πολλοῖς
τιθεῖσι: 3 pl. pres. of τίθημι (= Att. τιθέ-
ασι; cf. 83) 'they create'; the subject is
'the boys'

263 τούς them, i.e. the wasps
παρά … κίων as he goes past; tmesis of
pres. part. (m. nom. s.) found only in
this form
ἄνθρωπος -ου, ὁ man, person
ὁδίτης -αο/εω, ὁ traveller; ἄνθρωπος
ὁδίτης 'wayfaring man'

264 κινέω I move, stir, disturb; κινήσῃ is 3 s.
aor. subj., here generalising
δ(έ): apodotic (cf. 199)

265 πρόσ(σ)ω (adv.) forward
πᾶς each one of them; s. here picking up
οἱ δ' (264) with following s. verbs
πέτεται: cf. 149
ἀμύνω (here) I defend (+ dat.; cf. 32)
οἷσι their; n. dat. pl. of possessive ὅς (cf.
192)
τέκος -εος, τό child, young

266 τῶν: with κραδίην καὶ θυμὸν
ἔχοντες 'with their (i.e. the wasps')
heart and spirit'

267 βοή -ῆς, ἡ shout
ὄρνυμι I arouse; ὀρώρει is 3 s. intrans.
plup. 'arose'

268 κέλομαι I urge on, call out to (here + dat.
as oft.); ἐκέκλετο is 3 s. aor.
μακρός -ή -όν long; n. here as adv. 'so as
to be heard a long way off', i.e. loudly
ἀΰω I shout; ἀΰσας is aor. part. (m. nom. s.)

269 Μυρμίδονες: the last syllable is 'honorary
long', more conspicuous because not
preceding a liquid (cf. 21) and perhaps intended as the striking opening
to a speech.
Πηληϊάδης -αο/εω, ὁ son of Peleus.
Patroclus' speech is one of complete
loyalty to Achilles: the Myrmidons are
challenged to show what difference
they can make to the fighting, even
without their leader. They are to win
honour for Achilles, just as Agamemnon has deprived him of it.

270 ἀνέρες = ἄνδρες (cf. 44)
ἔστε: 2 pl. imper. of εἰμί
φίλος -ου, ὁ friend
μιμνήσκομαι I remember (+ gen.); μνήσασθε is 2 pl. aor. imper.
θοῦρις -ιδος (f. adj.) impetuous
ἀλκῆς: cf. 157

271 ὡς ἄν (+ subj.) in order that (introducing
purpose clause)
τιμήσομεν: 1 pl. aor. subj. of τιμάω (cf.
237); note the short vowel (= Att.
τιμήσωμεν; cf. on 19)
μέγ(α) (as adv. with sup.) by far

272 καί (here) too; with ἀγχέμαχοι θεράποντες understand μέγ' ἄριστοί εἰσίν

273 γνῶ: 3 s. aor. subj. of γιγνώσκω (cf. 119)
εὐρύς -εῖα -ύ wide; εὐρὺ (n. as adv.)
κρείων 'wide-ruling'

274 ἥν his; f. acc. s. of possessive ὅς (cf. 192)
ἄτη -ης, ἡ folly, delusion
ὅ τ(ε) in that
οὐδέν nothing; here as adv. 'not at all'
ἔτεισεν: 3 s. aor. of τίω (cf. 146)

276 ἐν … πέσον: tmesis of 3 pl. aor. of ἐμπίπτω (cf. 81)
ἀολλής -ές all together, in a mass
ἀμφί (as adv.) all around

σμερδαλέον κονάβησαν ἀϋσάντων ὑπ᾽ Ἀχαιῶν.

Τρῶες δ᾽ ὡς εἴδοντο Μενοιτίου ἄλκιμον υἱόν,
αὐτὸν καὶ θεράποντα, σὺν ἔντεσι μαρμαίροντας,
πᾶσιν ὀρίνθη θυμός, ἐκίνηθεν δὲ φάλαγγες,   280
ἐλπόμενοι παρὰ ναῦφι ποδώκεα Πηλεΐωνα
μηνιθμὸν μὲν ἀπορρῖψαι, φιλότητα δ᾽ ἑλέσθαι·
πάπτηνεν δὲ ἕκαστος ὅπῃ φύγοι αἰπὺν ὄλεθρον.

Πάτροκλος δὲ πρῶτος ἀκόντισε δουρὶ φαεινῷ
ἀντικρὺ κατὰ μέσσον, ὅθι πλεῖστοι κλονέοντο,   285
νηῒ πάρα πρύμνῃ μεγαθύμου Πρωτεσιλάου,
καὶ βάλε Πυραίχμην, ὃς Παίονας ἱπποκορυστὰς
ἤγαγεν ἐξ Ἀμυδῶνος ἀπ᾽ Ἀξιοῦ εὐρὺ ῥέοντος·
τὸν βάλε δεξιὸν ὦμον· ὁ δ᾽ ὕπτιος ἐν κονίῃσι
κάππεσεν οἰμώξας, ἕταροι δέ μιν ἀμφὶ φόβηθεν   290
Παίονες· ἐν γὰρ Πάτροκλος φόβον ἧκεν ἅπασιν
ἡγεμόνα κτείνας, ὃς ἀριστεύεσκε μάχεσθαι.
ἐκ νηῶν δ᾽ ἔλασεν, κατὰ δ᾽ ἔσβεσεν αἰθόμενον πῦρ.
ἡμιδαὴς δ᾽ ἄρα νηῦς λίπετ᾽ αὐτόθι· τοὶ δὲ φόβηθεν
Τρῶες θεσπεσίῳ ὁμάδῳ· Δαναοὶ δ᾽ ἐπέχυντο   295
νῆας ἀνὰ γλαφυράς· ὅμαδος δ᾽ ἀλίαστος ἐτύχθη.

---

277 σμερδαλέος -η -ον terrible; n. here as adv.
κοναβέω I resound; κονάβησαν is 3 pl. aor.
ἀϋσάντων: aor. part. (m. gen. pl.) of αὔω (cf. 268); tr. phrase 'at the shouting of the Achaeans'. The morale not just of the Myrmidons but of the whole Greek army has been boosted by the unexpected arrival of Achilles' troops under Patroclus.

278–418: The Trojans are alarmed by Patroclus' appearance, presuming him to be Achilles. They are driven back from the ships and flee in disorder back across the ditch. They suffer many losses.

278–96: The battle gets under way and Patroclus kills Pyraechmes the Paeonian.

278 ὡς when
εἴδοντο: 3 pl. aor. mid. of ὁράω (cf. 5); sense not discernibly different from act.
279 ἔντεα -ων, τά armour
μαρμαίρω I sparkle, gleam
280 ὀρίνω I throw into confusion; ὀρίνθη is 3 s. aor. pass.
ἐκίνηθεν: 3 pl. aor. pass. of κινέω (= ἐκινήθησαν; cf. 264), here 'began to waver' – a sign of things to come
φάλαγξ -αγγος, ἡ battle line, column

281 ἔλπομαι I suppose, think; ἐλπόμενοι m. (nom. pl.) part. follows sense (strict grammar would make it f. with φάλαγγες)
ναῦφι: dat. pl. of νηῦς (cf. 1)
282 ἀπορρίπτω I throw off, cast aside; ἀπορρῖψαι is aor. inf. in indirect statement
φιλότης -ητος, ἡ friendship, (here) reconciliation (i.e. with Agamemnon)

αἱρέομαι I choose (mid. of αἱρέω; cf. 58); ἑλέσθαι is aor. inf., again in indirect statement

283 παπταίνω I look about; πάπτηνεν is 3 s. aor.

ὅπη (adv.) where, by which way; πάπτηνεν ... ὅπη φύγοι 'looked about to see by what way he might avoid' (opt. in deliberative indirect question). Note the absolute terror among the Trojans at what they think is the arrival of Achilles. According to a fragmentary quotation, Aristotle thought this line the most terrifying (δεινότατον) in the whole of Homer.

αἰπύς -εῖα -ύ sheer, utter

ὄλεθρον: cf. 99

284 πρῶτος -η -ον first

ἀκοντίζω I hurl, let fly with (+ dat.); ἀκόντισε is 3 s. aor.

285 ἀντικρὺ κατὰ μέσσον straight into the midst

ὅθι (adv.) where

πλεῖστος -η -ον most

κλονέω I drive in confusion, mid. I rush about in confusion

286 πάρα: accented as postposition (cf. on 18)

πρυμνός -ή -ον end part of, stern of

μεγάθυμος -ον great-hearted

Πρωτεσίλαος -ου, ὁ Protesilaus. His was the first ship to be set on fire (15.704–26, and cf. on 1 above).

287 Πυραίχμης -αο/εω, ὁ Pyraechmes

Παίονες -ων, οἱ Paeonians. Paeonia is a district in north-eastern Greece, later Macedonia; the Paeonians were the most western allies of the Trojans.

ἱπποκορυστής -αο/εω, ὁ chariot-fighter

288 Ἀμυδών -ῶνος, ὁ Amydon, a city in Macedonia

Ἀξιός -οῦ, ὁ the Axius, a river in Macedonia. Homer's obituaries typically mention where the dead man came

from, oft. (though not here) adding a brief biography.

ῥέω I flow

289 τόν him

δεξιός -ή -όν right; δεξιὸν ὦμον 'on the right shoulder' (acc. of resp.)

ὕπτιος -η -ον on the back, backwards; i.e. he was facing Patroclus and got knocked backwards by the blow

κονίη -ης, ἡ dust (= Att. κονία -ας); here pl. for s.

290 καταπίπτω I fall down; κάππεσεν is 3 s. aor. (= κατέπεσεν)

οἰμώζω I cry, groan; οἰμώξας is aor. part. (m. nom. s.) 'with a groan'

φοβέομαι I flee, take flight (the usu. sense in Homer, rather than Att. 'I fear'); φόβηθεν is 3 pl. aor. (= ἐφοβήθησαν)

291 ἐνίημι I cause, implant X (acc.) in Y (dat.); ἐν ... ἧκεν is tmesis of 3 s. aor.

φόβος -ου/οιο, ὁ (here) fear, panic

ἅπας ἅπασα ἅπαν (ἅπαντ-) all (together)

292 κτείνω I kill; κτείνας is aor. part. (m. nom. s.) 'by killing'

ἀριστεύω I am the best at (+ inf.); ἀριστεύεσκε is 3 s. impf. iterative. Homer is as ready to praise Trojan warriors as Greek ones.

293 ἔλασεν: 3 s. aor. of ἐλαύνω (cf. 87)

κατασβέννυμι I extinguish; κατὰ ... ἔσβεσεν is tmesis of 3 s. aor.

294 ἡμιδαής -ές half-burnt

λείπω I leave; λίπετο is 3 s. aor. mid., here with pass. sense

αὐτόθι (adv.) there

τοί = οἱ; pron. redundant in tr., anticipating Τρῶες (295)

295 θεσπέσιος -η -ον tremendous, awful

ὅμαδος -ου, ὁ din, noise

ἐπιχέω I pour (something) over; ἐπέχυντο is 3 pl. aor. mid. 'came pouring'

296 ἀλίαστος -ον unceasing

ἐτύχθη: 3 s. aor. pass. of τεύχω (cf. 225), here 'arose'

ὡς δ᾽ ὅτ᾽ ἀφ᾽ ὑψηλῆς κορυφῆς ὄρεος μεγάλοιο
κινήσῃ πυκινὴν νεφέλην στεροπηγερέτα Ζεύς,
ἔκ τ᾽ ἔφανεν πᾶσαι σκοπιαὶ καὶ πρώονες ἄκροι
καὶ νάπαι, οὐρανόθεν δ᾽ ἄρ᾽ ὑπερράγη ἄσπετος αἰθήρ,   300
ὣς Δαναοὶ νηῶν μὲν ἀπωσάμενοι δήϊον πῦρ
τυτθὸν ἀνέπνευσαν, πολέμου δ᾽ οὐ γίγνετ᾽ ἐρωή·
οὐ γάρ πώ τι Τρῶες ἀρηϊφίλων ὑπ᾽ Ἀχαιῶν
προτροπάδην φοβέοντο μελαινάων ἀπὸ νηῶν,
ἀλλ᾽ ἔτ᾽ ἄρ᾽ ἀνθίσταντο, νεῶν δ᾽ ὑπόεικον ἀνάγκῃ.   305
   Ἔνθα δ᾽ ἀνὴρ ἕλεν ἄνδρα κεδασθείσης ὑσμίνης
ἡγεμόνων. πρῶτος δὲ Μενοιτίου ἄλκιμος υἱὸς
αὐτίκ᾽ ἄρα στρεφθέντος Ἀρηϊλύκου βάλε μηρὸν
ἔγχεϊ ὀξυόεντι, διαπρὸ δὲ χαλκὸν ἔλασσε·
ῥῆξεν δ᾽ ὀστέον ἔγχος, ὁ δὲ πρηνὴς ἐπὶ γαίῃ   310
κάππεσ᾽· ἀτὰρ Μενέλαος ἀρήϊος οὖτα Θόαντα
στέρνον γυμνωθέντα παρ᾽ ἀσπίδα, λῦσε δὲ γυῖα.
Φυλεΐδης δ᾽ Ἄμφικλον ἐφορμηθέντα δοκεύσας
ἔφθη ὀρεξάμενος πρυμνὸν σκέλος, ἔνθα πάχιστος
μυῶν ἀνθρώπου πέλεται· περὶ δ᾽ ἔγχεος αἰχμῇ   315
νεῦρα διεσχίσθη· τὸν δὲ σκότος ὄσσε κάλυψε.
Νεστορίδαι δ᾽ ὁ μὲν οὖτασ᾽ Ἀτύμνιον ὀξέϊ δουρὶ
Ἀντίλοχος, λαπάρης δὲ διήλασε χάλκεον ἔγχος·

297–305: In this first of three weather similes (cf. 364–5 and 384–92) the relief experienced by the Achaeans as the Trojans are driven back is compared with shafts of light breaking out from a cloudy sky – a striking image.

297 ἀφ᾽ = ἀπό (before vowel with rough breathing)

298 κινήσῃ: 3 aor. subj. of κινέω (cf. 264), again generalising in simile
πυκ(ι)νός -ή -όν (here) thick (cf. 212)
νεφέλη -ης, ἡ cloud
στεροπηγερέτα -αο/εω, ὁ gatherer of the lightning; used only here, instead of standard νεφεληγερέτα (cf. 666), which would be awkward in this context

299 ἐκφαίνω I reveal; ἐκ ... ἔφανεν is tmesis of 3 pl. aor. pass. (= ἐξεφάνησαν). The aorist is 'gnomic' ('like a proverb', Greek ones being oft. stated in past tense), i.e. expressing a general truth; tr. as pres. This is common in Homeric similes.
σκοπιή -ῆς, ἡ mountain peak (= Att. σκοπιά -ᾶς)

πρών πρωονος, ὁ headland; πρώονες ἄκροι 'pointed headlands'

300 νάπη -ης, ἡ glen
οὐρανόθεν (adv.) from the heavens
ὑπορρήγνυμαι I break out, burst through; ὑπερράγη is 3 s. aor., again gnomic
ἄσπετος -ον immense, beyond description
αἰθήρ -έρος, ἡ sky

301 ἀπωσάμενοι: aor. mid. part. (m. nom. pl.) of ἀπωθέω (cf. 251)

302 τυτθός -όν little, small; n. here as adv. 'just a little'
ἀνέπνευσαν: 3 pl. aor. of ἀναπνέω (cf. 42)
ἐρωή -ῆς, ἡ rest, relief from (+ gen.)

303 οὐ ... πω = οὔπω not yet
τι (n. as adv.) in any way
ἀρηΐφιλος -ον dear to Ares

304 προτροπάδην (adv.) in headlong
    flight
    μελαινάων: f. gen. pl. of μέλας
    (cf. 161)

305 ἀνθίσταμαι I resist; ἀνθίσταντο is 3 pl.
    impf.
    ὑποείκω I withdraw a little
    ἀνάγκη -ης, ἡ necessity

306–50: Nine Achaean leaders each kill an opponent and the rout begins.

306 ἕλεν: 3 s. aor. of αἱρέω (cf. 58); here 'over-
    came' or 'killed', as oft.
    κεδάννυμι I scatter, spread; κεδασθείσης
    is aor. pass. part. (f. gen. s.), here in
    gen. abs.
    ὑσμίνη -ης, ἡ battle
307 ἡγεμόνων: with ἀνὴρ ἕλεν ἄνδρα
    (306) 'man killed man among (lit. of)
    the leaders'
308 στρέφω I turn, twist; στρεφθέντος is aor.
    pass. part. (m. gen. s.) with mid. sense
    'just as he had turned round', i.e. tried
    to avoid the cast
    Ἀρηΐλυκος -ου, ὁ Areilycus, a Trojan
309 ὀξυόεις -εσσα -εν (-εντος) sharp-pointed
    διαπρό (adv.) right through
    ἔλασσε: 3 s. aor. of ἐλαύνω (cf. 87)
310 ῥήγνυμι I break; ῥῆξεν is 3 s. aor.
    ὀστέον -ου, τό bone
    πρηνής -ές headlong, on the face. Arei-
    lycus falls on his face because he is
    running away; the opposite happens
    to Pyraechmes at 289.
    ἐπί (+ dat.) (here) on
    γαῖα -ης, ἡ earth (= Att. γῆ γῆς, ἡ)
311 Μενέλαος -ου, ὁ Menelaus
    Θόας -αντος, ὁ Thoas, a Trojan
312 στέρνον -ου, τό chest; here acc. of resp.
    γυμνόω I strip, leave uncovered; γυμνω-
    θέντα is aor. pass. part. (m. acc. s.)
    'where his chest was unprotected'. We
    are probably to infer that the corselet
    (made only of cloth or leather?) is
    pierced.
    λῦσε: 3 s. aor. of λύω (cf. 100)
    γυῖον -ου, τό limb; 'loose the limbs'
    means 'kill', a graphic image of a
    man instantly collapsing. Homer has
    numerous ways of describing death
    in battle.
313 Φυλεΐδης -αο/εω, ὁ son of Phyleus; this is
    Meges, leader of the Achaean contin-
    gent from Dulichium
    Ἄμφικλος -ου, ὁ Amphiclus, a Trojan

    ἐφορμάομαι I make an attack; ἐφορμηθέ-
    ντα is aor. part. (m. acc. s.)
    δοκεύω I watch closely; δοκεύσας is aor.
    part. (m. nom. s.)
314 φθάνω I forestall, get in first; ἔφθη is 3 s.
    aor.
    ὀρέγομαι I lunge at, strike; ὀρεξάμενος is
    aor. part. (m. nom. s.)
    πρυμνός -η -ον (here) top part of (cf.
    286)
    σκέλος -εος, τό leg; tr. phrase 'in the
    thigh'. The two accusatives Ἀμφι-
    κλον and πρυμνὸν σκέλος indicate in
    turn 'whole and part': such expres-
    sions are a common version of acc.
    of resp.
    ἔνθα where
    πάχιστος -η -ον very thick, thickest
315 μυών -ῶνος, ὁ muscle
316 νεῦρον -ου, τό tendon, sinew
    διασχίζω I tear apart; διεσχίσθη is 3 s.
    aor. pass. (with n. pl. subject)
    σκότος -ου, ὁ darkness
    ὄσσε, τώ (dual) the two eyes; here acc.
    of resp.
    καλύπτω I cover, hide; κάλυψε is 3 s.
    aor. Realistically such a wound would
    not kill a man instantly, but it is a
    convention of epic that the deaths of
    unimportant characters are passed
    over in few words.
317 Νεστορίδης -αο/εω, ὁ son of Nestor.
    The two mentioned here are Anti-
    lochus and Thrasymedes, with ὁ μέν
    introducing Antilochus' action, and
    Thrasymedes following at 321; tr. 'As
    for the sons of Nestor, the one …'
    Ἀτύμνιος -ου, ὁ Atymnius, a Lycian
    ὀξύς -εῖα -ύ sharp
318 Ἀντίλοχος -ου, ὁ Antilochus
    λαπάρη -ης, ἡ flank, loins (= Att. λαπάρα
    -ας)
    διελαύνω I drive X (acc.) through Y
    (gen.); διήλασε is 3 s. aor.

ἤριπε δὲ προπάροιθε. Μάρις δ' αὐτοσχεδὰ δουρὶ
Ἀντιλόχῳ ἐπόρουσε κασιγνήτοιο χολωθείς,   320
στὰς πρόσθεν νέκυος· τοῦ δ' ἀντίθεος Θρασυμήδης
ἔφθη ὀρεξάμενος πρὶν οὐτάσαι, οὐδ' ἀφάμαρτεν,
ὦμον ἄφαρ· πρυμνὸν δὲ βραχίονα δουρὸς ἀκωκὴ
δρύψ' ἀπὸ μυώνων, ἀπὸ δ' ὀστέον ἄχρις ἄραξε·
δούπησεν δὲ πεσών, κατὰ δὲ σκότος ὄσσε κάλυψεν.   325
ὣς τὼ μὲν δοιοῖσι κασιγνήτοισι δαμέντε
βήτην εἰς Ἔρεβος, Σαρπηδόνος ἐσθλοὶ ἑταῖροι,
υἷες ἀκοντισταὶ Ἀμισωδάρου, ὅς ῥα Χίμαιραν
θρέψεν ἀμαιμακέτην, πολέσιν κακὸν ἀνθρώποισιν.
Αἴας δὲ Κλεόβουλον Ὀϊλιάδης ἐπορούσας   330
ζωὸν ἕλε, βλαφθέντα κατὰ κλόνον· ἀλλά οἱ αὖθι
λῦσε μένος, πλήξας ξίφει αὐχένα κωπήεντι.
πᾶν δ' ὑπεθερμάνθη ξίφος αἵματι· τὸν δὲ κατ' ὄσσε
ἔλλαβε πορφύρεος θάνατος καὶ μοῖρα κραταιή.
Πηνέλεως δὲ Λύκων τε συνέδραμον· ἔγχεσι μὲν γὰρ   335
ἤμβροτον ἀλλήλων, μέλεον δ' ἠκόντισαν ἄμφω·
τὼ δ' αὖτις ξιφέεσσι συνέδραμον. ἔνθα Λύκων μὲν
ἱπποκόμου κόρυθος φάλον ἤλασεν, ἀμφὶ δὲ καυλὸν
φάσγανον ἐρραίσθη· ὁ δ' ὑπ' οὔατος αὐχένα θεῖνε
Πηνέλεως, πᾶν δ' εἴσω ἔδυ ξίφος, ἔσχεθε δ' οἶον   340
δέρμα, παρηέρθη δὲ κάρη, ὑπέλυντο δὲ γυῖα.

---

319 ἐρείπω I throw down; ἤριπε is 3 s. aor.
with intrans. sense 'fell down'
προπάροιθε (here as adv.) forwards
Μάρις -ιος, ὁ Maris, a Lycian, brother of
Atymnius
αὐτοσχεδά (adv.) near at hand, in close
combat
320 ἐπορούω I rush at (+ dat.); ἐπόρουσε is 3
s. aor.
κασίγνητος -ου/οιο, ὁ brother; here gen.
of cause
χολωθείς: aor. part. (m. nom. s.) of χολόομαι (cf. 61) 'angry for his brother's
sake'
321 τοῦ: with ὦμον (323) 'his shoulder'
ἀντίθεος -ον godlike
Θρασυμήδης -εος, ὁ Thrasymedes
322 ἔφθη (cf. 314): here understand 'him' as
object

πρίν (as conj.) before (+ inf.); the iota
is here lengthened for the metre (cf.
on 57)
οὐτάσαι: aor. inf. of οὐτάω (cf. 24);
tr. phrase 'before he wounded him',
i.e. before Maris could wound
Antilochus
ἀφαμαρτάνω I miss; ἀφάμαρτεν is 3 s. aor.
323 ἄφαρ (adv.) at once
βραχίων -ονος, ὁ arm; tr. phrase 'the top
of his arm' (cf. 314)
ἀκωκή -ῆς, ἡ point
324 δρύπτω I tear; δρύψ(ε) is 3 s. aor.
ἀπὸ … ἄραξε: tmesis of 3 s. aor. of ἀπαράσσω (cf. 116)
ἄχρις (adv.) utterly
325 δουπέω I thud; δούπησεν is 3 s. aor.
πεσών: aor. part. (m. nom. s.) of πίπτω
(cf. 118); tr. phrase 'fell with a thud'

κατακαλύπτω I cover up, come down over; κατὰ … κάλυψεν is tmesis of 3 s. aor. Note another way of describing death.

326 τὼ μέν the two of them, i.e. Atymnius and Maris. The death of such a fighting pair, the one trying to save the other, is typical.
δοιοί -αί -ά two; δοιοῖσι κασιγνήτοισι is dat. of agent 'by two brothers'
δαμάζω I subdue, overcome (= δαμνάω, cf. 103); δαμέντε is aor. pass. part. (m. nom. dual)

327 βήτην: 3 dual aor. of βαίνω (cf. 221)
Ἔρεβος -εος, τό Erebus, a dark region in the Underworld
Σαρπηδών -όνος, ὁ Sarpedon, the Lycian leader. Homer here prepares the way for his entry into battle at 419.
ἐσθλός -ή -όν good, brave

328 ἀκοντιστής -ᾶο/έω, ὁ javelin-thrower, here as adj. with υἷες
Ἀμισώδαρος -ου, ὁ Amisodarus, a Lycian
ῥα: here implies 'as is well known'
Χίμαιρα -ας, ἡ the Chimaera, a monster with a lion's head, a goat's middle and a serpent's tail. It was killed by Bellerophon.

329 θρέψεν: 3 s. aor. of τρέφω (cf. 191)
ἀμαιμάκετος -η -ον huge, enormous
πολέσιν = πολλοῖς
κακόν as an evil (thing)

330 Κλεόβουλος -ου, ὁ Cleobulus, a Trojan
Ὀϊλιάδης -αο/εω, ὁ son of Oileus, i.e. the 'Lesser' Ajax, unrelated to Ajax son of Telamon, bulwark of the Greek army (cf. 102, 358 and 555)

331 ζωός -ή -όν alive. An enemy taken alive is normally given a chance to plead for his life, but not here.
βλάπτω I harm, (here) entangle; βλαφθέντα is aor. pass. part. (m. acc. s.)
κλόνος -ου, ὁ turmoil, confusion; κατὰ κλόνον 'in the confusion'
οἱ his (possessive dat., cf. 109), with μένος (332)
αὖθι (adv.) (right) there, on the spot

332 λῦσε μένος (cf. 189): equivalent to λῦσε … γυῖα (cf. 312)
πλήξας: aor. part. (m. nom. s.) of πλήσσω (cf. 115)

αὐχήν -ένος, ὁ neck
κωπήεις -εσσα -εν (-εντος) hilted

333 ὑποθερμαίνω I warm; ὑπεθερμάνθη is 3 s. aor. pass. A disturbing observation, as metal is usu. cold.
κατ' ὄσσε over both his eyes (cf. 316)

334 ἔλλαβε: 3 s. aor. of λαμβάνω (= ἔλαβε; cf. 30), here 'seized'
πορφύρεος -η -ον purple, dark
μοῖρα -ης, ἡ (here) fate, destiny (thought of as a person's 'portion', cf. 68)
κραταιός -ή -όν mighty, resistless

335 Πηνέλεως -ω, ὁ Peneleos, a leader of the contingent from Boeotia in central Greece (2.494)
Λύκων -ωνος, ὁ Lycon, a Trojan
συντρέχω I rush together; συνέδραμον is 3 pl. aor. This duel follows the common pattern of fighting in Homer: A misses B with a spear-throw, B likewise misses A, and then A kills B with a sword.

336 ἁμαρτάνω I miss (+ gen.); ἥμβροτον is 3 pl. aor.
μέλεον (adv.) in vain
ἠκόντισαν: 3 pl. aor. of ἀκοντίζω (cf. 284)

337 ἔνθα then, next

338 ἤλασεν: 3 s. aor. of ἐλαύνω (cf. 87), here 'struck at'
ἀμφί (+ acc.) (here) at
καυλός -οῦ, ὁ (here) hilt (cf. 115)

339 φάσγανον -ου, τό sword
ῥαίω I break, shatter (something); ἐρραίσθη is 3 s. aor. pass.
ὁ δ(έ): pron. redundant in tr., anticipating postponed subject Πηνέλεως (340; cf. on 67)
ὑπ(ό) (+ gen.) under
οὖς οὔατος, τό ear
θείνω I strike, slash

340 εἴσω (adv.) inside
ἔδυ went deep; 3 s. aor. of δύ(ν)ω (cf. 64)
ἔσχεθε: 3 s. aor. of ἔχω (= ἔσχε, cf. 68), here 'held fast'

341 δέρμα -ατος, τό skin
παραείρομαι I hang to one side; παρηέρθη is 3 s. aor. Another gruesome death.
ὑπολύω I loose; ὑπέλυντο is 3 pl. aor. pass. (cf. 312)

Μηριόνης δ' Ἀκάμαντα κιχεὶς ποσὶ καρπαλίμοισι
νύξ' ἵππων ἐπιβησόμενον κατὰ δεξιὸν ὦμον·
ἤριπε δ' ἐξ ὀχέων, κατὰ δ' ὀφθαλμῶν κέχυτ' ἀχλύς.
Ἰδομενεὺς δ' Ἐρύμαντα κατὰ στόμα νηλέϊ χαλκῷ   345
νύξε· τὸ δ' ἀντικρὺ δόρυ χάλκεον ἐξεπέρησε
νέρθεν ὑπ' ἐγκεφάλοιο, κέασσε δ' ἄρ' ὀστέα λευκά·
ἐκ δὲ τίναχθεν ὀδόντες, ἐνέπλησθεν δέ οἱ ἄμφω
αἵματος ὀφθαλμοί· τὸ δ' ἀνὰ στόμα καὶ κατὰ ῥῖνας
πρῆσε χανών· θανάτου δὲ μέλαν νέφος ἀμφεκάλυψεν.   350
    Οὗτοι ἄρ' ἡγεμόνες Δαναῶν ἕλον ἄνδρα ἕκαστος.
ὡς δὲ λύκοι ἄρνεσσιν ἐπέχραον ἢ ἐρίφοισι
σίνται, ὑπὲκ μήλων αἱρεύμενοι, αἵ τ' ἐν ὄρεσσι
ποιμένος ἀφραδίῃσι διέτμαγεν· οἱ δὲ ἰδόντες
αἶψα διαρπάζουσιν ἀνάλκιδα θυμὸν ἐχούσας·   355
ὣς Δαναοὶ Τρώεσσιν ἐπέχραον· οἱ δὲ φόβοιο
δυσκελάδου μνήσαντο, λάθοντο δὲ θούριδος ἀλκῆς.

4. Ajax and Achilles playing dice. Black-figure amphora by Exekias, c.540 BCE. Vatican Museum.

342 Μηριόνης -αο/εω, ὁ Meriones, a Cretan leader (2.651)

Ἀκάμας -αντος, ὁ Acamas, a Trojan

κιχάνω I catch up with; κιχείς is aor. part. (m. nom. s.)

καρπάλιμος -ον swift

343 νύσσω I stab; νύξ(ε) is 3 s. aor.

ἐπιβαίνω (here) I climb on to (+ gen.; cf. 69); ἐπιβησόμενον fut. part. (m. acc. s.) 'as he was about to mount his chariot' (a common meaning of the pl. of ἵππος). He is clearly trying to escape from the battlefield.

344 ὄχεα -έων, τά chariot. The word is pl. in form but can be s. (as here) or pl. in meaning.

κατὰ ... κέχυτ(o): tmesis of 3 s. plup. pass. of καταχέω (cf. 123), here 'spread over'

ἀχλύς -ύος, ἡ mist, darkness

345 Ἰδομενεύς -ῆος, ὁ Idomeneus, leader of the contingent from Crete (2.650)

Ἐρύμας -αντος, ὁ Erymas, a Trojan

στόμα -ατος, τό mouth

346 τὸ δ(έ): with δόρυ

ἐκπεράω I pass through; ἐξεπέρησε is 3 s. aor. A uniquely horrible death:

the spear passes through the mouth, under the brain and out at the back.

347 νέρθεν (adv.) down below

ὑπό (+ gen.) under

ἐγκέφαλος -ου/οιο, ὁ brain

κεάζω I split; κέασσε is 3 s. aor.

λευκός -ή -όν white

348 ἐκτινάσσω I shake out; ἐκ ... ἐτίναχθεν is tmesis of 3 pl. aor. pass.

ὀδούς -όντος, ὁ tooth

ἐμπίμπλημι I fill X (acc.) with Y (gen.); ἐνέπλησθεν is 3 pl. aor. pass. It is hard to see how the eyeballs could fill with blood; presumably Homer means eye sockets.

349 τό (acc.) it, i.e. blood

ἀνά (+ acc.) (here) up through

κατά (+ acc.) (here) down through

ῥίς ῥινός, ἡ nose, pl. nostrils

350 πρήθω I blow, spurt; πρῆσε is 3 s. aor. with 'he' (i.e. Erymas) understood as subject

χαίνω I gape; χανών is aor. part. (m. nom. s.)

ἀμφικαλύπτω I cover, enfold; ἀμφέκαλυψεν is 3 s. aor.

351–7: The Greeks fall upon the Trojans like ravening wolves upon lambs and kids. The simile neatly summarises the recent killings: the wolves (i.e. the Greeks) pick off individual scattered animals (i.e. the Trojans) who are without a shepherd (i.e. without their leader).

351 ἕλον: 3 pl. aor. of αἱρέω (cf. 58), used as at 306

ἕκαστος (cf. 169): with pl. subject and verb for sense rather than strict grammar

352 ἄρνα, τόν/τήν (no nom. s.) lamb, sheep; ἄρνεσσιν is dat. pl.

ἐπιχράω I attack (+ dat.); ἐπέχραον is 3 pl. aor., here gnomic

ἔριφος -ου, ὁ/ἡ kid, young goat

353 σίντης -αο/εω (m. adj.) ravening, predatory

ὑπέκ (+ gen.) out of, from among

μῆλον -ου, τό sheep, goat; pl. flocks, herds

αἱρεύμενοι = αἱρούμενοι: pres. part. (m. nom. pl.) of αἱρέομαι (cf. 282)

αἵ: rel. pron. f., as if the antecedent had been 'ewes'

354 ἀφραδία -ας, ἡ folly; here pl. for s.

διατμήγω I scatter; διέτμαγεν is 3 pl. aor. pass.

355 διαρπάζω I carry off as plunder, snatch

ἄναλκις -ιδος cowardly; ἀνάλκιδα θυμὸν ἐχούσας 'with their cowardly hearts'

356 φόβος -ου/οιο, ὁ flight (the usu. meaning in Homer; cf. 291)

357 δυσκέλαδος -ον harsh-sounding

μιμνήσκομαι I remember, turn my thoughts to (+ gen.); μνήσαντο is 3 pl. aor.

λανθάνομαι I forget (+ gen.); λάθοντο is 3 pl. aor.

Αἴας δ᾽ ὁ μέγας αἰὲν ἐφ᾽ Ἕκτορι χαλκοκορυστῇ
ἵετ᾽ ἀκοντίσσαι· ὁ δὲ ἰδρείη πολέμοιο,
ἀσπίδι ταυρείη κεκαλυμμένος εὐρέας ὤμους,   360
σκέπτετ᾽ ὀϊστῶν τε ῥοῖζον καὶ δοῦπον ἀκόντων.
ἦ μὲν δὴ γίγνωσκε μάχης ἑτεραλκέα νίκην·
ἀλλὰ καὶ ὣς ἀνέμιμνε, σάω δ᾽ ἐρίηρας ἑταίρους.
   Ὡς δ᾽ ὅτ᾽ ἀπ᾽ Οὐλύμπου νέφος ἔρχεται οὐρανὸν εἴσω
αἰθέρος ἐκ δίης, ὅτε τε Ζεὺς λαίλαπα τείνῃ,   365
ὣς τῶν ἐκ νηῶν γένετο ἰαχή τε φόβος τε,
οὐδὲ κατὰ μοῖραν πέραον πάλιν. Ἕκτορα δ᾽ ἵπποι
ἔκφερον ὠκύποδες σὺν τεύχεσι, λεῖπε δὲ λαὸν
Τρωϊκόν, οὓς ἀέκοντας ὀρυκτὴ τάφρος ἔρυκε.
πολλοὶ δ᾽ ἐν τάφρῳ ἐρυσάρματες ὠκέες ἵπποι   370
ἄξαντ᾽ ἐν πρώτῳ ῥυμῷ λίπον ἄρματ᾽ ἀνάκτων,
Πάτροκλος δ᾽ ἕπετο σφεδανὸν Δαναοῖσι κελεύων,
Τρωσὶ κακὰ φρονέων· οἱ δὲ ἰαχῇ τε φόβῳ τε
πάσας πλῆσαν ὁδούς, ἐπεὶ ἄρ τμάγεν· ὕψι δ᾽ ἀέλλη
σκίδναθ᾽ ὑπὸ νεφέων, τανύοντο δὲ μώνυχες ἵπποι   375
ἄψορρον προτὶ ἄστυ νεῶν ἄπο καὶ κλισιάων.
Πάτροκλος δ᾽ ᾗ πλεῖστον ὀρινόμενον ἴδε λαόν,
τῇ ῥ᾽ ἔχ᾽ ὁμοκλήσας· ὑπὸ δ᾽ ἄξοσι φῶτες ἔπιπτον
πρηνέες ἐξ ὀχέων, δίφροι δ᾽ ἀνακυμβαλίαζον.
ἀντικρὺ δ᾽ ἄρα τάφρον ὑπέρθορον ὠκέες ἵπποι   380
ἄμβροτοι, οὓς Πηλῆϊ θεοὶ δόσαν ἀγλαὰ δῶρα,
πρόσσω ἱέμενοι, ἐπὶ δ᾽ Ἕκτορι κέκλετο θυμός·
ἵετο γὰρ βαλέειν· τὸν δ᾽ ἔκφερον ὠκέες ἵπποι.

358–83: *Hector briefly holds his ground in the face of Ajax's efforts to strike him, but eventually there is a disorderly rout of the Trojans, further encouraged by Patroclus, who is eager to land a blow on Hector.*

358 Αἴας: note that the first letters of lines 358–61 also spell the name (though this may be no more than coincidence)
ὁ μέγας: distinguishing him from the Lesser Ajax (cf. 330 and 555)
ἐφ᾽ = ἐπί (+ dat.) at, against
χαλκοκορυστής -ᾱο/εω (m. adj.) bronze-helmeted, bronze-armoured
359 ἵεμαι (mid. of ἵημι, cf. 152) I am eager, long (to); ἵετ(ο) is 3 s. impf.
ἀκοντίσσαι: aor. inf. of ἀκοντίζω (cf. 284)
ἰδρείη -ης, ἡ skill (= Att. ἰδρεία -ας)
360 ταύρειος -η -ον of bull's hide
κεκαλυμμένος: perf. pass. part. (m. nom. s.) of καλύπτω (cf. 316); κεκαλυμμένος

εὐρέας ὤμους 'his broad shoulders covered' (acc. of resp.)
361 σκέπτομαι I watch out for, (here) am on the alert for
ῥοῖζος -ου, ὁ whistling, whirring. Note the onomatopoeia
δοῦπος -ου, ὁ thud, thudding. Onomatopoeia again. The noise of the weapons indicates the ferocity of the fighting.
ἄκων -οντος, ὁ javelin, spear
362 ἦ μὲν δή indeed; emphatic combination of particles, picked up by καὶ ὣς (363)
γίγνωσκε began to recognise ('inceptive' impf.)
ἑτεραλκής -ές inclining to the other side

363 καὶ ὧς even so
  ἀναμίμνω I wait, remain, (here) stand fast;
    ἀνέμιμνε is 3 s. impf., here conative
  σαόω I save (= Att. σῴζω); σάω is 3 s.
    impf., again conative
  ἐρίηρος -ον trusty; ἐρίηρας is 3rd decl.
    form m. acc. pl.
364 εἴσω (+ acc.) into; postposition. This
    second weather simile picks up the
    clear sky of 297–300, obliterated now
    by racing clouds. The shouting of the
    Trojans in flight is likened to the roar
    of a tempest.
365 δῖος -α -ον (here) bright, clear (cf. 5);
    αἰθέρος ἐκ δίης 'after clear weather'
  λαῖλαψ -απος, ἡ storm, tempest
  τείνω I spread out; τείνη is 3 s. aor. subj.,
    generalising with ὅτε
366 τῶν of these men
  γένετο: 3 s. aor. of γίγνομαι (cf. 39), here
    'arose'
  ἰαχή -ῆς, ἡ cry, shout
367 κατὰ μοῖραν in an orderly way
  περάω I cross over; understand 'the
    ditch' as object
368 ἐκφέρω I carry out
  ὠκύπους -πουν (-ποδος) (m.
    adj.) swift-footed
369 Τρωϊκός -ή -όν Trojan
  ὀρυκτός -ή -όν dug
  τάφρος -ου, ἡ ditch, trench. On Nestor's
    advice, the Achaeans had dug this
    ditch to defend their camp, reinforced
    it with vertical stakes and erected a
    gated wall (7.436–41).
  ἐρύκω I hold back
370 ἐρυσάρματος -ον chariot-drawing;
    ἐρυσάρματες is 3rd decl. form nom. m
    pl.
371 ἄγνυμι I break; ἄξαντε is aor. part. (m.
    nom. dual); dual (rather than expect-
    ed pl.) probably used here because
    there is a pair of horses for each
    chariot. The object is 'them', i.e. the
    chariots.
  ῥυμός -οῦ, ὁ pole (of a chariot); ἐν
    πρώτῳ ῥυμῷ 'at the end of the pole',
    i.e. the weak point where the chariot-
    pole joins the yoke.
  ἄρμα -ατος, τό chariot
372 σφεδανόν (adv.) eagerly
373 κακὰ φρονέων with evil intent

  ἰαχῇ τε φόβῳ τε with shouting and in
    flight
374 πλῆσαν: 3 pl. aor. of πίμπλημι (cf. 72)
  ἄρ = ἄρα
  τμήγω I scatter; τμάγεν is 3 pl. aor. pass.
  ὕψι (adv.) high above, on high
  ἀέλλη -ης, ἡ whirl of dust (= Att. ἄελλα -ης)
375 σκίδναμαι I spread out; σκίδναθ' = σκίδ-
    νατο is 3 s. impf.
  τανύω I stretch, strain; τανύοντο is 3 pl.
    impf. mid. 'ran at full stretch'
  μώνυχες -ων (m. pl. adj.) single-hoofed
    (i.e. not cloven). These are the horses
    that broke free from their chariots at
    370–1.
376 ἄψορρον (adv.) back again
  ἄπο: accented as postposition
377 ᾗ where (f. dat. of ὅς used as adv.), picked
    up by τῇ in 378
  ὀρινόμενον: pass. part. (m. acc. s.) of
    ὀρίνω (cf. 280); the last syllable is
    lengthened by the digamma with
    which ἴδε originally began
  ἴδε: 3 s. aor. of ὁράω (cf. 5)
378 τῇ there
  ἔχ(ε) held his course; Patroclus is attack-
    ing from his chariot
  ὁμοκλέω (here) I urge on with a shout;
    understand 'the horses' as object
  ὑπό (+ dat.) under
  ἄξων -ονος, ὁ axle
  φώς φωτός, ὁ man (distinguish from Att.
    φῶς φωτός, τό light)
379 δίφρος -ου/οιο, ὁ chariot
  ἀνακυμβαλιάζω I turn upside down
    (intrans.)
380 ὑπερθρώσκω I leap over; ὑπέρθορον is 3
    pl. aor.
381 ἄμβροτος -ον immortal
  δόσαν: 3 pl. aor. of δίδωμι (cf. 40)
382 πρόσ(σ)ω (adv.) forward
  ἱέμενοι: pres. part. (m. nom. pl.) of ἵεμαι
    (cf. 359) 'pressing forward'. Now
    that Patroclus has cleared the ditch,
    the battle action moves outside the
    Achaean defences and on to the
    Trojan plain.
  κέκλετο: reduplicated 3 s. aor. of κέλομαι
    (cf. 268); understand 'him to rush out'
    (with ἐπί used as at 358)
383 βαλέειν: aor. inf. of βάλλω (cf. 24)
  τὸν δ(έ) but him, i.e. Hector

ὡς δ᾽ ὑπὸ λαίλαπι πᾶσα κελαινὴ βέβριθε χθὼν
ἤματ᾽ ὀπωρινῷ, ὅτε λαβρότατον χέει ὕδωρ   385
Ζεύς, ὅτε δή ῥ᾽ ἄνδρεσσι κοτεσσάμενος χαλεπήνῃ,
οἳ βίῃ εἰν ἀγορῇ σκολιὰς κρίνωσι θέμιστας,
ἐκ δὲ δίκην ἐλάσωσι, θεῶν ὄπιν οὐκ ἀλέγοντες·
τῶν δέ τε πάντες μὲν ποταμοὶ πλήθουσι ῥέοντες,
πολλὰς δὲ κλιτῦς τότ᾽ ἀποτμήγουσι χαράδραι,   390
ἐς δ᾽ ἅλα πορφυρέην μεγάλα στενάχουσι ῥέουσαι
ἐξ ὀρέων ἐπικάρ, μινύθει δέ τε ἔργ᾽ ἀνθρώπων·
ὣς ἵπποι Τρῳαὶ μεγάλα στενάχοντο θέουσαι.
    Πάτροκλος δ᾽ ἐπεὶ οὖν πρώτας ἐπέκερσε φάλαγγας,
ἂψ ἐπὶ νῆας ἔεργε παλιμπετές, οὐδὲ πόληος   395
εἴα ἱεμένους ἐπιβαινέμεν, ἀλλὰ μεσηγὺ
νηῶν καὶ ποταμοῦ καὶ τείχεος ὑψηλοῖο
κτεῖνε μεταΐσσων, πολέων δ᾽ ἀπετίνυτο ποινήν.
ἔνθ᾽ ἤτοι Πρόνοον πρῶτον βάλε δουρὶ φαεινῷ,
στέρνον γυμνωθέντα παρ᾽ ἀσπίδα, λῦσε δὲ γυῖα·   400
δούπησεν δὲ πεσών. ὁ δὲ Θέστορα, Ἤνοπος υἱόν,
δεύτερον ὁρμηθείς — ὁ μὲν εὐξέστῳ ἐνὶ δίφρῳ
ἧστο ἀλείς· ἐκ γὰρ πλήγη φρένας, ἐκ δ᾽ ἄρα χειρῶν
ἡνία ἠΐχθησαν — ὁ δ᾽ ἔγχεϊ νύξε παραστὰς
γναθμὸν δεξιτερόν, διὰ δ᾽ αὐτοῦ πεῖρεν ὀδόντων,   405
ἕλκε δὲ δουρὸς ἑλὼν ὑπὲρ ἄντυγος, ὡς ὅτε τις φὼς
πέτρῃ ἔπι προβλῆτι καθήμενος ἱερὸν ἰχθὺν

384–93: This extended simile seems almost a continuation of the storm cloud simile at 364–5: Zeus punishes the crooked judgements of men with a violent and destructive storm, a concept of divine punishment for human injustice seen also in Hesiod's Works and Days, *219–21. It is only near the end that the real point of the simile becomes clear: the noise of the retreating chariots is just like the roar of mountain torrents rushing headlong to the sea.*

384 κελαινός -ή -όν dark, black
   βρίθω I am weighed down; βέβριθε is 3 s.
     perf., but tr. as pres.
   χθών -ονός, ἡ earth
385 ἦμαρ -ατος, τό day (= Att. ἡμέρα -ας, ἡ);
     ἤματ(ι) is dat. for time when
   ὀπωρινός -ή -όν of autumn
   λάβρος -ον furious, blustering; λαβρότα-
     τον is sup. (n. acc. s.)
   ὕδωρ -ατος, τό water, (here) rain
386 κοτέομαι I am angry with (+ dat.); κοτεσ-
     σάμενος is aor. part. (m. nom. s.)

χαλεπαίνω I rage, am harsh; χαλεπήνῃ
   is 3 s. aor. subj. with ὅτε, generalising
   in simile
387 εἰν = ἐν
   ἀγορή -ῆς, ἡ assembly (= Att. ἀγορά -ᾶς)
   σκολιός -ή -όν crooked
   κρίνω (here) I decide, give (cf. 199)
   θέμις -ιστος, ἡ judgement, decree
388 ἐξελαύνω I drive out; ἐκ … ἐλάσωσι is
     tmesis of 3 pl. aor. subj.
   δίκη -ης, ἡ justice
   ὄπις -ιδος, ἡ gaze, avenging eye

ἀλέγω I heed, care about. This passage provides a rare example of Zeus in the *Iliad* envisaged as the guardian of morality.

389 πλήθω I am full, am in flood

390 κλιτύς -ύος, ἡ hillside; κλιτῦς is acc. pl.
ἀποτμήγω I cut through, furrow
χαράδρη -ης, ἡ mountain torrent (= Att. χαράδρα -ας)

391 ἅλς ἁλός, ἡ sea

μεγάλα greatly; n. pl. of μέγας as adv.
στενάχω (here) I roar (cf. 20); mid. used with same sense in 393

392 ἐπικάρ (adv.) headlong
μινύθω I am destroyed
ἔργ(α) (here) farm labours (cf. 120), i.e. tilled fields

393 Τρῳός -ή -όν Trojan; there is no obvious reason why the horses are now f. (after m. adj. ὠκέες at 383)

394–418: *Patroclus goes on a killing spree.*

394 ἐπικείρω (here) I cut off (cf. 120); ἐπέκερσε is 3 s. aor.

395 ἔργω I hem in, confine (= Att. εἴργω); ἔεργε is 3 s. impf.
παλιμπετές (adv.) back, backwards; ἄψ ... παλιμπετές 'back again'. In his pursuit of Hector, Patroclus has cut through the fleeing Trojans and reached the front line of their flight. Now he turns and herds them back towards the Greek camp, blocking off their escape into the city.
πόληος: gen. s. of πόλις (cf. 57)

396 εἴα: impf. of ἐάω (cf. 60)
ἱεμένους: pres. part. (m. acc. pl.) of ἵεμαι (cf. 359), here concessive 'eager though they were'
ἐπιβαινέμεν: pres. inf. of ἐπιβαίνω (cf. 69 and 343), here 'to enter'
μεσηγύ (+ gen.) in the space between

397 τεῖχος -εος, τό wall

398 μεταΐσσω I attack, rush on
πολέων: gen. pl. of πολύς (cf. 110); tr. 'for many', i.e. 'for the deaths of many'
ἀποτίνυμαι I exact X (acc.) from Y (gen.); ἀπετίνυτο is 3 s. impf.
ποινή -ῆς, ἡ vengeance, retribution

399 ἔνθ(α) there
Πρόνοος -ου, ὁ Pronous, a Trojan, the first of twelve victims. Note the variety of the killings – a thrown spear (399), a stab (404) and a rock in the face (411).

400 = 312

401 ὁ δέ and he, i.e. Patroclus; anticipating second ὁ δ(έ) as subject of νύξε (404)
Θέστωρ -ορος, ὁ Thestor, a Trojan, and Pronous' charioteer

Ἦνοψ -οπος, ὁ Enops, Thestor's father

402 ὁρμάομαι I rush; ὁρμηθείς is aor. part. (m. nom. s.)
ὁ μέν he, i.e. Thestor
εὔξεστος -ον well-polished

403 ἧμαι I sit; ἧστο is 3 s. impf.
εἴλω I confine, roll up tight; ἀλείς is aor. pass. part. (m. nom. s.) 'hunched'
ἐκπλήσσω I terrify; ἐκ ... πλήγη is tmesis of 3 s. aor. pass., with φρένας acc. of resp. Not at all a heroic reaction: Patroclus treats him with contempt.

404 ἡνία -ων, τά reins
ἀΐσσω I move swiftly, dart; ἠΐχθησαν is 3 pl. aor. pass. here with act. sense 'slipped'
ὁ δ(έ): picking up ὁ δέ (401)
νύξε: 3 s. aor. of νύσσω (cf. 343)

405 γναθμός -οῦ/οῖο, ὁ jaw
δεξιτερός -ή -όν right
διά (+ gen.) through; here with ὀδόντων
αὐτοῦ: possessive gen. 'his'
πείρω I pierce

406 ἕλκω I drag
δουρὸς ἑλών taking him by the spear (i.e. as if it were part of his body)
ὑπέρ (+ gen.) over
ἄντυξ -υγος, ἡ rail (of chariot, to prevent driver from falling)
ὡς ὅτε τις φώς: understand ἕλκει

407 προβλής -ῆτος projecting, jutting out
κάθημαι I sit
ἱερόν (cf. 100): an apparently strange way to describe a fish, but perhaps here 'spirited' or 'vigorous'
ἰχθύς -ύος, ὁ fish

ἐκ πόντοιο θύραζε λίνῳ καὶ ἤνοπι χαλκῷ·
ὡς ἕλκ’ ἐκ δίφροιο κεχηνότα δουρὶ φαεινῷ,
κὰδ δ’ ἄρ’ ἐπὶ στόμ’ ἔωσε· πεσόντα δέ μιν λίπε θυμός.   410
αὐτὰρ ἔπειτ’ Ἐρύλαον ἐπεσσύμενον βάλε πέτρῳ
μέσσην κὰκ κεφαλήν· ἣ δ’ ἄνδιχα πᾶσα κεάσθη
ἐν κόρυθι βριαρῇ· ὃ δ’ ἄρα πρηνὴς ἐπὶ γαίῃ
κάππεσεν, ἀμφὶ δέ μιν θάνατος χύτο θυμοραϊστής.
αὐτὰρ ἔπειτ’ Ἐρύμαντα καὶ Ἀμφοτερὸν καὶ Ἐπάλτην,   415
Τληπόλεμόν τε Δαμαστορίδην Ἐχίον τε Πύριν τε,
Ἰφέα τ’ Εὔιππόν τε καὶ Ἀργεάδην Πολύμηλον,
πάντας ἐπασσυτέρους πέλασε χθονὶ πουλυβοτείρῃ.
    Σαρπηδὼν δ’ ὡς οὖν ἴδ’ ἀμιτροχίτωνας ἑταίρους
χέρσ’ ὕπο Πατρόκλοιο Μενοιτιάδαο δαμέντας,   420
κέκλετ’ ἄρ’ ἀντιθέοισι καθαπτόμενος Λυκίοισιν·
“αἰδώς, ὦ Λύκιοι· πόσε φεύγετε; νῦν θοοὶ ἔστε.
ἀντήσω γὰρ ἐγὼ τοῦδ’ ἀνέρος, ὄφρα δαείω
ὅς τις ὅδε κρατέει καὶ δὴ κακὰ πολλὰ ἔοργε
Τρῶας, ἐπεὶ πολλῶν τε καὶ ἐσθλῶν γούνατ’ ἔλυσεν.”   425
    Ἦ ῥα, καὶ ἐξ ὀχέων σὺν τεύχεσιν ἆλτο χαμᾶζε.
Πάτροκλος δ’ ἑτέρωθεν, ἐπεὶ ἴδεν, ἔκθορε δίφρου.
οἳ δ’ ὥς τ’ αἰγυπιοὶ γαμψώνυχες ἀγκυλοχεῖλαι
πέτρῃ ἐφ’ ὑψηλῇ μεγάλα κλάζοντε μάχωνται,
ὣς οἱ κεκλήγοντες ἐπ’ ἀλλήλοισιν ὄρουσαν.   430

408 πόντος -ου/οιο, ὁ sea
    θύραζε (adv.) out (here implying ‘of the water’)
    λίνον -ου, τό string, line
    ἤνοψ -οπος gleaming. The ‘gleaming bronze’ is of course a hook. Note that this adj. has the same form as Thestor’s father’s name (cf. 401).
409 κεχηνότα: perf. part. (m. acc. s.) of χαίνω (cf. 350) ‘gaping’
410 κατωθέω I thrust down; κὰδ (cf. 109) … ἔωσε is tmesis of 3 s. aor. In this extraordinary image Thestor is brutally hooked out of his chariot like a fish from the sea.
    στόμ(α) (here) face (cf. 345)
411 Ἐρύλαος -ου, ὁ Erylaus, a Trojan
    ἐπισ(σ)εύομαι I charge (at), rush (against); ἐπεσσύμενον is perf. part. (m. acc. s.)

πέτρος -ου, ὁ rock, stone
412 κὰκ = κατά (before κ)
    ἣ δ(έ) and it, i.e. his head
    ἄνδιχα (adv.) in two
    κεάσθη: 3 s. aor. pass. of κεάζω (cf. 347)
413 βριαρός -ή -όν strong. But presumably the helmet was broken too.
414 χύτο: 3 s. aor. pass. of χέω (cf. 3)
    θυμοραϊστής -ᾶο/έω (m. adj.) life-destroying
415 Ἐρύμας -αντος ὁ Erymas, a Lycian (cf. Erymas the Trojan at 345, killed at 350; Homer selects from stock names to make up numbers of ‘extras’ among Trojan allies). The following eight warriors are all Lycians.
    Ἀμφότερος -οῦ, ὁ Amphoterus
    Ἐπάλτης -αο/εω, ὁ Epaltes
416 Τληπόλεμος -ου, ὁ Tlepolemus
    Δαμαστορίδης -αο/εω, ὁ son of Damastor

Ἐχίος -ου, ὁ Echius
Πύρις -ιος, ὁ Pyris
417 Ἰφεύς -ῆος, ὁ Ipheus
Εὔιππος -ου, ὁ Euippus
Ἀργεάδης -αο/εω, ὁ son of Argeas
Πολύμηλος -ου, ὁ Polymelus
418 ἐπασσύτεροι -αι -α one after another,
in quick succession. This multiple

massacre prepares the ground for the
single combat with Sarpedon.
πελάζω I bring X (acc.) near to Y (dat.);
πέλασε is 3 s. aor.
πουλυβότειρα -ης (f. adj.) much-
nourishing; first syllable lengthened
(from πολ-) for the metre

419–683: Sarpedon, leader of the Lycians and a son of Zeus, now intervenes. Zeus is keen to avert his son's death, but Hera dissuades him from this. In the fight Sarpedon kills Patroclus' trace-horse, but is himself then killed by Patroclus. In the fierce fighting that ensues the Achaeans strip off Sarpedon's armour, and his body, recovered by Apollo, is eventually conveyed by Sleep and Death back to Lycia for burial.

419–30: Sarpedon enters the fray against Patroclus. The two rush on each other like vultures, the simile, as often, preparing the way for an encounter of high importance.

419 Σαρπηδών (cf. 327): he has already killed
a son of Heracles (5.628–59) and torn
down a parapet of the wall around the
Greek camp (12.290–399)
ἀμιτροχίτωνες -ων (m. pl. adj.) wearing
unbelted tunics
420 χέρσ(ι) ὕπο under/at the hands; ὕπο
accented as postposition
Μενοιτιάδης -αο/εω, ὁ son of Menoetius
δαμέντας: aor. pass. part. (m. acc. pl.) of
δαμάζω (cf. 326)
421 καθάπτομαι I chide, reprimand
Λύκιοι -ων, οἱ the Lycians, residents of
Lycia in Asia Minor (modern Turkey)
422 αἰδώς -οος, ἡ shame; nom. used here as
an exclamation 'for shame!', appealing
to the men's sense of honour
πόσε (adv.) to where? (= Att. ποῖ)
θοοί (cf. 123): here implies 'swift to fight'
(rather than 'to run', as they have been
doing)
423 ἀντάω I meet (+ gen.); ἀντήσω is 1 s.
fut.
ἀνέρος: Homeric gen. s. of ἀνήρ (cf. 44)
δάω I learn; δαείω is 1 s. aor. subj. in
purpose clause with ὄφρα
424 ὅς τις = ὅστις who (in indirect question)

κρατέω (here) I am strong, prevail (cf.
172); ὅς τις ὅδε κρατέει 'who this
man is who is carrying all before him'.
Sarpedon clearly doesn't think this is
Achilles, despite the armour.
ἔρδω I do, work; ἔοργε is 3 s. perf.
425 γόνυ -ατος, τό knee; γούνατα is acc. pl.
(with first syllable lengthened for the
metre). This way of describing death
is a variant of the one at 312.
426 ἠμί I speak (= φημί, cf. 14); ἦ is 3 s. impf.
(= ἔφη)
ἅλλομαι I leap; ἆλτο is 3 s. aor.
χαμᾶζε (adv.) to the ground
427 ἑτέρωθεν (adv.) from/on the other side
ἐκθρῴσκω I leap out of (+ gen.); ἔκθορε
is 3 s. aor.
428 αἰγυπιός -οῦ, ὁ vulture
γαμψῶνυξ -υχος (m. adj.) with crooked
claws
ἀγκυλοχείλης -εω (m. adj.) with crooked
beak
429 κλάζω I shriek, scream; κλάζοντε is pres.
part. (m. nom. dual)
μάχωνται: subj. generalising in simile
430 κεκλήγοντες: perf. part. (m. nom. pl.) of
κλάζω

τοὺς δὲ ἰδὼν ἐλέησε Κρόνου πάϊς ἀγκυλομήτεω,
Ἥρην δὲ προσέειπε κασιγνήτην ἄλοχόν τε·
"ὤ μοι ἐγών, ὅ τέ μοι Σαρπηδόνα, φίλτατον ἀνδρῶν,
μοῖρ᾽ ὑπὸ Πατρόκλοιο Μενοιτιάδαο δαμῆναι.
διχθὰ δέ μοι κραδίη μέμονε φρεσὶν ὁρμαίνοντι,   435
ἦ μιν ζωὸν ἐόντα μάχης ἄπο δακρυοέσσης
θείω ἀναρπάξας Λυκίης ἐν πίονι δήμῳ,
ἦ ἤδη ὑπὸ χερσὶ Μενοιτιάδαο δαμάσσω."
   Τὸν δ᾽ ἠμείβετ᾽ ἔπειτα βοῶπις πότνια Ἥρη·
"αἰνότατε Κρονίδη, ποῖον τὸν μῦθον ἔειπες.   440
ἄνδρα θνητὸν ἐόντα, πάλαι πεπρωμένον αἴσῃ,
ἂψ ἐθέλεις θανάτοιο δυσηχέος ἐξαναλῦσαι;
ἔρδ᾽· ἀτὰρ οὔ τοι πάντες ἐπαινέομεν θεοὶ ἄλλοι.
ἄλλο δέ τοι ἐρέω, σὺ δ᾽ ἐνὶ φρεσὶ βάλλεο σῆσιν·
αἴ κε ζὼν πέμψῃς Σαρπηδόνα ὅνδε δόμονδε,   445
φράζεο μή τις ἔπειτα θεῶν ἐθέλῃσι καὶ ἄλλος
πέμπειν ὃν φίλον υἱὸν ἀπὸ κρατερῆς ὑσμίνης·
πολλοὶ γὰρ περὶ ἄστυ μέγα Πριάμοιο μάχονται
υἱέες ἀθανάτων, τοῖσιν κότον αἰνὸν ἐνήσεις.
ἀλλ᾽ εἴ τοι φίλος ἐστί, τεὸν δ᾽ ὀλοφύρεται ἦτορ,   450
ἤτοι μέν μιν ἔασον ἐνὶ κρατερῇ ὑσμίνῃ
χέρσ᾽ ὕπο Πατρόκλοιο Μενοιτιάδαο δαμῆναι·
αὐτὰρ ἐπὴν δὴ τόν γε λίπῃ ψυχή τε καὶ αἰών,
πέμπειν μιν Θάνατόν τε φέρειν καὶ νήδυμον Ὕπνον,
εἰς ὅ κε δὴ Λυκίης εὐρείης δῆμον ἵκωνται,   455
ἔνθά ἑ ταρχύσουσι κασίγνητοί τε ἔται τε
τύμβῳ τε στήλῃ τε· τὸ γὰρ γέρας ἐστὶ θανόντων."

431–61: Zeus considers rescuing Sarpedon from Patroclus but is persuaded by Hera not to. This exchange raises, but does not resolve, the relation of his will to fate. It is typical of the poet to bring in the gods at such moments of high drama.

431 ἐλεέω I pity; ἐλέησε is 3 s. aor.
   Κρόνος -ου, ὁ Cronus, father of Zeus
   πάϊς = παῖς (here) son (cf. 260)
   ἀγκυλομήτης -εω (m. adj.) of crooked counsel, wily
432 προσλέγω I speak to, address; προσέειπε is 3 s. aor.
   κασιγνήτη -ης, ἡ sister. Both Zeus and Hera were children of the Titans Cronus and Rhea (who themselves were brother and sister as well as husband and wife).
   ἄλοχος -ου, ἡ wife. Zeus regularly uses Hera as a sounding board, but she

seems a strange choice of interlocutor here, since she is pro-Greek. She does not raise that issue in her reply, but argues instead (441–9) that Zeus must not set unworkable precedents.
433 ἐγών = ἐγώ; ὤ μοι ἐγών alas for me! (ἐγώ illogically nom. for emphasis)
   ὅ τε = ὅτε since
   φίλτατον: sup. (m. acc. s.) of φίλος (cf. 82)
434 μοῖρ(α) (here) fate (cf. 334); understand ἐστί 'it is fated'
   δαμῆναι: aor. pass. inf. of δαμάζω (cf. 326)

435 διχθά = δίχα (adv.) in two ways, at variance

μέμονα (perf. with pres. sense) I rage, strive

ὁρμαίνω I turn over, ponder; μοι … φρεσὶν ὁρμαίνοντι 'as I ponder in my mind'. Scenes of pondering, mortal and immortal, are typical; the second option is usu. taken, as here.

436 ἢ … ἦ (438) whether … or

δακρυοέσσης (cf. 10): note that battle can be tearful as well as glorious.

437 θείω: 1 s. aor. subj. of τίθημι (cf. 83) in deliberative indirect question; likewise δαμάσσω (438)

ἀναρπάζω I snatch up; ἀναρπάξας is aor. part. (m. nom. s.)

Λυκίη -ης, ἡ Lycia (= Att. Λυκία -ας)

πίων -ονος rich, fertile

δῆμος -ου, ὁ country, community

438 ἤδη (adv.) now

δαμάσσω: 1 s. aor. subj. of δαμάζω (cf. 326)

439 ἀμείβομαι I answer, reply to; ἠμείβετ(ο) is 3 s. impf.

βοῶπις -ιδος (f. adj.) ox-eyed

440 Κρονίδης -αο/εω ὁ son of Cronus; Κρονίδη is voc. s.

ποῖος -η -ον what sort of …?/what a …! (question or, more probably here, exclamation); the indignant Hera regularly addresses Zeus like this (cf. 18.360–1)

441 πάλαι (adv.) long ago

πεπρωμένος -η -ον destined, doomed (part. of πέπρωται 'it is destined, fated')

αἶσα -ης, ἡ fate, fate of death (in origin someone's 'portion', like μοῖρα; cf. 68 and 334)

442 δυσηχής -ές evil-sounding, hateful

ἐξαναλύω I set free; ἐξαναλῦσαι is aor. inf.

443 τοι (enclitic particle) I assure you (here strengthening the negative); distinguished only by context from τοι = σοι

ἐπαινέω I praise, approve; here with implied fut. sense. This line repeats 4.29 (Hera discouraging Zeus from ending the war immediately); it occurs again at 22.181 (Athena discouraging Zeus from saving Hector).

444 τοι = σοι

ἐρέω (= ἐρῶ): 1 s. fut. of λέγω (cf. 49)

βάλλεο: 2 s. mid. imper. of βάλλω (cf. 24), here 'put', but tr. phrase 'and you take it to heart'

445 ζώς = ζωός (cf. 331); ζών is m. acc. s.

δόμος -ου/οιο, ὁ house, home; ὄνδε δόμονδε 'to his home' (suffix -δε 'to' unusually added also to the possessive). Three spondees at the start of the line perhaps express Hera's forceful tone.

446 φράζομαι I consider; φράζεο is 2 s. imper.

ἔπειτα (here) in the future

ἐθέλησι: 3 s. pres. subj. of ἐθέλω (= Att. ἐθέλῃ; cf. 53) after μή 'in case …'

448 πολλοί: an exaggeration, as there are only nine (Achilles, Aeneas, Sarpedon, Machaon, Menestheus, Eudorus, Ialmenus, Ascalaphus and Podaleirius)

περί (+ acc.) about, around

Πρίαμος -ου/οιο, ὁ Priam, king of Troy

449 κότος -ου, ὁ resentment

ἐνήσεις: 2 s. fut. ἐνίημι (cf. 291), here 'you will cause'

450 τοι = σοι

τέος -η -ον = σός σή σόν (cf. 36)

451 ἔασον: 2 s. aor. imper. of ἐάω (cf. 60)

453 τόν him, i.e. Sarpedon

ψυχή -ῆς, ἡ breath, spirit

αἰών -ῶνος, ὁ/ἡ life, life force

454 πέμπειν: inf. as imper.

Θάνατος -ου, ὁ Death (personified)

φέρω I carry; φέρειν is inf. expressing purpose and μιν its object

νήδυμος -ον sweet

Ὕπνος -ου, ὁ Sleep (personified)

455 εἰς ὅ until

ἵκωνται: 3 pl. aor. subj. of ἱκνέομαι (cf. 247)

456 ἔνθα there

ἑ him (cf. 47 and 109)

ταρχύω I inter, bury solemnly; ταρχύσουσι is 3 pl. fut.

ἔτης -αο, ὁ kinsman

457 τύμβος -ου, ὁ grave-mound

στήλη -ης, ἡ pillar, gravestone

θανόντων: aor. part. (m. gen. pl.) of θνῇσκω (cf. 16). Hera's concession illustrates the importance given to proper burial.

Ὣς ἔφατ᾽, οὐδ᾽ ἀπίθησε πατὴρ ἀνδρῶν τε θεῶν τε·
αἱματοέσσας δὲ ψιάδας κατέχευεν ἔραζε
παῖδα φίλον τιμῶν, τόν οἱ Πάτροκλος ἔμελλε   460
φθίσειν ἐν Τροίῃ ἐριβώλακι, τηλόθι πάτρης.
    Οἱ δ᾽ ὅτε δὴ σχεδὸν ἦσαν ἐπ᾽ ἀλλήλοισιν ἰόντες,
ἔνθ᾽ ἤτοι Πάτροκλος ἀγακλειτὸν Θρασύμηλον,
ὅς ῥ᾽ ἠῢς θεράπων Σαρπηδόνος ἦν ἄνακτος,
τὸν βάλε νείαιραν κατὰ γαστέρα, λῦσε δὲ γυῖα.   465
Σαρπηδὼν δ᾽ αὐτοῦ μὲν ἀπήμβροτε δουρὶ φαεινῷ
δεύτερον ὁρμηθείς, ὃ δὲ Πήδασον οὔτασεν ἵππον
ἔγχεϊ δεξιὸν ὦμον· ὃ δ᾽ ἔβραχε θυμὸν ἀΐσθων,
κὰδ δὲ πέσ᾽ ἐν κονίῃσι μακών, ἀπὸ δ᾽ ἔπτατο θυμός.
τὼ δὲ διαστήτην, κρίκε δὲ ζυγόν, ἡνία δέ σφι   470
σύγχυτ᾽, ἐπεὶ δὴ κεῖτο παρήορος ἐν κονίῃσι.
τοῖο μὲν Αὐτομέδων δουρικλυτὸς εὕρετο τέκμωρ·
σπασσάμενος τανύηκες ἄορ παχέος παρὰ μηροῦ,
ἀΐξας ἀπέκοψε παρήορον οὐδὲ μάτησε·
τὼ δ᾽ ἰθυνθήτην, ἐν δὲ ῥυτῆρσι τάνυσθεν·   475
τὼ δ᾽ αὖτις συνίτην ἔριδος πέρι θυμοβόροιο.
    Ἔνθ᾽ αὖ Σαρπηδὼν μὲν ἀπήμβροτε δουρὶ φαεινῷ,
Πατρόκλου δ᾽ ὑπὲρ ὦμον ἀριστερὸν ἤλυθ᾽ ἀκωκὴ
ἔγχεος, οὐδ᾽ ἔβαλ᾽ αὐτόν· ὃ δ᾽ ὕστερος ὄρνυτο χαλκῷ
Πάτροκλος· τοῦ δ᾽ οὐχ ἅλιον βέλος ἔκφυγε χειρός,   480
ἀλλ᾽ ἔβαλ᾽ ἔνθ᾽ ἄρα τε φρένες ἔρχαται ἀμφ᾽ ἁδινὸν κῆρ.
ἤριπε δ᾽ ὡς ὅτε τις δρῦς ἤριπεν ἢ ἀχερωΐς,

458 ἀπιθέω I disobey; ἀπίθησε is 3 s. aor. Whether Zeus could in principle change fate is a matter of controversy, but in practice he never does so. Here he is persuaded by Hera's arguments and allows Sarpedon to die.

459 αἱματόεις -εσσα -εν (-εντος) bloody
ψιάς -άδος, ἡ raindrop
καταχεύω = καταχέω I pour down, shower down
ἔραζε (adv.) to the ground. Unnatural phenomena regularly accompany the death of special heroes: cf. 567–8, where Zeus covers the battlefield in darkness to hamper the fight over Sarpedon's body.

460 οἱ: dat. of ἑ (cf. 109); this ethic dat. (cf. 200) is hard to capture in tr. but perhaps 'in his sight' or 'to his distress'
μέλλω I am going to, intend to (usu. + fut. inf.)

461 φθίνω I cause to perish, kill; φθίσειν is fut. inf.
ἐριβῶλαξ -ακος deep-soiled, fertile
πάτρη -ης, ἡ native land (= Att. πάτρα -ας or πατρίς -ίδος). This line is full of pathos, but at least Sarpedon will be buried with honours in his native land.

462–507: Patroclus and Sarpedon fight, and Sarpedon is killed.

462 σχεδόν (adv.) near
   ἰόντες: pres. part. (m. nom. pl.) of εἶμι (I go)
463 ἔνθ(α) then
   ἀγακλειτός -ή -όν very famous, highly
      renowned
   Θρασύμηλος -ου, ὁ Thrasymelus, Sarpe-
      don's charioteer; object of βάλε (465)
464 ἠΰς ἠΰ noble, brave
   ἦεν = ἦν
465 τόν: picks up Θρασύμηλον (463), redun-
      dant in tr.
   νείαιρα -ης (f. adj.) lower (part of)
466 ἀπήμβροτε: 3 s. aor. of ἀφαμαρτάνω
      (here + gen.; cf. 322)
467 δεύτερον (as adv.) next, in turn
   οὔτασεν: 3 s. aor. of οὐτάω (cf. 24)
468 ἔβραχον (aor. only) I roared, shrieked
   ἀΐσθω I breathe out
469 κὰδ … πέσ(ε): tmesis of 3 s. aor. of κατα-
      πίπτω (cf. 290)
   μηκάομαι I shriek, cry; μακών is aor. part.
      (m. nom. s.)
   ἀποπέτομαι I fly away; ἀπὸ … ἔπτατο is
      tmesis of 3 s. aor.
470 τὼ δέ the (other) two, i.e. Xanthus and
      Balius, who (unlike Pedasus) were
      immortal
   διΐστημι I stand apart; διαστήτην is 3
      dual aor. 'pulled apart'
   κρίζω I creak; κρίκε is 3 s. aor. Note the
      onomatopoeia.
   σφεῖς (personal pron.) they, them; σφι is
      dat. pl. (= σφίσι)
471 συγχέω I pour together, (here) entangle
      with (+ dat.); σύγχυτο is 3 s. aor. mid.
   κεῖτο: 3 s. impf. of κεῖμαι (cf. 24)
   παρήορος -ου, ὁ trace-horse
472 τοῖο for this (situation)
   εὑρίσκω I find; εὕρετο is 3 s. aor. mid.
   τέκμωρ (nom./acc. only), τό end, goal,
      (here) solution (= Att. τέκμαρ)
473 σπάω I draw; σπασσάμενος is aor. mid.
      part. (m. nom. s.)
   τανυήκης -ες long-bladed
   παχύς -έος thick, sturdy
474 ἀΐξας: aor. part. (m. nom. s.) of ἀΐσσω (cf.
      404)
   ἀποκόπτω I cut off, cut loose; ἀπέκοψε
      is 3 s. aor.

ματάω I linger, delay; μάτησε is 3 s.
   aor. The verb can also mean 'I am
   unsuccessful', which may be its sense
   here.
475 τὼ δ(έ) the other two horses
   ἰθύνω I straighten (= Att. εὐθύνω);
      ἰθυνθήτην is 3 dual aor. pass. with act.
      sense 'straightened up'
   ῥυτήρ -ῆρος, ὁ rein
   τανύσθεν: 3 pl. aor. pass. of τανύω (cf.
      375) with act. sense 'strained forward'.
      Four spondees at the start of the line
      perhaps give a sense of the horses'
      power.
476 τὼ δ(έ) the two (men), on the other
      hand, i.e. Sarpedon and Patroclus
   σύνειμι I come together, meet; συνίτην is
      3 dual impf.
   ἔρις -ιδος, ἡ strife
   πέρι (+ gen.) (here) in, in the matter of
      (accented as postposition)
   θυμοβόρος -ον heart-devouring
478 ὑπέρ (+ acc.) over, beyond
   ἤλυθ(ε): aor. 3 s. of ἔρχομαι (= ἦλθε; cf.
      255)
479 ὕστερος -η -ον later, (here tr. as adv.)
      next, in turn
   ὤρνυτο: 3 s. impf. of ὄρνυμαι (cf. 126)
      'rose up'
480 ἅλιος -η -ον fruitless, in vain
   ἐκφεύγω I escape from, (here) fly from
      (+ gen.); ἔκφυγε is 3 s. aor.
481 ἔνθ(α): used as at 314
   φρένες (here) midriff (cf. 36)
   ἔρχαται: 3 pl. perf. pass. of ἔργω (cf.
      395) 'is closed in'
   ἀδινός -ή -όν repeated, (here) beating
   κῆρ κῆρος, τό heart
482 ὡς ὅτε … νήϊον εἶναι (484): the
      expected simile at a moment of high
      drama. The mighty but fallen trees
      reflect both the stature and fate of
      the fallen hero, while the scene of
      men productively at work contrasts
      poignantly with the τέλος θανάτοιο
      (502) about to befall Sarpedon.
   δρῦς -υός, ἡ oak
   ἤριπεν (cf. 319): gnomic aor. in simile
   ἀχερωΐς -ΐδος, ἡ poplar

ἠὲ πίτυς βλωθρή, τήν τ᾽ οὔρεσι τέκτονες ἄνδρες
ἐξέταμον πελέκεσσι νεήκεσι νήϊον εἶναι·
ὣς ὁ πρόσθ᾽ ἵππων καὶ δίφρου κεῖτο τανυσθείς,   485
βεβρυχώς, κόνιος δεδραγμένος αἱματοέσσης.
ἠΰτε ταῦρον ἔπεφνε λέων ἀγέληφι μετελθών,
αἴθωνα μεγάθυμον, ἐν εἰλιπόδεσσι βόεσσι,
ὤλετό τε στενάχων ὑπὸ γαμφηλῇσι λέοντος,
ὣς ὑπὸ Πατρόκλῳ Λυκίων ἀγὸς ἀσπιστάων   490
κτεινόμενος μενέαινε, φίλον δ᾽ ὀνόμηνεν ἑταῖρον·
"Γλαῦκε πέπον, πολεμιστὰ μετ᾽ ἀνδράσι, νῦν σε μάλα χρὴ
αἰχμητήν τ᾽ ἔμεναι καὶ θαρσαλέον πολεμιστήν·
νῦν τοι ἐελδέσθω πόλεμος κακός, εἰ θοός ἐσσι.
πρῶτα μὲν ὄτρυνον Λυκίων ἡγήτορας ἄνδρας,   495
πάντῃ ἐποιχόμενος, Σαρπηδόνος ἀμφιμάχεσθαι·
αὐτὰρ ἔπειτα καὶ αὐτὸς ἐμεῦ πέρι μάρναο χαλκῷ.
σοὶ γὰρ ἐγὼ καὶ ἔπειτα κατηφείη καὶ ὄνειδος
ἔσσομαι ἤματα πάντα διαμπερές, εἴ κέ μ᾽ Ἀχαιοὶ
τεύχεα συλήσωσι νεῶν ἐν ἀγῶνι πεσόντα.   500
ἀλλ᾽ ἔχεο κρατερῶς, ὄτρυνε δὲ λαὸν ἅπαντα."
  Ὣς ἄρα μιν εἰπόντα τέλος θανάτοιο κάλυψεν
ὀφθαλμοὺς ῥῖνάς θ᾽· ὁ δὲ λὰξ ἐν στήθεσι βαίνων
ἐκ χροὸς ἕλκε δόρυ, προτὶ δὲ φρένες αὐτῷ ἕποντο·
τοῖο δ᾽ ἅμα ψυχήν τε καὶ ἔγχεος ἐξέρυσ᾽ αἰχμήν.   505
Μυρμιδόνες δ᾽ αὐτοῦ σχέθον ἵππους φυσιόωντας,
ἱεμένους φοβέεσθαι, ἐπεὶ λίπον ἅρματ᾽ ἀνάκτων.

483 ἠέ = ἤ or
  πίτυς -υος, ἡ pine
  βλωθρός -ή -όν tall
  τέκτων -ονος, ὁ maker, carpenter;
    τέκτονες ἄνδρες 'craftsmen' or more
    specifically 'shipwrights'
484 ἐκτάμνω I fell, cut down; ἐξέταμον is 3 pl.
    aor., again here gnomic
  πέλεκυς -εος, ὁ axe
  νεηκής -ές newly sharpened, whetted
  νήϊον -ου, τό ship's timber
485 ὁ he, i.e. Sarpedon
  τανυσθείς: aor. pass. part. (m. nom. s.)
    of τανύω (cf. 375) 'stretched out'. A
    moment full of pathos. Four spondees
    starting the line slow the pace and
    impart solemnity.

486 βρυχάομαι I roar, bellow; βεβρυχώς is
    perf. part. (m. nom. s.) but tr. as pres.
  κόνις -ιος, ἡ dust
  δράσσομαι I clutch at (+ gen.); δεδραγμέ-
    νος is perf. part. (m. nom. s.) but again
    tr. as pres.
487 ἠΰτε just as. A second simile, triggered
    by Sarpedon's bellowing: typical ex-
    pansion of an important scene. Bulls
    and lions are both noble animals.
  ταῦρος -ου, ὁ bull
  ἔπεφνον (aor. only) I killed; again
    gnomic
  λέων -οντος, ὁ lion
  ἀγέλη -ης, ἡ herd; ἀγέληφι is dat.
  μετέρχομαι I come among (+ dat.); μετελ-
    θών is aor. part. (m. nom. s.)

488 αἴθων -ωνος tawny

εἰλίπους -οδος of rolling gait, shambling

βοῦς βοός, ὁ/ἡ ox, cow, pl. cattle

489 ὄλλυμαι I am killed, perish; ὤλετο is 3 s.
aor., once more gnomic in simile

ὑπό ... ὑπό (490): introducing broadly
parallel content, but natural sense first
time is 'under' and second time 'at the
hands of'

γαμφηλαί -ῶν, αἱ jaws

490 ἀγός -οῦ, ὁ leader

ἀσπιστής -ᾶο/έω, ὁ shield-bearer, warrior

491 κτεινόμενος: pres. pass. part. (m. nom. s.)
of κτείνω (cf. 292) lit. 'being killed' i.e.
'as he was dying'

μενεαίνω I struggle, rage

ὀνομαίνω I call by name; ὠνόμηνεν is 3 s.
aor. The following speech combines
a call to duty (492–4), a rallying
cry (495–7) and an appeal for help
(498–500).

492 Γλαῦκος -ου, ὁ Glaucus, second in
command of the Lycian troops. At
12.309–28 Sarpedon describes to him
what being a hero means; his final
words reflect that passage.

πέπον (+ voc.) dear friend

πολεμιστής -ᾶο/έω, ὁ warrior

χρή it is necessary for X (acc.) to do Y
(inf.)

493 αἰχμητής -ᾶο/έω, ὁ spearman, warrior

ἔμεναι = εἶναι

θαρσαλέος -η -ον bold, courageous (=
Att. θαρραλέος -α -ον)

494 τοι = σοι

ἔλδομαι I desire; ἐελδέσθω is 3 s. imper.
with pass. sense 'let war be your
desire'

θοός: used as at 422

ἐσσί: 2 s. pres. of εἰμί (= εἶ)

495 ὄτρυνον: 2 s. aor. imper. of ὀτρύνω (cf. 167)

496 πάντη (adv.) everywhere

ἀμφιμάχομαι (here) I fight for, fight over
(+ gen.; cf. 73)

497 ἐμεῦ = ἐμοῦ

πέρι: accented as postposition

μάρναο: 2 s. imper. of μάρναμαι (cf. 195)

498 καὶ ἔπειτα in the future also (cf. 446)

κατηφείη -ης, ἡ disgrace, shame

ὄνειδος -εος, τό (matter of) reproach.
This destruction of his reputation is
the very worst thing that could befall
a hero.

499 ἔσσομαι: 1 s. fut. of εἰμί (= ἔσομαι)

διαμπερές (adv.) continually, for ever.
Note the urgency of ἤματα πάντα and
διαμπερές piled on top of καὶ ἔπειτα
(498).

εἴ κέ: introducing fut. open condition
(cf. 87)

500 συλάω I strip off, plunder; συλήσωσι is 3
pl. aor. subj.

ἀγών -ῶνος, ὁ (here) contest (cf. 239);
νεῶν ἐν ἀγῶνι 'in the contest around
the ships'

501 ἔχομαι I hold on, (here) hold my ground;
ἔχεο is 2 s. imper.

502 τέλος θανάτοιο lit. the end of death, i.e.
the end that is death

503 ὁ δέ and he, i.e. Patroclus

λάξ (adv.) with the heel

βαίνων (here) stepping, treading:
a gesture of triumph which also
enables the spear to be withdrawn
more easily

504 χρώς χροός, ὁ flesh, body

προτί = πρός (here as adv.) in addition

φρένες: used as at 481

αὐτῷ it, i.e. the spear

505 τοῖο his, i.e. Sarpedon's

ἐξερύω I pull out; ἐξέρυσ(ε) is 3 s. aor.

506 αὐτοῦ (adv.) there, on the spot

σχέθον: 3 pl. aor. of ἔχω (= ἔσχον;
cf. 68)

φυσιάω I pant, snort; φυσιόωντας is pres.
part. (m. acc. pl.)

507 ἱεμένους: pres. part. (m. acc. pl.) of ἵεμαι
(cf. 359)

φοβέεσθαι: pres. inf. of φοβέομαι (cf.
290)

ἐπεί ... ἀνάκτων now that they had left
their lords' chariot. They hadn't, in
fact: this seems to be a formulaic
phrase carelessly used.

Γλαύκῳ δ᾽ αἰνὸν ἄχος γένετο φθογγῆς ἀΐοντι·
ὠρίνθη δέ οἱ ἦτορ, ὅ τ᾽ οὐ δύνατο προσαμῦναι.
χειρὶ δ᾽ ἑλὼν ἐπίεζε βραχίονα· τεῖρε γὰρ αὐτὸν   510
ἕλκος, ὃ δή μιν Τεῦκρος ἐπεσσύμενον βάλεν ἰῷ
τείχεος ὑψηλοῖο, ἀρὴν ἑτάροισιν ἀμύνων.
εὐχόμενος δ᾽ ἄρα εἶπεν ἑκηβόλῳ Ἀπόλλωνι·
"κλῦθι, ἄναξ, ὅς που Λυκίης ἐν πίονι δήμῳ
εἶς ἢ ἐνὶ Τροίῃ· δύνασαι δὲ σὺ πάντοσ᾽ ἀκούειν   515
ἀνέρι κηδομένῳ, ὡς νῦν ἐμὲ κῆδος ἱκάνει.
ἕλκος μὲν γὰρ ἔχω τόδε καρτερόν, ἀμφὶ δέ μοι χεὶρ
ὀξείῃς ὀδύνῃσιν ἐλήλαται, οὐδέ μοι αἷμα
τερσῆναι δύναται, βαρύθει δέ μοι ὦμος ὑπ᾽ αὐτοῦ·
ἔγχος δ᾽ οὐ δύναμαι σχεῖν ἔμπεδον, οὐδὲ μάχεσθαι   520
ἐλθὼν δυσμενέεσσιν. ἀνὴρ δ᾽ ὤριστος ὄλωλε,
Σαρπηδών, Διὸς υἱός· ὁ δ᾽ οὐδ᾽ οὗ παιδὸς ἀμύνει.
ἀλλὰ σύ πέρ μοι, ἄναξ, τόδε καρτερὸν ἕλκος ἄκεσσαι,
κοίμησον δ᾽ ὀδύνας, δὸς δὲ κράτος, ὄφρ᾽ ἑτάροισι
κεκλόμενος Λυκίοισιν ἐποτρύνω πολεμίζειν,   525
αὐτός τ᾽ ἀμφὶ νέκυι κατατεθνηῶτι μάχωμαι."
    Ὣς ἔφατ᾽ εὐχόμενος, τοῦ δ᾽ ἔκλυε Φοῖβος Ἀπόλλων.
αὐτίκα παῦσ᾽ ὀδύνας, ἀπὸ δ᾽ ἕλκεος ἀργαλέοιο
αἷμα μέλαν τέρσηνε, μένος δέ οἱ ἔμβαλε θυμῷ.
Γλαῦκος δ᾽ ἔγνω ᾗσιν ἐνὶ φρεσὶ γήθησέν τε,   530
ὅττί οἱ ὦκ᾽ ἤκουσε μέγας θεὸς εὐξαμένοιο.
πρῶτα μὲν ὤτρυνεν Λυκίων ἡγήτορας ἄνδρας,
πάντῃ ἐποιχόμενος Σαρπηδόνος ἀμφιμάχεσθαι·
αὐτὰρ ἔπειτα μετὰ Τρῶας κίε μακρὰ βιβάσθων,
Πουλυδάμαντ᾽ ἔπι Πανθοΐδην καὶ Ἀγήνορα δῖον,   535
βῆ δὲ μετ᾽ Αἰνείαν τε καὶ Ἕκτορα χαλκοκορυστήν.
ἀγχοῦ δ᾽ ἱστάμενος ἔπεα πτερόεντα προσηύδα·

*508–47: A grief-stricken Glaucus prays to Apollo for help, receives it, and brings
word to the Trojans of Sarpedon's death. Note here (514–26) the typical form taken
by a prayer: (i) invoke the god (514); (ii) appeal to him or her wherever he or she
may be (514–15); (iii) mention past or customary favours (515–16); (iv) explain
your present plight (517–22); (v) ask for help (523–6). It is interesting too to note
the lack of any humility on the part of the suppliant; Apollo may help or he may
not, and no amount of grovelling will change that.*

508 φθογγή -ῆς, ἡ voice
    ἀΐω I hear (+ gen.); ἀΐοντι is pres. part.
    (m. dat. s.)
509 ὠρίνθη: 3 s. aor. pass. of ὀρίνω (cf. 280)
    ὅ τ(ε) because

προσαμύνω I come to help, bring sup-
    port; προσαμῦναι is aor. inf.
510 πιέζω I press, squeeze
511 ὅ ... μιν: double acc. with βάλεν 'which
    Teucer had dealt him'

Τεῦκρος -ου, ὁ Teucer, a Greek archer. He wounded Glaucus at 12.387–91.

ἐπεσσύμενον: perf. part. (m. acc. s.) of ἐπισ(σ)εύομαι (here + gen.; cf. 411)

ἰός -οῦ, ὁ arrow

512 ἀρή -ῆς, ἡ ruin, destruction

513 ἑκηβόλος -ον far-shooting; the last syllable of ἑκηβόλῳ is shortened by correption, and the first syllable of Ἀπόλλωνι lengthened

514 κλῦθι: 2 s. aor. imper. of κλύω (cf. 13)
που (adv.) (here) probably, no doubt

515 εἶς: 2 s. pres. of εἰμί (= εἶ)
πάντοσ(ε) (adv.) in every direction, (here) from everywhere. Apollo is clearly just the god for the job.
ἀκούειν: here + dat. rather than usu. gen.

516 κήδομαι I am in distress
κῆδος -εος, τό trouble, distress, torment. Heroes in the *Iliad* very rarely complain about wounds, though Glaucus is also troubled by his inability to do anything for Sarpedon.

517 καρτερός -ή -όν = κρατερός (cf. 25) (here) stark, terrible
ἀμφί (as adv.) (here) all around (the wound), everywhere

518 ὀδύνη -ης, ἡ pain
ἐλήλαται: 3 s. perf. pass. of ἐλαύνω (cf. 87) here 'has been struck'

519 τερσαίνω I dry, dry up; τερσῆναι is aor. inf.
βαρύθω I am heavy, (here) am paralysed
αὐτοῦ: i.e. the wound

520 σχεῖν: aor. inf. of ἔχω (cf. 68) 'to hold'
ἔμπεδον (adv.) firmly

521 ἐλθών: tr. before μάχεσθαι, 'go and ...'
δυσμενής -ές hostile, (as m. noun) enemy; δυσμενέεσσιν is dat. pl. after μάχεσθαι
ὤριστος = ὁ ἄριστος
ὄλωλε: 3 s. perf. of ὄλλυμαι (cf. 489)

522 ὁ δ(έ) but he, i.e. Zeus
οὐδ(έ) not even
ἀμύνω (here) I protect (+ gen.; cf. 32). Glaucus could not know that Zeus had earlier tried to save Sarpedon.

523 ἀκέομαι I heal; ἄκεσσαι is 2 s. aor. imper.

524 κοιμάω I put to rest, (here) soothe; κοίμησον is 2 s. aor. imper.

525 κεκλόμενος: aor. part. (m. nom. s.) of κέλομαι (cf. 268)
ἐποτρύνω I stir up, urge on (+ dat.); here 1 s. subj. in purpose clause with ὄφρα

526 ἀμφὶ ... μάχωμαι: tmesis of 1 s. subj. of ἀμφιμάχομαι (here + dat.; cf. 496)
καταθνήσκω I die; κατατεθνηῶτι is perf. part. (m. dat. s.)

527 Φοῖβος -ου, ὁ Phoebus (epithet or alternative name of Apollo, probably meaning 'radiant')

528 αὐτίκα (cf. 184): gods usu. answer prayers immediately
παύω I stop (something); παῦσ(ε) is 3 s. aor.

529 τέρσηνε: 3 s. aor. of τερσαίνω (cf. 519), here trans.

530 γηθέω I rejoice, am glad; γήθησεν is 3 s. aor.

531 ὅττι = ὅτι (here) that
οἱ: here acts as gen. agreeing with εὐξαμένοιο

532-3 = 495-6

534 κίον (aor. only) I went
βιβάσθω I stride; μακρὰ βιβάσθων 'taking long strides', a sign of confident assurance

535 Πουλυδάμας -αντος, ὁ Polydamas (the first syllable of his name is lengthened for the metre), a Trojan who will have a major role in Book 18. At 535–6 Glaucus is summoning Troy's most outstanding leaders.
ἔπι: accented as postposition
Πανθοΐδης -αο/εω, ὁ son of Panthus
Ἀγήνωρ -ορος, ὁ Agenor, a Trojan

536 μετ(ά) (+ acc.) (here) to find
Αἰνείας -αο/εω, ὁ Aeneas, a Trojan, later to acquire great fame for leading Trojan survivors to Italy

537 ἀγχοῦ (adv.) near. Standing close makes communication more personal, as well as being necessary on a noisy battlefield.
ἱστάμενος: pres. part. (m. nom. s.) of ἵσταμαι (cf. 166)

"Ἕκτορ, νῦν δὴ πάγχυ λελασμένος εἰς ἐπικούρων,
οἳ σέθεν εἵνεκα τῆλε φίλων καὶ πατρίδος αἴης
θυμὸν ἀποφθινύθουσι· σὺ δ' οὐκ ἐθέλεις ἐπαμύνειν.   540
κεῖται Σαρπηδών, Λυκίων ἀγὸς ἀσπιστάων,
ὃς Λυκίην εἴρυτο δίκῃσί τε καὶ σθένεϊ ᾧ·
τὸν δ' ὑπὸ Πατρόκλῳ δάμασ' ἔγχεϊ χάλκεος Ἄρης.
ἀλλά, φίλοι, πάρστητε, νεμεσσήθητε δὲ θυμῷ,
μὴ ἀπὸ τεύχε' ἕλωνται, ἀεικίσσωσι δὲ νεκρὸν   545
Μυρμιδόνες, Δαναῶν κεχολωμένοι ὅσσοι ὄλοντο,
τοὺς ἐπὶ νηυσὶ θοῇσιν ἐπέφνομεν ἐγχείῃσιν."

    Ὣς ἔφατο, Τρῶας δὲ κατὰ κρῆθεν λάβε πένθος
ἄσχετον, οὐκ ἐπιεικτόν, ἐπεί σφισιν ἔρμα πόληος
ἔσκε καὶ ἀλλοδαπός περ ἐών· πολέες γὰρ ἅμ' αὐτῷ   550
λαοὶ ἕποντ', ἐν δ' αὐτὸς ἀριστεύεσκε μάχεσθαι·
βὰν δ' ἰθὺς Δαναῶν λελιημένοι· ἦρχε δ' ἄρά σφιν
Ἕκτωρ χωόμενος Σαρπηδόνος. αὐτὰρ Ἀχαιοὺς
ὦρσε Μενοιτιάδεω Πατροκλῆος λάσιον κῆρ·
Αἴαντε πρώτω προσέφη, μεμαῶτε καὶ αὐτώ·   555
"Αἴαντε, νῦν σφῶϊν ἀμύνεσθαι φίλον ἔστω,
οἷοί περ πάρος ἦτε μετ' ἀνδράσιν, ἢ καὶ ἀρείους.
κεῖται ἀνὴρ ὃς πρῶτος ἐσήλατο τεῖχος Ἀχαιῶν,
Σαρπηδών· ἀλλ' εἴ μιν ἀεικισσαίμεθ' ἑλόντες,
τεύχεά τ' ὤμοιιν ἀφελοίμεθα, καί τιν' ἑταίρων   560
αὐτοῦ ἀμυνομένων δαμασαίμεθα νηλέϊ χαλκῷ."

    Ὣς ἔφαθ', οἳ δὲ καὶ αὐτοὶ ἀλέξασθαι μενέαινον.
οἳ δ' ἐπεὶ ἀμφοτέρωθεν ἐκαρτύναντο φάλαγγας,
Τρῶες καὶ Λύκιοι καὶ Μυρμιδόνες καὶ Ἀχαιοί,
σύμβαλον ἀμφὶ νέκυι κατατεθνηῶτι μάχεσθαι   565

---

538 λελασμένος εἰς : 'periphrastic' (part. +
    auxiliary εἰμί) 2 s. perf. of λανθάνομαι
    (cf. 357)
    ἐπίκουρος -ον helping, (as m. pl. noun)
    allies
539 σέθεν = σοῦ
    εἵνεκα = ἕνεκα (cf. 18)
    τῆλε (here) far from (+ gen.)
    πατρίς -ίδος (as f. adj.) of one's fathers,
    native
    αἶα -ης, ἡ earth, land (= γαῖα)
540 θυμόν: acc. of resp.
    ἀποφθινύθω I waste away
    ἐπαμύνω I bring help to; understand
    'them' as object
541 κεῖται (cf. 24) (here) lies dead

542 ἐρύομαι I protect, guard; εἴρυτο is 3 s.
    impf. Sarpedon is recognised as a fine
    leader in both peace and war.
    δίκη -ης, ἡ (here) judgement
    (cf. 388)
    σθένος -εος, τό strength
543 ὑπό (+ dat.) (here) by the agency of.
    Note that Glaucus has recognised
    Patroclus for who he is.
    δάμασ(ε): 3 s. aor. of δαμάζω (cf. 326)
    χάλκεος (cf. 136) (here) bronze-
    armoured. It is unusual for a character
    (rather than the poet as narrator) to
    ascribe responsibility to a specific god,
    but 'killed by Ares' is often just a way
    of saying 'killed in battle'.

544 πάρστητε: variant form of παράστητε, 2 pl. aor. imper. of παρίσταμαι (cf. 2) here 'stand by him'

νεμεσσάομαι I am ashamed; νεμεσσήθητε is 2 pl. aor. imper.

θυμῷ at heart

545 ἀπό … ἕλωνται: tmesis of 3 pl. aor. mid. subj. of ἀφαιρέω (cf. 54)

ἀεικίζω I disfigure, abuse; ἀεικίσσωσι is 3 pl. aor. subj. mid. The abuse of the dead is a major theme of the *Iliad*;

it will reach its climax in Achilles' slaughter and treatment of Hector (22.214–404).

νεκρός -οῦ, ὁ corpse, dead body

546 κεχολωμένοι: perf. part. (m. nom. pl.) of χολόομαι (cf. 61); tr. phrase 'angry for all the Danaans who have perished'

ὄλοντο: 3 pl. aor. of ὄλλυμαι (cf. 489)

547 ἔπεφνον (aor. only) I killed

548–68: The Trojans are grief-stricken and Hector leads them against the Achaeans, themselves urged on by Patroclus.

548 κρῆθεν (adv.) from the head; κατὰ κρῆθεν 'from top to bottom', i.e. 'completely'

πένθος -εος, τό grief

549 ἄσχετος -ον irresistible, overwhelming

ἐπιεικτός -ή -όν yielding, ceasing

ἕρμα -ατος, τό support, bulwark

550 καί … πέρ although (cf. 154)

ἀλλοδαπός -ή -όν foreign

πολέες = πολλοί

551 ἐν (here as adv.) among (them)

552 βάν: 3 pl. aor. of βαίνω (cf. 221)

ἰθύς (+ gen.) straight for

λελιημένοι: perf. part. (m. nom. pl.) akin to λιλαίομαι (cf. 89); tr. as adv. 'eagerly'

553 χώομαι I am angered about (+ gen.)

554 ὦρσε: 3 s. aor. of ὄρνυμι (cf. 267)

Πατροκλῆος: gen. s. (cf. 7)

λάσιος -η -ον shaggy, (here) stout

555 Αἴαντε: acc. dual 'the two Ajaxes', i.e. Ajax the Great, son of Telamon (cf. 102), and Ajax the Lesser, son of Oileus (cf. 330). After 557 neither Ajax appears again in Book 16. Patroclus' exhortation effectively despatches them to another part of the fighting. This enables the spotlight to shine on Patroclus alone; if the greater Ajax had still been present, he would have been bound to intervene.

πρώτω: m. acc. dual of πρῶτος (cf. 284)

μέμαα (perf. with pres. sense) I am eager; μεμαῶτε is part. (m. acc. dual). Tr. phrase 'eager themselves also'.

556 σφῶϊν to the two of you; dat. dual of pron. σφεῖς (cf. 470; this form can be second person as well as third)

ἀμύνομαι I put up a defence; mid. of ἀμύνω (cf. 32)

ἔστω: 3 s. imper. of εἰμί; 'let it be dear to you' i.e. 'make it your job'

557 οἷοί περ just like (with preceding 'and to be' understood)

καί (here) even

ἀρείων -ον better, superior; ἀρείους is m. nom. pl. (= ἀρείονες)

558 εἰσάλλομαι I leap inside; ἐσήλατο is 3 s. aor.

559 ἀλλ' εἰ (here) come on, let's see if we can … (+ opt.)

ἀεικισσαίμεθ(α): 1 pl. aor. opt. mid. of ἀεικίζω (cf. 545). This is all exactly as Glaucus had feared.

560 ὤμοιιν: gen. dual of ὦμος (cf. 40) 'from his two shoulders'; the second iota is lengthened for the metre (cf. on 57)

ἀφελοίμεθα: 1 pl. aor. opt. mid. of ἀφαιρέω (cf. 54)

561 ἀμυνομένων: pres. part. (m. gen. pl.) of ἀμύνομαι (cf. 556, here + gen.) 'defending him', i.e. his body

δαμασαίμεθα: 1 pl. aor. opt. mid. of δαμάζω (cf. 326)

562 ἀλέξω I ward off; ἀλέξασθαι is aor. mid. inf. 'to put up a defence'

μενεαίνω I am eager

563 ἀμφοτέρωθεν (adv.) on both sides

καρτύνω I strengthen; ἐκαρτύναντο is 3 pl. aor. mid.

565 συμβάλλω lit. I throw together, (here) I join (battle); σύμβαλον is 3 pl. aor.

δεινὸν ἀΰσαντες· μέγα δ᾽ ἔβραχε τεύχεα φωτῶν.
Ζεὺς δ᾽ ἐπὶ νύκτ᾽ ὀλοὴν τάνυσε κρατερῇ ὑσμίνῃ,
ὄφρα φίλῳ περὶ παιδὶ μάχης ὀλοὸς πόνος εἴη.
    Ὦσαν δὲ πρότεροι Τρῶες ἑλίκωπας Ἀχαιούς·
βλῆτο γὰρ οὔ τι κάκιστος ἀνὴρ μετὰ Μυρμιδόνεσσιν,   570
υἱὸς Ἀγακλῆος μεγαθύμου, δῖος Ἐπειγεύς,
ὅς ῥ᾽ ἐν Βουδείῳ εὖ ναιομένῳ ἤνασσε
τὸ πρίν· ἀτὰρ τότε γ᾽ ἐσθλὸν ἀνεψιὸν ἐξεναρίξας
ἐς Πηλῆ᾽ ἱκέτευσε καὶ ἐς Θέτιν ἀργυρόπεζαν·
οἱ δ᾽ ἅμ᾽ Ἀχιλλῆϊ ῥηξήνορι πέμπον ἕπεσθαι   575
Ἴλιον εἰς εὔπωλον, ἵνα Τρώεσσι μάχοιτο.
τόν ῥα τόθ᾽ ἁπτόμενον νέκυος βάλε φαίδιμος Ἕκτωρ
χερμαδίῳ κεφαλήν· ἡ δ᾽ ἄνδιχα πᾶσα κεάσθη
ἐν κόρυθι βριαρῇ· ὁ δ᾽ ἄρα πρηνὴς ἐπὶ νεκρῷ
κάππεσεν, ἀμφὶ δέ μιν θάνατος χύτο θυμοραϊστής.   580
Πατρόκλῳ δ᾽ ἄρ᾽ ἄχος γένετο φθιμένου ἑτάροιο,
ἴθυσεν δὲ διὰ προμάχων ἴρηκι ἐοικὼς
ὠκέϊ, ὅς τ᾽ ἐφόβησε κολοιούς τε ψῆράς τε·
ὣς ἰθὺς Λυκίων, Πατρόκλεες ἱπποκέλευθε,
ἔσσυο καὶ Τρώων, κεχόλωσο δὲ κῆρ ἑτάροιο.   585

5. Battle scene from the oldest illustrated manuscript of the *Iliad*, fifth century CE. Biblioteca Ambrosiana, Milan.

566 ἀΰσαντες: aor. part. (m. nom. pl.) of ἀΰω
 (cf. 268)
 μέγα (here) loudly
567 ἐπιτανύω I spread X (acc.) over Y (dat.);
  ἐπὶ … τάνυσε is tmesis of 3 s. aor.
 νύξ νυκτός, ἡ night, (here) darkness.
  It here reflects Zeus's grief at his

son's death and makes the battle
for Sarpedon's body more
dramatic.
ὀλοός -ή -όν deadly
568 πόνος -ου, ὁ toil, labour
 εἴη: 3 s. opt. of εἰμί

569–601: Hector kills Epeigeus, but Patroclus kills Sthenelaus, briefly stopping the advance. Glaucus then responds by killing Bathycles. There is much to admire in the variety that Homer brings to these expanded battle scenes, though we miss any mention of Sarpedon.

569 ὦσαν: 3 pl. aor. of ὠθέω (cf. 45)
 πρότερος -η -ον first (of two); here adj.
  as adv.
 ἑλίκωψ -ωπος darting-eyed
570 βλῆτο: 3 s. aor. pass. of βάλλω (cf. 24)
 οὔ τι not at all
 κάκιστος: sup. (m. nom. s.) of κακός (cf.
  47)
571 Ἀγακλεής -ῆος ὁ Agacles, a Myrmidon,
  father of Epeigeus
 Ἐπειγεύς -ῆος, ὁ Epeigeus, a Myrmidon
572 Βούδειον -ου, τό Budeum, a town in
  Phthia
 ναιομένῳ: pres. pass. part. (n. dat. s.) of
  ναίω (cf. 233); with εὖ (cf. 191) here
  'where the living is good'
573 ἀνεψιός -οῦ, ὁ cousin
 ἐξεναρίζω I kill (lit. strip off armour);
  ἐξεναρίξας is aor. part. (m. nom. s.)
574 ἱκετεύω I supplicate, approach as suppliant; ἱκέτευσε is 3 s. aor. Patroclus
  himself came as a suppliant to Peleus;
  his later death is foreshadowed by the
  fate of Epeigeus here. Respect for sup-
  pliants is a main theme of the *Iliad*,
  culminating in Achilles' meeting with
  Hector's father Priam (24.477–676).
575 πέμπον: 3 pl. impf. of πέμπω (cf. 240)
576 εὔπωλος -ον with fine horses
577 τόθ' = τότε (before vowel with rough
  breathing)
 ἁπτόμενον: pres. part. (m. acc. s.) of
  ἅπτομαι (cf. 9), here used like a cona-

tive impf. 'as he was trying to put his
hand on' (+ gen.)
φαίδιμος -ον glorious
578 χερμάδιον -ου, τό stone
 κεφαλήν: acc. of resp.
 ἡ δ' ἄνδιχα … θυμοραϊστής (580): cf.
  412–14
581 φθίνομαι I perish, die; φθιμένου is aor.
  part. (m. gen. s.)
582 ἰθύω I go straight forward; ἴθυσεν is 3 s. aor.
 πρόμαχος -ου, ὁ foremost fighter
 ἴρηξ -ηκος, ὁ hawk
 ἐοικώς: part. (m. nom. s) of ἔοικα (cf. 259)
583 ὠκέϊ (cf. 48): note emphatic position. It
  is the speed of the hawk that counts
  in this brief simile, highlighting the
  speed of Patroclus' attack.
 φοβέω I put to flight; ἐφόβησε is 3 s. aor.,
  here gnomic
 κολοιός -οῦ, ὁ jackdaw
 ψήρ ψηρός, ὁ starling. Jackdaws and
  starlings appear in large flocks, ideal
  prey for the hawk.
584 Πατρόκλεες: voc. (again note the apostrophe)
 ἱπποκέλευθος -ον chariot-driving, driver
  of horses
585 ἔσσυο: 2 s. plup. of σεύομαι (cf. 9) 'you
  rushed'
 κεχόλωσο: 2 s. plup. of χολόομαι (cf. 61)
  'you were enraged'
 κῆρ: acc. of resp.
 ἑτάροιο for your companion

καί ῥ' ἔβαλε Σθενέλαον, Ἰθαιμένεος φίλον υἱόν,
αὐχένα χερμαδίῳ, ῥῆξεν δ' ἀπὸ τοῖο τένοντας.
χώρησαν δ' ὑπό τε πρόμαχοι καὶ φαίδιμος Ἕκτωρ.
ὅσση δ' αἰγανέης ῥιπὴ ταναοῖο τέτυκται,
ἥν ῥά τ' ἀνὴρ ἀφέῃ πειρώμενος ἢ ἐν ἀέθλῳ   590
ἠὲ καὶ ἐν πολέμῳ, δηΐων ὕπο θυμοραϊστέων,
τόσσον ἐχώρησαν Τρῶες, ὤσαντο δ' Ἀχαιοί.
Γλαῦκος δὲ πρῶτος, Λυκίων ἀγὸς ἀσπιστάων,
ἐτράπετ', ἔκτεινεν δὲ Βαθυκλῆα μεγάθυμον,
Χάλκωνος φίλον υἱόν, ὃς Ἑλλάδι οἰκία ναίων   595
ὄλβῳ τε πλούτῳ τε μετέπρεπε Μυρμιδόνεσσι.
τὸν μὲν ἄρα Γλαῦκος στῆθος μέσον οὔτασε δουρὶ
στρεφθεὶς ἐξαπίνης, ὅτε μιν κατέμαρπτε διώκων·
δούπησεν δὲ πεσών· πυκινὸν δ' ἄχος ἔλλαβ' Ἀχαιούς,
ὡς ἔπεσ' ἐσθλὸς ἀνήρ· μέγα δὲ Τρῶες κεχάροντο,   600
στὰν δ' ἀμφ' αὐτὸν ἰόντες ἀολλέες· οὐδ' ἄρ' Ἀχαιοὶ
ἀλκῆς ἐξελάθοντο, μένος δ' ἰθὺς φέρον αὐτῶν.
ἔνθ' αὖ Μηριόνης Τρώων ἕλεν ἄνδρα κορυστήν,
Λαόγονον, θρασὺν υἱὸν Ὀνήτορος, ὃς Διὸς ἱρεὺς
Ἰδαίου ἐτέτυκτο, θεὸς δ' ὣς τίετο δήμῳ.   605
τὸν βάλ' ὑπὸ γναθμοῖο καὶ οὔατος· ὦκα δὲ θυμὸς
ᾤχετ' ἀπὸ μελέων, στυγερὸς δ' ἄρα μιν σκότος εἷλεν.
Αἰνείας δ' ἐπὶ Μηριόνῃ δόρυ χάλκεον ἧκεν·
ἔλπετο γὰρ τεύξεσθαι ὑπασπίδια προβιβῶντος.
ἀλλ' ὃ μὲν ἄντα ἰδὼν ἠλεύατο χάλκεον ἔγχος·   610
πρόσσω γὰρ κατέκυψε, τὸ δ' ἐξόπιθεν δόρυ μακρὸν
οὔδει ἐνισκίμφθη, ἐπὶ δ' οὐρίαχος πελεμίχθη
ἔγχεος· ἔνθα δ' ἔπειτ' ἀφίει μένος ὄβριμος Ἄρης.
αἰχμὴ δ' Αἰνείαο κραδαινομένη κατὰ γαίης
ᾤχετ', ἐπεί ῥ' ἅλιον στιβαρῆς ἀπὸ χειρὸς ὄρουσεν.   615

586 Σθενέλαος -ου, ὁ Sthenelaus, a Lycian
   Ἰθαιμένης -εος, ὁ Ithaemenes, father of
   Sthenelaus
587 αὐχένα: acc. of resp.
   ἀπὸ τοῖο from it, i.e. the neck
   τένων -οντος, ὁ sinew, tendon
588 ὑποχωρέω I retreat, give ground; χώρησαν ... ὑπό is tmesis (with elements
   reversed) of 3 pl. aor.
589 ὅσ(σ)ος -η -ον as big as, (here) as far as
   αἰγανέη -ης, ἡ javelin
   ῥιπή -ῆς, ἡ flight, throw

ταναός -όν long
τέτυκται: 3 s. perf. pass. of τεύχω (cf.
   225), here no more than 'is'
590 ἀφίημι I send away, (here) let fly;
   ἀφέῃ is 3 s. aor. subj., generalising in
   simile
   πειράομαι I try, (here) try my strength
   ἤ ... ἠέ (591) either ... or
   ἄεθλος -ου, ὁ contest, competition (= Att.
   ἆθλος -ου)
591 δηΐων: m. gen. pl. of δήϊος (cf. 127) as
   noun 'enemies'

ὕπο (+ gen.) (here) under pressure from; accented as postposition

592 τόσ(σ)ος -η -ον so big; n. here as adv. 'so far' picking up ὅσση (589)

χωρέω I give way, withdraw; ἐχώρησαν is 3 pl. aor.

ὦσαντο: 3 pl. aor. mid. of ὠθέω (cf. 45)

594 τρέπω I turn; ἐτράπετ(ο) is 3 s. aor. mid.; tr. phrase 'was first to turn round'. Glaucus leads the counter-attack, suddenly turning (at 597) to take on his pursuer.

Βαθυκλῆς -ῆος, ὁ Bathycles, a Myrmidon

595 Χάλκων -ωνος, ὁ Chalcon, father of Bathycles

Ἑλλάς -άδος, ἡ Hellas, a region of north-west Greece including Achilles' kingdom (cf. on 21); here local dat. 'in Hellas'

οἰκία (cf. 261): here pl. for s.

596 ὄλβος -ου, ὁ happiness, prosperity
πλοῦτος -ου, ὁ wealth, riches

597 στῆθος μέσον: acc. of resp.

598 στρεφθείς: aor. pass. part. (m. nom. s.) of στρέφω (cf. 308) 'twisting around'
ἐξαπίνης (adv.) suddenly
καταμάρπτω I overtake, catch up with; impf. here 'was about to catch up with him'
διώκω I chase, pursue

599 πυκινὸν … ἄχος overwhelming (lit. thick) grief
ἔλλαβ(ε): double λ for the metre
χαίρω I rejoice; κεχάροντο is 3 pl. aor. mid.

600 χαίρω I rejoice; κεχάροντο is 3 pl. aor. mid.

601 στάν: 3 pl. aor. of ἵσταμαι (cf. 166), with ἰόντες 'they went and stood'
ἀμφ' αὐτόν around him, i.e. Glaucus (to continue the attack)

602–31: The Achaeans fight back and Meriones takes on the Trojan Aeneas.

602 ἐκλανθάνομαι I forget completely (+ gen.); ἐξελάθοντο is 3 pl. aor.
ἰθύς (here) straight ahead (cf. 552)

603 κορυστής -ᾶο/έω (m. adj.) helmeted, armed

604 Λαόγονος -ου, ὁ Laogonus, a Trojan
θρασύς -εῖα -ύ bold, daring
Ὀνήτωρ -ορος, ὁ Onetor, father of Laogonus
ἱρεύς -ῆος, ὁ priest (= Att. ἱερεύς -έως)

605 Ἰδαῖος -η -ον of Mount Ida, Idaean. Here a cult title of Zeus, i.e. as worshipped on this mountain close to Troy.
ἐτέτυκτο: 3 s. plup. pass. of τεύχω (cf. 225 and 589) here just 'was'
θεὸς δ' ὥς and like a god

607 οἴχομαι I go, depart; ᾤχετ(ο) is 3 s. impf.
στυγερός -ή -όν hateful
εἷλεν: 3 s. aor. of αἱρέω (cf. 58). Note yet another way of describing death.

608 ἐπί (+ dat.) (here) at
ἧκεν (here) let fly (3 s. aor. of ἵημι, cf. 152)

609 ἔλπετο: 3 s. impf. of ἔλπομαι (cf. 281), here 'he hoped'
τυγχάνω I hit (+ gen.); τεύξεσθαι is fut. inf.
ὑπασπίδια (adv.) under cover of a shield

προβιβῶντος: Homeric pres. part. (m. gen. s.) of προβαίνω (cf. 54) here 'as he advanced'

610 ἄντα (adv.) opposite, straight ahead
ἀλεύομαι I avoid; ἠλεύατο is 3 s. aor.

611 κατακύπτω I bend down, stoop; κατέκυψε is 3 s. aor.
ἐξόπιθεν (adv.) behind

612 οὖδας -εος, τό ground
ἐνισκίμπτω I stick X (acc.) in Y (dat.); ἐνισκίμφθη is 3 s. aor. pass.
ἐπί (here as adv.) above
οὐρίαχος -ου, ὁ butt end (of a spear)
πελεμίχθη: 3 s. aor. pass. of πελεμίζω (cf. 108) with act. sense 'quivered'

613 ἀφίει: 3 s. impf. of ἀφίημι (cf. 590) here 'took away'
ὄβριμος -η -ον heavy, mighty

614 κραδαίνομαι I quiver
κατὰ γαίης down into the ground

615 ἅλιον (cf. 480): n. as adv.
ὄρουσεν: 3 s. aor. of ὀρούω (cf. 258) here 'flew'
Lines 614–15 more or less repeat 612–13, and are themselves repeated from 13.504–5; they probably don't belong here.

Αἰνείας δ' ἄρα θυμὸν ἐχώσατο φώνησέν τε·
"Μηριόνη, τάχα κέν σε καὶ ὀρχηστήν περ ἐόντα
ἔγχος ἐμὸν κατέπαυσε διαμπερές, εἴ σ' ἔβαλόν περ."
    Τὸν δ' αὖ Μηριόνης δουρικλυτὸς ἀντίον ηὔδα·
"Αἰνεία, χαλεπόν σε καὶ ἴφθιμόν περ ἐόντα   620
πάντων ἀνθρώπων σβέσσαι μένος, ὅς κέ σευ ἄντα
ἔλθῃ ἀμυνόμενος· θνητὸς δέ νυ καὶ σὺ τέτυξαι.
εἰ καὶ ἐγώ σε βάλοιμι τυχὼν μέσον ὀξέϊ χαλκῷ,
αἶψά κε καὶ κρατερός περ ἐὼν καὶ χερσὶ πεποιθὼς
εὖχος ἐμοὶ δοίης, ψυχὴν δ' Ἄϊδι κλυτοπώλῳ."   625
    Ὣς φάτο, τὸν δ' ἐνένιπε Μενοιτίου ἄλκιμος υἱός·
"Μηριόνη, τί σὺ ταῦτα καὶ ἐσθλὸς ἐὼν ἀγορεύεις;
ὦ πέπον, οὔ τοι Τρῶες ὀνειδείοις ἐπέεσσι
νεκροῦ χωρήσουσι· πάρος τινὰ γαῖα καθέξει.
ἐν γὰρ χερσὶ τέλος πολέμου, ἐπέων δ' ἐνὶ βουλῇ·   630
τῶ οὔ τι χρὴ μῦθον ὀφέλλειν, ἀλλὰ μάχεσθαι."
    Ὣς εἰπὼν ὁ μὲν ἦρχ', ὁ δ' ἅμ' ἕσπετο ἰσόθεος φώς.
τῶν δ' ὥς τε δρυτόμων ἀνδρῶν ὀρυμαγδὸς ὄρωρεν
οὔρεος ἐν βήσσῃς, ἕκαθεν δέ τε γίγνετ' ἀκουή,
ὣς τῶν ὄρνυτο δοῦπος ἀπὸ χθονὸς εὐρυοδείης   635
χαλκοῦ τε ῥινοῦ τε βοῶν τ' εὐποιητάων,
νυσσομένων ξίφεσίν τε καὶ ἔγχεσιν ἀμφιγύοισιν.
οὐδ' ἂν ἔτι φράδμων περ ἀνὴρ Σαρπηδόνα δῖον
ἔγνω, ἐπεὶ βελέεσσι καὶ αἵματι καὶ κονίῃσιν
ἐκ κεφαλῆς εἴλυτο διαμπερὲς ἐς πόδας ἄκρους.   640
οἱ δ' αἰεὶ περὶ νεκρὸν ὁμίλεον, ὡς ὅτε μυῖαι

---

616 ἐχώσατο: 3 s. aor. of χώομαι (cf. 553)
617 τάχα κέν (+ aor.) would have soon … (in
    past unfulfilled condition)
    καί … περ although
    ὀρχηστής -ᾶο/έω, ὁ dancer. Aeneas is
    referring to Meriones' forward stoop
    at 611.
618 διαμπερές (adv.) (here) once and for all
    (cf. 499)
    εἴ … περ if (I had) really
619 ἀντίον (adv.) in reply. Exchanges of
    insults are common on the battlefield.
    ηὔδα: 3 s. impf. of αὐδάω (cf. 76)
620 χαλεπός -ή -όν hard, difficult; n. here
    (with ἐστί understood) 'it is difficult
    for X to' (+ acc. and inf.)
621 σβέννυμι I quench, extinguish; σβέσσαι is
    aor. inf.

ὅς κε (+ subj.) whoever
ἄντα (+ gen.) face to face with
622 ἔλθῃ: 3 s. aor. subj. of ἔρχομαι (cf. 255)
    δέ: used as at 262
    νυ = νύν well then, now then, I suppose
    τέτυξαι: 2 s. perf. pass. of τεύχω (cf. 225
    and 589) here 'you are'
623 εἰ (+ opt.) if (I were to … you would);
    fut. 'less likely' condition
    τυχών: aor. part. (m. nom. s.) of
    τυγχάνω (cf. 609); βάλοιμι τυχών lit.
    'strike having hit', i.e. 'hit and strike'
    μέσον lit. in the middle (of your body),
    i.e. 'full on'
624 πεποιθώς: part. (m. nom. s.) of πέποιθα
    (cf. 171)
625 εὖχος -εος, τό glory
    δοίης: 2 s. aor. opt. of δίδωμι (cf. 40)

Ἀΐδης -αο/εω, also Ἄϊδος, ὁ Hades, god of
    the Underworld (= Att. Ἀΐδης -ου)
κλυτόπωλος -ον with famous horses.
    Note the balanced expression in this
    line, with syllepsis ('give' used in two
    different senses).
626 ἐνίπτω I rebuke, reproach; ἐνένιπε is 3 s.
    aor. Patroclus alerts Meriones to his
    responsibilities, firmly bringing to
    an end what has so far been a purely
    verbal exchange.
627 τί why?
628 τοι: particle strengthening the negative
    (cf. 443)
ὀνείδειος -ον reproachful
ἐπέεσσι: dat. pl. of ἔπος (cf. 6)
629 χωρήσουσι: 3 pl. fut. of χωρέω (cf. 592),
    here + gen. 'withdraw from'
πάρος (here) before that (cf. 23)

τινά (here) many a one (m. acc. s. of
    τις, cf. 36). Note yet another way of
    describing death.
κατέχω I hold down, cover; καθέξει is 3
    s. fut. There is bitter irony here: the
    earth will soon hold down Patroclus
    himself.
630 ἐν ... χερσί: abbreviated expression
    implying 'in the deeds of men's hands'
τέλος -εος, τό (here) outcome, fulfilment
    (cf. 83); understood again in the sec-
    ond part of this balanced line
βουλή -ῆς, ἡ council. Words or action?
    The hero must exploit both (cf. Phoe-
    nix to Achilles at 9.443) – but at the
    right time.
631 τῶ therefore
ὀφέλλω I increase, multiply

632–55: *The fighting continues over Sarpedon's body until Zeus decides to take a
hand in the proceedings. The intensity of the fighting here is brilliantly summarised
in two fine similes: in the first (633–7) the sound of metal axes on wood is compared
with that of weapons on the leather of shields; and in the second (641–4) the throng
of warriors around Sarpedon's corpse is likened to flies in a farmyard buzzing
around splashing pails of milk.*

632 ὁ μὲν ... ὁ δ(έ) the one (i.e. Patroclus) ...
    and the other (i.e. Meriones)
ἕσπετο: 3 s. aor. of ἕπομαι (cf. 154)
ἰσόθεος -ον godlike
633 τῶν from them
δρυτόμος -ον wood-cutting
ὀρυμαγδός -οῦ, ὁ noise, din
ὄρωρεν: 3 s. intrans. perf. of ὄρνυμι (cf.
    267) 'arose'
634 βῆσσα -ης, ἡ glen, wooded valley
ἕκαθεν (adv.) from far away
ἀκουή -ῆς, ἡ hearing, sound; γίγνετ(αι)
    ἀκουή 'the sound is heard'
635 τῶν: picks up τῶν from 633
ὄρνυτο: 3 s. impf. mid. of ὄρνυμι, again
    'arose'
εὐρυόδεια -ης (f. adj.) with broad ways
636 ῥινός -οῦ, ὁ hide, skin
βοῦς βοός, ἡ (here) shield (of oxhide).
    Five spondees in this line express the
    noise of hammering blows.

637 νυσσομένων stabbing at each other; pres.
    mid. part. (m. gen. pl.) of νύσσω (cf.
    343), agreeing with τῶν (635)
ἀμφίγυος -ον double-edged
638 οὐδ(έ) ... ἔτι and no longer
φράδμων -ονος observant, shrewd
639 ἔγνω: 3 s. aor. of γιγνώσκω (cf. 119);
    with ἄν 'would have recognised'
βελέεσσι: suggests many Greeks
    triumphantly stabbed the already
    dead Sarpedon (cf. 22.371, where
    Hector gets the same
    treatment)
640 εἰλύω I wrap, envelop; εἴλυτο is 3 s. plup.
    pass.
διαμπερές (adv.) (here) completely (cf.
    499)
ἄκρος -ή -όν end part (of); ἐς πόδας
    ἄκρους 'to his toes'
641 ὁμιλέω I throng, gather
μυῖα -ας, ἡ fly

648 ἤ … ἤ (651) whether … or (cf. 243); each here + subj. or opt. in deliberative indirect question

κεῖνος -η -ο he, she, it; that (= ἐκεῖνος -η -ο); καὶ κεῖνον 'him too', i.e. Patroclus

649 αὐτου: used as at 506

ἐπ(ί) (+ dat.) (here) over

650 δηώσῃ: 3 s. aor. subj. of δηόω (cf. 158)

ἀπὸ … ἕληται: tmesis of 3 s. aor. mid. subj. of ἀφαιρέω (cf. 54)

651 πλέων πλέον (comp. of πολύς) more; καὶ πλεόνεσσιν 'for yet more men'

ὀφέλλειεν: 3 s. aor. opt. of ὀφέλλω (cf. 631)

652 δοάσσατο (impersonal 3 s. aor.) it seemed (= Att. ἔδοξε)

κερδίων -ον more profitable, i.e. better; as usual, the second option is selected (cf. on 435)

653 ὄφρ(α) (+ opt.) (here) that (X should happen)

654 ἐξαῦτις (adv.) once again

655 ὤσαιτο: 3 s. aor. opt. mid. of ὠθέω (cf. 45)

ἀπὸ … ἕλοιτο: tmesis of 3 s. aor. mid. opt. of ἀφαιρέω (cf. 54)

πολέων = πολλῶν

656–83: Hector takes flight and Patroclus takes Sarpedon's armour; but Zeus instructs Apollo to cleanse the body, and it is then conveyed to Lycia for burial.

656 πρώτιστος -η -ον first of all; here adj. as adv.

ἐνῆκεν: 3 s. aor. of ἐνίημι (cf. 291)

657 φύγαδε (adv.) to flight

ἔτραπε: 3 s. aor. of τρέπω (cf. 594); understand 'the horses' as object

658 φευγέμεναι: pres. inf. of φεύγω (cf. 71)

ἱρός -ή -όν holy, sacred (= ἱερός)

τάλαντα -ων, τά (pair of) scales. Hector realises that the tables are now turned and Zeus is against him.

659 φόβηθεν: 3 pl. aor. of φοβέομαι (cf. 290)

660 βασιλῆα: the poet refocuses our attention from Hector back to Sarpedon

βεβλαμμένον: perf. pass. part. (m. acc. s.) of βλάπτω (cf. 331); βεβλαμμένον ἦτορ 'struck in the heart' (acc. of resp.)

661 ἄγυρις -ιος, ἡ crowd, (here) heap

662 κάππεσον: 3 pl. aor. of καταπίπτω (cf. 290)

εὖτε (conj.) when

ἐτάνυσσε: 3 s. aor. of τανύω (cf. 375) here 'stretched tight' (implying 'intensified')

Κρονίων -ονος, ὁ son of Cronus, i.e. Zeus

663 οἱ δ(έ) but the others, i.e. the Achaeans

ἕλοντο: 3 pl. aor. mid. of αἱρέω (cf. 58)

664 τὰ μέν and this, i.e. the armour

κοῖλος -η -ον hollow

666 νεφεληγερέτα -αο/εω, ὁ cloud-gatherer (epithet of Zeus)

667 εἰ δ' ἄγε νῦν but come now; fossilised expression with 2 s. imper. of ἄγω (cf. 153), followed by another imper. Zeus now puts into effect the advice given by Hera at 453–7.

κελαινεφής -ές dark

κάθηρον: 2 s. aor. imper. of καθαίρω (cf. 228), here 'cleanse X (acc.) from Y (also acc.)'

668 ἐλθών: tr. before κάθηρον (667), 'go and …'

ἐκ (+ gen.) (here) out of range of

669 πολλὸν ἀποπρό very far away

λούω I wash, bathe; λοῦσον is 2 s. aor. imper.

670 χρίω I anoint; χρῖσον is 2 s. aor. imper.

ἀμβροσίη -ης, ἡ ambrosia, the food of the gods, also used as ointment (= Att. ἀμβροσία -ας)

περιέννυμι I put (clothing, acc.) on (someone, also acc.); περὶ … ἕσσον is tmesis of 2 s. aor. imper., with 'him' understood as object

ἄμβροτος -ον (here) of the immortals (cf. 381)

εἷμα -ατος, τό garment, pl. clothing

671–3 cf. 454–5

671 πέμπε: 2 s. imper. of πέμπω (cf. 240)

πομπός -οῦ, ὁ escort

κραιπνός -ή -όν swift

φέρεσθαι: pres. mid. inf. of φέρω (cf. 454), expressing purpose 'to bring with them'

672 διδυμάονες -ων, οἱ twins

θήσουσ' ἐν Λυκίης εὐρείης πίονι δήμῳ,
ἔνθά ἑ ταρχύσουσι κασίγνητοί τε ἔται τε
τύμβῳ τε στήλῃ τε· τὸ γὰρ γέρας ἐστὶ θανόντων."   675
    Ὣς ἔφατ', οὐδ' ἄρα πατρὸς ἀνηκούστησεν Ἀπόλλων.
βῆ δὲ κατ' Ἰδαίων ὀρέων ἐς φύλοπιν αἰνήν,
αὐτίκα δ' ἐκ βελέων Σαρπηδόνα δῖον ἀείρας
πολλὸν ἀποπρὸ φέρων λοῦσεν ποταμοῖο ῥοῇσι
χρῖσέν τ' ἀμβροσίῃ, περὶ δ' ἄμβροτα εἵματα ἕσσε·   680
πέμπε δέ μιν πομποῖσιν ἅμα κραιπνοῖσι φέρεσθαι,
Ὕπνῳ καὶ Θανάτῳ διδυμάοσιν, οἵ ῥά μιν ὦκα
κάτθεσαν ἐν Λυκίης εὐρείης πίονι δήμῳ.
    Πάτροκλος δ' ἵπποισι καὶ Αὐτομέδοντι κελεύσας
Τρῶας καὶ Λυκίους μετεκίαθε, καὶ μέγ' ἀάσθη   685
νήπιος· εἰ δὲ ἔπος Πηληϊάδαο φύλαξεν,
ἦ τ' ἂν ὑπέκφυγε κῆρα κακὴν μέλανος θανάτοιο.
ἀλλ' αἰεί τε Διὸς κρείσσων νόος ἠέ περ ἀνδρῶν·
ὅς τε καὶ ἄλκιμον ἄνδρα φοβεῖ καὶ ἀφείλετο νίκην
ῥηϊδίως, ὅτε δ' αὐτὸς ἐποτρύνῃσι μάχεσθαι·   690

6. Hermes directs Sleep and Death to carry the body of Sarpedon home for burial. Red-figure krater attributed to Euphronios, c.515 BCE. Archaeological Museum of Cerveteri. (Photo by Fine Art Images/Heritage Images/Getty Images.)

673 θήσουσ(ι): 3 pl. fut. of τίθημι (cf. 83)

674–5 = 456–7

676 ἀνηκουστέω I fail to listen to, am disobedient to (+ gen.); ἀνηκούστησεν is 3 s. aor.

678–83: cf. 668–73. Note that the last of Zeus's instructions (674–5) is not carried out here, probably because it would distract our attention from the main action.

678 ἀείρω I lift (= Att. αἴρω); ἀείρας is aor. part. (m. nom. s.)

680 χρῖσεν: 3 s. aor. of χρίω (cf. 670)

περὶ ... ἔσσε: tmesis of 3 s. aor. of περιέννυμι (cf. 670). A corpse has to be puri-fied before burial, and here Sarpedon, as a mortal son of Zeus, receives some rather special treatment; but he is not being made immortal.

681 πέμπε: 3 s. impf. of πέμπω (contrast in 671)

682 = 672

683 κατατίθημι I set down; κάτθεσαν is 3 pl. aor. None of the Greeks or Trojans seems to notice that the body has disappeared; necessarily, as this would have distracted attention from Patroclus. Sarpedon's death, and shortly that of Patroclus, lay the emotional groundwork for the death of Hector in Book 22.

684–776: Patroclus drives the Trojans back to the city wall. Apollo warns him that he cannot take Troy, and urges Hector to go against him. Patroclus then kills Cebriones, Hector's charioteer, and there is fierce fighting over the body.

684–711: Patroclus presses on against the Trojans, killing many of them. Apollo knocks him back from the city wall with a warning.

684 ἵπποισι καὶ Αὐτομέδοντι: hendiadys (one idea in two words), i.e. 'Automedon in his chariot'. We infer that Patroclus wants to be driven in pursuit of the Trojans, but the subsequent fighting takes place on foot, as usu. in the *Iliad* (cf. on 147).

κελεύσας: aor. part. (m. nom. s.) of κελεύω (cf. 78)

685 μετακιάθω I go after, go in pursuit of

ἀάω I delude; ἀάσθη is 3 s. aor. pass. The verb suggests a mental blindness which removes a man's judgement and leads him to make foolish decisions. This intrusion of the narrator (685–91) both raises the emotional temperature and deepens Patroclus' tragedy.

686 νήπιος fool that he was (cf. 46); note the emphasis given by enjambment ending a sense unit, as oft. with this adj.

φυλάσσω (here) I observe (cf. 30); φύλαξεν is 3 s. aor. in past unfulfilled condition 'if he had ...'

687 ἤ τ(ε) ἄν (+ aor.) most certainly (he) would have ...

ὑπεκφεύγω I escape; ὑπέκφυγε is 3 s. aor.

688 κρείσσων -ον stronger, better; understand ἐστί. The superior mind of Zeus will see to it that Patroclus does not observe Achilles' instruction.

ἠέ = ἤ than

689–90: some editors reject these two lines because they occur in almost identical form at 17.177–8 and in some manuscripts do not occur here.

689 ἀφείλετο: 3 s. aor. of ἀφαιρέω (cf. 54), here gnomic

690 ῥηϊδίως (adv.) easily (= Att. ῥᾳδίως)

ὅτε δέ but at another time

ἐποτρύνῃσι: 3 s. subj. of ἐποτρύνω (cf. 525); subj. perhaps indefinite, but may be a scribe's attempt to mend the metre (some manuscripts have indic. ἐποτρύνει here)

ὅς οἱ καὶ τότε θυμὸν ἐνὶ στήθεσσιν ἀνῆκεν.
   Ἔνθα τίνα πρῶτον, τίνα δ' ὕστατον ἐξενάριξας,
Πατρόκλεις, ὅτε δή σε θεοὶ θανατόνδε κάλεσσαν;
Ἄδρηστον μὲν πρῶτα καὶ Αὐτόνοον καὶ Ἔχεκλον
καὶ Πέριμον Μεγάδην καὶ Ἐπίστορα καὶ Μελάνιππον,   695
αὐτὰρ ἔπειτ' Ἔλασον καὶ Μούλιον ἠδὲ Πυλάρτην·
τοὺς ἕλεν· οἱ δ' ἄλλοι φύγαδε μνώοντο ἕκαστος.
   Ἔνθά κεν ὑψίπυλον Τροίην ἕλον υἷες Ἀχαιῶν
Πατρόκλου ὑπὸ χερσί· περιπρὸ γὰρ ἔγχεϊ θῦεν·
εἰ μὴ Ἀπόλλων Φοῖβος ἐϋδμήτου ἐπὶ πύργου   700
ἔστη, τῷ ὀλοὰ φρονέων, Τρώεσσι δ' ἀρήγων.
τρὶς μὲν ἐπ' ἀγκῶνος βῆ τείχεος ὑψηλοῖο
Πάτροκλος, τρὶς δ' αὐτὸν ἀπεστυφέλιξεν Ἀπόλλων,
χείρεσσ' ἀθανάτῃσι φαεινὴν ἀσπίδα νύσσων.
ἀλλ' ὅτε δὴ τὸ τέταρτον ἐπέσσυτο δαίμονι ἶσος,   705
δεινὰ δ' ὁμοκλήσας ἔπεα πτερόεντα προσηύδα·
"χάζεο, διογενὲς Πατρόκλεες· οὔ νύ τοι αἶσα
σῷ ὑπὸ δουρὶ πόλιν πέρθαι Τρώων ἀγερώχων,
οὐδ' ὑπ' Ἀχιλλῆος, ὅς περ σέο πολλὸν ἀμείνων."
   Ὣς φάτο, Πάτροκλος δ' ἀνεχάζετο πολλὸν ὀπίσσω,   710
μῆνιν ἀλευάμενος ἑκατηβόλου Ἀπόλλωνος.
   Ἕκτωρ δ' ἐν Σκαιῇσι πύλῃς ἔχε μώνυχας ἵππους·
δίζε γὰρ ἠὲ μάχοιτο κατὰ κλόνον αὖτις ἐλάσσας,
ἦ λαοὺς ἐς τεῖχος ὁμοκλήσειεν ἀλῆναι.
ταῦτ' ἄρα οἱ φρονέοντι παρίστατο Φοῖβος Ἀπόλλων,   715
ἀνέρι εἰσάμενος αἰζηῷ τε κρατερῷ τε,
Ἀσίῳ, ὃς μήτρως ἦν Ἕκτορος ἱπποδάμοιο,
αὐτοκασίγνητος Ἑκάβης, υἱὸς δὲ Δύμαντος,

---

691 οἱ to him, i.e. Patroclus
   ἀνίημι I send forth, make spring up;
      ἀνῆκεν is 3 s. aor.
692 ὕστατος -η -ον last; here adj. as adv.
   ἐξενάριξας: 2 s. aor. of ἐξεναρίζω (cf. 573;
      distinguished by accent from aor.
      part.), already signalling apostrophe
693 Πατρόκλεις: voc.
   θανατόνδε to death
   καλέω I call; κάλεσσαν is 3 pl. aor.
      Third-person narrative resumes after
      the question.
694 Ἄδρηστος -ου, ὁ Adrastus. He and the
      next eight warriors are all Trojans.
   Αὐτόνοος -ου, ὁ Autonous
   Ἔχεκλος -ου, ὁ Echeclus

695 Πέριμος -ου, ὁ Perimus
   Μεγάδης -αο/εω, ὁ son of Megas
   Ἐπίστωρ -ορος, ὁ Epistor
   Μελάνιππος -ου, ὁ Melanippus
696 Ἔλασος -ου, ὁ Elasus
   Μούλιος -ου, ὁ Mulius
   Πυλάρτης -αο/εω, ὁ Pylartes
697 τοὺς ἕλεν these he killed
   μνάομαι I turn my thoughts; μνώοντο is
      3 pl. impf.
698 κεν ... ἕλον would have taken (aor. in
      past unfulfilled condition)
   ὑψίπυλος -ον high-gated
699 περιπρό (adv.) around and in front
   θύω I rage, storm

700 εἰ μή (+ aor.) if … had not. This is pre-
cisely the outcome that Achilles fore-
saw at 93–4, if Patroclus disobeyed his
instructions.

ἐΰδμητος -ον well-built

πύργος -ου, ὁ tower

701 ἔστη: 3 s. aor. of ἵσταμαι (cf. 166 and
255)

τῷ for him, i.e. Patroclus

ὀλοὰ φρονέων with deadly intent (cf.
567)

ἀρήγω I aid, support (+ dat.)

702 τρίς (adv.) three times

ἐπ(ὶ) … βῆ: tmesis of 3 s. aor. of ἐπιβαίνω, here 'climbed up' (+ gen.). We are
left to imagine how Patroclus does
this.

ἀγκών -ῶνος, ὁ elbow, (here) corner

703 ἀποστυφελίζω I shove back, knock back;
ἀπεστυφέλιξεν is 3 s. aor.

705 τὸ τέταρτον the fourth time (cf. 196)

ἐπέσσυτο: 3 s. aor. of ἐπισ(σ)εύομαι (cf.
411)

δαίμων -ονος, ὁ god, divine power

ἶσος -η -ον like, equal to (+ dat.). Patroclus' extraordinary wall-scaling feat

suggests a power like that of a deity.
This is not the act of a sensible mortal.

706 δ(έ): apodotic (cf. 199). The subject
changes abruptly to Apollo.

ὁμοκλήσας: aor. part. (m. nom. s.) of
ὁμοκλέω (cf. 378), here 'calling out'

707 χάζεο: 2 s. imper. of χάζομαι (cf. 122)

708 σῷ: n. dat. s. of σός (cf. 36)

πέρθαι: irreg. aor. mid. inf. of πέρθω (cf.
57), with pass. sense; here in acc. +
inf. 'that the city … should be sacked'

ἀγέρωχος -ον lordly, proud

709 σέο = σοῦ

πολλόν much; 2nd decl. form n. of πολύς
as adv.

ἀμείνων -ον better; comp. of ἀγαθός (cf.
165)

710 ἀναχάζομαι I withdraw, draw back

ὀπίσ(σ)ω (adv.) backwards

711 μῆνις -ιος, ἡ wrath

ἀλευάμενος: aor. part. (m. nom. s.) of
ἀλεύομαι (cf. 610)

ἑκατηβόλος -ον far-shooting. Lines 707–9
were the final warning to Patroclus:
his reaction suggests that he knew it
came from Apollo.

---

*712–43: Apollo urges on Hector, who then, ignoring all the other Achaeans, makes
for Patroclus alone. Patroclus kills Cebriones, Hector's charioteer.*

712 Σκαιαί -ῶν, αἱ (with or without
πύλαι) the Scaean Gate; main
conduit from the city to the
battlefield, and location of key events
throughout the *Iliad* and beyond.
Hector's farewell to Andromache took
place there (6.393). The dying Hector
predicts that Achilles will be killed
near it (22.360).

πύλη -ης, ἡ gate; pl. here because of its
two wings

ἔχε (here) halted, held back

713 δίζω I am in doubt, at a loss

ἠέ … ἦ (714): each here + opt. in deliberative indirect question (cf. 243 and
648)

ἐλάσσας: aor. part. (m. nom. s.) of
ἐλαύνω (cf. 87) here 'riding'

714 ἐς τεῖχος inside the wall

ὁμοκλήσειεν: 3 s. aor. opt. of ὁμοκλέω
(cf. 378)

εἴλέω I confine, hem in; ἁλῆναι is aor.
pass. inf. 'to crowd together'

716 εἴδομαι I look like, take the form of (+
dat.); εἰσάμενος is aor. part. (m. nom. s.)

αἰζηός -οῦ (m. adj.) active, vigorous

717 Ἄσιος -ου, ὁ Asius, a Phrygian, Hector's
uncle. Gods regularly appear to mor-
tals in the guise of relatives.

μήτρως -ωος, ὁ maternal uncle

ἱππόδαμος -ον horse-taming

718 αὐτοκασίγνητος -ου, ὁ own brother

Ἑκάβη -ης, ἡ Hecuba, mother of Hector;
the name originally began with
digamma, so the last syllable of the
preceding word is lengthened

Δύμας -αντος, ὁ Dymas, a Phrygian,
father of Hecuba

ὃς Φρυγίῃ ναίεσκε ῥοῆς ἔπι Σαγγαρίοιο·
τῷ μιν ἐεισάμενος προσέφη Διὸς υἱὸς Ἀπόλλων·   720
"Ἕκτορ, τίπτε μάχης ἀποπαύεαι; οὐδέ τί σε χρή.
αἴθ' ὅσον ἥσσων εἰμί, τόσον σέο φέρτερος εἴην·
τῷ κε τάχα στυγερῶς πολέμου ἀπερωήσειας.
ἀλλ' ἄγε, Πατρόκλῳ ἔφεπε κρατερώνυχας ἵππους,
αἴ κέν πώς μιν ἕλῃς, δώῃ δέ τοι εὖχος Ἀπόλλων."   725
    Ὣς εἰπὼν ὃ μὲν αὖτις ἔβη θεὸς ἂμ πόνον ἀνδρῶν,
Κεβριόνῃ δ' ἐκέλευσε δαΐφρονι φαίδιμος Ἕκτωρ
ἵππους ἐς πόλεμον πεπληγέμεν. αὐτὰρ Ἀπόλλων
δύσεθ' ὅμιλον ἰών, ἐν δὲ κλόνον Ἀργείοισιν
ἧκε κακόν, Τρωσὶν δὲ καὶ Ἕκτορι κῦδος ὄπαζεν.   730
Ἕκτωρ δ' ἄλλους μὲν Δαναοὺς ἔα οὐδ' ἐνάριζεν·
αὐτὰρ ὁ Πατρόκλῳ ἔφεπε κρατερώνυχας ἵππους.
Πάτροκλος δ' ἑτέρωθεν ἀφ' ἵππων ἆλτο χαμᾶζε
σκαιῇ ἔγχος ἔχων· ἑτέρηφι δὲ λάζετο πέτρον
μάρμαρον ὀκριόεντα, τόν οἱ περὶ χεὶρ ἐκάλυψεν,   735
ἧκε δ' ἐρεισάμενος, οὐδὲ δὴν ἅζετο φωτός,
οὐδ' ἁλίωσε βέλος, βάλε δ' Ἕκτορος ἡνιοχῆα,
Κεβριόνην, νόθον υἱὸν ἀγακλῆος Πριάμοιο,
ἵππων ἡνί' ἔχοντα, μετώπιον ὀξέϊ λᾶϊ.
ἀμφοτέρας δ' ὀφρῦς σύνελεν λίθος, οὐδέ οἱ ἔσχεν   740
ὀστέον, ὀφθαλμοὶ δὲ χαμαὶ πέσον ἐν κονίῃσιν
αὐτοῦ πρόσθε ποδῶν· ὃ δ' ἄρ' ἀρνευτῆρι ἐοικὼς
κάππεσ' ἀπ' εὐεργέος δίφρου, λίπε δ' ὀστέα θυμός.
τὸν δ' ἐπικερτομέων προσέφης, Πατρόκλεες ἱππεῦ·
"ὢ πόποι, ἦ μάλ' ἐλαφρὸς ἀνήρ, ὡς ῥεῖα κυβιστᾷ.   745
εἰ δή που καὶ πόντῳ ἐν ἰχθυόεντι γένοιτο,
πολλοὺς ἂν κορέσειεν ἀνὴρ ὅδε τήθεα διφῶν,

---

719 Φρυγίη -ης, ἡ Phrygia
  ναίεσκε: 3 s. impf. iterative of ναίω (cf.
    233), here implying length of time
    rather than repetition
  Σαγγάριος -ου/οιο, ὁ the Sangarius, a
    river in Asia Minor
720 ἐεισάμενος = εἰσάμενος (cf. 716)
721 ἀποπαύομαι I cease from, desist from (+
    gen.); ἀποπαύεαι is 2 s. pres.
722 αἴθ(ε) (+ opt.) would that, if only (intro-
    ducing a wish, = Att. εἴθε)
  ὅσον … τόσον as much as … so much
  ἥσσων -ον inferior

φέρτερος -η -ον better, braver (here +
    gen. of comparison 'than')
  εἴην: 1 s. opt. of εἰμί
723 τῷ (adv.) in that case
  στυγερῶς (adv.) hatefully; here implying
    'at a heavy price' or 'with horrible
    consequences'
  ἀπερωέω I withdraw from (+ gen.);
    ἀπερωήσειας is 2 s. aor. opt., here
    potential with κε τάχα 'you would
    soon …'
724 ἄγε come! (cf. 667)
  ἐφέπω I drive on; ἔφεπε is 2 s. imper.

κρατερῶνυξ -υχος (m. adj.) strong-
hoofed

725 αἴ κέν πως (+ subj.) in the hope that
somehow (= ἐάν πως)

ἕλῃς: 2 s. aor. subj. of αἱρέω (cf. 58)

δώῃ: 3 s. aor. subj. of δίδωμι (cf. 40)

726 ἄμ = ἀνά. The contrast of θεός and ἀνδρῶν
underlines the effectiveness of the
illusion.

727 Κεβριόνης -αο/εω, ὁ Cebriones, son of
Priam, charioteer and half-brother of
Hector

δαΐφρων -ονος fiery-hearted

728 πεπληγέμεν: aor. inf. of πλήσσω (cf. 115)
here 'to whip'

729 δύομαι I enter, make my way into; δύσεθ᾿
(= δύσετο) is 3 s. aor.

ὅμιλος -ου, ὁ crowd, throng

ἐν: with Ἀργείοισιν

κλόνον (cf. 331): by creating confusion
among the Argives, Apollo helps the
Trojans rally.

730 ἧκε: 3 s. aor. of ἵημι (cf. 152)

ὀπάζω I give, grant

731 ἔα: 3 s. impf. of ἐάω (cf. 60)

ἐναρίζω I strip of armour, I kill; ἐνάριζεν
is 3 s. impf., here conative

732 ἔφεπε: here 3 s. impf. (contrast 724)

733 ἀφ᾿ ἵππων from his chariot. Presumably Patroclus retreated by chariot at
710–11.

734 σκαιός -ή -όν on the left; (f. as noun) left
hand

ἑτέρηφι with the other (hand)

λάζομαι I take

735 μάρμαρος -ον sparkling

ὀκριόεις -εσσα -εν (-εντος) jagged

περικαλύπτω I envelop; περὶ ... ἐκάλυψεν is tmesis of 3 s. aor.

736 ἐρείδομαι I lean on; ἐρεισάμενος is aor.
part. (m. nom. s.) here 'having braced
himself'

δήν (adv.) long, for a long time; originally δϝην (i.e. with digamma), so
the short final vowel of the preceding
word is lengthened

ἅζομαι I stand in awe of (+ gen.)

737 ἁλιόω I make fruitless, (here) throw in
vain; ἁλίωσε is 3 s. aor.

ἡνιοχεύς -ῆος, ὁ charioteer

738 νόθος -η -ον illegitimate

ἀγακλεής -ές very famous, highly renowned

739 μετώπιον -ου, τό forehead; here acc. of
resp.

λᾶας -ος, ὁ stone, rock

740 ὀφρύς -ύος, ἡ brow

συναιρέω I crush, destroy; σύνελεν is 3
s. aor.

οὐδέ οἱ ἔσχεν ὀστέον nor did his bone
hold

741 χαμαί = χαμᾶζε (cf. 426). What is
described here (and at 13.617) is
an anatomical impossibility, as the
eyeballs are held in their sockets by six
strap muscles on either side, and by
the optic nerve.

742 ἀρνευτήρ -ῆρος, ὁ diver

743 εὐεργής -ές well-made

λίπε δ᾿ ὀστέα θυμός: note yet another way
of describing death

**744–50: Patroclus' mocking words are not the only example of cruel and sarcastic
humour in the** Iliad. **At 14.456–7 Polydamas taunts Prothoënor, through whose
shoulder his spear has just gone, suggesting that he can use the spear as a staff to
lean on as he goes down to the Underworld.**

744 ἐπικερτομέω I mock. Apostrophe here
and at 754 frames the speech.

745 ὦ πόποι well now! (interjection)

ἐλαφρός -ή -ον light, nimble; ἦ μάλ᾿ ἐλαφρὸς ἀνήρ 'what a nimble fellow!'

ὡς how!

κυβιστάω I turn somersaults. A mocking
taunt, which Patroclus extends by reference to someone diving for oysters.

746 εἰ δή που (+ opt.) if he were perhaps (in
fut. 'less likely' condition)

ἰχθυόεις -εσσα -εν (-εντος) full of fish

γένοιτο: 3 s. aor. opt. of γίγνομαι
(cf. 39)

747 κορέννυμι I satisfy, (here) satisfy the
hunger of; κορέσειεν is 3 s. aor. opt.

τῆθος -εος, τό oyster

διφάω I dive after

νηὸς ἀποθρῴσκων, εἰ καὶ δυσπέμφελος εἴη,
ὡς νῦν ἐν πεδίῳ ἐξ ἵππων ῥεῖα κυβιστᾷ.
ἦ ῥα καὶ ἐν Τρώεσσι κυβιστητῆρες ἔασιν."   750
    Ὣς εἰπὼν ἐπὶ Κεβριόνῃ ἥρωϊ βεβήκει
οἶμα λέοντος ἔχων, ὅς τε σταθμοὺς κεραΐζων
ἔβλητο πρὸς στῆθος, ἑή τέ μιν ὤλεσεν ἀλκή·
ὣς ἐπὶ Κεβριόνῃ, Πατρόκλεες, ἆλσο μεμαώς.
Ἕκτωρ δ᾽ αὖθ᾽ ἑτέρωθεν ἀφ᾽ ἵππων ἆλτο χαμᾶζε.   755
τὼ περὶ Κεβριόναο λέονθ᾽ ὣς δηρινθήτην,
ὥ τ᾽ ὄρεος κορυφῇσι περὶ κταμένης ἐλάφοιο,
ἄμφω πεινάοντε, μέγα φρονέοντε μάχεσθον·
ὣς περὶ Κεβριόναο δύω μήστωρες ἀϋτῆς,
Πάτροκλός τε Μενοιτιάδης καὶ φαίδιμος Ἕκτωρ,   760
ἵεντ᾽ ἀλλήλων ταμέειν χρόα νηλέϊ χαλκῷ.
Ἕκτωρ μὲν κεφαλῆφιν ἐπεὶ λάβεν, οὐχὶ μεθίει·
Πάτροκλος δ᾽ ἑτέρωθεν ἔχεν ποδός· οἳ δὲ δὴ ἄλλοι
Τρῶες καὶ Δαναοὶ σύναγον κρατερὴν ὑσμίνην.
    Ὡς δ᾽ Εὖρός τε Νότος τ᾽ ἐριδαίνετον ἀλλήλοιιν   765
οὔρεος ἐν βήσσῃς βαθέην πελεμιζέμεν ὕλην,
φηγόν τε μελίην τε τανύφλοιόν τε κράνειαν,
αἵ τε πρὸς ἀλλήλας ἔβαλον τανυήκεας ὄζους
ἠχῇ θεσπεσίῃ, πάταγος δέ τε ἀγνυμενάων,
ὣς Τρῶες καὶ Ἀχαιοὶ ἐπ᾽ ἀλλήλοισι θορόντες   770
δῄουν, οὐδ᾽ ἕτεροι μνώοντ᾽ ὀλοοῖο φόβοιο.
πολλὰ δὲ Κεβριόνην ἀμφ᾽ ὀξέα δοῦρα πεπήγει
ἰοί τε πτερόεντες ἀπὸ νευρῆφι θορόντες,
πολλὰ δὲ χερμάδια μεγάλ᾽ ἀσπίδας ἐστυφέλιξαν
μαρναμένων ἀμφ᾽ αὐτόν· ὃ δ᾽ ἐν στροφάλιγγι κονίης   775
κεῖτο μέγας μεγαλωστί, λελασμένος ἱπποσυνάων.

---

748 ἀποθρῴσκω I leap from (+ gen.)   **750** κυβιστητήρ -ῆρος, ὁ acrobat
     δυσπέμφελος -ον rough, stormy; under-   ἔασιν = εἰσίν; ἦ ῥα … ἔασιν 'yes, among
     stand πόντος (cf. 408)   the Trojans too there are acrobats!'

751–76: Patroclus and Hector lead the fighting over Cebriones' body. With typical Homeric expansion at a moment of high tension, this passage leading up to the book's climax, the death of Patroclus, contains three powerful similes: first (752–3) a lion laying waste a farmstead, then (756–8) two lions fighting over a deer, and last (765–72) the East and South winds battling it out in a deep wood.

751 βεβήκει: 3 s. plup. of βαίνω (cf. 221),   **752** οἶμα -ατος, τό rush, spring
     but tr. as aor. Patroclus wants to strip   σταθμός -οῦ/οῖο, ὁ (here) cattle-fold (cf. 642)
     Cebriones of his armour.   κεραΐζω I lay waste, ravage

753 ἔβλητο: 3 s. aor. pass. of βάλλω (cf. 24), here gnomic in simile

ἑή his own; f. nom. s. of possessive ἑός (cf. 192). The lion's own courage destroys him, and Patroclus will soon suffer the same fate.

754 ἆλσο: 2 s. aor. of ἅλλομαι (cf. 426). Apostrophe is used more frequently as the climax approaches.

μεμαώς: part. (m. nom. s.) of μέμαα (cf. 555), tr. as adv. 'eagerly'

755 αὖθ' = αὖτε (adv.) again, too. Note the similarity of this line to 733.

756 τώ the two of them

λέονθ' ὥς like two lions; λέονθ' = λέοντε, nom. dual

δηρινθήτην: 3 dual aor. of δηρίομαι = δηριάομαι (cf. 96)

757 ὥ: m. nom. dual of rel. pron.

κταμένης: aor. mid. part. (f. gen. s.) of κτείνω (cf. 292), with pass. sense

ἔλαφος -ου/οιο, ἡ hind (female deer)

758 πεινάω I am hungry; πεινάοντε is pres. part. (m. nom. dual)

φρονέοντε: pres. part. (m. nom. dual) of φρονέω (cf. 258)

μάχεσθον: 3 dual pres. of μάχομαι (cf. 1)

759 μήστωρ -ωρος, ὁ leader; μήστωρες ἀϋτῆς 'raisers of the war cry'

761 ἵεντ(ο): 3 pl. impf. of ἵεμαι (cf. 359)

τάμνω I cut (= Att. τέμνω); ταμέειν is aor. inf.

χρόα: acc. s. of χρώς (cf. 504)

762 κεφαλῆφιν by the head

μεθίημι I let go; μεθίει is 3 s. impf.

763 ἔχεν: 3 s. impf. of ἔχω (cf. 68), here + gen. 'had hold of'

764 συνάγω I join (battle)

765 Εὖρος -ου, ὁ Eurus, the east wind

Νότος -ου, ὁ Notus, the south wind

ἐριδαίνω I compete with (+ dat.); ἐριδαίνετον is 3 dual pres.

ἀλλήλοιιν: dat. dual of ἀλλήλους (cf. 101)

766 βαθύς -εῖα -ύ deep

πελεμιζέμεν: pres. inf. of πελεμίζω (cf. 108)

ὕλη -ης, ἡ wood, forest

767 φηγός -οῦ, ἡ oak

τανύφλοιος -ον with smooth bark

κράνεια -ας, ἡ cornelian cherry

768 ἔβαλον: gnomic aor. in simile, here 'strike'

τανυήκης -ες (here) slender-pointed (cf. 473)

ὄζος -ου, ὁ branch

769 ἠχή -ῆς, ἡ noise

πάταγος -ου, ὁ crashing, din; understand ἐστί, and note the onomatopoeia

ἀγνυμενάων: pres. pass. part. (f. gen. pl.) of ἄγνυμι (cf. 371); understand 'trees' (all are f.). Hiatus after a short syllable is common, but the two successive examples in δέ τε ἀγνυμενάων seem particularly harsh, perhaps reflecting the sound of what is being described.

770 θρῴσκω I leap; θορόντες is aor. part. (m. nom. pl.)

771 ἕτεροι either side; οὐδ' ἕτεροι ... φόβοιο indicates the increasing intensity of the fighting

772 πήγνυμι I fix, plant firmly; πεπήγει is 3 s. plup. with pass. sense 'were fixed'

773 νευρή -ῆς, ἡ bowstring

θορόντες (here) flying (cf. 770)

774 στυφελίζω I strike, strike against; ἐστυφέλιξαν is 3 pl. aor.

775 μαρναμένων as men fought (one-word gen. abs.)

ὁ δ' ... ἱπποσυνάων (776): our attention is here drawn away from the noise and action of battle to the calm figure of Cebriones, lying dead in all his grandeur, his former skill now as nothing. The weight of these majestic words lends an air of solemnity to the close of this episode.

στροφάλιγξ -ιγγος, ἡ eddy, whirl

776 μεγαλωστί (adv.) (stretched) over a great space; with μέγας, a big phrase for a big man. It is used twice elsewhere by Homer, of dead heroes: Patroclus (18.26) and Achilles himself (*Odyssey* 24.40). It looks forward to Achilles' own death.

λελασμένος forgetful of (+ gen.); perf. part. (m. nom. s.) of λανθάνομαι (cf. 357)

ἱπποσύνη -ης, ἡ horsemanship; here pl. for s.

Ὄφρα μὲν Ἠέλιος μέσον οὐρανὸν ἀμφιβεβήκει,
τόφρα μάλ᾽ ἀμφοτέρων βέλε᾽ ἥπτετο, πῖπτε δὲ λαός·
ἦμος δ᾽ Ἠέλιος μετενίσετο βουλυτόνδε,
καὶ τότε δή ῥ᾽ ὑπὲρ αἶσαν Ἀχαιοὶ φέρτεροι ἦσαν.	780
ἐκ μὲν Κεβριόνην βελέων ἥρωα ἔρυσσαν
Τρώων ἐξ ἐνοπῆς, καὶ ἀπ᾽ ὤμων τεύχε᾽ ἕλοντο,
Πάτροκλος δὲ Τρωσὶ κακὰ φρονέων ἐνόρουσε.
τρὶς μὲν ἔπειτ᾽ ἐπόρουσε θοῷ ἀτάλαντος Ἄρηϊ,
σμερδαλέα ἰάχων, τρὶς δ᾽ ἐννέα φῶτας ἔπεφνεν·	785
ἀλλ᾽ ὅτε δὴ τὸ τέταρτον ἐπέσσυτο δαίμονι ἶσος,
ἔνθ᾽ ἄρα τοι, Πάτροκλε, φάνη βιότοιο τελευτή·
ἤντετο γάρ τοι Φοῖβος ἐνὶ κρατερῇ ὑσμίνῃ
δεινός· ὁ μὲν τὸν ἰόντα κατὰ κλόνον οὐκ ἐνόησεν·
ἠέρι γὰρ πολλῇ κεκαλυμμένος ἀντεβόλησε·	790
στῆ δ᾽ ὄπιθεν, πλῆξεν δὲ μετάφρενον εὐρέε τ᾽ ὤμω
χειρὶ καταπρηνεῖ, στρεφεδίνηθεν δέ οἱ ὄσσε.
τοῦ δ᾽ ἀπὸ μὲν κρατὸς κυνέην βάλε Φοῖβος Ἀπόλλων·
ἡ δὲ κυλινδομένη καναχὴν ἔχε ποσσὶν ὑφ᾽ ἵππων
αὐλῶπις τρυφάλεια, μιάνθησαν δὲ ἔθειραι	795
αἵματι καὶ κονίῃσι· πάρος γε μὲν οὐ θέμις ἦεν
ἱππόκομον πήληκα μιαίνεσθαι κονίῃσιν,
ἀλλ᾽ ἀνδρὸς θείοιο κάρη χαρίεν τε μέτωπον
ῥύετ᾽ Ἀχιλλῆος· τότε δὲ Ζεὺς Ἕκτορι δῶκεν
ᾗ κεφαλῇ φορέειν, σχεδόθεν δέ οἱ ἦεν ὄλεθρος.	800
πᾶν δέ οἱ ἐν χείρεσσιν ἄγη δολιχόσκιον ἔγχος,
βριθὺ μέγα στιβαρὸν κεκορυθμένον· αὐτὰρ ἀπ᾽ ὤμων
ἀσπὶς σὺν τελαμῶνι χαμαὶ πέσε τερμιόεσσα.
λῦσε δέ οἱ θώρηκα ἄναξ Διὸς υἱὸς Ἀπόλλων.
τὸν δ᾽ ἄτη φρένας εἷλε, λύθεν δ᾽ ὑπὸ φαίδιμα γυῖα,	805

777–867: The Achaeans win Cebriones' body, but Patroclus is now attacked, first by Apollo, who strips off his armour, and then by Euphorbus, who wounds him in the back. Seizing his chance, Hector then wounds him in the lower belly and utters taunting words. As he dies, Patroclus prophesies Hector's death at the hands of Achilles.

777–817: The Achaeans gain the upper hand and capture Cebriones' body, but time is now up for Patroclus: he manages to kill no fewer than twenty-seven men in quick succession but is then attacked in turn by the god Apollo and by the Trojan Euphorbus.

777 ὄφρα … τόφρα (778) as long as … so long
 Ἠέλιος: here personified (cf. 188)
 ἀμφιβεβήκει (here) bestrode; 3 s. plup. of
  ἀμφιβαίνω (cf. 66)

778 ἥπτετο struck home, hit their targets; 3 s. impf. of ἅπτομαι (cf. 9); note the continuous sense of the impf. here and in πῖπτε 'kept on …'

779 ἦμος (adv.) when

μετανίσσομαι I pass over, move over; μετενίσετο is 3 s. aor.

βουλυτός -οῦ, ὁ the time for loosing oxen, i.e. evening; βουλυτόνδε 'towards evening'. The mention of the time here helps to clarify the changing phases of the action.

780 ὑπὲρ αἶσαν (cf. 441): either (i) 'beyond what was fated' (i.e. the plan of Zeus, identified with fate, that the Achaeans should be brought to the brink of defeat) or (ii) in a weaker sense 'beyond measure/expectation' (i.e. their usual 'portion'). The first interpretation would be a unique example of the poet describing an event (rather than a fear or possibility) in this way. On either view, attention is drawn to the exceptional but temporary success of Patroclus.

781 ἐρύω I drag; ἔρυσσαν is 3 pl. aor.

783 ἐνορούω I rush upon, leap upon (+ dat.); ἐνόρουσε is 3 s. aor.

784 ἀτάλαντος -ον like, equal to (+ dat.)

785 σμερδαλέα (cf. 277): n. pl. as adv.

ἰάχω I cry, scream

ἐννέα nine

787 τοι = σοι. Once more, apostrophe (here closely following 3 s. ἐπέσσυτο (786)) adds pathos.

φαίνομαι I appear; φάνη is 3 s. aor.

βίοτος -ου/οιο, ὁ life

τελευτή -ῆς, ἡ end

788 ἄντομαι I meet (+ dat.); ἤντετο is 3 s. impf.

789 δεινός: emphatic enjambment ending a sense unit

ὁ μέν: the subject changes back to Patroclus

νοέω I notice, observe; ἐνόησεν is 3 s. aor.

790 ἀήρ ἠέρος, ἡ mist (= Att. ἀήρ ἀέρος)

ἀντιβολέω I encounter, come in the way of; ἀντεβόλησε is 3 s. aor.

791 ὄπιθεν = ὄπισθεν (cf. 115); στῆ ὄπιθεν '(came and) stood behind him'. Apollo attacks from behind and unseen, a ruthlessly chilling assault.

μετάφρενον -ου, τό the upper back

εὐρέε: m. acc. dual of εὐρύς (cf. 273), agreeing with ὤμω 'two broad shoulders'

792 καταπρηνής -ές downturned; χειρὶ καταπρηνεῖ 'with the flat of his hand'

στρεφεδινέω I whirl (something) round; στρεφεδίνηθεν is 3 pl. aor. pass.

793 κρατός: gen. of κάρη (cf. 137). Note how this 'disarming' scene (793–804) in effect reverses the sequence of the equivalent arming scene at 130–44.

794 κυλίνδομαι I roll along

795 αὐλῶπις -ιδος (f. adj.) with a tube to hold the plume, i.e. plumed

τρυφάλεια -ας, ἡ helmet

μιαίνω I stain, befoul; μιάνθησαν is 3 pl. aor. pass.

ἔθειραι -ῶν, αἱ horse-hair plume

796 θέμις -ιστος, ἡ (here) what is right, permitted (cf. 387)

798 θεῖος -η -ον godlike

χαρίεις -εσσα -εν (-εντος) pleasing, handsome

799 ῥύομαι I protect, save

800 ᾗ: f. dat. s. of possessive ὅς (cf. 192)

φορέω I bear, wear

σχεδόθεν (adv.) near at hand, close by

οἱ for him, i.e. Hector

801 οἱ his (possessive dat.); this time referring to Patroclus

ἄγη: 3 s. aor. pass. of ἄγνυμι (cf. 371)

δολιχόσκιος -ον long-shadowed

802 κεκορυθμένον pointed; perf. pass. part. (n. nom. s.) of κορύσσω (cf. 130), the tip thought of as the spear's helmet. Although described in very similar terms, this is not of course Achilles' own spear (cf. 140–1).

803 τελαμών -ῶνος, ὁ belt, strap

τερμιόεις -εσσα -εν (-εντος) fringed, tasselled

805 ἄτη (here) stupor (cf. 274)

φρένας: acc. of resp., with τόν (whole and part, cf. 314)

λύθεν ... ὑπό: tmesis (with elements reversed) of 3 pl. aor. pass. of ὑπολύω (cf. 341), here 'were made limp'

στῆ δὲ ταφών· ὄπιθεν δὲ μετάφρενον ὀξέϊ δουρὶ
ὤμων μεσσηγὺς σχεδόθεν βάλε Δάρδανος ἀνήρ,
Πανθοΐδης Εὔφορβος, ὃς ἡλικίην ἐκέκαστο
ἔγχεΐ θ᾽ ἱπποσύνῃ τε πόδεσσί τε καρπαλίμοισι·
καὶ γὰρ δὴ τότε φῶτας ἐείκοσι βῆσεν ἀφ᾽ ἵππων,   810
πρῶτ᾽ ἐλθὼν σὺν ὄχεσφι, διδασκόμενος πολέμοιο·
ὅς τοι πρῶτος ἐφῆκε βέλος, Πατρόκλεες ἱππεῦ,
οὐδὲ δάμασσ᾽· ὁ μὲν αὖτις ἀνέδραμε, μίκτο δ᾽ ὁμίλῳ,
ἐκ χροὸς ἁρπάξας δόρυ μείλινον, οὐδ᾽ ὑπέμεινε
Πάτροκλον γυμνόν περ ἐόντ᾽ ἐν δηϊοτῆτι.   815
Πάτροκλος δὲ θεοῦ πληγῇ καὶ δουρὶ δαμασθεὶς
ἂψ ἑτάρων εἰς ἔθνος ἐχάζετο κῆρ᾽ ἀλεείνων.
  Ἕκτωρ δ᾽ ὡς εἶδεν Πατροκλῆα μεγάθυμον
ἂψ ἀναχαζόμενον, βεβλημένον ὀξέϊ χαλκῷ,
ἀγχίμολόν ῥά οἱ ἦλθε κατὰ στίχας, οὖτα δὲ δουρὶ   820
νείατον ἐς κενεῶνα, διαπρὸ δὲ χαλκὸν ἔλασσε·
δούπησεν δὲ πεσών, μέγα δ᾽ ἤκαχε λαὸν Ἀχαιῶν.
ὡς δ᾽ ὅτε σῦν ἀκάμαντα λέων ἐβιήσατο χάρμῃ,
ὥ τ᾽ ὄρεος κορυφῇσι μέγα φρονέοντε μάχεσθον
πίδακος ἀμφ᾽ ὀλίγης· ἐθέλουσι δὲ πιέμεν ἄμφω·   825

7. Menelaus and Hector fight over the body of Euphorbus. Plate from Rhodes, c.600 BCE. British Museum.

806 ταφών -οῦσα -όν in a daze, as if paralysed. Patroclus' state here is a direct
  consequence both of Apollo's blow
  (791), and of his own realisation that
  he is now defenceless.

807 μεσσηγύς (+ gen.) between; μεσσηγύς
  ὤμων i.e. in the same place as Apollo
  struck him, on the back. There is,
  however, no suggestion that Patroclus
  is running away; he starts retreating
  only at 816–17.
  Δάρδανος -ου (as m. adj.) Dardanian,
  Trojan (here equated; cf. 18.122).
  Named from Dardanus, an ancestor of
  the Trojan kings.

808 Εὔφορβος -ου, ὁ Euphorbus, a Trojan; as
  Πανθοΐδης (cf. 535) he is brother of
  Polydamas.
  ἡλικίη -ης, ἡ age, (here) men of the same
  age, contemporaries (= Att. ἡλικία -ας)
  καίνυμαι I surpass, excel; ἐκέκαστο is 3 s.
  plup. (with impf. sense)

810 ἐείκοσι(ν) twenty (= Att. εἴκοσι(ν))
  βῆσεν (here) he dislodged; 3 s. 'causative'
  aor. of βαίνω (cf. 221)

811 ὄχεσφι: dat. of ὄχεα (cf. 344)

διδάσκω I teach, pass. I learn about (+
  gen.); πρῶτ' ἐλθὼν ... πολέμοιο 'at his
  first coming with his chariot, while
  learning the lessons of war'

812 τοι = σοι, introducing yet another apostrophe
  ἐφίημι I let X (acc.) fly at Y (dat.); ἐφῆκε
  is 3 s. aor.

813 δάμασσ(ε): 3 s. aor. of δαμάζω (cf. 326)
  ἀνατρέχω I run back; ἀνέδραμε is 3 s. aor.
  It says much for Patroclus' standing
  in Trojan eyes that Euphorbus is too
  scared of him, even stripped of his
  armour, to follow up and kill him.
  μίγνυμι I mix; μῖκτο is 3 s. aor. pass.
  'mingled with' (+ dat.)

814 ἁρπάζω I snatch, seize; ἁρπάξας is aor.
  part. (m. nom. s.)
  ὑπομένω I await, withstand; ὑπέμεινε is
  3 s. aor.

815 γυμνός -ή -όν naked, (here) unarmed; tr.
  phrase 'unarmed though he was'

816 πληγή -ῆς, ἡ blow
  δαμασθείς: aor. pass. part. (m. nom. s.) of
  δαμάζω (cf. 326)

817 ἔθνος -εος, τό company, people

*818–42: Hector, the third to attack Patroclus, mortally wounds him and makes a
boastful – and inaccurate – speech. With heavy tragic irony, Patroclus' death will
be closely paralleled by that of Hector in Book 22.*

820 ἀγχίμολον (adv.) near
  κατά (+ acc.) (here) through
  στίχες -ων, αἱ ranks (cf. 173)

821 νείατος -η -ον lowest part of (= Att. νέατος)
  κενεών -ῶνος, ὁ belly

822 ἀκαχίζω I bring grief to; ἤκαχε is 3 s. aor.

823 σῦς συός, ὁ/ἡ pig, wild boar

ἐβιήσατο: 3 s. aor. mid. of βιάζω (cf.
  102), here gnomic
  χάρμη -ης, ἡ battle, joy of battle

824–5: cf. 757–8

824 ὤ both of which; nom. dual of rel. pron. ὅς

825 πῖδαξ -ακος, ἡ spring
  ἀμφ(ί) (+ gen.) about, over
  πιέμεν: aor. inf. of πίνω (cf. 226)

πολλὰ δέ τ᾽ ἀσθμαίνοντα λέων ἐδάμασσε βίηφιν·
ὣς πολέας πεφνόντα Μενοιτίου ἄλκιμον υἱὸν
Ἕκτωρ Πριαμίδης σχεδὸν ἔγχεϊ θυμὸν ἀπηύρα,
καί οἱ ἐπευχόμενος ἔπεα πτερόεντα προσηύδα·
"Πάτροκλ᾽, ἦ που ἔφησθα πόλιν κεραϊξέμεν ἁμήν,   830
Τρωϊάδας δὲ γυναῖκας ἐλεύθερον ἦμαρ ἀπούρας
ἄξειν ἐν νήεσσι φίλην ἐς πατρίδα γαῖαν,
νήπιε· τάων δὲ πρόσθ᾽ Ἕκτορος ὠκέες ἵπποι
ποσσὶν ὀρωρέχαται πολεμίζειν· ἔγχεϊ δ᾽ αὐτὸς
Τρωσὶ φιλοπτολέμοισι μεταπρέπω, ὅ σφιν ἀμύνω   835
ἦμαρ ἀναγκαῖον· σὲ δέ τ᾽ ἐνθάδε γῦπες ἔδονται.
ἆ δείλ᾽, οὐδέ τοι ἐσθλὸς ἐὼν χραίσμησεν Ἀχιλλεύς,
ὅς πού τοι μάλα πολλὰ μένων ἐπετέλλετ᾽ ἰόντι·
'μή μοι πρὶν ἰέναι, Πατρόκλεες ἱπποκέλευθε,
νῆας ἔπι γλαφυράς, πρὶν Ἕκτορος ἀνδροφόνοιο   840
αἱματόεντα χιτῶνα περὶ στήθεσσι δαΐξαι.'
ὣς πού σε προσέφη, σοὶ δὲ φρένας ἄφρονι πεῖθε."
    Τὸν δ᾽ ὀλιγοδρανέων προσέφης, Πατρόκλεες ἱππεῦ·
"ἤδη νῦν, Ἕκτορ, μεγάλ᾽ εὔχεο· σοὶ γὰρ ἔδωκε
νίκην Ζεὺς Κρονίδης καὶ Ἀπόλλων, οἵ με δάμασσαν   845
ῥηϊδίως· αὐτοὶ γὰρ ἀπ᾽ ὤμων τεύχε᾽ ἕλοντο.
τοιοῦτοι δ᾽ εἴ πέρ μοι ἐείκοσιν ἀντεβόλησαν,
πάντές κ᾽ αὐτόθ᾽ ὄλοντο ἐμῷ ὑπὸ δουρὶ δαμέντες.
ἀλλά με μοῖρ᾽ ὀλοὴ καὶ Λητοῦς ἔκτανεν υἱός,
ἀνδρῶν δ᾽ Εὔφορβος· σὺ δέ με τρίτος ἐξεναρίζεις.   850
ἄλλο δέ τοι ἐρέω, σὺ δ᾽ ἐνὶ φρεσὶ βάλλεο σῇσιν·
οὔ θην οὐδ᾽ αὐτὸς δηρὸν βέῃ, ἀλλά τοι ἤδη
ἄγχι παρέστηκεν θάνατος καὶ μοῖρα κραταιή,
χερσὶ δαμέντ᾽ Ἀχιλῆος ἀμύμονος Αἰακίδαο."
    Ὣς ἄρα μιν εἰπόντα τέλος θανάτοιο κάλυψε·   855

---

826 ἀσθμαίνω I pant; with πολλὰ ... ἀσθμαίνοντα understand 'the boar'
βίηφιν = βίη by force
827 πολέας: m. acc. pl. of πολύς (cf. 110)
πεφνόντα: part. (m. acc. s.) of ἔπεφνον
(cf. 547)
828 Πριαμίδης -αο/εω, ὁ son of Priam
ἀπαυράω I rob, deprive X (acc.) of Y
(also acc.); ἀπηύρα is 3 s. impf.
829 ἐπεύχομαι I boast over, exult
830 ἦ που doubtless, I presume

ἔφησθα: 2 s. impf. of φημί (cf. 14) here
'you thought'. Patroclus of course
expressed no such hopes.
κεραϊξέμεν: fut. inf. of κεραΐζω
(cf. 752)
ἁμός -η -ον = ἡμέτερος our
831 Τρωϊάς -άδος, ἡ Trojan woman (= Att.
Τρῳάς -άδος); here as adj. with
γυναῖκας
ἐλεύθερος -η -ον free; ἐλεύθερον ἦμαρ 'the
day of freedom'

ἀπούρας: aor. part. (m. nom. s.) of ἀπαυράω (cf. 828)

832 ἄξειν: fut. inf. of ἄγω (cf. 153)

833 νήπιε: emphatic enjambment
τάων (= τῶν) … πρόσθ(ε) in front of
them, i.e. to protect them

834 ὀρέγω I stretch, strain; ὀρωρέχαται is 3
pl. perf. mid. (= ὠρεγμένοι εἰσίν)

835 ὁ I who (article as rel. pron. with 1 s. verb)

836 ἀναγκαῖος -η -ον necessary, inevitable;
ἦμαρ ἀναγκαῖον 'the day of necessity'
(implying slavery)
ἐνθάδε (adv.) here
γύψ γυπός, ὁ vulture
ἔδω I eat, devour (= Att. ἐσθίω); ἔδονται
is 3 pl. fut. Hector is wrong here:
Patroclus' body will be retrieved by
the Achaeans.

837 ἄ ah!
δειλός -ή -όν wretched, miserable; ἄ
δειλέ 'poor wretch!' (here mocking
rather than sympathetic)

χραισμέω I am useful to, help (+ dat.);
χραίσμησεν is 3 s. aor.

838 ἐπετέλλετ(ο): 3 s. impf. mid. of ἐπιτέλλω
(cf. 199). Achilles' instructions were
of course the opposite of what Hector
imagines.
ἰόντι going out; pres. part. (m. dat. s.)
of εἶμι (I go). Note the contrast with
μένων.

839 πρίν: anticipating πρίν in 840; redundant
in tr.
ἰέναι: inf. as imper. with μή 'do not come
back'

841 δαΐζω I slash, cut to shreds; δαΐξαι is aor.
inf.

842 ὡς … προσέφη: the end of the speech
within Hector's speech is marked in
the same way as that of a speech in the
main narrative
ἄφρων -ον foolish, deluded; σοὶ … ἄφρονι is possessive dat. In fact it is Hector
who is, tragically, deluding himself.
πείθω I persuade; πεῖθε is 3 s. impf.

---

*843–67: With the prophetic gift of the dying (cf. Hector himself at 22.358–60),
Patroclus accurately predicts Hector's later death at the hands of Achilles. Hector,
less convinced of this, replies (even though his opponent is already dead) and sets
off in pursuit of Automedon, Achilles' charioteer.*

843 ὀλιγοδρανέων (m. part., nom. only) failing in strength. A final apostrophe
introduces Patroclus' final words.

844 ἤδη νῦν for now
εὔχεο: 2 s. imper. of εὔχομαι (= εὔχου; cf.
231) here 'boast'

846 ῥηϊδίως (cf. 690): emphatic enjambment

847 τοιοῦτοι men such as you; subject of past
unfulfilled condition

848 αὐτόθ(ι) (here) on the spot, right here
(cf. 294)
δαμέντες: aor. pass. part. (m. nom. pl.) of
δαμάζω (cf. 326)

849 Λητώ -οῦς, ἡ Leto, mother of Apollo and
Artemis
ἔκτανεν: 3 s. aor. of κτείνω (cf. 292), s.
agreeing with the nearest of three
subjects but understood also with the
other two

850 σὺ δὲ … ἐξεναρίζεις you are the third
in my killing. It has taken a god and
two men to bring Patroclus down; he
is quick to point out that this rather
diminishes Hector's achievement.

851 = 444

852 θήν surely, certainly
δηρόν (adv.) long, for a long time
βέομαι I shall live; βέῃ is 2 s.
ἤδη (here) already (cf. 438)

853 παρέστηκεν: 3 s. perf. of παρίσταμαι (cf.
2) here 'stands near'

854 δαμέντ(ι): aor. pass. part. (m. dat. s.) of
δαμάζω (cf. 326) agreeing with τοί
(852); rare elision of dat. s. -ι
Ἀχιλῆος ἀμύμονος Αἰακίδαο: only
here does the hero get these two
epithets together, with conspicuous
assonance

ψυχὴ δ' ἐκ ῥεθέων πταμένη Ἄϊδόσδε βεβήκει,
ὃν πότμον γοόωσα, λιποῦσ' ἀνδροτῆτα καὶ ἥβην.
τὸν καὶ τεθνηῶτα προσηύδα φαίδιμος Ἕκτωρ·
"Πατρόκλεις, τί νύ μοι μαντεύεαι αἰπὺν ὄλεθρον;   860
τίς δ' οἶδ', εἴ κ' Ἀχιλεύς, Θέτιδος πάϊς ἠϋκόμοιο,
φθήῃ ἐμῷ ὑπὸ δουρὶ τυπεὶς ἀπὸ θυμὸν ὀλέσσαι;"
    Ὣς ἄρα φωνήσας δόρυ χάλκεον ἐξ ὠτειλῆς
εἴρυσε λὰξ προσβάς, τὸν δ' ὕπτιον ὦσ' ἀπὸ δουρός.
αὐτίκα δὲ ξὺν δουρὶ μετ' Αὐτομέδοντα βεβήκει,   865
ἀντίθεον θεράποντα ποδώκεος Αἰακίδαο·
ἵετο γὰρ βαλέειν· τὸν δ' ἔκφερον ὠκέες ἵπποι
ἄμβροτοι, οὓς Πηλῆϊ θεοὶ δόσαν ἀγλαὰ δῶρα.

856 ῥέθος -εος, τό limb
  πταμένη: aor. part. (f. nom. s.) of πέτομαι
    (cf. 149)
  Ἄϊδόσδε to Hades
857 πότμος -ου, ὁ fate, death
  γοάω I bewail, lament; γοόωσα is pres.
    part. (f. nom. s.)
  ἀνδροτής -ῆτος, ἡ manhood, manliness.
    Note that the first syllable is scanned
    short though followed by three conso-
    nants, an apparent breach of metrical
    rules.
  ἥβη -ης, ἡ youth
858 τεθνηῶτα: perf. part. (m. acc. s.) of
    θνήσκω; καὶ τεθνηῶτα 'though he was
    already dead'
859 τί why?
  μαντεύομαι I prophesy, predict; μαντεύεαι
    is 2 s. pres.
860 ἠΰκομος -ον with beautiful hair (= Att.
    εὔκομος -ον)
861 φθήῃ: 3 s. aor. subj. of φθάνω (cf. 314) in
    indirect question

τύπτω I strike, hit; τυπείς is aor. pass.
  part. (m. nom. s.); φθήῃ τυπείς 'may
  be struck first'
ἀπόλλυμι I lose, destroy; ἀπο ... ὀλέσσαι
  is tmesis of aor. inf., here expressing
  result 'so as to lose his life'. A tragically
  over-confident view of the future on
  Hector's part.
862 ὠτειλή -ῆς, ἡ wound
863 εἴρυσε: 3 s. aor. of ἐρύω (cf. 781), here
    'pulled'
  προσβαίνω (here) I step on; προσβάς is
    aor. part. (m. nom. s.)
  ὦσε: 3 s. aor. of ὠθέω (cf. 45). A brutal
    image.
866 ἵετο: 3 s. impf. of ἵεμαι (cf. 359)
866-7 ὠκέες ἵπποι ἄμβροτοι: the immortality
    of the horses which carry Automedon
    off stands in stark contrast with the
    mortality of Patroclus, now lying dead
    on the field of battle.

Iliad Book 18

Iliad Book 18 (ancient title Ὁπλοποιία: Making of the arms)

Book 16 has told how Hector, with Apollo's aid, killed Patroclus. This is the hinge on which the plot of the epic turns. Its importance rests on Achilles' reaction to it, and throughout Book 17 we are kept waiting for this while a fierce battle is fought over Patroclus' body. Hector acquires Patroclus' armour, which is in fact Achilles', but after a long struggle the Achaeans rescue the body and carry it slowly back to their camp. No messenger is sent to Achilles until, late in the book, Menelaus asks Nestor's son Antilochus to run from the battlefield and bring the news.

> Ὣς οἱ μὲν μάρναντο δέμας πυρὸς αἰθομένοιο,
> Ἀντίλοχος δ᾽ Ἀχιλῆϊ πόδας ταχὺς ἄγγελος ἦλθε.
> τὸν δ᾽ εὗρε προπάροιθε νεῶν ὀρθοκραιράων
> τὰ φρονέοντ᾽ ἀνὰ θυμὸν ἃ δὴ τετελεσμένα ἦεν·
> ὀχθήσας δ᾽ ἄρα εἶπε πρὸς ὃν μεγαλήτορα θυμόν·   5
> "ὤ μοι ἐγώ, τί τ᾽ ἄρ᾽ αὖτε κάρη κομόωντες Ἀχαιοὶ
> νηυσὶν ἔπι κλονέονται ἀτυζόμενοι πεδίοιο;
> μὴ δή μοι τελέσωσι θεοὶ κακὰ κήδεα θυμῷ,

1–34: Achilles receives the news of Patroclus' death.

1–14: Antilochus is approaching Achilles. Achilles contemplates the disastrous scene of battle before him and guesses rightly what Antilochus has to tell him.

1 ὥς (accented) so, thus (= Att. οὕτως)
οἱ they, these men. The article (ὁ ἡ τό) in Homer usu. has its original role as a personal or demonstrative pronoun. It refers here to the Achaean and Trojan armies in action at the end of Book 17.
μέν: sets up a contrast with δέ (2)
μάρναμαι I fight; μάρναντο is 3 pl. impf. with the augment omitted, as very oft. in Homer.
δέμας (+ gen.) like, in the form of (acc. of n. noun meaning 'form' used as adv.)
πῦρ πυρός, τό fire
αἴθω I set on fire; αἰθομένοιο is pass. part. (n. gen. s.) 'blazing'. Note that -οιο is an alternative gen. ending, frequent in Homer, for 2nd decl. genitives in -ου.

2 Ἀντίλοχος -ου/οιο, ὁ Antilochus. He brings bad news to Achilles here as Patroclus did at the beginning of Book 16. In the sequel he takes over from Patroclus the role of the charismatic young hero.

He comes second only to Diomedes in the chariot race in Book 23. In the epic tradition following on from the *Iliad* he is killed defending his father against the Ethiopian Memnon; in the following tumult Achilles kills Memnon and is himself killed by Paris.

δ(έ) and, but; a short vowel at the end of a word is normally elided when the next word starts with a vowel. See Introduction Section E for metre and scansion.

Ἀχιλ(λ)εύς -ῆος, ὁ Achilles; Ἀχιλῆϊ is dat., the diaeresis (two dots) above the last letter indicating that it constitutes a separate syllable. Alternative spellings with single or double consonant give the poet greater metrical flexibility.

πούς ποδός, ὁ foot; the acc. πόδας limits the application of the adj. (lit.) 'swift with respect to his feet', i.e. 'swift-footed' (this is called 'accusative of respect'). This phrase is a synonymous variant

σταθμῷ ἔνι βρομέωσι περιγλαγέας κατὰ πέλλας
ὥρῃ ἐν εἰαρινῇ, ὅτε τε γλάγος ἄγγεα δεύει·
ὡς ἄρα τοὶ περὶ νεκρὸν ὁμίλεον, οὐδέ ποτε Ζεὺς
τρέψεν ἀπὸ κρατερῆς ὑσμίνης ὄσσε φαεινώ,   645
ἀλλὰ κατ᾽ αὐτοὺς αἰὲν ὅρα καὶ φράζετο θυμῷ,
πολλὰ μάλ᾽ ἀμφὶ φόνῳ Πατρόκλου μερμηρίζων,
ἢ ἤδη καὶ κεῖνον ἐνὶ κρατερῇ ὑσμίνῃ
αὐτοῦ ἐπ᾽ ἀντιθέῳ Σαρπηδόνι φαίδιμος Ἕκτωρ
χαλκῷ δῃώσῃ ἀπό τ᾽ ὤμων τεύχε᾽ ἕληται,   650
ἦ ἔτι καὶ πλεόνεσσιν ὀφέλλειεν πόνον αἰπύν.
ὧδε δέ οἱ φρονέοντι δοάσσατο κέρδιον εἶναι,
ὄφρ᾽ ἠῢς θεράπων Πηληϊάδεω Ἀχιλῆος
ἐξαῦτις Τρῶάς τε καὶ Ἕκτορα χαλκοκορυστὴν
ὤσαιτο προτὶ ἄστυ, πολέων δ᾽ ἀπὸ θυμὸν ἕλοιτο.   655
Ἕκτορι δὲ πρωτίστῳ ἀνάλκιδα θυμὸν ἐνῆκεν·
ἐς δίφρον δ᾽ ἀναβὰς φύγαδ᾽ ἔτραπε, κέκλετο δ᾽ ἄλλους
Τρῶας φευγέμεναι· γνῶ γὰρ Διὸς ἱρὰ τάλαντα.
ἔνθ᾽ οὐδ᾽ ἴφθιμοι Λύκιοι μένον, ἀλλὰ φόβηθεν
πάντες, ἐπεὶ βασιλῆα ἴδον βεβλαμμένον ἦτορ,   660
κείμενον ἐν νεκύων ἀγύρει· πολέες γὰρ ἐπ᾽ αὐτῷ
κάππεσον, εὖτ᾽ ἔριδα κρατερὴν ἐτάνυσσε Κρονίων.
οἱ δ᾽ ἄρ᾽ ἀπ᾽ ὤμοιιν Σαρπηδόνος ἔντε᾽ ἕλοντο
χάλκεα μαρμαίροντα, τὰ μὲν κοίλας ἐπὶ νῆας
δῶκε φέρειν ἑτάροισι Μενοιτίου ἄλκιμος υἱός.   665
καὶ τότ᾽ Ἀπόλλωνα προσέφη νεφεληγερέτα Ζεύς·
᾿εἰ δ᾽ ἄγε νῦν, φίλε Φοῖβε, κελαινεφὲς αἷμα κάθηρον
ἐλθὼν ἐκ βελέων Σαρπηδόνα, καί μιν ἔπειτα
πολλὸν ἀποπρὸ φέρων λοῦσον ποταμοῖο ῥοῇσι
χρῖσόν τ᾽ ἀμβροσίῃ, περὶ δ᾽ ἄμβροτα εἵματα ἕσσον·   670
πέμπε δέ μιν πομποῖσιν ἅμα κραιπνοῖσι φέρεσθαι,
Ὕπνῳ καὶ Θανάτῳ διδυμάοσιν, οἵ ῥά μιν ὦκα

642 σταθμός -οῦ/οῖο, ὁ farmyard
ἔνι: accented as postposition
βρομέω I buzz; βρομέωσι is 3 pl. pres.
    subj., generalising in simile
περιγλαγής -ές filled with milk
κατά (+ acc.) (here) around
πέλλα -ης, ἡ milking-pail
643 ὥρη -ης, ἡ season, time (= Att. ὥρα -ας)
εἰαρινός -ή -όν of spring (= Att. ἐαρινός)
γλάγος -εος, τό milk
ἄγγος -εος, τό bucket
δεύω I wet, (here) fill

644 τοί = οἱ they
οὐδέ ποτε nor ever, never
645 τρέψεν: 3 s. aor. of τρέπω (cf. 594)
646 καθοράω I look down on; κατ᾽ ... ὅρα is
    tmesis of 3 s. impf.
647 ἀμφί (+ dat.) (here) about, concerning
φόνος -ου, ὁ (here) death (cf. 144 and
    162)
μερμηρίζω I ponder. A (very rare) mo-
    ment of divine deliberation: we are
    reminded that as Sarpedon has died,
    so too must Patroclus.

of πόδας ὠκύς, the standard epithet of Achilles (cf. 78).

ταχύς -εῖα -ύ quick, swift

ἄγγελος -ου, ὁ messenger; here predicative 'as a messenger'

ἔρχομαι I come, go; ἦλθε is 3 s. aor.

3 τόν him; again the article as personal pron.

εὑρίσκω I find; εὗρε is 3 s. aor., again unaugmented

προπάροιθε (+ gen.) in front of

νηῦς νηός, ἡ ship (= Att. ναῦς νεώς)

ὀρθόκραιρος -η -ον with upright beaks (lit. horns); originally used of oxen, but here referring to pointed projections at prow and stern of Bronze Age ships

4 τά … ἅ … those things which …; τά is again the article as demonstrative pron., ἅ is n. nom. pl. of the rel. pron. ὅς ἥ ὅ who, which

φρονέω I think; φρονέοντ(α) is pres. part. (m. acc. s.), agreeing with τόν (3)

ἀνά (+ acc.) (here) in

θυμός -οῦ, ὁ mind, heart, soul (location of emotions and mental processes)

δή indeed, in fact

τελέω I fulfil, accomplish; τετελεσμένα is perf. pass. part. (n. nom. pl.), here used with auxiliary verb εἰμί to make a plup. pass.

ἦεν: 3 s. impf. of εἰμί I am (= Att. ἦν)

5 ὀχθέω I am disturbed, upset; ὀχθήσας is aor. part. (m. nom. s.)

ἄρα then (ἄρα is oft. hard to translate, but typically expresses a consequence)

λέγω I say; εἶπε is 3 s. aor. The preceding ἄρα is not elided to ἄρ' because εἶπε originally began with the obsolete consonant digamma (ϝ = w). Further examples at 9, 16, 57 and many more.

πρός (+ acc.) to

ὅς ἥ ὅν his (own), her (own); third-person possessive pron./adj., usu. reflexive (distinguish from rel. ὅς ἥ ὅ), also found in the form ἑός ἑή ἑόν

μεγαλήτωρ -ορος (m. adj.) great-hearted

6 ἐγώ (dat. μοι) I, me; ὤ μοι ἐγώ alas for me! Note that μοι scans short (a long vowel or diphthong ending a word in Homer oft. undergoes 'correption'

('shortening') when the next word starts with a vowel); ἐγώ is illogically nom. for emphasis.

τί; why?

τ(ε) ἄρ(α): this combination of particles gives emphasis to τί; ('Why on earth …?')

αὖτε (adv.) again

κάρη κρατός, τό head

κομάω I have long hair; κομόωντες is Homeric pres. part. (m. nom. pl.) with κάρη acc. of resp. This formulaic phrase distinguishes the Achaeans from the Trojans (implied to have close-cropped or shaved heads).

Ἀχαιοί -ῶν, οἱ Achaeans. The regular term in Homer for Greeks. Ἕλληνες (the usual term in classical Greek) occurs only once in the *Iliad*, at 2.684, for inhabitants of Hellas, a then insignificant region of north-west Greece. Achaea was a region of the more important Peloponnese in southern Greece (cf. on 111 and 449).

7 νηυσίν: dat. pl. of νηῦς (cf. 3)

ἐπί (+ dat.) towards, on to; here with the preceding word, so accented ἔπι (when a two-syllable prep. is used as postposition, i.e. follows its noun, the accent moves back from the second syllable to the first)

κλονέω I drive in confusion; κλονέονται is 3 pl. pres. pass.

ἀτυζόμενοι running wildly; part. (m. nom. pl.) of verb not otherwise used

πεδίον -ου/οιο, τό plain; note again the Homeric gen. ending. The gen. with verbs of motion in Homer oft. indicates the space within which something happens, so here 'over the plain'.

8 μή not; here + aor. subj. as main clause expresses the hope that something has not happened ('May it not be that …').

μοι: here possessive with θυμῷ 'for my heart'

τελέσωσι: 3 pl. aor. subj. of τελέω (cf. 4)

θεός -οῦ, ὁ god

κακός -ή -όν bad, cruel

κῆδος -εος, τό trouble

ὡς ποτέ μοι μήτηρ διεπέφραδε, καί μοι ἔειπε
Μυρμιδόνων τὸν ἄριστον ἔτι ζώοντος ἐμεῖο   10
χερσὶν ὕπο Τρώων λείψειν φάος ἠελίοιο.
ἦ μάλα δὴ τέθνηκε Μενοιτίου ἄλκιμος υἱός,
σχέτλιος· ἦ τ' ἐκέλευον ἀπωσάμενον δήϊον πῦρ
ἂψ ἐπὶ νῆας ἴμεν, μηδ' Ἕκτορι ἶφι μάχεσθαι."
    Ἧος ὁ ταῦθ' ὥρμαινε κατὰ φρένα καὶ κατὰ θυμόν,   15
τόφρα οἱ ἐγγύθεν ἦλθεν ἀγαυοῦ Νέστορος υἱός,
δάκρυα θερμὰ χέων, φάτο δ' ἀγγελίην ἀλεγεινήν·
"ὤ μοι, Πηλέος υἱὲ δαΐφρονος, ἦ μάλα λυγρῆς
πεύσεαι ἀγγελίης, ἣ μὴ ὤφελλε γενέσθαι.
κεῖται Πάτροκλος, νέκυος δὲ δὴ ἀμφιμάχονται   20
γυμνοῦ· ἀτὰρ τά γε τεύχε' ἔχει κορυθαίολος Ἕκτωρ."

9 ὡς as. Note that ὡς in this sense usu. has no accent, but here acquires one because the next word is an 'enclitic' (lit. 'leaning on'), i.e. a short unemphatic word joined closely in pronunciation to the one before it.

πoτέ (adv.) once. This word in turn has acquired an accent because the following μοι is also enclitic.

μήτηρ μητρός, ἡ mother

διαφράζω I tell clearly; διεπέφραδε is 3 s. aor.

καί and

ἔειπε = εἶπε (cf. 5): this earlier, uncontracted form (convenient for the metre) originally had another digamma between the first two vowels; here introducing indirect statement with acc. + inf.

10 Μυρμιδόνες -ων, οἱ Myrmidons. They are Achilles' people, from Phthia in Thessaly, a region of north-eastern Greece.

ἄριστος -η -ον best

ἔτι (adv.) still

ζώω I live (= Att. ζάω); pres. part. ζώοντος (m. gen. s.) here as gen. abs. with ἐμεῖο

ἐμεῖο: Homeric gen. of ἐγώ (cf. 6) (= Att. ἐμοῦ)

11 χείρ χειρός/χερός, ἡ hand

ὑπό (+ dat.) under; ὕπο here accented as postposition (cf. on 7)

Τρῶες -ων, οἱ Trojans

λείπω I leave; λείψειν is fut. inf.

φάος -εος, τό light (= Att. φῶς φωτός)

ἠέλιος -ου/οιο, ὁ the sun (= Att. ἥλιος -ου); note again the Homeric gen. ending. 'Leaving the light of the sun' is one of numerous expressions for death, but no such prophecy by Thetis is mentioned in the *Iliad*. (At 9.410–16 Achilles recalls her offering him a choice of lives: short and glorious, or long and obscure. At 17.409 we hear that she often told him about Zeus's plans.) Prophecies in epic (and in the Bible) are typically remembered when they become relevant, but the poet may well have invented this one for the present passage.

12 ἦ μάλα for sure

θνήσκω I die; τέθνηκε is 3 s. perf.

Μενοίτιος -ου, ὁ Menoetius, father of Patroclus

ἄλκιμος -ον brave

υἱός -οῦ/έος, ὁ son

13 σχέτλιος -η -ον stubborn, headstrong; note the emphasis given by enjambment (syntactical continuity over a line end) and by ending a sense unit, making the word almost an exclamation. Achilles has seen that his friend did not follow the instruction he gave at 16.83–96, to drive the Trojans away from the ships and come straight back.

ἦ τ(ε) and yet … certainly

κελεύω I order; understand 'him' as object

ἀπωθέω I push away, drive away; ἀπωσάμενον is aor. mid. part. (m. acc. s.), mid.
implying 'from' or 'to the advantage of'
the doer

δήϊος (-η) -ον hostile, (of fire) destructive
(= Att. δάϊος -α -ον); the η is short by
correction even though not at the end
of the word (cf. on 6).

14 ἄψ (adv.) back

ἐπί (+ acc.) to

νῆας: acc. pl. of νηῦς (cf. 3)

εἶμι I go, come; ἴμεν is inf. (= Att. ἰέναι)

μηδ(έ) and not

Ἕκτωρ -ορος, ὁ Hector

ἶφι with force; 'instrumental' case of obsolete f. noun ἴς (cf. Latin *vis*)

μάχομαι I fight (+ dat.); μάχεσθαι is pres.
inf.

15–35: *Antilochus delivers the news; Achilles is in despair.*

15 ἧος while (= Att. ἕως)

ὁ: again the article as personal pron. (cf. 1)

ταῦθ' = ταῦτα (before vowel with rough
breathing)

ὁρμαίνω I turn over, ponder; ὥρμαινε is 3
s. impf.

κατά (+ acc.) (here) in

φρήν φρενός, ἡ mind, heart, soul
(location of emotions and mental
processes); virtually synonymous with
θυμός (cf. 4)

16 τόφρα in the meantime (answering ἧος);
the α is not elided (cf. on 2) because
an older form of the following word
οἱ began with digamma (cf. on 5).
This line makes clear that Achilles'
monologue in 6–14 precedes the
appearance of Antilochus.

οἱ to him; dat. of personal pron. ἕ (acc.)
οὗ (gen.) οἷ (dat.) him, her, it; here in
unaccented enclitic form (cf. on 9)

ἐγγύθεν (adv.) near

ἀγαυός -ή -όν illustrious

Νέστωρ -ορος, ὁ Nestor, king of Pylos in
the Peloponnese; the oldest, wisest and
most loquacious of the Achaean heroes

17 δάκρυ (no gen. s.), τό tear

θερμός -ή -όν hot. Tears are hot because
freshly welling up (not as a symbol
of anger). Homeric heroes regularly
express emotion by weeping.

χέω I pour, shed

φημί I say; φάτο is unaugmented 3 s. impf.

ἀγγελίη -ης, ἡ message, news (= Att.
ἀγγελία -ας)

ἀλεγεινός -ή -όν painful

18 ὤ μοι: Antilochus is in distress as well as
Achilles (cf. 6)

Πηλεύς -έος/ῆος, ὁ Peleus, father of
Achilles

δαΐφρων -ονος fiery-hearted

ἦ μάλα (cf. 12): here intensifies λυγρῆς

λυγρός -ή -όν sad, dreadful

19 πυνθάνομαι I learn, hear (+ gen.); πεύσεαι
is 2 s. fut.

ὅς ἥ ὅ (rel. pron.) who, which; ἥ picks up
ἀγγελίης but refers to its contents

ὀφέλλω I owe, ought (= Att. ὀφείλω); ὤφελλε is 3 s. impf. (Greek says 'oughted not
to' for English 'ought not to have')

γίγνομαι I become, happen; γενέσθαι is
aor. inf.

20 κεῖμαι I lie; here a euphemism for 'is
dead'. The asyndeton (omission of con-
junction) makes the statement abrupt:
Antilochus blurts out the terrible
news.

Πάτροκλος -ου/οιο, ὁ Patroclus

νέκυς -υος, ὁ dead body

ἀμφιμάχομαι I fight for, fight over
(+ gen.)

21 γυμνός -ή -όν naked; note again emphasis
by enjambment ending a sense unit. It is
a shocking detail, explained by the rest
of the line.

ἀτάρ but

γε at least, at any rate. Presumably the
word qualifies our reading of γυμνοῦ:
the dead Patroclus is effectively naked
without his armour.

τεύχε(α) -έων, τά arms, armour

ἔχω I have, hold

κορυθαίολος -ον with shining helmet.
Hector is the only human character of
whom this epithet is used; it is applied
to Ares at 20.38.

Ὣς φάτο, τὸν δ᾽ ἄχεος νεφέλη ἐκάλυψε μέλαινα·
ἀμφοτέρῃσι δὲ χερσὶν ἑλὼν κόνιν αἰθαλόεσσαν
χεύατο κὰκ κεφαλῆς, χαρίεν δ᾽ ᾔσχυνε πρόσωπον·
νεκταρέῳ δὲ χιτῶνι μέλαιν᾽ ἀμφίζανε τέφρη.   25
αὐτὸς δ᾽ ἐν κονίῃσι μέγας μεγαλωστὶ τανυσθεὶς
κεῖτο, φίλῃσι δὲ χερσὶ κόμην ᾔσχυνε δαΐζων.
δμῳαὶ δ᾽ ἃς Ἀχιλεὺς ληΐσσατο Πάτροκλός τε
θυμὸν ἀκηχέμεναι μεγάλ᾽ ἴαχον, ἐκ δὲ θύραζε
ἔδραμον ἀμφ᾽ Ἀχιλῆα δαΐφρονα, χερσὶ δὲ πᾶσαι   30
στήθεα πεπλήγοντο, λύθεν δ᾽ ὑπὸ γυῖα ἑκάστης.

8. Achilles mourning the dead Patroclus. Roman marble sarcophagus, c.160 BCE. Museo
Archeologico Ostiense, Ostia Antica.

22 τὸν δ(έ): i.e. Achilles

ἄχος -εος, τό grief

νεφέλη -ης, ἡ cloud. The η is not shortened by correption (cf. on 6) even though the next word begins with a vowel. This (or the non-elision of a short final vowel) is called 'hiatus' ('gap').

καλύπτω I cover, hide; ἐκάλυψε is 3 s. aor.

μέλας -αινα -αν black, dark

23 ἀμφότεροι -αι -α both; ἀμφοτέρῃσι is f. dat. pl. Note that the ending -ῃσ(ι) is the norm in Homer for 1st decl. dat. pl. (= Att. -αις).

αἱρέω I take, seize; ἑλών is aor. part. (m. nom. s.). The subject is now Achilles.

κόνις -ιος, ἡ dust

αἰθαλόεις -εσσα -εν (-εντος) smoky, grimy. 'Smoky dust' already suggests 'ashes', confirmed by τέφρη (25).

24 χεύατο: 3 s. aor. mid. of χέω (cf. 17)

κάκ = κατά (before κ) (+ gen.) down over

κεφαλή -ῆς, ἡ head

χαρίεις -εσσα -εν (-εντος) pleasing, handsome

αἰσχύνω I disfigure, defile; ᾔσχυνε is 3 s. aor.

πρόσωπον -ου, τό face

25 νεκτάρεος -η -ον nectar-like, fragrant. Achilles' clothing was packed in his trunk by his goddess mother Thetis (16.222–4), so it may well have been scented with nectar, the drink of the gods. There is a sharp contrast between this word and τέφρη at the end of the line.

χιτών -ῶνος, ὁ tunic

ἀμφιζάνω I settle on (+ dat.)

τέφρη -ης, ἡ ashes (= Att. τέφρα -ας)

26 αὐτός (here) he himself, as contrasted with the slave women (δμῳαί) in 28

ἐν (+ dat.) in

κονίη -ης, ἡ dust, here pl. for s. (= Att. κονία -ας); note again the Homeric dat. pl. ending (cf. on 23)

μέγας μεγάλη μέγα big, great

μεγαλωστί (adv.) (stretched) over a great space; with μέγας, a big phrase for a big man. It is used twice elsewhere by Homer, of dead heroes: Hector's charioteer Cebriones (16.776) and Achilles himself (Odyssey 24.40). It looks forward to Achilles' own death.

τανύω I stretch out; τανυσθείς is aor. pass. part. (m. nom. s.). This is a ritual action to mourn a dead person.

27 κεῖτο: 3 s. impf. of κεῖμαι (cf. 20); once more, enjambment ending a sense unit

φίλος -η -ον dear, (here and oft. in Homer) one's own; φίλῃσι is f. dat. pl., again with the Homeric ending

κόμη -ης, ἡ hair

ᾔσχυνε: here probably 3 s. impf. rather than aor. (cf. 24); the forms are the same

δαΐζω I tear

28 δμῳή -ῆς, ἡ female slave

ληΐζομαι I carry off as booty; ληΐσσατο is 3 s. aor.

τε and (tr. before the word it follows); a second subject is added, s. verb agreeing with the first but understood with both, as oft.

29 θυμόν: here acc. of resp. 'in their hearts'

ἀχέομαι I am distressed; ἀκηχέμεναι is perf. part. (f. nom. pl.)

μεγάλ(α) greatly; n. pl. as adv.

ἰάχω I cry, scream; ἴαχον is 3 pl. impf.

ἐκτρέχω I run out; in ἐκ … ἔδραμον (30) (3 pl. aor.) the two parts of the compound verb are separated by 'tmesis' ('cutting'), though this is strictly a misnomer, as in Homer's time they had not yet fully coalesced.

θύραζε (adv.) out, outside

30 ἀμφ(ί) (+ acc.) around

πᾶς πᾶσα πᾶν (παντ-) all

31 στῆθος -εος, τό breast, chest

πλήσσω I beat; πεπλήγοντο is 3 pl. aor. mid. Striking the breasts is a usual action in female lamentation.

λύω I loose, loosen; λύθεν is 3 pl. aor. pass. (= Att. ἐλύθησαν). Homer does not consistently observe the rule that n. pl. subject takes s. verb.

ὑπό (as adv.) below, (here) beneath them

γυῖον -ου, τό limb. Loosening of limbs (i.e. the knees buckle) here describes a strong emotional reaction (elsewhere the same expression oft. implies death). The reaction of captive slaves indicates a general affection for Patroclus, evidently shared by the poet (cf. on 16.20).

ἕκαστος -η -ον each

Ἀντίλοχος δ᾽ ἑτέρωθεν ὀδύρετο δάκρυα λείβων,
χεῖρας ἔχων Ἀχιλῆος· ὁ δ᾽ ἔστενε κυδάλιμον κῆρ·
δείδιε γὰρ μὴ λαιμὸν ἀπαμήσειε σιδήρῳ.
σμερδαλέον δ᾽ ᾤμωξεν· ἄκουσε δὲ πότνια μήτηρ   35
ἡμένη ἐν βένθεσσιν ἁλὸς παρὰ πατρὶ γέροντι,
κώκυσέν τ᾽ ἄρ᾽ ἔπειτα· θεαὶ δέ μιν ἀμφαγέροντο,
πᾶσαι ὅσαι κατὰ βένθος ἁλὸς Νηρηΐδες ἦσαν.
ἔνθ᾽ ἄρ᾽ ἔην Γλαύκη τε Θάλειά τε Κυμοδόκη τε,
Νησαίη Σπειώ τε Θόη θ᾽ Ἁλίη τε βοῶπις,   40
Κυμοθόη τε καὶ Ἀκταίη καὶ Λιμνώρεια
καὶ Μελίτη καὶ Ἴαιρα καὶ Ἀμφιθόη καὶ Ἀγαύη,
Δωτώ τε Πρωτώ τε Φέρουσά τε Δυναμένη τε,
Δεξαμένη τε καὶ Ἀμφινόμη καὶ Καλλιάνειρα,
Δωρὶς καὶ Πανόπη καὶ ἀγακλειτὴ Γαλάτεια,   45
Νημερτής τε καὶ Ἀψευδὴς καὶ Καλλιάνασσα·
ἔνθα δ᾽ ἔην Κλυμένη Ἰάνειρά τε καὶ Ἰάνασσα,
Μαῖρα καὶ Ὠρείθυια ἐϋπλόκαμός τ᾽ Ἀμάθεια,
ἄλλαι θ᾽ αἲ κατὰ βένθος ἁλὸς Νηρηΐδες ἦσαν.

32 ἑτέρωθεν (adv.) on the other side
   ὀδύρομαι I lament
   λείβω I pour, shed
33 ὁ δ(έ): the subject is probably still Antilochus, though it could be Achilles (with an abrupt change back to Antilochus in 34)
   στένω I sigh, groan
   κυδάλιμος -ον noble, glorious
   κῆρ κῆρος, τό heart; acc. of resp. 'in his noble heart'
34 δείδια (perf. with pres. sense) I fear, am afraid; δείδιε is 3 s. plup. with impf. sense

γάρ for, because
μή (+ opt.) lest, that (introducing an expression of fear)
λαιμός -οῦ, ὁ throat
ἀπαμάω I cut; ἀπαμήσειε is 3 s. aor. opt.
σίδηρος -ου, ὁ iron, iron weapon. Here probably a knife or short sword. Weapons in the *Iliad* are usually bronze, but the use of iron is known to the poet.
35 σμερδαλέον (adv.) terribly
   οἰμώζω I cry, groan; ᾤμωξεν is 3 s. aor. The subject is now Achilles.

35–147: Thetis visits Achilles. There can be no consolation, but Thetis promises to have armour made for her son.

35–49: Thetis and her sisters hear Achilles' cry; she directs them to come with her, to visit Achilles and learn what his trouble is.

35 ἀκούω I hear
   πότνια, ἡ (noun or f. adj.) lady; respectful title for a woman or goddess
   μήτηρ: Achilles' mother is the sea-goddess Thetis. Both Zeus and his brother Poseidon had wished to possess her.

But there existed a prophecy that Thetis' son would be greater than his father, so Zeus forced her to marry the mortal Peleus (as she acknowledges at 432–4). Their son was indeed greater than his father. At some point Thetis left Peleus and returned to live with her father, the sea-god Nereus, along with her sisters. Nereus' daughters are collectively known as Nereids.

36 ἧμαι I sit; ἡμένη is pres. part. (f. nom. s.), with η scanned short by correption (cf. on 6).

βένθος -εος, τό depth (= Att. βάθος -ους)

ἅλς ἁλός, ἡ sea

παρά (+ dat.) beside

πατήρ πατρός, ὁ father

γέρων -οντος, ὁ old man; here as adj. 'aged'. Nereus is a god, but given (here and in the similar circumstances of 1.358) the human characteristic of age, perhaps for pathos.

37 κωκύω I wail; κώκυσεν is 3 s. aor.

ἄρ' = ἄρα (cf. 5): here 'indeed' (reinforcing ἔπειτα)

ἔπειτα (adv.) then

θεά -ᾶς, ἡ goddess

μιν him, her, it (acc. s. personal pron., = αὐτόν -ήν -ό), here 'her'

ἀμφαγείρομαι I gather around; ἀμφαγέρο-ντο is 3 pl. aor.

38 ὅσος -η -ον as much as, pl. as many as; πᾶσαι ὅσαι 'all those who …'

κατά (+ acc.) all over

Νηρηΐδες -ων, αἱ daughters of Nereus, Nereids

ἧσαν: 3 pl. impf. of εἰμί

39 ἔνθ(α) (adv.) there

ἔην: 3 s. impf. of εἰμί (= ἦν). The Nereids are now listed. Some names have associations with the sea, with the power of prophecy associated with sea-gods, or with other divine attributes. Some seem to be there mainly for assonance. They are joined by τε or καί, in runs of one or the other, or paired, for variety, euphony and metrical convenience. The list (perhaps at least partly traditional) provides relief from the scene of sorrow, and underlines the importance of what follows.

Γλαύκη -ης, ἡ Glauce (Gleaming)

Θάλεια -ας, ἡ Thaleia (Flourishing)

Κυμοδόκη -ης, ἡ Cymodoce (Wave-smoother)

40 Νησαίη -ης, ἡ Nesaeë (From the Island)

Σπειώ -οῦς, ἡ Speio (From the Cave)

Θόη -ης, ἡ Thoë (Swift)

θ' = τε (before vowel with rough breathing)

Ἁλίη -ης, ἡ Halië (From the Sea)

βοῶπις (f. adj.) ox-eyed. Halië shares this epithet with Hera.

41 Κυμοθόη -ης, ἡ Cymothoë (Wave-swift)

Ἀκταίη -ης, ἡ Actaeë (From the Shore)

Λιμνώρεια -ας, ἡ Limnoreia (From the Marshes)

42 Μελίτη -ης, ἡ Melite (Honeyed)

Ἴαιρα -ας, ἡ Iaera (Joyous)

Ἀμφιθόη -ης, ἡ Amphithoë (Very Swift)

Ἀγαύη -ης, ἡ Agauë (Noble)

43 Δωτώ -οῦς, ἡ Doto (Giver)

Πρωτώ -οῦς, ἡ Proto (Leader)

Φέρουσα -ης, ἡ Pherousa (Ship-bearer)

Δυναμένη -ης, ἡ Dynamene (Able to Help)

44 Δεξαμένη -ης, ἡ Dexamene (She who Wel-comes)

Ἀμφινόμη -ης, ἡ Amphinome (Rich in Pasture)

Καλλιάνειρα -ας, ἡ Callianeira (She of the Fair Husband)

45 Δωρίς -ίδος, ἡ Doris (Giver). This is also the name of Thetis' mother.

Πανόπη -ης, ἡ Panope (All-seeing)

ἀγακλειτός -ή -όν very famous, highly renowned

Γαλάτεια -ας, ἡ Galateia (Milk-white). She is indeed highly renowned in later po-etry for her romance with the one-eyed giant Polyphemus.

46 Νημερτής (only nom.), ἡ Nemertes (Infalli-ble)

Ἀψευδής -οῦς, ἡ Apseudes (Truthful)

Καλλιάνασσα -ης, ἡ Callianassa (Fair Queen)

47 Κλυμένη -ης, ἡ Clymene (Famous)

Ἰάνειρα -ας, ἡ Ianeira (Mighty Lady)

Ἰάνασσα -ης, ἡ Ianassa (Mighty Queen)

48 Μαῖρα -ας, ἡ Maera (Sparkler)

Ὠρείθυια -ας, ἡ Oreithyia (Mountain Runner)

ἐϋπλόκαμος -ον with beautiful hair

Ἀμάθεια -ας, ἡ Amatheia (Sandy)

49 ἄλλος -η -ο other

αἵ who (f. nom. pl. of rel. pron.; cf. 4) This line nearly repeats 38, rounding off the passage ('ring composition').

τῶν δὲ καὶ ἀργύφεον πλῆτο σπέος· αἳ δ᾽ ἅμα πᾶσαι   50
στήθεα πεπλήγοντο, Θέτις δ᾽ ἐξῆρχε γόοιο·
"κλῦτε, κασίγνηται Νηρηΐδες, ὄφρ᾽ ἐῢ πᾶσαι
εἴδετ᾽ ἀκούουσαι ὅσ᾽ ἐμῷ ἔνι κήδεα θυμῷ.
ὤ μοι ἐγὼ δειλή, ὤ μοι δυσαριστοτόκεια,
ἥ τ᾽ ἐπεὶ ἂρ τέκον υἱὸν ἀμύμονά τε κρατερόν τε,   55
ἔξοχον ἡρώων· ὁ δ᾽ ἀνέδραμεν ἔρνεϊ ἶσος·
τὸν μὲν ἐγὼ θρέψασα, φυτὸν ὣς γουνῷ ἀλωῆς,
νηυσὶν ἐπιπροέηκα κορωνίσιν Ἴλιον εἴσω
Τρωσὶ μαχησόμενον· τὸν δ᾽ οὐχ ὑποδέξομαι αὖτις
οἴκαδε νοστήσαντα δόμον Πηλήϊον εἴσω.   60
ὄφρα δέ μοι ζώει καὶ ὁρᾷ φάος ἠελίοιο,
ἄχνυται, οὐδέ τί οἱ δύναμαι χραισμῆσαι ἰοῦσα.
ἀλλ᾽ εἶμ᾽, ὄφρα ἴδωμι φίλον τέκος, ἠδ᾽ ἐπακούσω
ὅττι μιν ἵκετο πένθος ἀπὸ πτολέμοιο μένοντα."

50–64: Thetis' lament. In Book 9 Achilles considered leaving Troy and returning home. It seems to follow that he has not yet fully made the choice referred to in line 11. Patroclus' death commits him to making it, so this is the point where his death becomes assured. Hence Thetis' words are a lament not for Patroclus but for Achilles (cf. on 95). They echo the words of Andromache at 6.407–39, foretelling the death of Hector. The presence of the Nereids with Thetis at Troy also foreshadows the death of Achilles: they were present at his funeral (Odyssey 24.47–62).

50 τῶν of them (f. gen. pl.; again the article as personal pron.)
  ἀργύφεος -η -ον white, glittering
  πίμπλημι I fill X (acc.) with Y (gen.); πλῆτο is 3 s. aor. pass. (= Att. ἐπλήσθη)
  σπέος -είους, τό cave
  ἅμα (adv.) at the same time
51 Θέτις -ιδος, ἡ Thetis; only now named (cf. 35)
  ἐξάρχω I begin, lead (+ gen.); ἐξῆρχε is 3 s. impf.
  γόος -ου/οιο, ὁ lamentation
52 κλύω I hear, listen; κλῦτε is 2 pl. imper.
  κασιγνήτη -ης, ἡ sister
  ὄφρ(α) (+ subj.) in order that (introducing purpose clause)
  ἐΰ = εὖ (adv.) well
53 οἶδα (perf. with pres. sense) I know; εἴδετε is 2 pl. subj. (= Att. εἴδητε). Note that subj. forms in Homer oft. have a short vowel in the ending.

ὅσοι -αι -α how many; ὅσ᾽ = ὅσα
ἐμός -ή -όν my
ἔνι = ἔνεστι: '(troubles) there are in'
54 ὤ μοι ἐγὼ ... ὤ μοι: the language of lament (cf. 6) is intensified by repetition
  δειλός -ή -όν wretched, miserable
  δυσαριστοτόκεια (f. adj.) unhappy mother of an excellent son; δυσ- (badly) + ἀριστο- (excellent) + τοκεια (mother). A remarkable compound adjective with three elements, found only here in surviving Greek literature.
55 ἥ τ(ε) I who. The first τε in this line indicates the cause of the speaker's passion; the second and third are 'both ... and'.
  ἐπεί when, after
  ἄρ = ἄρα
  τίκτω I give birth to; τέκον is 1 s. aor.
  ἀμύμων -ον blameless, excellent
  κρατερός -ή -όν strong, mighty

56 ἔξοχος -ον prominent among (+ gen.)

ἥρως -ωος, ὁ hero, warrior. In Homer the term can be used of any leader or fighter whose prowess is acknowledged.

ἀνατρέχω (here) I shoot up; ἀνέδραμεν is 3 s. aor.

ἔρνος -εος, τό shoot, young tree

ἴσος -η -ον like, equal to (+ dat.)

57 τὸν μέν: this and τὸν δ(έ) (59) refer not (as they usu. would) to different people, but both to Achilles; the contrast is between the two verbs ἐπιπροέηκα (58) and ὑποδέξομαι (59)

τρέφω I bring up, rear; θρέψασα is aor. part. (f. nom. s.)

φυτόν -ου, τό plant; the second syllable is long here because of the memory of the digamma (cf. on 5) with which ὥς originally began.

ὥς like; accented when it follows the noun to which it refers

γουνός -οῦ, ὁ fruitful land

ἀλωή -ῆς, ἡ orchard; the gen. is 'defining' (implying 'consisting of')

58 ἐπιπροίημι I send out X (acc.) with Y (dat.); ἐπιπροέηκα is 1 s. aor.

κορωνίς -ίδος (f. adj.) curved; always of ships (the curve is the ship's profile seen from the side)

Ἴλιος -ου, ἡ or Ἴλιον -ου, τό Ilium, another name for Troy

εἴσω (+ acc.) to; postposition

59 μαχησόμενον in order to fight; fut. part. (m. acc. s.) of μάχομαι (cf. 14) agreeing with τόν (57) and expressing purpose

οὐ/οὐκ/οὐχ not; οὐκ before vowel with smooth breathing, οὐχ before vowel with rough breathing

ὑποδέχομαι I receive, welcome; ὑποδέξομαι is 1 s. fut.

αὖτις (adv.) again, back again; here with either ὑποδέξομαι or νοστήσαντα. Thetis' words are echoed by Achilles at 89–90.

60 οἴκαδε (adv.) home, homeward

νοστέω I return; νοστήσαντα is aor. part. (m. acc. s.)

δόμος -ου, ὁ house

Πηλήϊος -η -ον of Peleus

61 ὄφρα (+ indic.) while, so long as

μοι: 'ethic' dative ('of feeling'), expressing the involvement of the speaker ('for me'), though the nuance is oft. hard to tr.

ὁράω I see

62 ἄχνυμαι I am distressed; from ὄφρα (61) understand τόφρα (cf. 16), here 'for all that time'

οὐδέ and … not

τι at all, in any way; n. of τις (some, any) as adv., here accented because the next word is an enclitic

οἱ: to him (cf. 16)

δύναμαι I am able

χραισμέω I am useful to, help (+ dat.); χραισμῆσαι is aor. inf.

ἰοῦσα: part. (f. nom. s.) of εἶμι (I go, cf. 14), here implying 'even if I go'

63 εἶμ(ι): indic. usu. has fut. sense, as here

ὄφρα (+ subj.) in order that, so that (introducing purpose clause)

ἴδωμι: 1 s. subj. of ὁράω (cf. 61)

τέκος -εος, τό child

ἠδ(έ) and

ἐπακούω I listen to, hear; ἐπακούσω is 1 s. aor. subj.

64 ὅττι = ὅ τι what (with πένθος); n. of ὅστις who, what (used in indirect question)

μιν (here) him (cf. 37)

ἱκνέομαι I arrive at, reach, (here) come over; ἵκετο is 3 s. aor. (with μιν as object)

πένθος -εος, τό grief

ἀπό (+ gen.) away from

πτόλεμος = πόλεμος, -ου/οιο, ὁ war; πτ- for π- is another common type of variant spelling (cf. on 2), again for metrical flexibility (πτ- allows short vowel ending preceding word to create a long syllable)

μένω I stay, remain; μένοντα is pres. part. (m. acc. sg.), here either temporal 'while he stays' or concessive 'although he stays'

Ὣς ἄρα φωνήσασα λίπε σπέος· αἱ δὲ σὺν αὐτῇ   65
δακρυόεσσαι ἴσαν, περὶ δέ σφισι κῦμα θαλάσσης
ῥήγνυτο· ταὶ δ᾿ ὅτε δὴ Τροίην ἐρίβωλον ἵκοντο,
ἀκτὴν εἰσανέβαινον ἐπισχερώ, ἔνθα θαμειαὶ
Μυρμιδόνων εἴρυντο νέες ταχὺν ἀμφ᾿ Ἀχιλῆα.
τῷ δὲ βαρὺ στενάχοντι παρίστατο πότνια μήτηρ,   70
ὀξὺ δὲ κωκύσασα κάρη λάβε παιδὸς ἑοῖο,
καί ῥ᾿ ὀλοφυρομένη ἔπεα πτερόεντα προσηύδα·
"τέκνον, τί κλαίεις; τί δέ σε φρένας ἵκετο πένθος;
ἐξαύδα, μὴ κεῦθε· τὰ μὲν δή τοι τετέλεσται
ἐκ Διός, ὡς ἄρα δὴ πρίν γ᾿ εὔχεο χεῖρας ἀνασχών,   75
πάντας ἐπὶ πρύμνῃσιν ἀλήμεναι υἷας Ἀχαιῶν
σεῦ ἐπιδευομένους, παθέειν τ᾿ ἀεκήλια ἔργα."
    Τὴν δὲ βαρὺ στενάχων προσέφη πόδας ὠκὺς Ἀχιλλεύς·
"μῆτερ ἐμή, τὰ μὲν ἄρ μοι Ὀλύμπιος ἐξετέλεσσεν·
ἀλλὰ τί μοι τῶν ἦδος, ἐπεὶ φίλος ὤλεθ᾿ ἑταῖρος,   80
Πάτροκλος, τὸν ἐγὼ περὶ πάντων τῖον ἑταίρων,

65–77: Thetis asks Achilles what his trouble is. The climax and centre of this whole scene is Thetis' two-line prophecy at 95–6. It is doubly framed by Achilles' two speeches (79–93 and 98–126) and Thetis' two speeches (73–7 and 128–37) – even triply framed if Thetis' two speeches to the Nereids (52–64 and 140–4) are included: complex ring composition.

65 φωνέω I speak; φωνήσασα is aor. part. (f. nom. s.)
  λίπε: 3 s. aor. of λείπω (cf. 11)
  σύν (+ dat.) with
  αὐτόν -ήν -ό him, her, it (personal pron., not used in nom.)
66 δακρυόεις -εσσα -εν (-εντος) weeping, in tears
  ἴσαν: 3 pl. impf. of εἶμι (I go, cf. 14; = Att. ἦσαν)
  περί (+ dat.) around
  σφεῖς (personal pron.) they, them; σφίσι is dat.
  κῦμα -τος, τό wave
  θάλασσα -ης, ἡ sea
67 ῥήγνυμι I break; ῥήγνυτο is 3 s. impf. mid. The wash gives a strong visual indication of the strength and speed of the swimmers on an urgent mission.
  ταί = αἱ; note that m. and f. nom. pl. forms of the article/pron. oft. have initial τ in Homer

ὅτε (adv.) when
Τροίη -ης, ἡ Troy (= Att. Τροία -ας)
ἐρίβωλος -ον fertile
ἵκοντο: 3 pl. aor. of ἱκνέομαι (cf. 64)
68 ἀκτή -ῆς, ἡ shore
εἰσαναβαίνω I go up on to
ἐπισχερώ (adv.) one after another
ἔνθα (here) where (cf. 39)
θαμέες -ειαί (m. and f. pl. adj.) crowded together
69 ἐρύω (here) I draw up; εἴρυντο is 3 pl. plup. pass.
νέες: nom. pl. of νηῦς (cf. 3)
70 τῷ to him
βαρύς -εῖα -ύ heavy; n. here as adv.
στενάχω I sigh, groan
παρίσταμαι I come and stand beside (+ dat.); παρίστατο is 3 s. impf.
71 ὀξύς -εῖα -ύ sharp; again n. as adv.
κωκύσασα: aor. part. (f. nom. s.) of κωκύω (cf. 37)
λαμβάνω I take, take hold of; λάβε is 3 s. aor.

παῖς παιδός, ὁ boy, (here and oft.) son

ἑός ἑή ἑόν his (own), her (own); ἑοῖο is m. gen. s. Achilles is prostrate, Thetis holding his head in her hands. This too foreshadows Achilles' death (cf. 23.136, where Achilles holds the head of the dead Patroclus, and 24.724, where Andromache holds that of the dead Hector).

72 ῥ(ά) = ἄρα (cf. 5)

ὀλοφύρομαι I lament, mourn; ὀλοφυρομένη is pres. part. (f. nom. s.)

ἔπος -εος, τό word

πτερόεις -εσσα -εν (-εντος) winged (words are so called in this formulaic phrase because they fly from speaker to hearer)

προσαυδάω I speak to, address; προσηύδα is 3 s. impf.

73 τέκνον -ου, τό child

κλαίω I weep, cry

σε you (s.); acc. of σύ. The two accusatives σε and φρένας indicate in turn 'whole and part': such expressions are a common version of acc. of resp. Note also that φρένας is here (as oft.) pl. for s.

74 ἐξαυδάω I speak out

μή (+ imper.) don't …!

κεύθω I hide, cover. Thetis' words (73 and first part of 74) are the same as she used at 1.362–3. The distress Achilles now

feels has arisen from the help Thetis offered then.

τὰ μὲν δή these things evidently (i.e. the content of the prayer referred to in 75); no δέ follows, but there is an implied contrast with what he may ask for now

τοι = σοι; dat. of σύ (cf. 73) in unaccented enclitic form

τετέλεσται: 3 s. perf. pass. τελέω (cf. 4)

75 ἐκ (+ gen.) (here) by

Ζεύς Διός, ὁ Zeus

πρίν (adv.) before, formerly

εὔχομαι I pray; εὔχεο is 2 s. impf.

ἀνέχω I hold up; ἀνασχών is aor. part. (m. nom. s.). Raising the hands skywards was the ancient gesture of prayer.

76 πάντας … ἀλήμεναι … παθέειν τ' (77): acc. + inf. for indirect statement, expressing the content of the prayer 'that (X should happen)'

πρύμνη -ης, ἡ stern (of a ship)

εἴλω I confine, hem in; ἀλήμεναι is aor. pass. inf.

υἷας: 3rd decl. form acc. pl. of υἱός (cf. 12)

77 σεῦ = σοῦ (gen. of σύ)

ἐπιδεύομαι I am in need of (+ gen.); ἐπιδευομένους is pres. part. (m. acc. pl.)

πάσχω I suffer; παθέειν is aor. inf. (= Att. παθεῖν)

ἀεκήλιος -ον unwelcome

ἔργον -ου, τό deed, pl. (here) treatment

78–93: Achilles explains his grief.

78 πρόσφημι I speak to, address; προσέφη is 3 s. impf. (used like aor.)

ὠκύς -εῖα/έα -ύ swift; πόδας is acc. of resp. i.e. 'swift-footed'. This formulaic phrase is a frequent epithet for Achilles and unique to him, though synonymous variants are sometimes used of others: cf. 2 (Antilochus as πόδας ταχύς) and 202 (Iris as πόδας ὠκέα).

79 τὰ μὲν ἄρ those things indeed; again no δέ follows (cf. on 74), but ἀλλά (80) provides an even stronger contrast

Ὀλύμπιος -ον Olympian, of Olympus; 'the Olympian (god)' is Zeus

ἐκτελέω I fulfil, accomplish; ἐξετέλεσσεν is 3 s. aor. Zeus accomplished Achilles' wishes as conveyed to him by Thetis at 1.503–10.

80 τίς τί (interrogative) who? what? which?

ἦδος -εος, τό enjoyment

ὄλλυμαι I perish; ὄλεθ' (= ὤλετο) is 3 s. aor. mid.

ἑταῖρος/ἕταρος -ου, ὁ companion, comrade

81 Πάτροκλος: emphatic enjambment

τόν: here rel. pron. (= Att. ὅν)

περί (+ gen.) (here) above, more than

τίω I honour, value; τῖον is 1 s. impf.

ἶσον ἐμῇ κεφαλῇ· τὸν ἀπώλεσα, τεύχεα δ᾽ Ἕκτωρ
δηώσας ἀπέδυσε πελώρια, θαῦμα ἰδέσθαι,
καλά· τὰ μὲν Πηλῆϊ θεοὶ δόσαν ἀγλαὰ δῶρα
ἤματι τῷ ὅτε σε βροτοῦ ἀνέρος ἔμβαλον εὐνῇ.   85
αἴθ᾽ ὄφελες σὺ μὲν αὖθι μετ᾽ ἀθανάτης ἁλίῃσι
ναίειν, Πηλεὺς δὲ θνητὴν ἀγαγέσθαι ἄκοιτιν.
νῦν δ᾽ ἵνα καὶ σοὶ πένθος ἐνὶ φρεσὶ μυρίον εἴη
παιδὸς ἀποφθιμένοιο, τὸν οὐχ ὑποδέξεαι αὖτις
οἴκαδε νοστήσαντ᾽, ἐπεὶ οὐδ᾽ ἐμὲ θυμὸς ἄνωγε   90
ζώειν οὐδ᾽ ἄνδρεσσι μετέμμεναι, αἴ κε μὴ Ἕκτωρ
πρῶτος ἐμῷ ὑπὸ δουρὶ τυπεὶς ἀπὸ θυμὸν ὀλέσσῃ,
Πατρόκλοιο δ᾽ ἕλωρα Μενοιτιάδεω ἀποτείσῃ."
    Τὸν δ᾽ αὖτε προσέειπε Θέτις κατὰ δάκρυ χέουσα·
"ὠκύμορος δή μοι, τέκος, ἔσσεαι, οἶ᾽ ἀγορεύεις·   95
αὐτίκα γάρ τοι ἔπειτα μεθ᾽ Ἕκτορα πότμος ἑτοῖμος."
    Τὴν δὲ μέγ᾽ ὀχθήσας προσέφη πόδας ὠκὺς Ἀχιλλεύς·
"αὐτίκα τεθναίην, ἐπεὶ οὐκ ἄρ᾽ ἔμελλον ἑταίρῳ
κτεινομένῳ ἐπαμῦναι· ὁ μὲν μάλα τηλόθι πάτρης

82 κεφαλῇ: the head is the most precious part of the body, so this expression is equivalent to 'my own life'

ἀπόλλυμι I lose, destroy; ἀπώλεσα is 1 s. aor. The verb is ambiguous: Achilles is probably saying here 'I have lost him' rather than the starker 'I have killed him' (by sending him into battle), though he does at 98–103 accept responsibility for Patroclus' death.

83 δηόω/δηϊόω I kill; δηώσας is aor. part. (m. nom. s.)

ἀποδύω I strip off; ἀπέδυσε is 3 s. aor.
πελώριος -η -ον huge
θαῦμα -ατος, τό wonder
ἰδέσθαι: aor. mid. inf. of ὁράω (cf. 61), here explanatory 'to behold'

84 κᾱλός -ή -όν beautiful, fine (long α in Homer, short in Att.). The formulaic phrase τεύχεα καλά is here separated by two lines with enjambment, putting striking emphasis on the adj.

τὰ μέν: again δέ could have followed ('and he in turn gave them to me'), but Achilles moves on to other thoughts

δίδωμι I give; δόσαν is 3 pl. aor.

ἀγλαός -ή -όν splendid, shining
δῶρον -ου, τό gift

85 ἦμαρ -ατος, τό day (= Att. ἡμέρα -ας, ἡ); dat. for time when
βροτός -οῦ, ὁ mortal; here as m. adj.
ἀνήρ ἀνδρός/ἀνέρος, ὁ man
ἐμβάλλω (here) I put X (acc.) in Y (dat.); ἔμβαλον is 3 pl. aor. (= Att. ἐνέβαλον)
εὐνή -ῆς, ἡ bed

86 αἴθ(ε): introducing a wish along with ὄφελες
ὄφελες: 2 s. aor. of ὀφέλλω (cf. 19), introducing a wish expressed by inf. 'if only you were living …'
αὖθι (adv.) just there
μετ(ά) (+ dat.) among
ἀθάνατος -η -ον immortal; ἀθανάτης is f. dat. pl., here as noun
ἅλιος -η -ον of the sea

87 ναίω I live, dwell
Πηλεύς: subject of ὄφελε understood from ὄφελες in 86, with another wish expressed by inf. 'and that Peleus had married'
θνητός -ή -όν mortal
ἄγομαι I marry; ἀγαγέσθαι is aor. inf.
ἄκοιτις -ιος, ἡ wife

88 νῦν now; νῦν δ(ἐ) conveys the idea 'but as things are', here implying 'Peleus did in fact marry you, a goddess'

ἵνα (+ opt.) in order that, so that (introducing purpose clause)

καὶ σοί for you too (i.e. as well as for me)

φρεσί: dat. pl. of φρήν, again pl. for s. (cf. 15 and 73)

μυρίος -η -ον measureless

εἴη: 3 s. opt. of εἰμί

89 ἀποφθίομαι I perish, die; ἀποφθιμένοιο is aor. part. (m. gen. s.). Tr. phrase 'grief … for your dead son'.

τόν: again rel. pron. (cf. 81)

ὑποδέξεαι: 2 s. fut. of ὑποδέχομαι (cf. 59); note how the phrasing echoes 59–60

90 οὐδ(ε) (here) not even (me), implying 'I too should be dead, as Patroclus is'

ἄνωγα (perf. with pres. sense) I order

91 ἄνδρεσσι (cf. 85): Homeric dat. pl. (= Att. ἀνδράσι)

μέτειμι I am among (+ dat.); μετέμμεναι is inf. (= Att. μετεῖναι)

αἰ if (= Att. εἰ)

κε: particle indicating potential or conditional action, κεν before a vowel or elided κ' (= Att. ἄν; Homer uses both, but more often κε); αἴ κε μή (+ subj.) 'unless' (in fut. open condition; = Att. ἐάν (εἰ + ἄν) μή)

92 πρῶτος -η -ον first; here equivalent to πρότερος (first of two), and implying 'sooner'

δόρυ -ατος, τό spear; δουρί is an alternative dat. s.

τύπτω I strike, hit; τυπείς is aor. pass. part. (m. nom. s.)

ἀπό … ὀλέσσῃ: tmesis (cf. on 29) of 3 s. aor. subj. of ἀπόλλυμι (cf. 82)

θυμός -οῦ, ὁ (here) life

93 ἕλωρ, τό prey, spoil; (pl. here) penalty for killing, blood price of (+ gen.)

Μενοιτιάδης -αο/εω, ὁ son of Menoetius

ἀποτίνω I pay; ἀποτείσῃ is 3 s. aor. subj.

94–6: Thetis' stark response

94 προσέειπον (aor. only) I spoke to (= Att. προσεῖπον)

καταχέω I pour down; κατὰ … χέουσα is tmesis of pres. part. (f. nom. s.)

95 ὠκύμορος -ον short-lived, doomed to an early death

μοι: ethic dat. (cf. 61)

ἔσσεαι: 2 s. fut. of εἰμί (= Att. ἔσῃ)

οἶος -η -ον such

ἀγορεύω I say, declare (usu. in public); 'such things you say' implies 'judging from what you say'. The expression suggests that it is only by Achilles' decision to kill Hector (hitherto left open)

that his death is made imminent. At 9.410–16 the crucial factor was his decision to stay in Troy. Reported prophecy is oft. used to sharpen our appreciation of crucial points in the narrative.

96 αὐτίκα (adv.) at once, straight away

τοι = σοι

ἔπειτα (here of cause rather than time) so then

μεθ' = μετά (+ acc.) after

πότμος -ου, ὁ death, fate

ἑτοῖμος -η -ον ready, at hand; understand ἐστί

97–113: Achilles' grief at his own failure.

97 μέγ(α) greatly; n. s. as adv. (cf. 29)

ὀχθήσας: the verb (cf. 5) covers a large range of negative emotions (anxiety, resentment, irritation, consternation). Which is it here?

98 τεθναίην: 1 s. perf. opt. of θνήσκω (cf. 12), expressing a wish

μέλλω I am going to, (here) fated to (+ inf.)

99 κτείνω I kill; κτεινομένῳ is pres. pass. part. (m. dat. s.)

ἐπαμύνω I bring help to (+ dat.); ἐπαμῦναι is aor. inf.

μάλα (adv.) very

τηλόθι (+ gen.) far away from

πάτρη -ης, ἡ native land (= Att. πάτρα -ας or πατρίς -ίδος)

ἔφθιτ᾽, ἐμεῖο δὲ δῆσεν ἀρῆς ἀλκτῆρα γενέσθαι.   100
νῦν δ᾽ ἐπεὶ οὐ νέομαί γε φίλην ἐς πατρίδα γαῖαν,
οὐδέ τι Πατρόκλῳ γενόμην φάος οὐδ᾽ ἑτάροισι
τοῖς ἄλλοις, οἳ δὴ πολέες δάμεν Ἕκτορι δίῳ,
ἀλλ᾽ ἧμαι παρὰ νηυσὶν ἐτώσιον ἄχθος ἀρούρης,
τοῖος ἐὼν οἷος οὔ τις Ἀχαιῶν χαλκοχιτώνων   105
ἐν πολέμῳ· ἀγορῇ δέ τ᾽ ἀμείνονές εἰσι καὶ ἄλλοι.
ὡς ἔρις ἔκ τε θεῶν ἔκ τ᾽ ἀνθρώπων ἀπόλοιτο,
καὶ χόλος, ὅς τ᾽ ἐφέηκε πολύφρονά περ χαλεπῆναι,
ὅς τε πολὺ γλυκίων μέλιτος καταλειβομένοιο
ἀνδρῶν ἐν στήθεσσιν ἀέξεται ἠΰτε καπνός·   110
ὡς ἐμὲ νῦν ἐχόλωσεν ἄναξ ἀνδρῶν Ἀγαμέμνων.
ἀλλὰ τὰ μὲν προτετύχθαι ἐάσομεν ἀχνύμενοί περ,
θυμὸν ἐνὶ στήθεσσι φίλον δαμάσαντες ἀνάγκῃ·
νῦν δ᾽ εἶμ᾽, ὄφρα φίλης κεφαλῆς ὀλετῆρα κιχείω,
Ἕκτορα· κῆρα δ᾽ ἐγὼ τότε δέξομαι, ὁππότε κεν δὴ   115
Ζεὺς ἐθέλῃ τελέσαι ἠδ᾽ ἀθάνατοι θεοὶ ἄλλοι.
οὐδὲ γὰρ οὐδὲ βίη Ἡρακλῆος φύγε κῆρα,

100 φθίνομαι I perish; ἔφθιτ(ο) is 3 s. aor.
δέω I need, have need of (+ gen.); δῆσεν
   is 3 s. aor. Patroclus is the subject.
γενέσθαι (cf. 19) expresses purpose
   'to be'.
ἀρή -ῆς, ἡ ruin, destruction
ἀλκτήρ -ῆρος, ὁ defender against, protector from (+ gen.)
101 νέομαι I go; pres. indic. usu. has fut.
   sense, as here
γε (cf. 21): tr. closely with ἐπεί
ἐς = εἰς (+ acc.) to
πατρίς -ίδος (as f. adj.) native
γαῖα -ης, ἡ land (= Att. γῆ γῆς, ἡ)
102 τι: used as at 62
γενόμην: 1 s. aor. of γίγνομαι (cf. 19)
φάος (here) (a light of) deliverance (cf.
   11)
ἑτάροισι (cf. 80): note Homeric dat. pl.
   ending -οισι (= Att. -οις)
103 πολύς πολλή πολύ much, pl. many;
πολέες is 3rd decl. form m. nom. pl. (=
   Att. πολλοί)
δαμάζω I subdue, overcome; δάμεν is 3
   pl. aor. pass. (= Att. ἐδάμησαν), with

Ἕκτορι dat. of agent. With Patroclus
   dead, Hector becomes the focus of
   Achilles' rage, and his victims now
   receive sympathy.
δῖος -α -ον noble, glorious, godlike
104 ἧμαι: cf. 36
ἐτώσιος -ον useless
ἄχθος -εος, τό burden
ἄρουρα -ης, ἡ earth
105 τοῖος -η -ον of such a sort
ἐών: pres. part. (m. nom. s.) of εἰμί (= Att.
   ὤν), here implying 'although I am …'
οἷος -η -ον (such) as
οὔ τις no one (here implying 'no one else')
χαλκοχίτων -ωνος bronze-clad
106 πόλεμος -ου, ὁ war, battle
ἀγορή -ῆς, ἡ assembly (= Att. ἀγορά -ᾶς)
δέ τ(ε) but of course; τε is here 'generalising', implying 'as regularly happens', 'as
   everyone knows'. Further examples at
   108, 201, 219 and many more.
ἀμείνων -ον better; comp. of ἀγαθός
   (good)
καί: here affirmative particle 'yes, there
   are'

107 ὡς (+ opt.) I wish that
ἔρις -ιδος, ἡ strife
ἐκ (+ gen.) (here) from among
ἄνθρωπος -ου, ὁ man, person
ἀπόλλυμαι I perish; ἀπόλοιτο is 3 s. aor.
    opt. mid.
108 χόλος -ου, ὁ anger, wrath
τ(ε): again generalising, as in 106
ἐφίημι (here) I incite; ἐφέηκα is 3 s. aor.,
    here 'gnomic' ('like a proverb', Greek
    ones being oft. stated in past tense),
    i.e. expressing a general truth; tr. as
    pres.
πολύφρων -ον very thoughtful; here 'a
    very thoughtful man'
περ: enclitic particle emphasising
    preceding word and oft. suggesting
    'even' or 'although'
χαλεπαίνω I rage, am angry; χαλεπῆναι
    is aor. inf.
109 ὅς: picking up χόλος
γλυκύς -εῖα -ύ sweet; γλυκίων -ον is
    comp., here + gen. of comparison
    'sweeter than'
μέλι -ιτος, τό honey
καταλείβω I pour down; καταλειβομένοιο
    is pass. part. (m. gen. s.)
110 ἀέξομαι I grow, increase (= Att. αὔξομαι)
ἠΰτε (adv.) like
καπνός -ου, ὁ smoke. The sweetness of
    anger is strikingly described.

111 νῦν (here) in this case; ἐμέ and νῦν pull
    us roughly from the general to the
    particular
χολόω I enrage, anger; ἐχόλωσεν is 3 s. aor.
ἄναξ -ακτος, ὁ lord
Ἀγαμέμνων -ονος, ὁ Agamemnon, king
    of Argos (in the Peloponnese) and
    overall leader of the Achaean expedi-
    tion against Troy. Achilles now regrets
    his quarrel with Agamemnon, having
    seen its disastrous consequences –
    though, as he puts it, he regrets not
    having become angry, but that Agam-
    emnon made him angry.
112 προτεύχω I do beforehand; προτετύχθαι
    is perf. pass. inf., lit. 'to have been
    done beforehand', i.e. 'to be over and
    done with' (cf. 16.60)
ἐάω I allow, leave (something) be;
    ἐάσομεν is 1 pl. aor. subj., here 'jussive'
    ('let us …') and again with short vowel
    (= Att. ἐάσωμεν). The pl. associates
    Achilles with all who have similar
    feelings.
ἀχνύμενοί: pres. part. (m. nom. pl.) of
    ἄχνυμαι (cf. 62); here with second
    accent because of following enclitic
    περ 'though we are grieving'
113 φίλον (our) own (cf. 27)
δαμάσαντες: aor. part. (m. nom. pl.) of
    δαμάζω (cf. 103)
ἀνάγκη -ης, ἡ necessity; dat. here 'by
    necessity'

114–26: Achilles will go and avenge Patroclus even at the cost of his own life.

114 κεφαλῆς: 'dear head' implies 'dear one'
    (cf. on 82), i.e. Patroclus
ὀλετήρ -ῆρος, ὁ destroyer
κιχάνω I catch up with; κιχείω is 1 s. aor.
    subj.
115 Ἕκτορα: emphatic enjambment again,
    the stronger for coming before a sense
    break
κήρ κηρός, ἡ death, fate
τότε (adv.) then
δέχομαι I receive, accept; δέξομαι is 1 s.
    fut.
ὁππότε κεν whenever (+ subj.)
116 ἐθέλω I wish; ἐθέλη is 3 s. subj.

117 οὐδέ: repeated for emphasis 'nor did …
    no, not even'
βίη -ης, ἡ force, might (= Att. βία -ας)
Ἡρακλέης -ῆος, ὁ Heracles (= Att. Ἡρα-
    κλῆς -έους); βίη Ἡρακλῆος lit. 'might of
    Heracles' i.e. 'mighty Heracles'
φεύγω (here) I escape from; φύγε is 3 s.
    aor. The circumstances of Heracles'
    death (on a pyre on Mount Oeta) and
    its consequence (his apotheosis) are
    irrelevant and perhaps unknown to
    the poet of the *Iliad*: all that matters
    is that no human was greater than he,
    and yet he died.

ὅς περ φίλτατος ἔσκε Διὶ Κρονίωνι ἄνακτι·
ἀλλά ἑ μοῖρ' ἐδάμασσε καὶ ἀργαλέος χόλος Ἥρης.
ὡς καὶ ἐγών, εἰ δή μοι ὁμοίη μοῖρα τέτυκται,   120
κείσομ' ἐπεί κε θάνω· νῦν δὲ κλέος ἐσθλὸν ἀροίμην,
καί τινα Τρωϊάδων καὶ Δαρδανίδων βαθυκόλπων
ἀμφοτέρῃσιν χερσὶ παρειάων ἀπαλάων
δάκρυ' ὀμορξαμένην ἁδινὸν στοναχῆσαι ἐφείην,
γνοῖεν δ' ὡς δὴ δηρὸν ἐγὼ πολέμοιο πέπαυμαι·   125
μηδέ μ' ἔρυκε μάχης φιλέουσά περ· οὐδέ με πείσεις."
    Τὸν δ' ἠμείβετ' ἔπειτα θεὰ Θέτις ἀργυρόπεζα·
"ναὶ δὴ ταῦτά γε, τέκνον, ἐτήτυμον οὐ κακόν ἐστι,
τειρομένοις ἑτάροισιν ἀμυνέμεν αἰπὺν ὄλεθρον.
ἀλλά τοι ἔντεα καλὰ μετὰ Τρώεσσιν ἔχονται,   130
χάλκεα μαρμαίροντα· τὰ μὲν κορυθαίολος Ἕκτωρ
αὐτὸς ἔχων ὤμοισιν ἀγάλλεται· οὐδέ ἕ φημι
δηρὸν ἐπαγλαϊεῖσθαι, ἐπεὶ φόνος ἐγγύθεν αὐτῷ.
ἀλλὰ σὺ μὲν μή πω καταδύσεο μῶλον Ἄρηος,
πρίν γ' ἐμὲ δεῦρ' ἐλθοῦσαν ἐν ὀφθαλμοῖσιν ἴδηαι·   135
ἠῶθεν γὰρ νεῦμαι ἅμ' ἠελίῳ ἀνιόντι
τεύχεα καλὰ φέρουσα παρ' Ἡφαίστοιο ἄνακτος."

118 φίλτατος: sup. of φίλος (cf. 27)
    ἔσκε: 3 s. impf. of εἰμί (= Att. ἦν). This is an 'iterative' form of the impf. (identified by -σκ-) to indicate regular or repeated action, here implying 'was always'.
    Διὶ: dat. of Ζεύς (cf. 75)
    Κρονίων -ωνος, ὁ son of Cronus, i.e. Zeus
119 ἑ (acc.) him (cf. 16)
    μοῖρα -ης, ἡ fate
    ἐδάμασσε: 3 s. aor. of δαμάζω (cf. 103) (= Att. ἐδάμασε)
    ἀργαλέος -η -ον painful, cruel
    Ἥρη -ης, ἡ Hera, wife of Zeus (= Att. Ἥρα -ας). Hera hated Heracles, resenting Zeus's love for his mother Alcmene.
120 καί (here) too. Achilles, like Heracles, will die despite having one divine parent. ἐγών = ἐγώ (before vowel)
    εἰ if
    ὁμοῖος -η -ον like, similar
    τεύχω I make, prepare; τέτυκται is 3 s. perf. pass.
121 κείσομαι: 1 s. fut. of κεῖμαι (cf. 20), here implying 'lie still/inactive'

ἐπεί κε (+ subj.) when; with fut. main verb, suggesting indefinite 'whenever' (again note κε used like ἄν in Att.)
    θάνω: 1 s. aor. subj. of θνήσκω (cf. 12)
    νῦν δέ: here returning from imagined future to present intention
    κλέος (nom. and acc. only), τό glory
    ἐσθλός -ή -όν good
    ἄρνυμαι I win, earn; ἀροίμην is 1 s. aor. opt., expressing a wish
122 τινα: s. but implying collective 'some', picked up by pl. γνοῖεν (125)
    Τρωϊάς -άδος, ἡ Trojan woman (= Att. Τρωάς)
    Δαρδανίς -ίδος, ἡ Dardanian woman. The Dardanians are neighbours and allies of the Trojans, effectively indistinguishable from them (cf. 16.807). They are named from Dardanus, an ancestor of the Trojan kings.
    βαθύκολπος -ον deep-bosomed
123 παρειαί -ῶν, αἱ cheeks
    ἁπαλός -ή -όν tender; ἁπαλάων is f. gen. pl.

124 ὀμόργνυμι I wipe away X (acc.) from Y (gen.); ὀμορξαμένην is aor. mid. part. (f. acc. s.)

ἀδινός -ή -όν dense, repeated; (n. here as adv.) repeatedly, abundantly

στοναχέω I lament; στοναχῆσαι is aor. inf.

ἐφίημι (here) I cause; ἐφείην is 1 s. aor. opt., again expressing a wish. Achilles is brutally clear that his glory consists in killing many men and thereby making many women lament.

125 γιγνώσκω I know; γνοῖεν is 3 pl. aor. opt., expressing another wish, with 'Trojan women' understood as subject (cf. on 122)

ὡς (here) that

δηρόν (adv.) for a long time

παύομαι I cease from (+ gen.); πέπαυμαι is 1 s. perf.

126 ἐρύκω I hold X (acc.) back from Y (gen.), here 2 s. imper.

μάχη -ης, ἡ battle

φιλέω I love

πείθω I persuade; πείσεις is 2 s. fut., constructed as if ἔρυκε had been indic. ('You will not restrain me and you will not persuade me'). Achilles' words here take the form of a ring composition within the wider ring (cf. on 65–77): (A) I will kill Hector (B) and then die (C) as Heracles did (B) so I too will die (A) but win glory (by killing Hector).

127–37: Thetis promises to bring new armour.

127 ἀμείβομαι I answer, reply; ἠμείβετ(ο) is 3 s. impf.

ἀργυρόπεζα -ης (f. adj.) silver-footed; in Homer used only of Thetis

128 ναί yes; ταῦτα is acc. of resp., lit. 'yes in respect of these things' i.e. 'that is right'

ἐτήτυμος -ον true; n. here as adv.

129 τείρω I wear out, exhaust; τειρομένοις is pres. pass. part. (m. dat. pl.)

ἀμύνω I ward off X (acc.) from Y (dat.); ἀμυνέμεν is pres. inf.

αἰπύς -εῖα -ύ sheer, utter

ὄλεθρος -ου, ὁ destruction

130 τοι = σοι (here) your (possessive dat.)

ἔντεα -ων, τά armour

ἔχονται: 3 pl. pres. pass. of ἔχω (cf. 21); n. pl. subject taking pl. verb (cf. on 31)

131 χάλκεος -ον of bronze

μαρμαίρω I sparkle, gleam. The three epithets for the armour draw attention to the shameful fact of it being in the hands of the enemy.

μέν: here emphatic particle ('certainly'), without corresponding contrast

132 ὦμος -ου, ὁ shoulder; dat. pl. here 'on his shoulders'; note again Homeric dat. pl. ending -οισι, here with movable ν before vowel

ἀγάλλομαι I take delight in

133 ἐπαγλαΐζομαι I glory in; ἐπαγλαΐεῖσθαι is fut. inf., with acc. subject ἕ (132) (cf. 16) in indirect statement after φημί

φόνος -ου, ὁ violent death

ἐγγύθεν (adv.) near at hand; understand ἐστί

134 μή πω not yet

καταδύω I go down into; καταδύσεο is 2 s. aor. mid. imper.

μῶλος -ου, ὁ toil, struggle

Ἄρης -ηος, ὁ Ares, the god of war

135 πρίν (conj.) until (+ subj.), here as oft. in Homer without ἄν (which Att. would have) or κε

δεῦρο (adv.) (to) here

ὀφθαλμός -οῦ, ὁ eye

ἴδηαι: 2 s. aor. subj. mid. of ὁράω (cf. 61); tautology with ἐν ὀφθαλμοῖσιν stresses an important condition for Achilles rejoining the conflict (cf. 190)

136 ἠῶθεν (adv.) in the morning (= Att. ἕωθεν)

νεῦμαι = νέομαι (cf. 101)

ἅμα (+ dat.) along with, at the same time as

ἄνειμι I rise; ἀνίοντι is pres. part. (m. dat. s.)

137 φέρω I carry, bring; φέρουσα is pres. part. (f. nom. s.)

παρά (+ gen.) from

Ἥφαιστος -ου/οιο, ὁ Hephaestus, the blacksmith god

Ὣς ἄρα φωνήσασα πάλιν τράπεθ' υἷος ἑοῖο,
καὶ στρεφθεῖσ' ἁλίῃσι κασιγνήτῃσι μετηύδα·
"ὑμεῖς μὲν νῦν δῦτε θαλάσσης εὐρέα κόλπον,   140
ὀψόμεναί τε γέρονθ' ἅλιον καὶ δώματα πατρός,
καί οἱ πάντ' ἀγορεύσατ'· ἐγὼ δ' ἐς μακρὸν Ὄλυμπον
εἶμι παρ' Ἥφαιστον κλυτοτέχνην, αἴ κ' ἐθέλησιν
υἱεῖ ἐμῷ δόμεναι κλυτὰ τεύχεα παμφανόωντα."
   Ὣς ἔφαθ', αἱ δ' ὑπὸ κῦμα θαλάσσης αὐτίκ' ἔδυσαν·   145
ἡ δ' αὖτ' Οὔλυμπόνδε θεὰ Θέτις ἀργυρόπεζα
ἤϊεν, ὄφρα φίλῳ παιδὶ κλυτὰ τεύχε' ἐνείκαι.
   Τὴν μὲν ἄρ' Οὔλυμπόνδε πόδες φέρον· αὐτὰρ Ἀχαιοὶ
θεσπεσίῳ ἀλαλητῷ ὑφ' Ἕκτορος ἀνδροφόνοιο
φεύγοντες νῆάς τε καὶ Ἑλλήσποντον ἵκοντο.   150
οὐδέ κε Πάτροκλόν περ ἐϋκνήμιδες Ἀχαιοὶ
ἐκ βελέων ἐρύσαντο νέκυν, θεράποντ' Ἀχιλῆος·
αὖτις γὰρ δὴ τόν γε κίχον λαός τε καὶ ἵπποι
Ἕκτωρ τε Πριάμοιο πάϊς, φλογὶ εἴκελος ἀλκήν.
τρὶς μέν μιν μετόπισθε ποδῶν λάβε φαίδιμος Ἕκτωρ   155
ἑλκέμεναι μεμαώς, μέγα δὲ Τρώεσσιν ὁμόκλα·
τρὶς δὲ δύ' Αἴαντες, θοῦριν ἐπιειμένοι ἀλκήν,

138–47: *The Nereids depart.*

138 πάλιν (here) away from (+ gen.)
   τρέπω I turn; τράπεθ' (= τράπετο) is 3 s.
      aor. mid.
   υἷος: 3rd decl. form gen. of υἱός (cf. 12;
      distinguished from nom. only by
      accent)
   ἑοῖο: m. gen. s. of ἑός (cf. 71)
139 στρέφω I turn; στρεφθεῖσ(α) is aor. pass.
      part. (f. nom. s.) with mid. sense
   μεταυδάω I speak among (+ dat.); μετηύ-
      δα is 3 s. impf.
140 ὑμεῖς you (pl.)
   δύω I go into, (here) plunge into
   εὐρύς -εῖα -ύ wide, broad
   κόλπος -ου, ὁ bosom
141 ὀψόμεναι: fut. part. (f. nom. pl.) of ὁράω
      (cf. 61), here expressing purpose
   γέρονθ' = γέροντα (cf. 36); the Old Man
      of the Sea is of course Nereus
   δῶμα -τος, τό house, palace; here pl. for
      s.

142 οἱ to him (cf. 16)
   ἀγορεύσατ(ε): 2 pl. aor. imper. of ἀγο-
      ρεύω (cf. 95)
   μακρός -ή -όν long, (here) high
   Ὄλυμπος/Οὔλυμπος -ου/οιο, ὁ Mount
      Olympus, home of the gods; first
      syllable oft. lengthened for the metre
      (cf. 146)
143 παρά (+ acc.) to (the side of)
   κλυτοτέχνης -ου (m. adj.) renowned for
      craftsmanship
   αἴ κ(ε) (+ subj.) in the hope that
   ἐθέλησιν: 3 s. subj. of ἐθέλω (= Att. ἐθέλῃ;
      cf. 116)
144 υἱεῖ: 3rd decl. form dat. of υἱός
      (cf. 12)
   δόμεναι: aor. inf. of δίδωμι (cf. 84; = Att.
      δοῦναι)
   κλυτός -ή -όν glorious, famous
   παμφανόων -ωσα -ον (-ωντος) shining
      brightly

145 ἔφαθ' = ἔφατο: 3 s. impf. of φημί (cf. 17)
   ὑποδύω I plunge beneath; ὑπό ... ἔδυσαν
   is tmesis of 3 pl. aor.
146 αὖτ(ε) (adv.) (here) on the other hand
   Οὔλυμπόνδε to Olympus; the suffix
   -δε (on acc. noun) indicates motion
   towards

147 ἤϊεν: 3 s. impf. of εἶμι (I go; =
   Att. ἤει)
   ὄφρα (+ opt.) in order to (purpose
   clause)
   ἐνείκαι: 3 s. aor. opt. of φέρω
   (cf. 137)

148–242: Achilles halts the rout of the Achaeans.

148–64: The battle over Patroclus' body.

148 πόδες φέρον: a curious statement, as
   Thetis presumably flies to Olympus
   αὐτάρ (conj.) but, however. The change
   of scene is abrupt.
149 θεσπέσιος -η -ον tremendous, awful
   ἀλαλητός -οῦ, ὁ yell, cry; note the onomatopoeia
   ὑφ' = ὕπο (+ gen.) (here) at the hands of
   ἀνδροφόνος -ον man-slaying; a standard
   epithet of Hector
150 φεύγω I run away, flee
   Ἑλλήσποντος -ου, ὁ the Hellespont
   (modern Dardanelles), the strait
   between Europe and Asia on whose
   shore the Achaeans were camped.
   Here the Achaeans as a group have
   reached the ships; those round
   Patroclus seem to be left further back,
   struggling to follow.
151 οὐδέ κε (+ aor. indic.) 'would not have ...'
   (κε again acting like ἄν in Att.); the
   expected 'if' element of a past unfulfilled condition does not appear (but
   cf. on 166). The syntactical suspense
   reflects the action.
   περ: the thought seems to be 'even
   though it was Patroclus ...'
   ἐϋκνήμις -ιδος (m. adj.) well-greaved
   (greaves are shin-protecting armour);
   a standard epithet of the Achaeans
152 ἐκ (+ gen.) (here) out of range of
   βέλος -εος, τό missile
   ἐρύω I drag; ἐρύσαντο is 3 pl. aor. mid.
   θεράπων -οντος, ὁ aide, battle companion; both νέκυν and θεράποντ(α) are
   in apposition to Πάτροκλον (151)
153 κίχον: 3 pl. aor. of κιχάνω (cf. 114)
   λαός -οῦ, ὁ people, army (= Att. λεώς -ώ);
   here the Trojan army

ἵππος -ου, ὁ horse, pl. chariots
154 Πρίαμος -ου/οιο, ὁ Priam, king of Troy
   πάϊς = παῖς (cf. 71)
   φλόξ φλογός, ἡ flame
   εἴκελος -η -ον like (+ dat.)
   ἀλκή -ῆς, ἡ fighting spirit; ἀλκήν is acc.
   of resp.
155 τρίς (adv.) three times. A common
   number for unsuccessful attempts, e.g.
   Patroclus' three attempts to scale the
   Trojan wall (16.702–4)
   μετόπισθε (adv.) from behind
   ποδῶν: gen. pl. of πούς (cf. 2); here 'by
   the feet' (gen. for object aimed at)
   φαίδιμος -ον illustrious
156 ἕλκω I drag; ἑλκέμεναι is inf.
   μέμαα (perf. with pres. sense) I am eager;
   μεμαώς is part. (m. nom. s.)
   μέγα (here) loudly
   ὁμοκλάω I urge on with a shout (here +
   dat.); ὁμόκλα is 3 s. impf.
157 δύο two
   Αἴας -αντος, ὁ Ajax, pl. Αἴαντες. There
   are two Ajaxes among the Achaean
   heroes: the Great, son of Telamon,
   and the Lesser, son of Oileus.
   θοῦρις -ιδος (acc. -ιν; f. adj.) impetuous.
   The second syllable, by nature short,
   is here treated as 'honorary long'; likewise κατά (159) and μέγα (160), the
   last with hiatus too (cf. on 22). This
   accumulation of unusual metrical features perhaps reflects the violence of
   the scene, with the body being jerked
   to and fro.
   ἐπιέννυμι I clothe (someone), mid. I
   wear; ἐπιειμένοι is perf. mid. part. (m.
   nom. pl.) 'clothed in' (here metaphor-
   ical)

νεκροῦ ἀπεστυφέλιξαν· ὁ δ’ ἔμπεδον ἀλκὶ πεποιθὼς
ἄλλοτ’ ἐπαΐξασκε κατὰ μόθον, ἄλλοτε δ’ αὖτε
στάσκε μέγα ἰάχων· ὀπίσω δ’ οὔ χάζετο πάμπαν.   160
ὡς δ’ ἀπὸ σώματος οὔ τι λέοντ’ αἴθωνα δύνανται
ποιμένες ἄγραυλοι μέγα πεινάοντα δίεσθαι,
ὣς ῥα τὸν οὐκ ἐδύναντο δύω Αἴαντε κορυστὰ
Ἕκτορα Πριαμίδην ἀπὸ νεκροῦ δειδίξασθαι.
καί νύ κεν εἴρυσσέν τε καὶ ἄσπετον ἤρατο κῦδος,   165
εἰ μὴ Πηλεΐωνι ποδήνεμος ὠκέα Ἶρις
ἄγγελος ἦλθε θέουσ’ ἀπ’ Ὀλύμπου θωρήσσεσθαι,
κρύβδα Διὸς ἄλλων τε θεῶν· πρὸ γὰρ ἧκέ μιν Ἥρη.
ἀγχοῦ δ’ ἱσταμένη ἔπεα πτερόεντα προσηύδα·
“ὄρσεο, Πηλεΐδη, πάντων ἐκπαγλότατ’ ἀνδρῶν·   170
Πατρόκλῳ ἐπάμυνον, οὗ εἵνεκα φύλοπις αἰνὴ
ἕστηκε πρὸ νεῶν· οἱ δ’ ἀλλήλους ὀλέκουσιν
οἱ μὲν ἀμυνόμενοι νέκυος πέρι τεθνηῶτος,
οἱ δὲ ἐρύσσασθαι ποτὶ Ἴλιον ἠνεμόεσσαν
Τρῶες ἐπιθύουσι· μάλιστα δὲ φαίδιμος Ἕκτωρ   175
ἑλκέμεναι μέμονεν· κεφαλὴν δέ ἑ θυμὸς ἄνωγε

---

158 νεκρός -ου, ὁ corpse, dead body
  ἀποστυφελίζω I shove back, knock back
    from (+ gen.); ἀπεστυφέλιξαν is 3 pl.
    aor.; understand ‘him’ as object
  ἔμπεδος -ον firm; n. here as adv.
  ἀλκί: 3rd decl. form dat. of ἀλκή (cf. 154)
  πέποιθα (perf. with pres. sense) I trust,
    rely on (+ dat.); πεποιθώς is part. (m.
    nom. s.)
159 ἄλλοτ(ε) ... ἄλλοτε now ... now, one
    moment ... the next
  ἐπαΐσσω I dart forth, attack; ἐπαΐξασκε is
    3 s. aor. in iterative form (cf. on 118)
  κατά (+ acc.) (here) through
  μόθος -ου, ὁ fray
  αὖτε: cf. 6
160 ἵσταμαι I stand; στάσκε is 3 s. aor., again
    iterative
  ἰάχων: cf. 29
  ὀπίσω (adv.) backwards
  χάζομαι I give way

πάμπαν (adv.) at all
161 σῶμα -ατος, τό body (here that of an
    animal the lion has just killed)
  οὔ τι in no way
  λέων -οντος, ὁ lion
  αἴθων -ωνος tawny
162 ποιμήν -ένος, ὁ shepherd
  ἄγραυλος -ον living in open country
  πεινάω I am hungry
  δίομαι I drive away
163 ῥα = ἄρα (cf. 5)
  τόν: redundant in tr., anticipating post-
    poned object Ἕκτορα (164)
  δύω = δύο (cf. 157)
  Αἴαντε the two Ajaxes; nom. dual of Αἴας
    (cf. 157)
  κορυστής -ᾶο/έω (m. adj.) helmeted,
    armed; κορυστά is nom. dual.
164 Πριαμίδης -αο/εω, ὁ son of Priam
  δειδίσσομαι I scare away; δειδίξασθαι is
    aor. inf.

165–201: Iris, messenger of the gods, visits Achilles and urges him to make his presence felt by the fighters.

165 νυ now; enclitic form of νῦν, here accented because another enclitic follows

κεν = κε (before vowel), again indicating 'would have'

εἴρυσσεν: Homeric 3 s. aor. of ἐρύω (cf. 152)

τε καί both … and; here joining the two verbs

ἄσπετος -ον immense, beyond description

ἤρατο: 3 s. aor. of ἄρνυμαι (cf. 121)

κῦδος -εος, τό glory

166 εἰ μή (+ aor. indic.) 'if … had not …' (past unfulfilled condition); this clause perhaps also completes the sentence left hanging at 152

Πηλεΐων -ωνος, ὁ son of Peleus, i.e. Achilles

ποδήνεμος -ον wind-footed

ὠκύς -εῖα/έα -ύ swift

Ἶρις (voc. Ἶρι), ἡ Iris, the messenger goddess

167 ἄγγελος ἦλθε: again predicative 'came as a messenger' (cf. 2), here implying 'telling him to' (+ inf. in indirect command)

θέω I run; θέουσ(α) is pres. part. (f. nom. s.)

θωρήσσω I arm, prepare for battle; θωρήσσεσθαι is pres. mid. inf. Iris is aware that Achilles has no armour.

168 κρύβδα (adv.) in secret from, without the knowledge of (+ gen.)

προΐημι I send out, send forth; πρό … ἧκε is tmesis of 3 s. aor. Hera has not been pleased by Zeus's decision to favour the Trojans. At 14.153–351 she seduced him into an afternoon of lovemaking in order to distract him. By this stage we know that Zeus's plan has had the desired effect: Achilles will return to the battle. But Hera may still suspect that he will go too far.

169 ἀγχοῦ (adv.) near

ἱσταμένη: pres. part. (f. nom. s.) of ἵσταμαι (cf. 160)

170 ὄρνυμι I arouse, mid. I rise, get up; ὄρσεο is 2 s. aor. mid. imper.

Πηλεΐδης -αο/εω, ὁ son of Peleus, i.e. Achilles; Πηλεΐδη is voc.

ἔκπαγλος -ον terrifying, extraordinary; here sup. (m. voc. s.)

171 ἐπαμύνω I bring help to (+ dat.); ἐπάμυνον is 2 s. aor. imper.

οὗ (of) whom; m. gen. s. of rel. pron. ὅς

εἵνεκα = ἕνεκα (+ gen. of preceding word) for the sake of

φύλοπις -ιδος, ἡ combat

αἰνός -ή -όν dreadful

172 ἕστηκε: 3 s. perf. of ἵσταμαι (cf. 160), here 'has arisen'

πρό (+ gen.) in front of

ἀλλήλους -ας -α (no nom.) each other, one another

ὀλέκω I destroy

173 οἱ μέν some, one side (i.e. the Achaeans)

ἀμύνομαι I put up a defence; mid. of ἀμύνω (cf. 129)

πέρι (+ gen.): here suggests both 'around' and 'for'; accented as postposition (cf. on 7)

τεθνηῶτος: perf. part (m. gen. s.) of θνήσκω (cf. 12)

174 οἱ δέ … Τρῶες (175) the others, the Trojans

ἐρύσσασθαι: aor. mid. inf. of ἐρύω (cf. 152)

ποτί = πρός (cf. 5)

ἠνεμόεις -εσσα -εν (-εντος) windy; a standard epithet of Troy

175 ἐπιθύω I am eager; part. to balance ἀμυνόμενοι might have been expected, but the construction has changed

μάλιστα (adv.) most, especially

176 μέμονα (perf. with pres. sense) I rage, strive

πῆξαι ἀνὰ σκολόπεσσι ταμόνθ᾽ ἀπαλῆς ἀπὸ δειρῆς.
ἀλλ᾽ ἄνα μηδ᾽ ἔτι κεῖσο· σέβας δέ σε θυμὸν ἱκέσθω
Πάτροκλον Τρῳῆσι κυσὶν μέλπηθρα γενέσθαι·
σοὶ λώβη, αἴ κέν τι νέκυς ᾐσχυμμένος ἔλθῃ."   180
     Τὴν δ᾽ ἠμείβετ᾽ ἔπειτα ποδάρκης δῖος Ἀχιλλεύς·
"Ἶρι θεά, τίς γάρ σε θεῶν ἐμοὶ ἄγγελον ἧκε;"
     Τὸν δ᾽ αὖτε προσέειπε ποδήνεμος ὠκέα Ἶρις·
"Ἥρη με προέηκε, Διὸς κυδρὴ παράκοιτις·
οὐδ᾽ οἶδε Κρονίδης ὑψίζυγος οὐδέ τις ἄλλος   185
ἀθανάτων, οἳ Ὄλυμπον ἀγάννιφον ἀμφινέμονται."
     Τὴν δ᾽ ἀπαμειβόμενος προσέφη πόδας ὠκὺς Ἀχιλλεύς·
"πῶς τ᾽ ἄρ ἴω μετὰ μῶλον; ἔχουσι δὲ τεύχεα κεῖνοι·
μήτηρ δ᾽ οὔ με φίλη πρίν γ᾽ εἴα θωρήσσεσθαι,
πρίν γ᾽ αὐτὴν ἐλθοῦσαν ἐν ὀφθαλμοῖσιν ἴδωμαι·   190
στεῦτο γὰρ Ἡφαίστοιο πάρ᾽ οἰσέμεν ἔντεα καλά.
ἄλλου δ᾽ οὔ τευ οἶδα τεῦ ἂν κλυτὰ τεύχεα δύω,
εἰ μὴ Αἴαντός γε σάκος Τελαμωνιάδαο.
ἀλλὰ καὶ αὐτὸς ὅ γ᾽, ἔλπομ᾽, ἐνὶ πρώτοισιν ὁμιλεῖ,
ἔγχεϊ δηϊόων περὶ Πατρόκλοιο θανόντος."   195
     Τὸν δ᾽ αὖτε προσέειπε ποδήνεμος ὠκέα Ἶρις·
"εὖ νυ καὶ ἡμεῖς ἴδμεν ὅ τοι κλυτὰ τεύχε᾽ ἔχονται·
ἀλλ᾽ αὔτως ἐπὶ τάφρον ἰὼν Τρώεσσι φάνηθι,
αἴ κέ σ᾽ ὑποδείσαντες ἀπόσχωνται πολέμοιο

---

177 πήγνυμι I fix, plant firmly; πῆξαι is aor.
     inf.
     ἀνά (+ dat.) on
     σκόλοψ -οπος, ὁ stake; here either pl.
          for s. or implying 'palisade' (on or in
          addition to the city walls)
     τάμνω I cut (= Att. τέμνω); ταμόνθ᾽ (=
          ταμόντα) is aor. part. (m. acc. s.)
          agreeing with ἑ (i.e. Hector)
     δειρή -ῆς, ἡ neck (= Att. δέρη -ης). At
          17.126 the poet says that Hector
          intended to cut off dead Patroclus'
          head. We are left to wonder whether
          this further atrocity is Hector's actual
          intention or an invention of Hera's to
          spur Achilles to action.
178 ἄνα (adv.) up! (here used like imper.)
     ἔτι (here) any longer
     κεῖμαι I lie, lie idle; κεῖσο is 2 s. imper.
     σέβας, τό respect, sense of shame (here
          introducing acc. + inf. 'lest' or 'at the
          thought that')

ἱκέσθω: 3 s. aor. imper. of ἱκνέομαι
     (cf. 64) 'let (shame) come over',
     objects σε and θυμόν ('whole and
     part', cf. 73)
179 κύων κυνός, ὁ/ἡ dog; κυσί is dat. pl., here
     f.
     Τρῳός -ή -όν Trojan; Τρῳῆσι is f. dat.
     pl.
     μέλπηθρα, τά plaything. To have his
          dead body eaten by dogs is one of the
          worst fates that a Homeric warrior can
          suffer. Achilles threatens Hector with
          it at 22.354.
180 λώβη -ης, ἡ disgrace; understand ἔσται, 3
     s. fut. of εἰμί
     αἴ κέν (+ subj.) if; fut. open condition
     (cf. 91)
     τι in any way, at all (with ᾐσχυμμένος)
     ᾐσχυμμένος: perf. pass. part. (m. nom. s.)
          of αἰσχύνω (cf. 24) 'disfigured'
     ἔλθῃ: 3 s. aor. subj. of ἔρχομαι (cf. 2), here
          'come back' i.e. be brought

181 ποδάρκης -ες swift-footed
182 γάρ: the train of thought seems to be
 'Which of the gods has sent you (for
 one of them must have)?'
 ἵημι I send; ἧκε is 3 s. aor.
184 προέηκε: 3 s. aor. of προΐημι (cf. 168)
 κυδρός -ή -όν venerable, honoured
 παράκοιτις -ιος, ἡ wife. Hera is 'Zeus's
 wife' here; cf. Zeus as 'Hera's husband'
 at 16.88.
185 Κρονίδης -αο/εω ὁ son of Cronus, i.e.
 Zeus
 ὑψίζυγος -ον high-throned
186 ἀγάννιφος -ον snow-capped. Olympus is
 mainly imagined as in the sky, but this
 epithet fits the physical mountain in
 northern Greece.
 ἀμφινέμομαι I live around
187 ἀπαμείβομαι I answer, reply
188 πῶς (adv.) how?
 τ(ε): perhaps adds a note of furious im-
 patience (cf. on 55) 'And how …?'
 ἴω: 1 s. subj. of εἶμι (I go), here deliberative 'how am I to go?'
 μετά (+ acc.) into the midst of
 δέ: perhaps suggests 'I wish I could go,
 but …'
 κεῖνος -η -ο he, she, it; that (= ἐκεῖνος -η
 -ο); here 'those men', i.e. the enemy (as
 in English 'them and us')
189 πρίν: here adv. 'sooner'; in 190 conj.
 'until' (+ subj.)
 εἴα: 3 s. impf. of ἐάω (cf. 112)
190 ἐλθοῦσαν: aor. part. (f. acc. s.) of ἔρχομαι
 (cf. 2)
 ἴδωμαι: 1 s. aor. subj. of ὁράω (for the
 expression cf. 135)
191 στεῦμαι I undertake, promise (+ fut.
 inf.); στεῦτο is 3 s. impf.
 παρά (+ gen.) from; πάρα here accented
 as postposition
 οἰσέμεν: fut. inf. φέρω (cf. 137)
192 τευ: m. gen. s. of τις 'anyone'
 τεῦ: gen. of τίς (interrogative, but tr. here
 as rel.) 'whose'; ἄλλου … τευ has been
 attracted (from the expected acc. after
 οἶδα) into the case of τεῦ

ἄν: particle suggesting potential or conditional action; Homer more oft. uses
 κε (cf. 91)
 δύω (here) I put on (cf. 140); here 1 s.
 subj. with ἄν 'I could put on'. Ajax
 the Great is second only to Achilles in
 strength, and is his cousin too (their
 fathers being sons of Aeacus).
193 σάκος -εος, τό shield. Ajax's shield is an
 iconic piece of armour, 'like a tower',
 with eight layers, seven of oxhide and
 one of bronze (7.219–23).
 Τελαμωνιάδης -αο/εω, ὁ son of Telamon
194 αὐτὸς ὅ he himself, i.e. Ajax
 ἔλπομ(αι) (here) I suppose; parenthetical
 in the sentence
 ἐνί = ἐν; tr. phrase 'among the front-fight-
 ers'
 ὁμιλέω I join battle
195 ἔγχος -εος, τό spear
 δηϊόων: part. (m. nom. s.) of δηϊόω (cf.
 83), here intrans. 'causing havoc'
 περί (+ gen.) (here) over, for the sake of
 θανόντος: aor. part. (m. gen. s.) of θνήσκω (cf. 12)
197 ἡμεῖς we; καὶ ἡμεῖς 'we too', i.e. the gods
 ἴδμεν: 1 pl. pres. of οἶδα (cf. 53; = Att.
 ἴσμεν)
 ὅ = ὅτι that
 τοι: used as at 130
 ἔχονται (lit.) are held, i.e. are in their
 possession (cf. 130)
198 αὔτως (adv.) just as you are
 τάφρος -ου, ὁ ditch, trench. On Nestor's
 advice, the Achaeans had dug this
 ditch to defend their camp, reinforced
 it with vertical stakes, and erected a
 gated wall (7.436–41).
 ἰών: part. (m. nom. s.) of εἶμι (I go), here
 'go and'
 φαίνομαι I appear, show myself; φάνηθι is
 2 s. aor. imper.
199 αἴ κε (+ subj.) in the hope that (cf. 143)
 ὑποδείδω I come to fear; ὑποδείσαντες is
 aor. part. (m. nom. pl.)
 ἀπέχομαι I hold back from (+ gen.);
 ἀπόσχωνται is 3 pl. aor. subj.

Τρῶες, ἀναπνεύσωσι δ᾽ ἀρήϊοι υἷες Ἀχαιῶν   200
τειρόμενοι· ὀλίγη δέ τ᾽ ἀνάπνευσις πολέμοιο."
    Ἡ μὲν ἄρ᾽ ὡς εἰποῦσ᾽ ἀπέβη πόδας ὠκέα Ἶρις,
αὐτὰρ Ἀχιλλεὺς ὦρτο Διῒ φίλος· ἀμφὶ δ᾽ Ἀθήνη
ὤμοις ἰφθίμοισι βάλ᾽ αἰγίδα θυσσανόεσσαν,
ἀμφὶ δέ οἱ κεφαλῇ νέφος ἔστεφε δῖα θεάων   205
χρύσεον, ἐκ δ᾽ αὐτοῦ δαῖε φλόγα παμφανόωσαν.
ὡς δ᾽ ὅτε καπνὸς ἰὼν ἐξ ἄστεος αἰθέρ᾽ ἵκηται,
τηλόθεν ἐκ νήσου, τὴν δήϊοι ἀμφιμάχωνται,
οἵ τε πανημέριοι στυγερῷ κρίνονται Ἄρηϊ
ἄστεος ἐκ σφετέρου· ἅμα δ᾽ ἠελίῳ καταδύντι   210
πυρσοί τε φλεγέθουσιν ἐπήτριμοι, ὑψόσε δ᾽ αὐγὴ
γίγνεται ἀΐσσουσα περικτιόνεσσιν ἰδέσθαι,
αἴ κέν πως σὺν νηυσὶν ἄρεω ἀλκτῆρες ἵκωνται·
ὡς ἀπ᾽ Ἀχιλλῆος κεφαλῆς σέλας αἰθέρ᾽ ἵκανε·
στῆ δ᾽ ἐπὶ τάφρον ἰὼν ἀπὸ τείχεος, οὐδ᾽ ἐς Ἀχαιοὺς   215

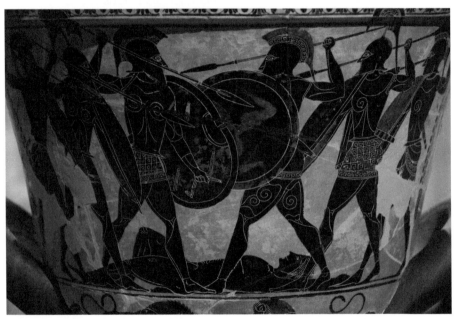

9. Homeric battle over body of a dead warrior, possibly Patroclus. Attic black-figure krater, c.530 BCE. National Archaeological Museum, Athens.

200 ἀναπνέω I breathe again, rest myself;
    ἀναπνεύσωσι is 3 pl. aor. subj.
    ἀρήϊος -η -ον warlike (= Att. ἄρειος -α -ον)
    υἷες: 3rd decl. form nom. pl. of υἱός (cf. 12)
201 ὀλίγος -η -ον little, small
    τ(ε): generalising in a proverbial statement 'any respite in war is little', implying 'but valuable'

ἀνάπνευσις -εως, ἡ respite in, rest from (+ gen.). Nestor used words almost identical with 199–201 at 11.799–801, recommending that Patroclus go to battle in Achilles' armour; Patroclus relayed them to Achilles at 16.41–3.

202–21: Athena enhances Achilles' power.

202 εἰποῦσ(α): aor. part. (f. nom. s.) of λέγω (cf. 5)

ἀποβαίνω I go away; ἀπέβη is 3 s. aor.

πόδας ὠκέα: Iris is here given f. version of Achilles' standard epithet (cf. on 78)

203 ὦρτο: 3 s. aor. mid. of ὄρνυμι (cf. 170). Achilles here abandons the quarrel he has maintained since Book 1. He has no armour and he is not going to fight immediately, but the aegis and the crown constitute a symbolic, divine arming scene.

ἀμφί (+ dat.) around

Ἀθήνη -ης, ἡ Athena (= Att. Ἀθηνᾶ -ᾶς). She is a warrior goddess and represented by Homer as probably the most powerful divinity after Zeus. She is determinedly on the side of the Achaeans throughout the *Iliad* (though not always in other parts of the Epic Cycle).

204 ὤμοις (cf. 132): i.e. Achilles' shoulders

ἴφθιμος -η -ον strong

βάλλω I throw; βάλ(ε) is 3 s. aor.

αἰγίς -ίδος, ἡ the aegis. In the *Iliad* it belongs to Zeus; he uses it himself or lends it to other gods. It takes the form of a tasselled protective cloak which inspires terror when shaken in the face of the enemy (5.738–42). Only here is it worn by a living mortal (cf. on 215). At 24.20 it is used by Apollo to protect the body of Patroclus. The term 'Aegis' has been adopted by the US military as the name of an anti-missile system capable of spreading a defensive shield over a target.

θυσσανόεις -εσσα -εν (-εντος) tasselled

205 οἱ κεφαλῇ on to him (dat. of pron.) on the head ('whole and part')

νέφος -εος, τό cloud

στέφω (here) I put … as a crown

θεάων: gen. pl. of θεά (cf. 37); δῖα (cf. 103) θεάων lit. 'noble among goddesses', i.e. 'noble goddess'

206 χρύσε(ι)ος -η -ον golden

δαίω I set ablaze

207 ἄστυ -εος, τό city. The blaze from Achilles' head is compared first to smoke rising from a besieged city, then to fire signals calling for rescue. The content of a simile usu. contrasts with the narrative. Here it is close, though with complex implications: the city suggests Troy, but it is the Achaeans who will be rescued by Achilles.

αἰθήρ -έρος, ὁ/ἡ upper air, sky

ἵκηται: 3 s. aor. subj. of ἱκνέομαι (cf. 64). The subj. here and in ἀμφιμάχωνται (208) is 'indefinite' (giving the sense 'whenever'). It occurs frequently in Homeric similes without the ἄν it would have in Att. (cf. on 135).

208 τηλόθεν (adv.) from far away

νῆσος -ου, ἡ island

δήϊος -η -ον hostile; pl. here as noun 'enemies'

ἀμφιμάχομαι (here) I fight around (+ acc.; cf. 20)

209 πανημέριος -η -ον (adj. used like adv.) all day long

στυγερός -ή -όν hateful

κρίνομαι I contend

Ἄρηϊ: dat. of Ἄρης (cf. 134); metonymy (naming by something associated) for 'war'

210 σφέτερος -η -ον their

καταδύω I sink, set; καταδύντι is aor. part. (m. dat. s.)

211 πυρσός -οῦ, ὁ beacon, fire signal

φλεγέθω I blaze, flare up

ἐπήτριμος -ον close together, one after another

ὑψόσε (adv.) upward

αὐγή -ῆς, ἡ brightness

212 ἀΐσσω I move swiftly, dart

περικτίονες -ων, οἱ those who live nearby

213 αἴ κεν (+ subj.) (here) in the hope that

πως (adv.) somehow, perhaps

ἄρεω: alternative gen. s. of Ἄρης (cf. 134), here treated as a common noun

ἵκωνται: 3 pl. aor. subj. of ἱκνέομαι (cf. 64)

214 σέλας, τό gleam

ἱκάνω I arrive at, reach; ἵκανε is 3 s. impf.

215 στῆ: 3 s. aor. of ἵσταμαι (cf. 160)

τεῖχος -εος, τό wall. Achilles is standing between the wall and the ditch. His appearance there is almost like the epiphany of a god.

μίσγετο· μητρὸς γὰρ πυκινὴν ὠπίζετ' ἐφετμήν.
ἔνθα στὰς ἤϋσ', ἀπάτερθε δὲ Παλλὰς Ἀθήνη
φθέγξατ'· ἀτὰρ Τρώεσσιν ἐν ἄσπετον ὦρσε κυδοιμόν.
ὡς δ' ὅτ' ἀριζήλη φωνή, ὅτε τ' ἴαχε σάλπιγξ
ἄστυ περιπλομένων δηΐων ὕπο θυμοραϊστέων,   220
ὣς τότ' ἀριζήλη φωνὴ γένετ' Αἰακίδαο.
οἱ δ' ὡς οὖν ἄϊον ὄπα χάλκεον Αἰακίδαο,
πᾶσιν ὀρίνθη θυμός· ἀτὰρ καλλίτριχες ἵπποι
ἂψ ὄχεα τρόπεον· ὄσσοντο γὰρ ἄλγεα θυμῷ.
ἡνίοχοι δ' ἔκπληγεν, ἐπεὶ ἴδον ἀκάματον πῦρ   225
δεινὸν ὑπὲρ κεφαλῆς μεγαθύμου Πηλείωνος
δαιόμενον· τὸ δὲ δαῖε θεὰ γλαυκῶπις Ἀθήνη.
τρὶς μὲν ὑπὲρ τάφρου μεγάλ' ἴαχε δῖος Ἀχιλλεύς,
τρὶς δὲ κυκήθησαν Τρῶες κλειτοί τ' ἐπίκουροι.
ἔνθα δὲ καὶ τότ' ὄλοντο δυώδεκα φῶτες ἄριστοι   230
ἀμφὶ σφοῖς ὀχέεσσι καὶ ἔγχεσιν. αὐτὰρ Ἀχαιοὶ
ἀσπασίως Πάτροκλον ὑπὲκ βελέων ἐρύσαντες
κάτθεσαν ἐν λεχέεσσι· φίλοι δ' ἀμφέσταν ἑταῖροι
μυρόμενοι· μετὰ δέ σφι ποδώκης εἵπετ' Ἀχιλλεὺς
δάκρυα θερμὰ χέων, ἐπεὶ εἴσιδε πιστὸν ἑταῖρον   235
κείμενον ἐν φέρτρῳ δεδαϊγμένον ὀξέϊ χαλκῷ,
τόν ῥ' ἤτοι μὲν ἔπεμπε σὺν ἵπποισιν καὶ ὄχεσφιν
ἐς πόλεμον, οὐδ' αὖτις ἐδέξατο νοστήσαντα.

216 μίσγω I mix, mingle; μίσγετο is 3 s. impf. mid.
πυκ(ι)νός -ή -όν (here) shrewd, wise (lit. 'close-packed', hence 'closely thought out')
ὀπίζομαι I respect, heed; ὠπίζετ(ο) is 3 s. impf.
ἐφετμή -ῆς, ἡ command. Thetis gave this at 134–5.
217 στάς: aor. part. (m. nom. s.) of ἵσταμαι (cf. 160)
αὔω I shout, cry out; ἤϋσ(ε) is 3 s. aor.
ἀπάτερθε (adv.) apart, at a distance
Παλλάς -άδος, ἡ Pallas (epithet of Athena of uncertain meaning, perhaps 'maiden' or 'weapon-brandishing')
218 φθέγγομαι I call out; φθέγξατ(ο) is 3 s. aor.
ἀτάρ (here) and so (cf. 21)
ἐνόρνυμι I arouse X (acc.) among Y (dat.); ἐν ... ὦρσε is tmesis of 3 s. aor.

κυδοιμός -ου, ὁ uproar, confusion. Achilles' heroic status is enhanced, not diminished, by divine support.
219 ἀρίζηλος -η -ον very clear, piercing (ἀρι- is an intensifying prefix)
φωνή -ῆς, ἡ voice, (here) sound (of trumpet)
τε: here generalising (cf. 106), as oft. in similes, where it is usu. redundant in tr.
ἴαχε (here) sounds; 3 s. impf. of ἰάχω (cf. 29) acting as gnomic aor. in a second, shorter simile involving a besieged city
σάλπιγξ -ιγγος, ἡ trumpet. Ancient scholars identified this as an anachronism, because trumpets are not used on the Homeric battlefield. As oft. in similes, the poet seems to be thinking of his own time.

220 περιπλόμενος -η -ον moving round, circling; usu. of time ('the circling years'),
  here uniquely of people (and trans.)
  ὕπο (+ gen.) (here) because of; accented
  as postposition

222–38: *Patroclus' body is rescued.*

222 ὡς (here) when
  οὖν (here) well then; the particle picks up
  the narrative from before the simile
  ἀΐω I hear; ἄϊον is 3 pl. impf.
  ὄψ ὀπός, ἡ voice
  χάλκεον (cf. 131): the adj. is more
  applicable to the trumpet to
  which Achilles' voice has just been
  compared
223 πᾶσιν: possessive dat.
  ὀρίνω I throw into confusion; ὀρίνθη is 3
  s. aor. pass.
  καλλίθριξ -τριχος (m. adj.) with beautiful
  mane
224 ὄχεα -ων, τά chariot(s). The word is pl.
  in form but can be s. or (as here) pl. in
  meaning.
  τροπέω I turn (something) round
  ὄσσομαι I foresee; ὄσσοντο is 3 pl. impf.
  ἄλγος -εος, τό pain, sorrow, pl. troubles
225 ἡνίοχος -ου, ὁ charioteer
  ἐκπλήσσω I terrify; ἔκπληγεν is 3 pl. aor.
  pass.
  ἴδον: 3 pl. aor. of ὁράω (cf. 61)
  ἀκάματος -ον untiring
226 δεινός -ή -όν terrible; n. here as adv. with
  δαιόμενον (227)
  ὑπέρ (+ gen.) over, above
  μεγάθυμος -ον great-hearted
227 δαιόμενον: pres. pass. part. (n. acc. s.) of
  δαίω (cf. 206) 'blazing'
  γλαυκῶπις -ιδος (f. adj.) gleaming-eyed,
  from γλαυκός ('gleaming'); the word
  also suggests γλαῦξ 'owl' and possibly
  gave rise to Athena's association with
  the bird. The reference to Athena
  rounds off the passage which began
  at 203.
229 κυκάω I stir up, throw into confusion;
  κυκήθησαν is 3 pl. aor. pass.
  κλειτός -ή -όν famous, renowned
  ἐπίκουρος -ον helping, (as m. pl. noun)
  allies

θυμοραϊστής -ᾱο/έω (m. adj.) life-
  destroying
221 Αἰακίδης -αο/εω, ὁ son or descendant
  of Aeacus (Achilles is his grandson)

230 ὄλοντο: 3 pl. aor. of ὄλλυμαι (cf. 80)
  δυώδεκα/δώδεκα twelve
  φώς φωτός, ὁ man (distinguish from Att.
  φῶς φωτός, τό light)
231 ἀμφί (+ dat.) (here) entangled in
  σφός -ή -όν their, their own. The Trojan
  charioteers are killed by their own or
  their comrades' weapons and chariots
  while retreating. Achilles dominates
  the battlefield to such effect that his
  mere presence causes death in the
  Trojan army.
232 ἀσπασίως (adv.) happily
  ὑπέκ (+ gen.) out from under (= ὑπό + ἐκ)
  ἐρύσαντες: aor. part. (m. nom. pl.) of
  ἐρύω (cf. 152)
233 κατατίθημι I lay (something) down;
  κάτθεσαν is 3 pl. aor.
  λέχος -εος, τό litter, bier; λεχέεσσι is dat.
  pl., here for s.
  ἀμφίσταμαι I stand around; ἀμφέσταν is
  3 pl. aor.
234 μύρομαι I weep
  μετά (+ dat.) (here) with
  σφι: dat. of σφεῖς (cf. 66)
  ποδώκης -ες swift-footed
  ἕπομαι I follow; εἵπετ(ο) is 3 s. impf.
235 εἰσοράω I look at; εἴσιδε is 3 s. aor.
  πιστός -ή -όν trusty, faithful
236 φέρτρον -ου, τό litter, bier
  δαΐζω I slash, cut to shreds; δεδαϊγμένον
  is perf. pass. part. (m. acc. s.)
  χαλκός -οῦ, ὁ bronze
237 τόν: here as rel. pron.
  ἤτοι truly, indeed. The particle emphasises that sending Patroclus into battle
  was Achilles' idea, and that he now
  feels the guilt of it.
  πέμπω I send; impf. here perhaps gives
  a sense of Achilles going over what
  happened
  ὄχεσφιν: Homeric dat. of ὄχεα (cf. 224)
238 ἐδέξατο: 3 s. aor. of δέχομαι (cf. 115)

Ἥλιον δ' ἀκάμαντα βοῶπις πότνια Ἥρη
πέμψεν ἐπ' Ὠκεανοῖο ῥοὰς ἀέκοντα νέεσθαι·   240
ἠέλιος μὲν ἔδυ, παύσαντο δὲ δῖοι Ἀχαιοὶ
φυλόπιδος κρατερῆς καὶ ὁμοιίου πτολέμοιο.

Τρῶες δ' αὖθ' ἑτέρωθεν ἀπὸ κρατερῆς ὑσμίνης
χωρήσαντες ἔλυσαν ὑφ' ἅρμασιν ὠκέας ἵππους,
ἐς δ' ἀγορὴν ἀγέροντο, πάρος δόρποιο μέδεσθαι.   245
ὀρθῶν δ' ἑσταότων ἀγορὴ γένετ', οὐδέ τις ἔτλη
ἕζεσθαι· πάντας γὰρ ἔχε τρόμος, οὕνεκ' Ἀχιλλεὺς
ἐξεφάνη, δηρὸν δὲ μάχης ἐπέπαυτ' ἀλεγεινῆς.
τοῖσι δὲ Πουλυδάμας πεπνυμένος ἦρχ' ἀγορεύειν
Πανθοΐδης· ὁ γὰρ οἶος ὅρα πρόσσω καὶ ὀπίσσω·   250
Ἕκτορι δ' ἦεν ἑταῖρος, ἰῇ δ' ἐν νυκτὶ γένοντο,
ἀλλ' ὁ μὲν ἂρ μύθοισιν, ὁ δ' ἔγχεϊ πολλὸν ἐνίκα·
ὅ σφιν ἐϋφρονέων ἀγορήσατο καὶ μετέειπεν·
"ἀμφὶ μάλα φράζεσθε, φίλοι· κέλομαι γὰρ ἔγωγε
ἄστυδε νῦν ἰέναι, μὴ μίμνειν ἠῶ δῖαν   255
ἐν πεδίῳ παρὰ νηυσίν· ἑκὰς δ' ἀπὸ τείχεός εἰμεν.
ὄφρα μὲν οὗτος ἀνὴρ Ἀγαμέμνονι μήνιε δίῳ,
τόφρα δὲ ῥηΐτεροι πολεμίζειν ἦσαν Ἀχαιοί·

239–42: Early sunset.

239 ἀκάμας -αντος (m. adj.) untiring
240 Ὠκεανός -ου/οῖο, ὁ Oceanus, the mighty
     river believed to surround the whole
     (flat) earth
     ῥοή -ῆς, ἡ stream
     ἀέκων -ουσα -ον (-οντος) (adj. tr. as
     adv.) unwillingly, reluctantly (= Att.
     ἄκων). The gods can quicken or slow
     down the sun's movement (Athena de-
     lays dawn in *Odyssey* 23.241–6). This

long day has been going on since the
sun rose at 11.1–2. It is Hector's day of
glory (as Zeus promised, 11.191–4);
it is appropriate that jealous Hera
should prematurely end it.
241 ἔδυ (here) sank, went down (into
     Oceanus); 3 s. aor. of δύω (cf. 140)
242 ὁμοιῖος = ὁμοῖος (cf. 120) (here) equally
     balanced; the second ι has to be
     scanned long.

243–314: Debate among the Trojans: they will stay out on the plain overnight.

243–8: The Trojans meet for a discussion. The urgency of this discussion is emphasised by the fact that they hold it at night, hungry, and standing up: another dramatic purpose achieved by Hera's acceleration of nightfall.

243 αὖθ' = αὖτε (cf. 6) before rough
     breathing
     ὑσμίνη -ης, ἡ battle
244 χωρέω I give way, withdraw; χωρήσαντες
     is aor. part. (m. nom. pl.)

ὑφ' = ὕπο (+ dat.) (here) from under; the
     expected gen. would not fit the metre
     ἅρμα -ατος, τό chariot
245 ἀγείρω I gather; ἀγέροντο is 3 pl. aor.
     mid.

πάρος (conj.) before (+ inf.)
δόρπον -ου/οιο, τό evening meal, supper
μέδομαι I think about (+ gen.)

246 ὀρθός -ή -όν upright
ἑσταότων: perf. part. (m. gen. pl.) of
    ἵσταμαι (cf. 160)
γένετ(ο): 3 s. aor. of γίγνομαι (cf. 19),
    here 'took place'
τλάω I dare, have the courage; ἔτλη is 3
    s. aor.

249–83: Polydamas' judicious speech.

249 Πουλυδάμας -αντος, ὁ Polydamas (the
    first syllable of his name is lengthened
    for the metre). At 16.535 he was one
    of the Trojan leaders called on by
    Glaucus to protect the dead Sarpedon.
    He is Hector's exact contemporary, to
    the day. The two are contrasted: Hec-
    tor the impetuous fighter, Polydamas
    the cautious counsellor. Polydamas
    offers advice on four occasions: 12.61–
    79, 12.211–28 (a confirmation of their
    uneasy relationship), 13.726–47 and
    here. Twice his advice is acceptable,
    and twice it is offensively rejected (as
    in this passage).
πεπνυμένος -η -ον prudent
ἄρχω I begin; ἦρχ(ε) is 3 s. impf.

250 Πανθοΐδης -αο/εω, ὁ son of Panthus.
    Panthus is one of the Trojan elders
    sitting with Priam on the city wall at
    3.146, whose talk is like the chirping
    of cicadas.
οἶος -η -ον alone
ὅρα: 3 s. impf. of ὁράω (cf. 61)
πρόσσω (adv.) ahead
ὀπίσσω (adv.) behind. The past is ahead
    of you (you can see it), the future
    behind (you can't see it). The phrase is
    used of practical rather than prophetic
    wisdom.

251 ἰῆ = μιᾷ, f. dat. of εἷς one
νύξ νυκτός, ἡ night
γένοντο: 3 pl. aor. of γίγνομαι (cf. 19),
    here 'were born'

252 ὁ μέν ... ὁ δέ one (i.e. Polydamas) ... the
    other (i.e. Hector)
μῦθος -ου, ὁ speech, word

247 ἕζομαι I sit down
τρόμος -ου, ὁ trembling
οὕνεκ(α) because

248 ἐκφαίνω I bring to light, mid. I
    appear; ἐξεφάνη is 3 s. aor. pass. with
    mid. sense
δέ: almost a parenthesis 'and it was a
    long time ...'
ἐπέπαυτ(ο): 3 s. plup. of παύομαι (cf.
    125)

πολλόν = πολύ (as adv.) much, very
νικάω (here) I am superior

253 σφιν: dat. of σφεῖς (cf. 66)
ἐϋφρονέων -ουσα -ον (-οντος) with good
    intent
ἀγοράομαι I speak in assembly; ἀγορή-
    σατο is 3 s. aor.
μετεῖπον (aor.) I spoke among, spoke to
    (+ dat.)

254 ἀμφί (as adv.) (here) on both sides (of the
    question)
μάλα (here) hard, seriously
φράζομαι I consider, think; φράζεσθε is 2
    pl. imper.
κέλομαι I urge
ἔγωγε = ἐγώ + γε; emphatic, 'I for my
    part'

255 ἄστυδε to the city
ἰέναι: inf. of εἶμι (I go)
μίμνω = μένω (cf. 64), here trans. 'wait for'
ἠώς ἠοῦς (acc. ἠῶ), ἡ dawn (= Att. ἕως ἕω)

256 ἑκάς (adv.) far
δ(έ): rather than the expected γάρ, as
    Polydamas is pointing out a separate
    disadvantage of their present position
τείχεος (cf. 215): here the city wall, not
    the wall round the Achaean ships
εἶμεν = ἐσμεν

257 ὄφρα μέν ... τόφρα δέ as long as ... so
    long
οὗτος αὕτη τοῦτο this; Polydamas avoids
    naming Achilles
μηνίω I am angry at (+ dat.); μήνιε is 3 s.
    impf.

258 ῥηΐτερος -η -ον easier (= Att. ῥᾴων -ον)
πολεμίζω I make war against; inf. here
    explanatory

χαίρεσκον γὰρ ἔγωγε θοῇς ἐπὶ νηυσὶν ἰαύων
ἐλπόμενος νῆας αἱρησέμεν ἀμφιελίσσας.   260
νῦν δ᾽ αἰνῶς δείδοικα ποδώκεα Πηλείωνα·
οἷος ἐκείνου θυμὸς ὑπέρβιος, οὐκ ἐθελήσει
μίμνειν ἐν πεδίῳ, ὅθι περ Τρῶες καὶ Ἀχαιοὶ
ἐν μέσῳ ἀμφότεροι μένος Ἄρηος δατέονται,
ἀλλὰ περὶ πτόλιός τε μαχήσεται ἠδὲ γυναικῶν.   265
ἀλλ᾽ ἴομεν προτὶ ἄστυ, πίθεσθέ μοι· ὧδε γὰρ ἔσται·
νῦν μὲν νὺξ ἀπέπαυσε ποδώκεα Πηλεΐωνα
ἀμβροσίη· εἰ δ᾽ ἄμμε κιχήσεται ἐνθάδ᾽ ἐόντας
αὔριον ὁρμηθεὶς σὺν τεύχεσιν, εὖ νύ τις αὐτὸν
γνώσεται· ἀσπασίως γὰρ ἀφίξεται Ἴλιον ἱρὴν   270
ὅς κε φύγῃ, πολλοὺς δὲ κύνες καὶ γῦπες ἔδονται
Τρώων· αἲ γὰρ δή μοι ἀπ᾽ οὔατος ὧδε γένοιτο.
εἰ δ᾽ ἂν ἐμοῖς ἐπέεσσι πιθώμεθα κηδόμενοί περ,
νύκτα μὲν εἰν ἀγορῇ σθένος ἕξομεν, ἄστυ δὲ πύργοι
ὑψηλαί τε πύλαι σανίδες τ᾽ ἐπὶ τῆς ἀραρυῖαι   275
μακραὶ ἐΰξεστοι ἐζευγμέναι εἰρύσσονται·
πρῶϊ δ᾽ ὑπηοῖοι σὺν τεύχεσι θωρηχθέντες
στησόμεθ᾽ ἂμ πύργους· τῷ δ᾽ ἄλγιον, αἴ κ᾽ ἐθέλησιν
ἐλθὼν ἐκ νηῶν περὶ τείχεος ἄμμι μάχεσθαι.
ἂψ πάλιν εἶσ᾽ ἐπὶ νῆας, ἐπεί κ᾽ ἐριαύχενας ἵππους   280
παντοίου δρόμου ἄσῃ ὑπὸ πτόλιν ἠλασκάζων·
εἴσω δ᾽ οὔ μιν θυμὸς ἐφορμηθῆναι ἐάσει,
οὐδέ ποτ᾽ ἐκπέρσει· πρίν μιν κύνες ἀργοὶ ἔδονται."

259 χαίρω I rejoice, enjoy (+ part.); χαίρε-σκον is 1 s. aor. iterative
γάρ: the train of thought seems to be 'For I did enjoy sleeping out here when I hoped to capture the Achaean ships – but now (261) …', though in fact the Trojans have only spent one night out of the city, the one that began at the end of Book 8 with a marvellous description of the Trojan campfires dotted over the plain in the dark (8.555–61)
θοός -ή -όν swift, fast
ἰαύω I sleep
260 ἔλπομαι I hope
αἱρησέμεν: fut. inf. of αἱρέω (cf. 23)
ἀμφιέλισσα -ης (f. adj.) curved
261 αἰνῶς (adv.) terribly
δείδοικα (perf. with pres. sense) I fear; alternative form of δείδια (cf. 34)

262 οἷος …: 'such is … (that) …' (cf. 95)
ὑπέρβιος -ον over-violent
οὐκ ἐθελήσει he will not be willing; 3 s. fut. of ἐθέλω (cf. 116)
263 ὅθι (adv.) where; περ here gives emphasis 'just where'
264 μέσ(σ)ος -η -ον (adj.) middle (part of); ἐν μέσῳ 'in the middle'
μένος -εος, τό fighting spirit
δατέομαι I divide, share
265 περί: used as at 195
π(τ)όλις -ιος, ἡ city (= Att. πόλις -εως)
μαχήσεται: 3 s. fut. of μάχομαι (cf. 14)
ἠδέ and
γυνή -αικός, ἡ woman, wife
266 ἴομεν: 1 pl. subj. of εἶμι (I go), here jussive and again with short vowel
προτί = πρός (cf. 5)
πείθομαι I trust, obey (+ dat.); πίθεσθε is 2 pl. aor. imper.

ὧδε (adv.) so, in this way

ἔσται: 3 s. fut. of εἰμί. The three short clauses in this line express Polydamas' sense of urgency.

267 ἀποπαύω I hold in check; ἀπέπαυσε is 3 s. aor.

268 ἀμβρόσιος -η -ον divine

ἄμμε us (acc., = Att. ἡμᾶς)

κιχήσεται: 3 s. fut. of κιχάνω (cf. 114)

ἐνθάδε (adv.) here

ἐόντας: part. (m. acc. pl.) of εἰμί (= ὄντας)

269 αὔριον (adv.) tomorrow

ὁρμάομαι I rush, charge out; ὁρμηθείς is aor. part. (m. nom. s.)

νυ: emphatic particle, suggesting 'surely', 'of course'

270 γνώσεται: 3 s. fut. of γιγνώσκω (cf. 125), here 'will recognise'

ἀφικνέομαι I arrive at, reach; ἀφίξεται is 3 s. fut.

ἱ(ε)ρός -ή -όν sacred

271 ὅς κε (+ subj.) whoever

φύγῃ: 3 s. aor. subj. of φεύγω (cf. 117), here indefinite

γύψ γυπός, ὁ vulture

ἔδω I eat (= Att. ἐσθίω); ἔδονται is 3 pl. fut.

272 αἴ γάρ (+ opt.) may ...! (introducing a wish)

οὖς οὔατος, τό ear

γένοιτο: 3 s. aor. opt. of γίγνομαι (cf. 19); 'may it happen away from my ear', i.e. 'may I never hear that news'

273 εἰ ... ἄν = ἐάν (+ subj.) if (introducing fut. open condition)

ἐπέεσσι: dat. pl. of ἔπος (cf. 72)

πιθώμεθα: 1 pl. aor. subj. of πείθομαι (cf. 266)

κήδομαι I am in distress; κηδόμενοί is part. (m. nom. pl.) with περ 'distressed though we are'

274 νύκτα: acc. of time how long, i.e. 'the whole night'

εἰν = ἐν

ἀγορή -ῆς, ἡ (here) meeting-place (cf. 106)

σθένος εος, τό strength, (here) 'our forces'

ἕξομεν: 1 pl. fut. of ἔχω (cf. 21), here 'we shall keep'

ἄστυ: object of εἰρύσσονται (276)

πύργος -ου, ὁ tower

275 ὑψηλός -ή -όν high

πύλη -ης, ἡ gate, (here) gatepost

σανίς -ίδος, ἡ board, (pl. here) door

ἐπί (+ dat.) to, on to

τῆς = ταῖς (f. dat. pl.) them, i.e. the gateposts

ἀραρίσκω I fit; ἀραρυῖαι is perf. part. (f. nom. pl.) with pass. sense 'fitted'

276 ἐΰξεστος -η -ον well-polished

ζεύγνυμι I yoke, join; ἐζευγμέναι is perf. pass. part. (f. nom. pl.) 'closed' (of the doors)

ἐρύομαι I protect, guard; εἰρύσσονται is 3 pl. fut. Polydamas devotes more than two lines to the security the city will offer, indicating the vehemence with which he makes his point.

277 πρῶϊ (adv.) early, in the morning

ὑπηοῖος -η -ον (adj. used like adv.) at dawn

θωρηχθέντες: aor. pass. part. (m. nom. pl.) of θωρήσσω (cf. 167)

278 στησόμεθ(α): 1 pl. fut. of ἵσταμαι (cf. 160)

ἄμ = ἀνά (+ acc.) up on

τῷ for him, i.e. Achilles

ἄλγιον more painful, worse (n. comp. adj. formed from ἄλγος, cf. 224); understand ἔσται, 3 s. fut. of εἰμί – 'it will be ...'

αἴ κε (+ subj.) (here) if

279 περί (+ gen.) (here) around

ἄμμι (with) us (dat., = Att. ἡμῖν)

280 ἄψ πάλιν back again

εἶσ(ι): 3 s. of εἶμι (I go), with fut. sense

ἐπεί κε (+ subj.) when; with fut. main verb (cf. 121)

ἐριαύχην -ενος (m. adj.) high-necked

281 παντοῖος -η -ον of every kind; here implying 'in every direction'

δρόμος -ου, ὁ running

ἄω I give X (acc.) a fill of Y (gen.); ἄσῃ is 3 s. aor. subj.

ὑπό (+ acc.) (here) under the walls of

ἠλασκάζω I wander about

282 εἴσω (adv.) inside

ἐφορμάομαι I make an attack; ἐφορμηθῆναι is aor. inf.

ἐάσει: 3 s. fut. of ἐάω (cf. 112)

283 ποτ(έ) (adv.) (here) ever

ἐκπέρθω I sack, destroy; ἐκπέρσει is 3 s. fut.

πρίν before (that happens)

ἀργός -ή -όν swift

Τὸν δ' ἄρ' ὑπόδρα ἰδὼν προσέφη κορυθαίολος Ἕκτωρ·
"Πουλυδάμα, σὺ μὲν οὐκέτ' ἐμοὶ φίλα ταῦτ' ἀγορεύεις,   285
ὃς κέλεαι κατὰ ἄστυ ἀλήμεναι αὖτις ἰόντας.
ἦ οὔ πω κεκόρησθε ἐελμένοι ἔνδοθι πύργων;
πρὶν μὲν γὰρ Πριάμοιο πόλιν μέροπες ἄνθρωποι
πάντες μυθέσκοντο πολύχρυσον πολύχαλκον·
νῦν δὲ δὴ ἐξαπόλωλε δόμων κειμήλια καλά,   290
πολλὰ δὲ δὴ Φρυγίην καὶ Μῃονίην ἐρατεινὴν
κτήματα περνάμεν' ἵκει, ἐπεὶ μέγας ὠδύσατο Ζεύς.
νῦν δ' ὅτε πέρ μοι ἔδωκε Κρόνου πάϊς ἀγκυλομήτεω
κῦδος ἀρέσθ' ἐπὶ νηυσί, θαλάσσῃ τ' ἔλσαι Ἀχαιούς,
νήπιε, μηκέτι ταῦτα νοήματα φαῖν' ἐνὶ δήμῳ·   295
οὐ γάρ τις Τρώων ἐπιπείσεται· οὐ γὰρ ἐάσω.
ἀλλ' ἄγεθ' ὡς ἂν ἐγὼ εἴπω, πειθώμεθα πάντες.
νῦν μὲν δόρπον ἕλεσθε κατὰ στρατὸν ἐν τελέεσσι,
καὶ φυλακῆς μνήσασθε, καὶ ἐγρήγορθε ἕκαστος·
Τρώων δ' ὃς κτεάτεσσιν ὑπερφιάλως ἀνιάζει,   300
συλλέξας λαοῖσι δότω καταδημοβορῆσαι·
τῶν τινα βέλτερόν ἐστιν ἐπαυρέμεν ἤ περ Ἀχαιούς.
πρῶϊ δ' ὑπηοῖοι σὺν τεύχεσι θωρηχθέντες
νηυσὶν ἔπι γλαφυρῇσιν ἐγείρομεν ὀξὺν Ἄρηα.
εἰ δ' ἐτεὸν παρὰ ναῦφιν ἀνέστη δῖος Ἀχιλλεύς,   305

284–96: Hector harshly dismisses Polydamas' proposal.

284 ὑπόδρα (adv.) sternly, with a frown
 ἰδών: aor. part. (m. nom. s.) of ὁράω (cf. 61), here 'looking at'
285 οὐκέτι (adv.) no longer; tr. with φίλα
 φίλος -η -ον (here) pleasing
286 κέλεαι: 2 s. of κέλομαι (cf. 254)
 κατὰ ἄστυ: hiatus because ἄστυ originally began with digamma (cf. on 5)
 ἀλήμεναι: aor. pass. inf. of εἴλω (cf. 76)
 ἰόντας: pres. part. (m. acc. pl.) of εἶμι (I go), here 'go and …' (cf. on 62)
287 ἦ: introduces question
 οὔ πω not yet
 κορέννυμι I satisfy; κεκόρησθε is 2 pl. perf. pass. 'had enough of'
 ἐελμένοι: perf. pass. part. (m. nom. pl.) of εἴλω (cf. 76)
 ἔνδοθι (+ gen.) within

288 πρὶν μὲν … νῦν δέ (290) in the past … but now
 μέροπες -ων (m. pl. adj.) mortal
289 μυθέομαι I speak of as, call; μυθέσκοντο is 3 pl. impf. iterative 'used to …'
 πολύχρυσος -ον rich in gold
 πολύχαλκος -ον rich in bronze
290 ἐξαπόλλυμαι I perish, (here) vanish; ἐξαπόλωλε is 3 s. perf.
 κειμήλιον -ου, τό treasure
291 Φρυγίη -ης, ἡ Phrygia (= Att. Φρυγία -ας)
 Μῃονίη -ης, ἡ Maeonia (= Att. Μαιονία -ας). These are regions of Asia Minor: Phrygia to the north and east of Troy, and Maeonia to the south of Phrygia. They have presumably acquired Trojan wealth in return for military aid, or as ransom for Trojans sold by the Achaeans as slaves.
 ἐρατεινός -ή -όν lovely

292 κτῆμα -ατος, τό possession, pl. treasures

πέρνημι I sell; περνάμεν(α) is pres. pass. part. (n. nom. pl.)

ἵκω I come to, reach

ὀδύσσομαι I become angry; ὠδύσατο is 3 s. aor.

293 περ: with ὅτε 'just at the moment when' (cf. 263)

ἔδωκε: 3 s. aor. of δίδωμι (cf. 84), here 'has granted'

Κρόνος -ου, ὁ Cronus, father of Zeus

ἀγκυλομήτης -εω (m. adj.) of crooked counsel, wily

294 ἀρέσθ(αι): aor. inf. of ἄρνυμαι (cf. 121)

ἐπί (+ dat.) at, by

θαλάσσῃ: here dat. of destination 'towards the sea'. The two expressions of location are emphatically juxtaposed as expressions of Hector's pride.

ἔλσαι: aor. inf. of εἴλω (cf. 76)

297–313: Hector's own proposal.

297 ἄγεθ' = ἄγετε come on, …!

εἴπω: 1 s. subj. of εἶπον, aor. of λέγω (cf. 5); here 'prospective' (i.e. like fut.). This standard line (eight times in the *Iliad*) makes a transition between two passages of high intensity.

πειθώμεθα: 1 pl. subj. of πείθομαι (cf. 266), here jussive

298 ἔλεσθε: 2 pl. aor. mid. imper. of αἱρέω (cf. 23)

κατά (+ acc.) throughout

στρατός -οῦ, ὁ army, camp (usu. sense in the *Iliad*)

τέλος -εος, τό (here) unit, company

299 φυλάκη -ης, ἡ watch, guard

μιμνήσκομαι I turn my thoughts to (+ gen.); μνήσασθε is 2 pl. aor. imper.

ἐγείρομαι I wake up; ἐγρήγορθε is 2 pl. perf. imper. 'stay awake'

ἕκαστος (cf. 31): with pl. verb for sense rather than strict grammar

300 κτεάτεσσιν (dat. pl. only), τοῖς (n.) possessions

ὑπερφιάλως (adv.) excessively

ἀνιάζω I am burdened with (+ dat.)

301 συλλέγω I collect, gather up; συλλέξας is aor. part. (m. nom. s.)

295 νήπιος -η -ον childish, foolish; (voc. here) 'you fool!' The train of thought is 'just when we are winning, you tell us to give it all up!' In his fury Hector breaks off and switches to a sharp command.

μηκέτι (adv.) no longer

νόημα -τος, τό thought, idea

φαίνω I reveal, (here) put forward; there is angry sarcasm in Hector's use of the word

δῆμος -ου, ὁ people, community

296 οὐ … τις none

ἐπιπείθομαι I am convinced; ἐπιπείσεται is 3 s. fut.

ἐάσω: 1 s. fut. of ἐάω (cf. 112). Hector's words are probably an understatement. At 12.250 he threatened to kill Polydamas if he persisted in giving unwarlike advice.

λαοῖσι (cf. 153): note that this word is usu. pl. (as here), with collective s. sense

δότω: 3 s. aor. imper. of δίδωμι (cf. 84)

καταδημοβορέω I consume in common; καταδημοβορῆσαι is aor. inf. expressing purpose

302 τῶν of them, i.e. the Trojans

βέλτερος -η -ον better; n. here with ἐστιν introducing acc. + inf. ('it is better for X to …')

ἐπαυρίσκω I enjoy, get the benefit of; ἐπαυρέμεν is aor. inf.

ἤ than

περ: contributes to the sardonic tone of Hector's words

303 = 277: Hector sarcastically echoes Polydamas' words to preface his own very different suggestion

304 ἔπι: accented as postposition

γλαφυρός -ή -όν hollow

ἐγείρω (here) I stir up; ἐγείρομεν is 1 pl. aor. subj., here jussive and again with short vowel

305 ἐτεόν (adv.) truly

ναῦφιν: dat. pl. of νηῦς (cf. 3)

ἀνίσταμαι I stand up, rise up; ἀνέστη is 3 s. aor.

ἄλγιον, αἴ κ' ἐθέλησι, τῷ ἔσσεται· οὔ μιν ἔγωγε
φεύξομαι ἐκ πολέμοιο δυσηχέος, ἀλλὰ μάλ' ἄντην
στήσομαι, ἤ κε φέρησι μέγα κράτος, ἤ κε φεροίμην.
ξυνὸς Ἐνυάλιος, καί τε κτανέοντα κατέκτα."

    Ὣς Ἕκτωρ ἀγόρευ', ἐπὶ δὲ Τρῶες κελάδησαν,   310
νήπιοι· ἐκ γάρ σφεων φρένας εἵλετο Παλλὰς Ἀθήνη·
Ἕκτορι μὲν γὰρ ἐπήνησαν κακὰ μητιόωντι,
Πουλυδάμαντι δ' ἄρ' οὔ τις, ὃς ἐσθλὴν φράζετο βουλήν.
δόρπον ἔπειθ' εἵλοντο κατὰ στρατόν· αὐτὰρ Ἀχαιοὶ
παννύχιοι Πάτροκλον ἀνεστενάχοντο γοῶντες.   315
τοῖσι δὲ Πηλεΐδης ἁδινοῦ ἐξῆρχε γόοιο,
χεῖρας ἐπ' ἀνδροφόνους θέμενος στήθεσσιν ἑταίρου,
πυκνὰ μάλα στενάχων, ὥς τε λὶς ἠϋγένειος,
ᾧ ῥά θ' ὑπὸ σκύμνους ἐλαφηβόλος ἁρπάσῃ ἀνὴρ
ὕλης ἐκ πυκινῆς· ὁ δέ τ' ἄχνυται ὕστερος ἐλθών,   320
πολλὰ δέ τ' ἄγκε' ἐπῆλθε μετ' ἀνέρος ἴχνι' ἐρευνῶν,
εἴ ποθεν ἐξεύροι· μάλα γὰρ δριμὺς χόλος αἱρεῖ·
ὣς ὁ βαρὺ στενάχων μετεφώνεε Μυρμιδόνεσσιν·
"ὢ πόποι, ἦ ῥ' ἅλιον ἔπος ἔκβαλον ἤματι κείνῳ
θαρσύνων ἥρωα Μενοίτιον ἐν μεγάροισι·   325

306 ἄλγιον ...: Hector again echoes Polyda-
    mas (cf. 278)
    ἔσσεται: 3 s. fut. of εἰμί
307 φεύγω (here) I run away from; φεύξομαι
    is 1 s. fut., here with μιν as object.
    This is exactly what he will do at
    22.136–7.
    δυσηχής -ές evil-sounding, hateful
    ἄντην (adv.) opposite, in front
308 στήσομαι: 1 s. fut. of ἵσταμαι (cf. 160)
    ἤ ... ἤ whether ... or (here equivalent to
    Att. εἴτε ... εἴτε)
    φέρησι: 3 s. subj. of φέρω (cf. 137), here
    prospective (cf. on 297)
    κράτος -εος, τό (here) victory
    φεροίμην: 1 s. opt. mid. of φέρω, with
    mid. sense 'win'; κε + opt. indicates a
    less likely possibility than κε + subj.,
    so perhaps mock-modest 'I might just
    possibly win'
309 ξυνός -ή -όν common, even-handed (=
    Att. κοινός)
    Ἐνυάλιος -ου, ὁ Enyalius (a title of Ares;
    in origin a separate war god)

κτανέοντα: fut. part. (m. acc. s.) of κτείνω
    (cf. 99) 'the one who is about to kill'
κατακτείνω I kill; κατέκτα is 3 s. aor.,
    here gnomic. This (along with the
    generalising τε and striking allit-
    eration of κ) marks a proverbial
    expression, suitable for winding up
    the speech. In it Hector makes his
    own death certain, as Achilles made
    his own death certain by his resolve
    to avenge Patroclus. Achilles knows
    it; Hector does not. There is pathos
    in both.
310 ἐπί (as adv.) thereupon
    κελαδέω I shout in applause; κελάδησαν
    is 3 pl. aor.
311 νήπιοι fools that they were (cf. 295); em-
    phasis by enjambment ending a sense
    unit is particularly common with this
    adj.
    ἐξαιρέω I take away, remove; ἐκ ... εἵλετο
    is tmesis of 3 s. aor. mid. The gods
    often help their favourites by affecting
    their opponents' judgement.

σφέων: gen. of σφεῖς (cf. 66)

φρένες -ῶν, αἱ (here) wits

312 ἐπαινέω I give approval to (+ dat.);
ἐπήνησαν is 3 pl. aor.
μητιάω I devise, plan; μητιόωντι is pres.
part. (m. dat. s.)

313 φράζετο: 3 s. of φράζομαι (cf. 254), here
'devised'
βουλή -ης, ἡ plan. Lines 311–13 constitute a rare comment by the poet,
steering the listener to see Hector's
policy as ill-advised and ill-fated.

314–55: Patroclus' body is brought to Achilles and cared for.

314–22: Achilles leads the lament for Patroclus; lion simile.

314 The abrupt mid-line transition allows
us no time to draw breath between
scenes. Contrast the substantial transition passage 239–42.

315 παννύχιος -η -όν (adj. used like adv.) all
night long
ἀναστενάχω I groan aloud for; ἀνεστενάχοντο is 3 pl. impf. mid.
γοάω I wail, lament

316 τοῖσι among them
ἐξῆρχε: cf. 51

317 ἐπιτίθημι I lay X (acc.) on Y (dat.); ἐπ(ί)
... θέμενος is tmesis of aor. mid. part.
(m. nom. s.)
στήθεσσιν: dat. pl. of στῆθος (cf. 31); here
pl. for s.

318 πυκνά: n. pl. of πυκ(ι)νός (cf. 216) as adv.
'repeatedly'
μάλα (adv.) very much, (here) loudly
στενάχω I groan
λίς acc. λῖν, ὁ lion. The simile's point of
contact with the narrative is the sound
made by Achilles. In addition, both
he and the lion have suffered a loss
that could have been avoided, and
both are furiously in search of the one
responsible.

ἠϋγένειος -ον with fine beard and/or
mane (= Att. εὐγένειος)

319 ᾧ (here) from whom (dat. of disadvan-
tage)
ὑφαρπάζω I snatch away; ὑπό ... ἁρπάσῃ is tmesis of 3 s. aor. subj. Note
that ὑπό in compounds often suggests
stealth; also again subj. in a simile (cf.
207).
σκύμνος -ου, ὁ cub
ἐλαφηβόλος -ου, ὁ deer hunter; ἐλαφηβόλος ἀνήρ 'hunter-man' (noun as adj.)

320 ὕλη -ης, ἡ wood, forest
πυκ(ι)νός -ή -όν (here) dense (cf. 216)
ὁ δέ: i.e. the lion
ὕστερος -η -ον (adj. used like adv.) later,
(here) too late

321 ἄγκε(α), τά valleys, gorges
ἐπέρχομαι I pass through; ἐπῆλθε is 3 s.
aor., here gnomic
μετ(ά) (+ acc.) after, in pursuit of
ἴχνια -ων, τά footprints
ἐρευνάω I trace, track

322 εἴ ποθεν (+ opt.) to see if ... somewhere
ἐξευρίσκω I find, come upon; ἐξεύροι is 3
s. aor. opt.
δριμύς -εῖα -ύ sharp

323–42: Achilles addresses the Myrmidons and the dead Patroclus. Another carefully balanced speech, with four lines of how things might have been, one line of proverbial generalisation, and four lines of how things are.

323 ὁ: i.e. Achilles
μεταφωνέω I speak among (+ dat.)

324 ὢ πόποι well, now! (expressing grief
and/or disagreeable surprise)
ἦ ῥα so after all
ἅλιος -η -ον fruitless

ἐκβάλλω I throw out, (here) let fall

325 θαρσύνω I encourage, cheer (= Att. θαρρύνω)
ἥρωα: acc. of ἥρως (cf. 56)
μέγαρον -ου/οιο, τό hall, pl. house,
palace

φῆν δέ οἱ εἰς Ὀπόεντα περικλυτὸν υἱὸν ἀπάξειν
Ἴλιον ἐκπέρσαντα, λαχόντα τε ληΐδος αἶσαν.
ἀλλ᾽ οὐ Ζεὺς ἄνδρεσσι νοήματα πάντα τελευτᾷ·
ἄμφω γὰρ πέπρωται ὁμοίην γαῖαν ἐρεῦσαι
αὐτοῦ ἐνὶ Τροίῃ, ἐπεὶ οὐδ᾽ ἐμὲ νοστήσαντα   330
δέξεται ἐν μεγάροισι γέρων ἱππηλάτα Πηλεύς
οὐδὲ Θέτις μήτηρ, ἀλλ᾽ αὐτοῦ γαῖα καθέξει.
νῦν δ᾽ ἐπεὶ οὖν, Πάτροκλε, σεῦ ὕστερος εἶμ᾽ ὑπὸ γαῖαν,
οὔ σε πρὶν κτεριῶ, πρίν γ᾽ Ἕκτορος ἐνθάδ᾽ ἐνεῖκαι
τεύχεα καὶ κεφαλήν, μεγαθύμου σοῖο φονῆος·   335
δώδεκα δὲ προπάροιθε πυρῆς ἀποδειροτομήσω
Τρώων ἀγλαὰ τέκνα, σέθεν κταμένοιο χολωθείς.
τόφρα δέ μοι παρὰ νηυσὶ κορωνίσι κείσεαι αὔτως,
ἀμφὶ δὲ σὲ Τρῳαὶ καὶ Δαρδανίδες βαθύκολποι
κλαύσονται νύκτας τε καὶ ἤματα δάκρυ χέουσαι,   340
τὰς αὐτοὶ καμόμεσθα βίηφί τε δουρί τε μακρῷ,
πιείρας πέρθοντε πόλεις μερόπων ἀνθρώπων."
   Ὣς εἰπὼν ἑτάροισιν ἐκέκλετο δῖος Ἀχιλλεύς
ἀμφὶ πυρὶ στῆσαι τρίποδα μέγαν, ὄφρα τάχιστα
Πάτροκλον λούσειαν ἄπο βρότον αἱματόεντα.   345
οἱ δὲ λοετροχόον τρίποδ᾽ ἵστασαν ἐν πυρὶ κηλέῳ,
ἐν δ᾽ ἄρ᾽ ὕδωρ ἔχεαν, ὑπὸ δὲ ξύλα δαῖον ἑλόντες.

---

326 φῆν: 1 s. impf. of φημί (cf. 17)
   Ὀπόεις -εντος, ὁ Opus, a city in Locris
   (central Greece), Patroclus' birth-
   place. When he was very young,
   Patroclus accidentally killed another
   boy (23.85–8) and was brought by
   his father to live in Phthia (cf. on 10)
   with Achilles. Menoetius was also
   present when Patroclus left Phthia for
   Troy (11.765–89). Only here do we
   hear (for pathetic effect) of a possible
   homecoming for Patroclus to Opus.
   περικλυτός -ον highly renowned, famous
   ἀπάγω I bring back; ἀπάξειν is fut. inf.
   (in indirect statement after φῆν)
327 ἐκπέρσαντα: aor. part. (m. acc. s.) of
   ἐκπέρθω (cf. 283)
   λαγχάνω I obtain by lot, receive; λαχόντα is aor. part. (m. acc. s.)

ληΐς -ΐδος, ἡ booty (= Att. λεία -ας)
αἶσα -ης, ἡ share, lot
328 τελευτάω I fulfil
329 ἄμφω (here m. acc.) both, the two of us
   πέπρωται (impersonal 3 s. perf. pass.
   with pres. sense) it is destined (here
   introducing indirect statement with
   acc. + inf.)
   ὁμοῖος -η -ον the same
   γαῖα -ης, ἡ (here and in 332–3) earth (cf.
   101)
   ἐρεύθω I make (something) red; ἐρεῦσαι
   is aor. inf.
330 αὐτοῦ (adv.) right here
   ἐνί = ἐν
   νοστήσαντα: aor. part. (m. acc. s.) of
   νοστέω (cf. 60)
331 δέξεται: 3 s. fut. of δέχομαι (cf. 115)
   ἱππηλάτα -εω, ὁ horseman, charioteer

332 κατέχω I hold; καθέξει is 3 s. fut. with ἐμέ (330) understood again as object. In 36 Thetis is found living in the depths of the sea, but here (as in 59–60 and 440–1) the possibility is envisaged of her welcoming Achilles home: a pathetic touch, as with Patroclus' imagined homecoming above.

333 οὖν (here) well then (cf. 222), implying 'back to practicalities'
σεῦ (cf. 77): here gen. of comparison 'than you'
εἶμι: here with fut. sense (as in Att. but not usu. in Homer)
ὑπό (+ acc.) below (implying motion towards)

334 πρίν ... πρίν: the first πρίν is redundant in tr.; the second (+ inf.) is 'before' (cf. on 189–90)
κτερίζω I bury with solemn honours; κτεριῶ is 1 s. fut.
ἐνεῖκαι: aor. inf. of φέρω (cf. 137)

335 τεύχεα (cf. 21): the arms Hector is wearing belong to Achilles. The words sound like a formulaic threat.
σός σή σόν your, of you (s.); σοῖο is m. gen. s.
φονεύς -ῆος, ὁ killer, murderer. The complimentary adj. μεγαθύμου (cf. 226) adds dignity to Patroclus' death.

336 πυρή -ῆς, ἡ pyre (= Att. πυρά -ᾶς)
ἀποδειροτομέω I cut the throat of, slaughter; ἀποδειροτομήσω is 1 s. fut. An emphatically horrible word, taking up more than a third of the line, used only here and at 23.22 (again Achilles to the dead Patroclus). He duly fulfils his promise at 23.175–6.

337 σέθεν: Homeric gen. of σύ (cf. 73)
κταμένοιο: aor. pass. part. (m. gen. s.) of κτείνω (cf. 99); σέθεν κταμένοιο is gen. of cause with χολωθείς
χολωθείς: aor. pass. part. (m. nom. s.) of χολόω (cf. 111)

338 τόφρα δέ in the meantime, until then
μοι: ethic dat. (cf. 61)
κείσεαι: 2 s. fut. of κεῖμαι (cf. 20)
αὔτως: used as at 198

339 Τρῳαί -ῶν, αἱ Trojan women

340 κλαύσονται: 3 pl. fut. of κλαίω (cf. 73)

341 αὐτοί we ourselves
κάμνω I work hard at; καμόμεσθα is 1 pl. aor. mid. 'we won by effort'
βίηφι: Homeric dat. s. of βίη (cf. 117)

342 πίειρα -ας (f. adj.) fertile, rich
πέρθω I sack, plunder; πέρθοντε is pres. part. (m. nom. dual). Use of the dual adds pathos by claiming the achievement for Achilles and Patroclus alone.

343–55: Patroclus' funeral rites begin with washing and anointing of the body. This scene releases the tension but also emphasises the grief for Patroclus.

343 ἐκέκλετο: 3 s. 'reduplicated' (where first consonant sound is repeated) aor. of κέλομαι (cf. 254)

344 ἵστημι I set up; στῆσαι is aor. inf.
τρίπους -οδος, ὁ tripod (cauldron plus three-legged stand)
ὄφρα (+ opt.) in order that, so that (introducing purpose clause)
τάχιστα (adv.) very quickly

345 ἀπολούω I wash X (acc.) off Y (also acc.); λούσειαν ... ἄπο is tmesis (with the elements reversed) of 3 pl. aor. opt.
βρότος -ου, ὁ gore, clotted blood

αἱματόεις -εσσα -εν (-εντος) bloody

346 λοετροχόος -ον holding water for washing (= Att. λουτροχόος)
ἵστασαν: 3 pl. impf. of ἵστημι (cf. 344)
κήλεος -ον blazing

347 ἐγχέω I pour in; ἐν ... ἔχεαν is tmesis of 3 pl. aor.
ὕδωρ -ατος, τό water
ὑπό (as adv.) underneath
ξύλον -ου, τό (piece of) wood, pl. wood, firewood
ἐλόντες: aor. part. (m. nom. pl.) of αἱρέω (cf. 23)

γάστρην μὲν τρίποδος πῦρ ἄμφεπε, θέρμετο δ' ὕδωρ·
αὐτὰρ ἐπεὶ δὴ ζέσσεν ὕδωρ ἐνὶ ἤνοπι χαλκῷ,
καὶ τότε δὴ λοῦσάν τε καὶ ἤλειψαν λίπ' ἐλαίῳ,   350
ἐν δ' ὠτειλὰς πλῆσαν ἀλείφατος ἐννεώροιο·
ἐν λεχέεσσι δὲ θέντες ἑανῷ λιτὶ κάλυψαν
ἐς πόδας ἐκ κεφαλῆς, καθύπερθε δὲ φάρεϊ λευκῷ.
παννύχιοι μὲν ἔπειτα πόδας ταχὺν ἀμφ' Ἀχιλῆα
Μυρμιδόνες Πάτροκλον ἀνεστενάχοντο γοῶντες·   355
Ζεὺς δ' Ἥρην προσέειπε κασιγνήτην ἄλοχόν τε·
"ἔπρηξας καὶ ἔπειτα, βοῶπις πότνια Ἥρη,
ἀνστήσασ' Ἀχιλῆα πόδας ταχύν· ἦ ῥά νυ σεῖο
ἐξ αὐτῆς ἐγένοντο κάρη κομόωντες Ἀχαιοί."
     Τὸν δ' ἠμείβετ' ἔπειτα βοῶπις πότνια Ἥρη·   360
"αἰνότατε Κρονίδη, ποῖον τὸν μῦθον ἔειπες.
καὶ μὲν δή πού τις μέλλει βροτὸς ἀνδρὶ τελέσσαι,
ὅς περ θνητός τ' ἐστὶ καὶ οὐ τόσα μήδεα οἶδε·
πῶς δὴ ἔγωγ', ἥ φημι θεάων ἔμμεν ἀρίστη,
ἀμφότερον, γενεῇ τε καὶ οὕνεκα σὴ παράκοιτις   365
κέκλημαι, σὺ δὲ πᾶσι μετ' ἀθανάτοισιν ἀνάσσεις,
οὐκ ὄφελον Τρώεσσι κοτεσσαμένη κακὰ ῥάψαι;"
     Ὣς οἱ μὲν τοιαῦτα πρὸς ἀλλήλους ἀγόρευον·
Ἡφαίστου δ' ἵκανε δόμον Θέτις ἀργυρόπεζα
ἄφθιτον ἀστερόεντα, μεταπρεπέ' ἀθανάτοισι,   370
χάλκεον, ὅν ῥ' αὐτὸς ποιήσατο κυλλοποδίων.
τὸν δ' εὗρ' ἱδρώοντα ἑλισσόμενον περὶ φύσας

348 γάστρη -ης, ἡ belly (of cauldron)
   ἀμφιέπω I move round, envelop; ἄμφεπε
      is 3 s. impf.
   θέρμω I warm, heat; θέρμετο is 3 s. impf.
      mid.
349 ζέω I boil; ζέσσεν is 3 s. aor.
   ἤνοψ -οπος (m. adj.) gleaming
   χαλκῷ (cf. 236): possibly here 'copper'
      (as at 474), which would withstand
      repeated heating and cooling better
      than bronze
350 λούω I wash; λοῦσαν is 3 pl. aor.
   ἀλείφω I anoint; ἤλειψαν is 3 pl. aor.
   λίπ(α) (adv.) richly
   ἔλαιον -ου, τό olive oil

351 ἐμπίμπλημι I fill X (acc.) with Y (gen.); ἐν
      ... πλῆσαν is tmesis of 3 pl. aor.
   ὠτειλή -ῆς, ἡ wound
   ἄλειφαρ -ατος, τό ointment, unguent
   ἐννέωρος -ον nine years old, i.e. seasoned
352 τίθημι I put, place; θέντες is aor. part. (m.
      nom. pl.)
   ἑανός -ή -όν fine, soft
   λιτί (dat. only), τῷ (m.) linen cloth
   κάλυψαν: 3 pl. aor. of καλύπτω (cf. 22)
353 καθύπερθε (adv.) above, on top
   φᾶρος -εος, τό robe, shroud
   λευκός -ή -όν white
354 πόδας: acc. of resp.
355: note the similarity of this line to 315

356–67: Interlude on Olympus

356 κασιγνήτην: cf. 52. Both Zeus and Hera were children of the Titans Cronus and Rhea (who themselves were brother and sister as well as husband and wife).

ἄλοχος -ου, ἡ wife

357 πρήσσω I do, accomplish (= Att. πράσ-σω); ἔπρηξας is 2 s. aor.; tr. phrase 'you've done it again' (lit. 'you did it then also')

358 ἀνίστημι I rouse; ἀνστήσασ(α) is aor. part. (f. nom. s.)

ἦ ῥά νυ evidently then. The words give a teasing tone to what Zeus says.

σεῖο: Homeric gen. of σύ (cf. 73)

359 ἐγένοντο: 3 pl. aor. of γίγνομαι, here 'were born' (cf. 19 and 251), imply-ing 'you are behaving like a mother towards them'

360–1 = 16.439–40, in a similarly tense ex-change between Zeus and Hera

361 αἰνότατε most dread; sup. (m. voc. s.) of αἰνός (cf. 171)

Κρονίδη: voc. of Κρονίδης (cf. 185)

ποῖος -η -ον what sort of …?/what a …! (question or, more probably here, exclamation); Hera's response is indignant

ἔειπες: 2 s. aor. of λέγω (cf. 5 and 9)

362 καὶ … τις … βροτός even any mortal

μέν: prepares the contrast between human and god, taken up by Hera's indignant question (364)

που (adv.) no doubt. Hera's indignant tone comes out again in the succes-sion of five monosyllabic words, and three spondees starting the line.

μέλλω (here) I am likely to (+ inf.)

τελέσσαι: aor. inf. of τελέω (cf. 4), here 'achieve his purpose for' (+ dat.)

363 τόσ(σ)ος -η -ον so great, pl. so many (understand 'as we gods do')

μήδεα -έων, τά plans, counsels

364 φημί (here) I claim

ἔμμεν: inf. of εἰμί (= εἶναι)

365 ἀμφότερον (n. as adv.) in both respects (cf. 23)

γενεή -ῆς, ἡ birth (= Att. γενεᾶ -ᾶς)

οὕνεκα because

366 καλέω I call; κέκλημαι is 1 s. perf. pass. with pres. sense

μετ(ά) (+ dat.): cf. 86; here implying 'over'

ἀνάσσω I rule, am lord

367 ὄφελον: 1 s. aor. of ὀφέλλω (cf. 19); πῶς (364) … οὐκ ὄφελον here 'how should I not have …?' (+ inf.)

κοτέομαι I am angry with (+ dat.); κοτεσσαμένη is aor. part. (f. nom. s.)

ῥάπτω I stitch up, devise; ῥάψαι is aor. inf.

368–467: Thetis' appeal to Hephaestus

368–81: Thetis arrives at Hephaestus' house with its multiple curious gadgets.

368 τοιοῦτος τοιαύτη τοιοῦτο(ν) such, of such a kind. This line occurs seven times in the *Iliad*, forming a neat formulaic transition from one scene to another.

369 ἵκανε: 3 s. impf. of ἱκάνω (cf. 214)

370 ἄφθιτος -ον imperishable

ἀστερόεις -εσσα -εν (-εντος) shining like a star

μεταπρεπής -ές conspicuous among (+ dat.). The other gods admire the house that Hephaestus the technician has built for himself.

371 χάλκεον (cf. 131): the Phaeacian king Alcinous also has a bronze-built house (*Odyssey* 7.81–94)

ποιέω I make; ποιήσατο is 3 s. aor. mid. (implying 'for himself')

κυλλοποδίων -ονος (m. adj.) club-footed, lame

372 ἱδρόω I sweat; ἱδρώοντα is pres. part. (m. acc. s.)

ἑλίσσομαι I bustle about

φῦσαι -ῶν, αἱ (pair of) bellows

σπεύδοντα· τρίποδας γὰρ ἐείκοσι πάντας ἔτευχεν
ἑστάμεναι περὶ τοῖχον ἐϋσταθέος μεγάροιο,
χρύσεα δέ σφ' ὑπὸ κύκλα ἑκάστῳ πυθμένι θῆκεν,   375
ὄφρα οἱ αὐτόματοι θεῖον δυσαίατ' ἀγῶνα
ἠδ' αὖτις πρὸς δῶμα νεοίατο, θαῦμα ἰδέσθαι.
οἱ δ' ἤτοι τόσσον μὲν ἔχον τέλος, οὔατα δ' οὔ πω
δαιδάλεα προσέκειτο· τά ῥ' ἤρτυε, κόπτε δὲ δεσμούς.
ὄφρ' ὅ γε ταῦτ' ἐπονεῖτο ἰδυίῃσι πραπίδεσσι,   380
τόφρα οἱ ἐγγύθεν ἦλθε θεὰ Θέτις ἀργυρόπεζα.
τὴν δὲ ἴδε προμολοῦσα Χάρις λιπαροκρήδεμνος
καλή, τὴν ὤπυιε περικλυτὸς ἀμφιγυήεις·
ἔν τ' ἄρα οἱ φῦ χειρὶ ἔπος τ' ἔφατ' ἔκ τ' ὀνόμαζε·
"τίπτε, Θέτι τανύπεπλε, ἱκάνεις ἡμέτερον δῶ   385
αἰδοίη τε φίλη τε; πάρος γε μὲν οὔ τι θαμίζεις.
ἀλλ' ἔπεο προτέρω, ἵνα τοι πὰρ ξείνια θείω."
      Ὣς ἄρα φωνήσασα πρόσω ἄγε δῖα θεάων.
τὴν μὲν ἔπειτα καθεῖσεν ἐπὶ θρόνου ἀργυροήλου
καλοῦ δαιδαλέου· ὑπὸ δὲ θρῆνυς ποσὶν ἦεν·   390
κέκλετο δ' Ἥφαιστον κλυτοτέχνην εἶπέ τε μῦθον·
"Ἥφαιστε, πρόμολ' ὧδε· Θέτις νύ τι σεῖο χατίζει."

373 σπεύδω I hurry. The three participles unconnected and in succession emphasise the intense activity.
ἐείκοσι(ν) twenty (= Att. εἴκοσι(ν)); ἐείκοσι πάντας 'twenty in all' (as if this were an item on Hephaestus' list of commissions)
374 ἑστάμεναι: perf. inf. of ἵσταμαι (cf. 160) with pres. sense, expressing purpose
περί (+ acc.) around
τοῖχος -ου, ὁ wall
ἐϋσταθής -ές well-built. The μέγαρον (cf. 325) is probably that of Hephaestus' house, where the tripods will be kept (cf. 377).
375 σφ(ι) ... ἑκάστῳ each of them (dat. 'whole and part'). There is archaeological evidence for wheeled tripods; cf. also the wheeled work basket from Egypt given to Helen (*Odyssey* 4.131–2).
ὑποτίθημι I fix X (acc.) under Y (dat.); ὑπὸ ... θῆκεν is tmesis of 3 s. aor.
κύκλος -ου, ὁ; pl. κύκλοι or κύκλα (τά) (here) wheel
πυθμήν -ένος, ὁ base, bottom; dat. here 'on the base'

376 οἱ for him (cf. 16); here dat. of advantage
αὐτόματος -η -ον self-moving. These mobile stands were perhaps less elaborate than the ones described at 1 Kings 7:27–37 (perhaps sixth century BCE), but to make them automotive is to go one step further.
θεῖος -η -ον divine, of the gods
δυσαίατ(ο): 3 pl. aor. opt. mid. of δύω (cf. 140), mid. perhaps reinforcing the idea of independent movement
ἀγών -ος, ὁ assembly place (either out of doors or in the palace of Zeus)
377 νεοίατο: 3 pl. opt. of νέομαι (cf. 101)
θαῦμα ἰδέσθαι: cf. 83
378 τέλος -εος, τό (here) completeness, finish; τόσσον ... ἔχον 'they had just so much finish (but ...)'
οὖς οὔατος, τό ear, (here) handle
οὔ πω not yet
379 δαιδάλεος -η -ον skilfully made, skilfully decorated
πρόσκειμαι I am attached; προσέκειτο is 3. s. impf. (with n. pl. subject)
ἀρτύω I make ready; ἤρτυε is 3 s. impf.

κόπτω (here) I forge; κόπτε is 3 s. impf.

δεσμός -οῖο, ὁ fastening, rivet

380 ὄφρ(α) ... τόφρα (381) (here) while ... in the meantime

πονέομαι I toil at; ἐπονεῖτο is 3 s. impf.

ἰδυίῃσι knowing, i.e. skilful; part. (f. dat. pl.) of οἶδα

πραπίδες -ων, αἱ mind

382–92: Charis receives Thetis. It might not be proper for Thetis to bump into Hephaestus (probably half-dressed) at his forge, so she is greeted by his wife.

382 ἴδε: 3 s. aor. of ὁράω (cf. 61; = Att. εἶδε)

προβλώσκω I come forward; προμολοῦ-σα is aor. part. (f. nom. s.)

Χάρις -ιτος, ἡ Charis (Grace). The name suggests attractiveness befitting the hospitable house of Hephaestus and the artefacts he creates. In the *Odyssey* and elsewhere his wife is Aphrodite, but as a supporter of the Trojans she would be unsuitable here. It is uncertain whether the three Graces of Hesiod (*Theogony* 907–9) and later tradition were known to Homer (cf. 398).

λιπαροκρήδεμνος -ον with shining veil

383 ὀπυίω I have as wife, am married to; ὤπυιε is 3 s. impf.

ἀμφιγυήεις (m. adj.): traditional epithet for Hephaestus, of uncertain meaning, perhaps 'bow-legged'

384 ἐμφύω I grow into (+ dat.); ἐν ... φῦ is tmesis of 3 s. aor., lit. 'she grew into' i.e. 'clasped her hand' (οἱ is possessive dat.)

ἐξονομάζω I address; ἐκ ... ὀνόμαζε is tmesis of 3 s. impf.

385 τίπτε why ever? ('syncopated' i.e. telescoped form of τί ποτε)

Θέτι: voc. of Θέτις (cf. 51)

τανύπεπλος -ον with trailing robe

ἡμέτερος -η -ον our

δῶ = δῶμα (cf. 141); here acc. without prep. for motion towards. Two metrical features of this line – 'honorary long' (cf. on 157) for the second syllable of Θέτι, hiatus (cf. on 22) between τανύπεπλε and ἱκάνεις – perhaps represent the surprise and warmth of the greeting.

386 αἰδοῖος -η -ον honoured

πάρος (adv.) previously, in the past (cf. 245)

γε μέν: both particles create a contrast between past and future, neatly and hospitably implying 'but we hope you'll be coming often after this'

θαμίζω I come/go frequently; θαμίζεις is 2 s. pres., here with impf. sense

387 ἕπεο: 2 s. imper. of ἕπομαι (cf. 234)

προτέρω (adv.) onward, forward

ἵνα (+ subj.) in order that, so that (introducing purpose clause)

τοι = σοι

παρατίθημι I put X (acc.) beside/before Y (dat.); πάρ (= παρά) ... θείω is tmesis of 1 s. aor. subj.

ξείνιον -ου, τό gift of hospitality (= Att. ξένιον). This line is repeated at *Odyssey* 5.91 (Calypso welcoming Hermes).

388 φωνήσασα: aor. part. (f. nom. s.) of φωνέω (cf. 65)

πρόσω (adv.) forward

ἄγω I lead; ἆγε is 3 s. impf.

δῖα θεάων: cf. 205

389 τήν: i.e. Thetis

καθίζω I sit (someone) down; καθεῖσεν is 3 s. aor.

ἐπί (+ gen.) on

θρόνος -ου, ὁ armchair

ἀργυρόηλος -ον silver-studded

390 ὕπειμι I am under (+ dat.); ὑπό ... ἦεν is tmesis of 3 s. impf.

θρῆνυς -υος, ὁ footstool

ποσίν: dat. pl. of πούς (cf. 2)

391 κέκλετο: 3 s. aor. of κέλομαι (cf. 254), here 'she called out to'

392 πρόμολε: 2 s. aor. imper. of προβλώσκω (cf. 382)

ὧδε (adv.) (here) this way

χατίζω I have need of (+ gen.); with τι σεῖο here 'some need of you'

τὴν δ᾽ ἠμείβετ᾽ ἔπειτα περικλυτὸς ἀμφιγυήεις·
"ἦ ῥά νύ μοι δεινή τε καὶ αἰδοίη θεὸς ἔνδον,
ἥ μ᾽ ἐσάωσ᾽, ὅτε μ᾽ ἄλγος ἀφίκετο τῆλε πεσόντα   395
μητρὸς ἐμῆς ἰότητι κυνώπιδος, ἥ μ᾽ ἐθέλησε
κρύψαι χωλὸν ἐόντα· τότ᾽ ἂν πάθον ἄλγεα θυμῷ,
εἰ μή μ᾽ Εὐρυνόμη τε Θέτις θ᾽ ὑπεδέξατο κόλπῳ,
Εὐρυνόμη, θυγάτηρ ἀψορρόου Ὠκεανοῖο.
τῇσι παρ᾽ εἰνάετες χάλκευον δαίδαλα πολλά,   400
πόρπας τε γναμπτάς θ᾽ ἕλικας κάλυκάς τε καὶ ὅρμους
ἐν σπῆϊ γλαφυρῷ· περὶ δὲ ῥόος Ὠκεανοῖο
ἀφρῷ μορμύρων ῥέεν ἄσπετος· οὐδέ τις ἄλλος
ᾔδεεν οὔτε θεῶν οὔτε θνητῶν ἀνθρώπων,
ἀλλὰ Θέτις τε καὶ Εὐρυνόμη ἴσαν, αἵ μ᾽ ἐσάωσαν.   405
ἥ νῦν ἡμέτερον δόμον ἵκει· τώ με μάλα χρεὼ
πάντα Θέτι καλλιπλοκάμῳ ζῳάγρια τίνειν.
ἀλλὰ σὺ μὲν νῦν οἱ παράθες ξεινήϊα καλά,
ὄφρ᾽ ἂν ἐγὼ φύσας ἀποθείομαι ὅπλα τε πάντα."
Ἦ, καὶ ἀπ᾽ ἀκμοθέτοιο πέλωρ αἴητον ἀνέστη   410
χωλεύων· ὑπὸ δὲ κνῆμαι ῥώοντο ἀραιαί.
φύσας μέν ῥ᾽ ἀπάνευθε τίθει πυρός, ὅπλά τε πάντα
λάρνακ᾽ ἐς ἀργυρέην συλλέξατο, τοῖς ἐπονεῖτο·

*393–409: Hephaestus' debt to Thetis. Two falls of Hephaestus from heaven are
described in the Iliad. The first arose from Hera's persecution of Heracles. Zeus
took violent action against her, and when Hephaestus tried to help his mother, Zeus
flung him from Olympus (1.590–4). If that story explained his lameness, this one
sits uneasily with it. But Thetis needs to be provided with a claim on Hephaestus'
gratitude. Like Charis as Hephaestus' wife, the story is likely to have been specially
invented for this episode.*

394 ἦ ῥα νύ well now (there is …); understand ἐστί
δεινός -ή -όν awe-inspiring
θεός -οῦ, ἡ goddess
ἔνδον (adv.) (here) in the house
395 σαόω I save (= Att. σῴζω); ἐσάωσ(ε) is 3
s. aor.
ἀφίκετο: 3 s. aor. of ἀφικνέομαι (cf. 270),
here 'came upon'
τῆλε (adv.) a long way
πίπτω I fall; πεσόντα is aor. part. (m.
acc. s.)
396 ἰότης -ητος, ἡ will, wish; dat. here 'by the
will'

κυνῶπις -ιδος (f. adj.) dog-faced, shameless. Some ancient scribes, surprised
by the coarse insult, substituted
Hera's traditional epithet βοώπιδος
(cf. 40).
ἐθέλησε: 3 s. aor. of ἐθέλω (cf. 116)
397 κρύπτω I hide; κρύψαι is aor. inf.
χωλός -ή όν lame
πάθον: 1 s. aor. of πάσχω (cf. 77); with
ἄν 'I would have …'
398 Εὐρυνόμη -ης, ἡ Eurynome. In Hesiod
(*Theogony* 907) she is mother of the
Graces, which would make her Hephaestus' mother-in-law.

ὑπεδέξατο: 3 s. aor. of ὑποδέχομαι (cf. 59); εἰ μή 'if … had not …' (past unfulfilled condition). The s. verb perhaps indicates Thetis as the more important of the two.

κόλπῳ: the poet here plays on two meanings, the bosom (cf. 140) of Thetis and an inlet of the sea

399 θυγάτηρ -έρος/ρός, ἡ daughter

ἀψόρροος -ον back-flowing. Oceanus (cf. 240) encircles the earth and therefore at some point flows back into itself. This line is decorative but redundant, a compliment to Eurynome from Hephaestus. There follows a remarkable picture, full of contrasts: the huge smith-god at secret work in his forge with the sea roaring around, making tiny delicate items of jewellery.

400 τῇσι: f. dat. pl. of article as personal pron.

παρ(ά) (+ dat.) with, beside

εἰνάετες (adv.) for nine years

χαλκεύω I fashion in metal

δαίδαλον -ου, τό skilfully made ornament

401 πόρπη -ης, ἡ brooch

γναμπτός -ή -όν curved

ἕλικες -ων, αἱ armbands

κάλυξ κάλυκος, ἡ earring

ὅρμος -ου, ὁ necklace

402 σπῆϊ: dat. of σπέος (cf. 50)

περί (as adv.) all around

ῥόος -ου, ὁ stream

403 ἄφρος -ου, ὁ foam

μορμύρω I roar

ῥέω I flow

ἄσπετος -ον (here adj. tr. as adv.) unceasingly (cf. 165)

404 ᾔδεεν: 3 s. past of οἶδα. Four spondees ending the line perhaps emphasise Hephaestus' isolation.

405 ἴσαν: 3 pl. past of οἶδα. The line closes this little narrative passage (ring composition).

406 τώ so, therefore

χρεώ -όος, ἡ need; here understand ἐστί, introducing acc. + inf. 'there is need for me to …'

407 Θέτι: here dat. (cf. 51)

καλλιπλόκαμος -ον with beautiful hair

ζῳάγρια, τά reward for saving life. The suggestion that a god's life might be endangered is paradoxical, but emphasises the scale of his debt to Thetis.

τίνω I pay

408 σὺ μέν: i.e. Charis; Hephaestus follows not with 'and I (δέ) shall (tidy up here)', but switches to the dependent clause ὄφρα … (409)

παράθες: 2 s. aor. imper. of παρατίθημι (cf. 387)

ξεινήϊα = ξείνια (n. pl., cf. 387)

409 ἀποτίθημι I put away; ἀποθείομαι is 1 s. aor. subj. mid., with ὄφρ(α) ἄν expressing purpose

ὅπλον -ου, τό tool, implement

410–20: Hephaestus prepares to meet Thetis.

410 ἦ he spoke; 3 s. impf. of ἠμί I speak, found in Homer only in this form

ἀκμόθετον -ου/οιο, τό anvil block

πέλωρ (nom. only), τό monstrous figure

ἄητος -ον gasping, panting

ἀνέστη: aor. 3 s. of ἀνίσταμαι (cf. 305)

411 χωλεύω I limp; part. here m. (nom. s.) for sense rather than strict grammar after n. πέλωρ (410)

κνήμη -ης, ἡ shin

ῥώομαι I move quickly; ῥώοντο is 3 pl. impf.

ἀραιός -ή -όν slender, stunted. Hephaestus' monstrous hugeness must lie in his arms and torso (another striking contrast).

412 ἀπάνευθε (+ gen.) away from

τίθει: 3 s. impf. of τίθημι (cf. 352)

413 λάρναξ -ακος, ἡ chest, box

ἀργύρεος -η -ον made of silver (= Att. ἀργυροῦς -ᾶ -οῦν)

συλλέξατο: 3 s. aor. mid. of συλλέγω (cf. 301)

τοῖς with which (dat. pl. rel. pron.)

πονέομαι I am busy, work

σπόγγῳ δ᾽ ἀμφὶ πρόσωπα καὶ ἄμφω χεῖρ᾽ ἀπομόργνυ
αὐχένα τε στιβαρὸν καὶ στήθεα λαχνήεντα,   415
δῦ δὲ χιτῶν᾽, ἕλε δὲ σκῆπτρον παχύ, βῆ δὲ θύραζε
χωλεύων· ὑπὸ δ᾽ ἀμφίπολοι ῥώοντο ἄνακτι
χρύσειαι, ζωῇσι νεήνισιν εἰοικυῖαι.
τῇς ἐν μὲν νόος ἐστὶ μετὰ φρεσίν, ἐν δὲ καὶ αὐδὴ
καὶ σθένος, ἀθανάτων δὲ θεῶν ἄπο ἔργα ἴσασιν.   420
αἱ μὲν ὕπαιθα ἄνακτος ἐποίπνυον· αὐτὰρ ὁ ἔρρων
πλησίον, ἔνθα Θέτις περ, ἐπὶ θρόνου ἷζε φαεινοῦ,
ἔν τ᾽ ἄρα οἱ φῦ χειρὶ ἔπος τ᾽ ἔφατ᾽ ἔκ τ᾽ ὀνόμαζε·
"τίπτε, Θέτι τανύπεπλε, ἱκάνεις ἡμέτερον δῶ
αἰδοίη τε φίλη τε; πάρος γε μὲν οὔ τι θαμίζεις.   425
αὔδα ὅ τι φρονέεις· τελέσαι δέ με θυμὸς ἄνωγεν,
εἰ δύναμαι τελέσαι γε καὶ εἰ τετελεσμένον ἐστίν."
    Τὸν δ᾽ ἠμείβετ᾽ ἔπειτα Θέτις κατὰ δάκρυ χέουσα·
"Ἥφαιστ᾽, ἦ ἄρα δή τις, ὅσαι θεαί εἰσ᾽ ἐν Ὀλύμπῳ,
τοσσάδ᾽ ἐνὶ φρεσὶν ᾗσιν ἀνέσχετο κήδεα λυγρά,   430
ὅσσ᾽ ἐμοὶ ἐκ πασέων Κρονίδης Ζεὺς ἄλγε᾽ ἔδωκεν;
ἐκ μέν μ᾽ ἀλλάων ἁλιάων ἀνδρὶ δάμασσεν,
Αἰακίδῃ Πηλῆϊ, καὶ ἔτλην ἀνέρος εὐνὴν
πολλὰ μάλ᾽ οὐκ ἐθέλουσα. ὁ μὲν δὴ γήραϊ λυγρῷ
κεῖται ἐνὶ μεγάροις ἀρημένος, ἄλλα δέ μοι νῦν·   435
υἱὸν ἐπεί μοι δῶκε γενέσθαί τε τραφέμεν τε,
ἔξοχον ἡρώων· ὁ δ᾽ ἀνέδραμεν ἔρνεϊ ἶσος·
τὸν μὲν ἐγὼ θρέψασα φυτὸν ὣς γουνῷ ἀλωῆς,
νηυσὶν ἐπιπροέηκα κορωνίσιν Ἴλιον εἴσω
Τρωσὶ μαχησόμενον· τὸν δ᾽ οὐχ ὑποδέξομαι αὖτις   440
οἴκαδε νοστήσαντα δόμον Πηλήϊον εἴσω.
ὄφρα δέ μοι ζώει καὶ ὁρᾷ φάος ἠελίοιο,
ἄχνυται, οὐδέ τί οἱ δύναμαι χραισμῆσαι ἰοῦσα.

---

414 σπόγγος -ου, ὁ sponge
    ἀμφί (adv.) (here) on both sides
    πρόσωπα: here pl. for s. (cf. 24)
    ἄμφω both (here f. acc.)
    χεῖρ(ε): acc. dual of χείρ (cf. 11)
    ἀπομόργνυμι I wipe clean; ἀπομόργνῡ is
        3 s. impf.
415 αὐχήν -ένος, ὁ neck
    στιβαρός -ή -όν firm, strong
    στήθεα: acc. pl. of στῆθος (cf. 31); here
        again pl. for s.
    λαχνήεις -εσσα -εν (-εντος) hairy,
        shaggy

416 δῦ: 3 s. aor. of δύω (cf. 192)
    ἕλε: 3 s. aor. of αἱρέω (cf. 23)
    σκῆπτρον -ου, τό staff
    παχύς -εῖα -ύ thick, sturdy
    βαίνω I go; βῆ is 3 s. aor.
    θύραζε (adv.) to the door, out of doors
417 ὑπό (+ dat.) (here) supporting
    ἀμφίπολος -ου, ἡ female servant. Robotic
        golden girls are the smith-god's assis-
        tants, and presumably also products
        of his workshop.
418 ζωός -ή -όν living, alive
    νεῆνις -ιδος, ἡ young girl (= Att. νεᾶνις)

ἔοικα (perf. with pres. sense) I am like,
   resemble (+ dat.); εἰοικυῖαι is part. (f.
   nom. pl.)

419 τῆς = ταῖς
   ἔνεστι (there) is in (+ dat.); ἐν ... ἐστί
   here tmesis, the second ἐν suggesting a
   repetition of the verb

νόος -ου, ὁ thought, intelligence
μετά (+ dat.) (here) in
αὐδή -ῆς, ἡ voice

420 ἄπο: accented as postposition
   ἔργον -ου, τό (here) skill
   ἴσασιν: 3 pl. of οἶδα (cf. 53)

421–7: Hephaestus welcomes and encourages Thetis.

421 ὕπαιθα (+ gen.) in support of
   ποιπνύω I bustle about
   ἔρρω I move with difficulty

422 πλησίον (adv.) near
   ἔνθα: used as at 68
   ἵζω I sit down
   φαεινός -ή -όν shining

423–5 = 384–6, the hospitable unanimity of
   Hephaestus and Charis contrasting
   with the tetchiness of Zeus and Hera
   (356–67)

426 αὐδάω I speak, tell; αὔδα is 2 s. imper.
   ὅ τι what

τελέσαι: aor. inf. of τελέω (cf. 4)

427 τετελεσμένον: perf. pass. part. (n. nom.
   s.) of τελέω (cf. 4), lit. 'having been
   accomplished' here implying 'possible'.
   Even the gods cannot do 'what is not
   to be', i.e. what fate does not allow,
   such as preventing Achilles' death.
   The same words (426–7) were used by
   Aphrodite to Hera at 14.195–6 when
   Hera asked Aphrodite for some of her
   sex appeal so that she could seduce
   Zeus.

428–61: Thetis explains her distress and puts her request to Hephaestus.

429 ἦ ἄρα δή τις is there really anyone …?
   The accumulated particles emphasise
   Thetis' aggrieved question.
   ὅσαι θεαί: elliptical expression (lit. 'as
   many goddesses') equivalent to 'of all
   the goddesses who'

430 τοσσάδ(ε) ... ὅσσ(α) (431) as many ... as
   (both n. acc. pl.)
   ᾗσι(ν): f. dat. pl. of possessive pron. ὅς
   (cf. 5)
   ἀνέσχετο: 3 s. aor. mid. of ἀνέχω (cf. 75),
   here 'endured'

431 πασέων: f. gen. pl. of πᾶς (cf. 30)

432 ἀλλάων: f. gen. pl. of ἄλλος (cf. 49)
   ἅλιαι -άων, αἱ sea-goddesses
   δαμάζω (here) I subject X (acc.) as a wife
   to Y (dat.); δάμασσεν is 3 s. aor. (cf.
   103)

433 Πηλῆϊ: dat. of Πηλεύς (cf. 18)
   ἔτλην: 1 s. aor. of τλάω (cf. 246), here 'I
   endured'

434 πολλά μάλ(α) very much (with οὐκ ἐθέλουσα). Divinities of the sea have the
   capacity to change shape at will. Thetis'
   reluctance to marry is depicted in vase
   paintings which show Peleus struggling to keep hold of her during her
   many changes (cf. the story of Proteus
   and Menelaus at Odyssey 4.455–9).
   γῆρας -αος, τό old age

435 ἀρημένος -η -ον overcome, worn out
   ἄλλα: understand ἄλγε(α) ἔδωκεν from
   431. Thetis speaks in a rather breath-
   less style.

436 δῶκε: here introducing acc. + inf.
   γενέσθαι: aor inf. of γίγνομαι (cf. 19 and
   251), 'to be born'
   τραφέμεν: aor. inf. of τρέφω (cf. 57), here
   with pass. sense

437–43 = 56–62, Thetis repeating to Hephaestus what she said to her sea-goddess
   sisters

κούρην ἣν ἄρα οἱ γέρας ἔξελον υἷες Ἀχαιῶν,
τὴν ἂψ ἐκ χειρῶν ἕλετο κρείων Ἀγαμέμνων.   445
ἤτοι ὁ τῆς ἀχέων φρένας ἔφθιεν· αὐτὰρ Ἀχαιοὺς
Τρῶες ἐπὶ πρύμνῃσιν ἐείλεον, οὐδὲ θύραζε
εἴων ἐξιέναι· τὸν δὲ λίσσοντο γέροντες
Ἀργείων, καὶ πολλὰ περικλυτὰ δῶρ' ὀνόμαζον.
ἔνθ' αὐτὸς μὲν ἔπειτ' ἠναίνετο λοιγὸν ἀμῦναι,   450
αὐτὰρ ὁ Πάτροκλον περὶ μὲν τὰ ἃ τεύχεα ἕσσε,
πέμπε δέ μιν πόλεμόνδε, πολὺν δ' ἅμα λαὸν ὄπασσε.
πᾶν δ' ἦμαρ μάρναντο περὶ Σκαιῇσι πύλῃσι·
καί νύ κεν αὐτῆμαρ πόλιν ἔπραθον, εἰ μὴ Ἀπόλλων
πολλὰ κακὰ ῥέξαντα Μενοιτίου ἄλκιμον υἱὸν   455
ἔκταν' ἐνὶ προμάχοισι καὶ Ἕκτορι κῦδος ἔδωκε.
τοὔνεκα νῦν τὰ σὰ γούναθ' ἱκάνομαι, αἴ κ' ἐθέλῃσθα
υἱεῖ ἐμῷ ὠκυμόρῳ δόμεν ἀσπίδα καὶ τρυφάλειαν
καὶ καλὰς κνημῖδας ἐπισφυρίοις ἀραρυίας,
καὶ θώρηχ'· ὃ γὰρ ἦν οἱ ἀπώλεσε πιστὸς ἑταῖρος   460
Τρωσὶ δαμείς· ὁ δὲ κεῖται ἐπὶ χθονὶ θυμὸν ἀχεύων."
    Τὴν δ' ἠμείβετ' ἔπειτα περικλυτὸς ἀμφιγυήεις·
"θάρσει· μή τοι ταῦτα μετὰ φρεσὶ σῇσι μελόντων.
αἲ γάρ μιν θανάτοιο δυσηχέος ὧδε δυναίμην
νόσφιν ἀποκρύψαι, ὅτε μιν μόρος αἰνὸς ἱκάνοι,   465

444 κούρη -ης, ἡ girl, young woman (= Att.
        κόρη -ης)
    γέρας -αος, τό gift of honour
    ἔξελον: 3 pl. aor. of ἐξαιρέω (cf. 311), here
        'picked out'
445 ἂψ (adv.) back again
    ἕλετο: 3 s. aor. mid. of αἱρέω (cf. 23), here
        'took for himself'
    κρείων -οντος, ὁ lord, ruler
446 ἤτοι ... αὐτάρ: sets up a contrast (be-
        tween Achilles and the Achaeans)
        much as μέν ... δέ would
    ἀχέω I grieve about (+ gen.)
    φθίω I waste away; ἔφθιεν is 3 s. impf,
        with φρένας acc. of resp. 'in his heart'
447 ἐείλεον: 3 pl. impf. of εἴλω (cf. 76)
448 εἴων: 3 pl. impf. of ἐάω (cf. 112)
    ἔξειμι I go out; ἐξιέναι is inf.
    λίσσομαι I beg, beseech
    γέροντες (pl. here) elders
449 Ἀργεῖοι -ων, οἱ Argives, i.e. Greeks.
        Named from the city of Argos in
        southern Greece (cf. on 111) but used
        as a general term for all those fighting

against the Trojans and their allies,
    synonymous with 'Achaeans' (cf. 6)
    ὀνομάζω I name
450 ἔνθ(α) (here) thereupon (reinforcing
        ἔπειτα)
    ἀναίνομαι I refuse; ἠναίνετο is 3 s. impf.
    λοιγός -οῦ ὁ destruction, death
    ἀμῦναι: aor. inf. of ἀμύνω (cf. 129)
451 περιέννυμι I put (clothing or armour,
        acc.) on (someone, also acc.); περὶ ...
        ἕσσε is tmesis of 3 s. aor.
    ἅ his own (n. pl.; cf. 5)
452 πόλεμόνδε into the war
    ὀπάζω I grant, provide as followers;
        ὄπασσε is 3 s. aor. Thetis here gives an
        abbreviated account of events, mis-
        leadingly implying that the initiative
        for Patroclus going into battle came
        from Achilles: from 16.1–45 it is clear
        that it came from Patroclus himself.
        The summary is for Hephaestus' ben-
        efit, but also marks the point where
        the first 'anger' section (Achilles
        against Agamemnon) ends and is re-

placed by the second (Achilles against Hector).

453 πᾶν ... ἦμαρ all day long (acc. of time how long)

Σκαιαί -ῶν, αἱ (with or without πύ-λαι) the Scaean Gate; main conduit from the city to the battlefield and location of key events throughout the *Iliad* and beyond. Hector's farewell to Andromache took place there (6.393). Thetis' reference here recalls its mention just before the death of Patroclus (16.712). The dying Hector predicts that Achilles will be killed near it (22.360).

454 αὐτῆμαρ on the same day

ἔπραθον: 3 pl. aor. of πέρθω (cf. 342); κεν gives the sense 'would have ...'

εἰ μή: 'if ... had not ...' (past unfulfilled condition; cf. on 398)

Ἀπόλλων -ωνος, ὁ Apollo

455 πολλὰ κακά much damage

ῥέζω I do; ῥέξαντα is aor. part. (m. acc. s.)

456 ἔκταν(ε): 3 s. aor. of κτείνω (cf. 99)

πρόμαχος -ου, ὁ foremost fighter

457 τοὔνεκα = τοῦ ἕνεκα therefore

γόνυ γούνατος, τό knee

ἱκάνομαι: 1 s. mid. of ἱκάνω (cf. 214). Grasping someone's knees (literally or, as here, metaphorically) was the traditional gesture of supplication, usu. directed to a more powerful person: Hephaestus as an Olympian god outranks Thetis.

αἴ κ(ε) (+ subj.) (here) in the hope that ...

ἐθέλησθα: 2 s. subj. of ἐθέλω (cf. 116)

458 υἱεῖ: 3rd decl. form dat. of υἱός (cf. 12). The first part of the line is metrically unusual, requiring -ῷ ὠ- to be scanned as one long syllable (ignoring the iota subscript).

δόμεν: aor. inf. of δίδωμι (cf. 84)

ἀσπίς -ίδος, ἡ shield

τρυφάλεια -ης, ἡ helmet

459 κνημίς -ίδος, ἡ greave, shin guard

ἐπισφύριον -ου, τό ankle protector

ἀραρυίας: perf. part. (f. acc. pl.) of ἀραρίσκω with pass. sense (cf. 275), here 'fitted with' (+ dat.)

460 θώρηξ -ηκος, ὁ breastplate (= Att. θώραξ -ακος); θώρηχ' = θώρηκα (elided and aspirated before vowel with rough breathing)

ὅ (n. of rel. ὅς) ... ἦν οἱ what belonged to him (possessive dat.); the whole phrase is the object of ἀπώλεσε

ἀπώλεσε: 3 s. aor. of ἀπόλλυμι (cf. 82), here 'lost' (not 'destroyed': Achilles recovers the armour at 22.368–9)

461 Τρωσί by the Trojans; dat. of agent

δαμείς: aor. pass. part. (m. nom. s.) of δαμάζω (cf. 103)

ὁ δέ but he (i.e. Achilles). Thetis ends her speech by remembering her son's condition when she left him.

χθών χθονός, ἡ earth, ground

ἀχεύω I grieve; θυμόν is acc. of resp.

462–7: Hephaestus will do as Thetis asks. The contrast between the glorious and imperishable armour now made and the short time for which it will serve comes out strongly in the wish expressed by Hephaestus. He also uses the tragic certainty of Achilles' death as a guarantee to Thetis of his goodwill and co-operation.

463 θαρσέω I take courage, cheer up (= Att. θαρρέω); θάρσει is 2 s. imper. τοι = σοι; reinforcing φρεσὶ σῇσι

μετά (+ dat.) (here) in

σῇσι = σαῖς

μέλω I am an object of care to (+ dat.); μελόντων is 3 pl. imper.

464 αἲ γάρ ... ὧδε ... ὥς (466) if only I could (+ opt. expressing wish) ... as surely as

θάνατος -ου/οιο, ὁ death

δυναίμην: 1 s. opt. of δύναμαι (cf. 62)

465 νόσφιν (+ gen.) far away from

ἀποκρύπτω I hide (something/someone) away; ἀποκρύψαι is aor. inf.

μόρος -ου, ὁ fate, doom

ἱκάνοι: 3 s. opt. of ἱκάνω (cf. 214); opt. either indefinite (regarding the time, not the fact) or attracted into the mood of δυναίμην (464)

ὥς οἱ τεύχεα καλὰ παρέσσεται, οἷά τις αὖτε
ἀνθρώπων πολέων θαυμάσσεται, ὅς κεν ἴδηται."
    Ὣς εἰπὼν τὴν μὲν λίπεν αὐτοῦ, βῆ δ᾿ ἐπὶ φύσας·
τὰς δ᾿ ἐς πῦρ ἔτρεψε κέλευσέ τε ἐργάζεσθαι.
φῦσαι δ᾿ ἐν χοάνοισιν ἐείκοσι πᾶσαι ἐφύσων,   470
παντοίην εὔπρηστον ἀϋτμὴν ἐξανιεῖσαι,
ἄλλοτε μὲν σπεύδοντι παρέμμεναι, ἄλλοτε δ᾿ αὖτε,
ὅππως Ἥφαιστός τ᾿ ἐθέλοι καὶ ἔργον ἄνοιτο.
χαλκὸν δ᾿ ἐν πυρὶ βάλλεν ἀτειρέα κασσίτερόν τε
καὶ χρυσὸν τιμῆντα καὶ ἄργυρον· αὐτὰρ ἔπειτα   475

10. Hephaestus and Cyclopes forging the shield of Achilles. Greco-Roman marble. Pinacoteca Capitolino, Rome.

466 πάρειμι I am present, at hand; παρέσσε-
      ται is 3 s. fut.
   τις (here) anyone at all
   αὖτε (adv.) (here) in the future
467 πολέων: Homeric gen. pl. of πολύς (cf.
      103), here 'of the many (that there are)'

θαυμάζω I admire; θαυμάσσεται is 3 s.
   fut.
ὅς κε(ν) (+ subj.) whoever
ἴδηται: 3 s. aor. subj. mid. of ὁράω (cf.
   61)

468–617: Hephaestus makes Achilles' armour.

The poet describes the construction of the new armour, in particular the shield and
the scenes depicted on it. This divinely fashioned artefact is by definition extraordinary: contrast the more typical shield of Agamemnon, adorned with the monstrous
face of the Gorgon and demonic figures of Fear and Terror (11.32–40). After several
books of bloody conflict, and in the first half of this book dramatic anger from Achilles and then between Hector and Polydamas, the action quietened down with the
peaceful domestic life of Hephaestus and Charis, only for Thetis' emotional intensity
on her son's behalf to raise the tempo again. Now we have a controlled, constructive
process in which Hephaestus methodically portrays the range of human existence:
the universe, city life, warfare, peaceful and productive farming, and country fes-
tivals. The description gives the listener a break from high tension (as the list of
Nereids at 39–49 more briefly did), and paves the way for the public reconciliation
of Agamemnon and Achilles (19.40–275). Achilles will then carry into battle a pan-
orama of the life he has renounced.

468–77: Hephaestus prepares to make the shield.

468 αὐτοῦ (adv.) there
469 ἔτρεψε: 3 s. aor. of τρέπω (cf. 138)
   ἐργάζομαι I work, perform. The bellows
      are automatic.
470 χόανος -ου, ὁ melting-pit
   φυσάω I blow; ἐφύσων is 3 pl. impf.
471 παντοῖος -η -ον (here) from all directions
      (cf. 281), i.e. the twenty bellows were
      positioned all around the melting-pits
   εὔπρηστος -ον strong-blowing
   ἀϋτμή -ῆς ἡ breath, blast
   ἐξανίημι I emit; ἐξανιεῖσαι is pres. part. (f.
      nom. pl.)
472 ἄλλοτε (cf. 159) μέν … ἄλλοτε δ'
      αὖτε: contrasts times when Hephaes-
      tus was in a hurry and other times
   σπεύδοντι: pres. part. (m. dat. s.) of
      σπεύδω (cf. 373), referring to Hep-
      haestus 'for him as he hurried'
   παρέμμεναι: inf. of πάρειμι (cf. 466), here
      'so as to be available'

473 ὅπ(π)ως (adv.) as, according to how
   ἐθέλοι: 3 s. opt. of ἐθέλω (cf. 116), here
      indefinite
   ἔργον -ου, τό (here) work
   ἄνω I finish; ἄνοιτο is 3 s. opt. mid.,
      again indefinite 'in whatever way the
      work would come to an end'
474 χαλκός -οῦ, ὁ (here) copper; it will
      become bronze (the usual meaning
      of the word: cf. 236) when alloyed
      with the tin. Images will be created by
      inlaying other metals on the bronze
      surface of the shield.
   ἀτειρής -ές that does not wear out; ἀτει-
      ρέα is m. acc. s. (uncontracted form),
      with χαλκόν
   κασσίτερος -ου/οιο, ὁ tin
475 χρυσός -οῦ/οῖο, ὁ gold
   τιμήεις -εσσα -εν (-εντος) precious; τιμῆ-
      ντα is m. acc. s. (contracted form)
   ἄργυρος -ου, ὁ silver

θῆκεν ἐν ἀκμοθέτῳ μέγαν ἄκμονα, γέντο δὲ χειρὶ
ῥαιστῆρα κρατερήν, ἑτέρηφι δὲ γέντο πυράγρην.

Ποίει δὲ πρώτιστα σάκος μέγα τε στιβαρόν τε
πάντοσε δαιδάλλων, περὶ δ’ ἄντυγα βάλλε φαεινὴν
τρίπλακα μαρμαρέην, ἐκ δ’ ἀργύρεον τελαμῶνα.   480
πέντε δ’ ἄρ’ αὐτοῦ ἔσαν σάκεος πτύχες· αὐτὰρ ἐν αὐτῷ
ποίει δαίδαλα πολλὰ ἰδυίῃσι πραπίδεσσιν.

Ἐν μὲν γαῖαν ἔτευξ’, ἐν δ’ οὐρανόν, ἐν δὲ θάλασσαν,
ἠέλιόν τ’ ἀκάμαντα σελήνην τε πλήθουσαν,
ἐν δὲ τὰ τείρεα πάντα, τά τ’ οὐρανὸς ἐστεφάνωται,   485
Πληϊάδας θ’ Ὑάδας τε τό τε σθένος Ὠρίωνος
Ἄρκτον θ’, ἣν καὶ Ἄμαξαν ἐπίκλησιν καλέουσιν,
ἥ τ’ αὐτοῦ στρέφεται καί τ’ Ὠρίωνα δοκεύει,
οἴη δ’ ἄμμορός ἐστι λοετρῶν Ὠκεανοῖο.

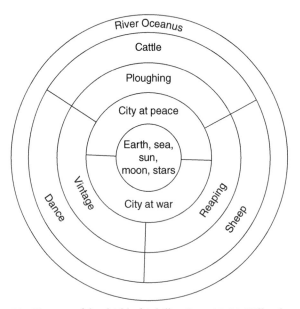

11. Diagram of the shield of Achilles. From M. M. Willcock,
A Companion to the Iliad, University of Chicago Press 1976.

476 θῆκε(ν): 3 s. aor. of τίθημι (cf. 352)
  ἄκμων -ονος, ὁ anvil
  γέντο (3 s. aor. only) he took, grasped
477 ῥαιστήρ -ῆρος, ἡ hammer

ἕτερος -η -ον the other (of two);
  ἑτέρηφι is f. dat. s. with χειρί
  understood
πυράγρη -ης, ἡ fire tongs

478–82: *Materials for the shield.*

478 πρώτιστα (adv.) first of all

σάκος: Ajax's shield (referred to by this
  word at 193) is described at 7.219 as
  'like a tower', i.e. curving and covering
  the whole body; but Achilles' shield
  as described in this passage is clearly
  circular (both types are attested
  archaeologically)

στιβαρός -ή -όν firm, strong

479 πάντοσε (adv.) all over

δαιδάλλω I decorate

περιβάλλω I place around; περί ... βάλλε
  is tmesis of 3 s. impf.

ἄντυξ -υγος, ἡ rim

480 τρίπλαξ -ακος with three layers

μαρμάρεος -η -ον flashing, glittering; the
  word repeats and emphasises the idea
  in φαεινήν (cf. 422)

ἐκ (as adv.) from it, i.e. attached to it

τελαμών -ῶνος, ὁ shield strap

481 πέντε five

αὐτοῦ (here) 'of the shield itself' (rather
  than the decorated surface); ἐν αὐτῷ
  is the unemphatic 'on it'

ἔσαν: 3 pl. impf. of εἰμί (= Att. ἦσαν)

πτύξ πτυχός, ἡ fold, (here) layer. Other
  shields in the *Iliad* seem to be made
  of concentric layers of oxhide of
  decreasing diameter, making the
  central part the sturdiest. A layer of
  bronze, hammered on to the surface
  of such a construction, would give the
  appearance of five separate rings. In
  what follows the poet perhaps invites
  us to see each separate element as
  presented on a different ring.

483–9: *Scenes on the shield (1) Earth and Sky.*

483 ἐν (as adv.) on it

ἔτευξ(ε): 3 s. aor. of τεύχω (cf. 120). The
  different scenes on the shield are introduced by a variety of words: ἔτευξε
  here, ποίησε (490), (ἐ)τίθει (541, 550,
  561), ποίησε again (573, 587), ποίκιλλε
  (590) and τίθει again (607). Each
  change of introductory word perhaps
  indicates a separate ring/layer, with
  the rim of the shield as a sixth.

οὐρανός -οῦ, ὁ sky, heaven

484 σελήνη -ης, ἡ moon

πλήθω I am full

485 τείρεα, τά constellations; Homeric pl. of
  τέρας -ατος, τό (sign, portent). They
  served as signs in navigation and to plot
  the course of the year in agriculture.

στεφανόω I put on as a crown; ἐστεφάνωται is 3 s. perf. mid. Tr. phrase 'which
  the sky has put on itself as a crown';
  τ(ε) with rel. pron. expressing a per-
  manent characteristic.

486 Πληϊάδες -ων, αἱ the Pleiades (a prominent constellation, like the next three)

Ὑάδες -ων, αἱ the Hyades

Ὠρίων -ωνος, ὁ Orion; σθένος Ὠρίωνος lit. 'the strength of Orion' i.e.
  'mighty Orion' (cf. on 117)

487 Ἄρκτος -ου, ἡ the Great Bear

Ἄμαξα -ης, ἡ Wagon (the older form
  'Wain' is another name in English for
  the Great Bear)

ἐπίκλησις, ἡ extra name; for the acc. cf.
  Matthew 1:21 (AV) 'Thou shalt call
  his name Jesus'

488 αὐτοῦ (adv.) (here) in the same place

στρέφομαι I turn round

δοκεύω I watch closely

489 ἄμμορος -ον without a share in (+ gen.)

λοετρόν -ου, τό bath (= Att. λουτρόν).
  The Great Bear for viewers in the
  northern hemisphere never dips
  below the horizon.

Ἐν δὲ δύω ποίησε πόλεις μερόπων ἀνθρώπων   490
καλάς· ἐν τῇ μέν ῥα γάμοι τ᾽ ἔσαν εἰλαπίναι τε,
νύμφας δ᾽ ἐκ θαλάμων δαΐδων ὕπο λαμπομενάων
ἠγίνεον ἀνὰ ἄστυ, πολὺς δ᾽ ὑμέναιος ὀρώρει·
κοῦροι δ᾽ ὀρχηστῆρες ἐδίνεον, ἐν δ᾽ ἄρα τοῖσιν
αὐλοὶ φόρμιγγές τε βοὴν ἔχον· αἱ δὲ γυναῖκες   495
ἱστάμεναι θαύμαζον ἐπὶ προθύροισιν ἑκάστη.
λαοὶ δ᾽ εἰν ἀγορῇ ἔσαν ἀθρόοι· ἔνθα δὲ νεῖκος
ὠρώρει, δύο δ᾽ ἄνδρες ἐνείκεον εἵνεκα ποινῆς
ἀνδρὸς ἀποφθιμένου· ὁ μὲν εὔχετο πάντ᾽ ἀποδοῦναι
δήμῳ πιφαύσκων, ὁ δ᾽ ἀναίνετο μηδὲν ἑλέσθαι·   500
ἄμφω δ᾽ ἱέσθην ἐπὶ ἴστορι πεῖραρ ἑλέσθαι.
λαοὶ δ᾽ ἀμφοτέροισιν ἐπήπυον, ἀμφὶς ἀρωγοί·
κήρυκες δ᾽ ἄρα λαὸν ἐρήτυον· οἱ δὲ γέροντες
ἥατ᾽ ἐπὶ ξεστοῖσι λίθοις ἱερῷ ἐνὶ κύκλῳ,
σκῆπτρα δὲ κηρύκων ἐν χέρσ᾽ ἔχον ἠεροφώνων·   505
τοῖσιν ἔπειτ᾽ ἤϊσσον, ἀμοιβηδὶς δὲ δίκαζον.
κεῖτο δ᾽ ἄρ᾽ ἐν μέσσοισι δύω χρυσοῖο τάλαντα,
τῷ δόμεν ὃς μετὰ τοῖσι δίκην ἰθύντατα εἴποι.

490–508: Scenes on the shield (2) A city at peace. *Two features of the city at peace are described: a marriage ceremony (490–6) and a dispute being resolved peacefully by litigation (497–508).*

490 δύω = δύο (cf. 157)
ποίησε: 3 s. aor. of ποιέω (cf. 371)

491 καλάς: emphatic enjambment, again almost like an exclamation
ἐν τῇ μέν in the one
γάμος -ου, ὁ marriage, wedding
εἰλαπίνη -ης, ἡ feast, banquet

492 νύμφη -ης ἡ bride
θάλαμος -ου, ὁ bedroom. The reference here is to rooms in parental homes.
δαΐς -ίδος, ἡ torch
ὕπο (+ gen.) (here) to the accompaniment of; accented as postposition
λάμπομαι I shine; λαμπομενάων is pres. part. (f. gen. pl.)

493 ἀγινέω I lead, conduct; ἠγίνεον is 3 pl. impf. (scanned as three long syllables, running the last two short ones together)
ἀνά (+ acc.) (here) all round
ὑμέναιος -ου, ὁ wedding song
ὀρώρει: 3 s. plup. of ὄρνυμι (cf. 170), here intrans. 'arose'

494 κοῦρος -ου, ὁ young man (= Att. κόρος)
ὀρχηστήρ -ῆρος, ὁ dancer; here as adj. (cf. on 319)
δινέω I turn round and round, whirl

495 αὐλός -οῦ, ὁ pipe, flute
φόρμιγξ -ιγγος, ἡ lyre
βοή -ῆς, ἡ (here) loud sound (of the musical instruments)
ἔχον: 3 pl. impf. of ἔχω (cf. 21)

496 ἱστάμεναι: pres. part. (f. nom. pl.) of ἵσταμαι (cf. 160)
πρόθυρον -ου, τό front porch, doorway
ἑκάστη (cf. 31): s. (with pl. part. and verb) for sense rather than strict grammar (cf. on 299)

497–508 The litigation. A man has been killed, and there is a dispute over the penalty to be paid. The parties submit their dispute to a meeting of elders who are described in the process of debate.

497 ἀθρόοι -αι -α all together, in crowds
νεῖκος -εος, τό dispute, quarrel

498 ὠρώρει: augmented form of ὀρώρει (cf.
493) 'had arisen'
νεικέω I quarrel
ποινή -ῆς, ἡ blood price, compensation

499 ἀποφθιμένου: aor. part. (m. gen. s.) of
ἀποφθίομαι (cf. 89), here 'who had
been killed'
εὔχομαι (here) I declare
ἀποδίδωμι I pay, deliver up; ἀποδοῦναι
is aor. inf. The meaning of 499–500 is
debated. Either (i) one litigant promised to pay a blood price, but the other
refused to accept it, or (ii) one said he
had paid it, but the other denied having received it. The difficulty arises because aor. inf. can mean either (i) 'to
do X (once)' or (ii) 'to have done X'.

500 πιφαύσκω I make known; part. πῑφαύ-
σκων (m. nom. s.) here scanned with
long ι. The point of δήμῳ (cf. 295) is
that this first session is a general (and
probably rowdy) meeting, before the
case comes to the ἵστωρ (501).
ἀναίνομαι I refuse (cf. 450) or I deny;
ἀναίνετο (3 s. impf.) either (i) 'refused
(to accept anything)', or (ii) 'denied
(that he had received anything)', in either case with redundant neg. (μηδέν,
lit. 'nothing') for emphasis, as oft.
ἑλέσθαι: aor. mid. inf. of αἱρέω (cf. 23)

501 ἱέσθην: 3 dual impf. mid. of ἵημι (cf. 182),
here 'were eager'
ἐπί (+ dat.) (here) on the authority of
ἵστωρ -ορος, ὁ judge (lit. one who
knows)
πεῖραρ -ατος, τό decision, judgement
ἑλέσθαι (here) 'to win (the verdict)'

502 ἐπηπύω I applaud, give assent to (+ dat.);
ἐπήπυον is 3 pl. impf.
ἀμφίς (adv.) on both sides
ἀρωγός -οῦ, ὁ supporter

503 κῆρυξ -υκος, ὁ herald
ἐρητύω I hold back, restrain

504 ἧατ(ο): 3 pl. impf. of ἧμαι (cf. 36); note
-ατο as an alternative to -ντο as 3 pl.
ending
ἐπί (+ dat.) (here) on
ξεστός -ή -όν smoothed, polished
λίθος -ου, ὁ stone
κύκλος -ου, ὁ circle. It is sacred because
Zeus presides over the administration
of justice (cf. 9.98–9: it is from Zeus that
Agamemnon gets his judicial authority).

505 ἠερόφωνος -ον loud-voiced (lit. sounding
through the air)

506 τοῖσιν with them (i.e. the staffs, which
signal the right to speak)
ἤϊσσον: 3 pl. impf. of ἀΐσσω (cf. 212),
here 'they sprang up'
ἀμοιβηδίς (adv.) in turn
δικάζω I give judgement

507 τάλαντον -ου, τό talent (a unit of weight,
in Homer always of gold). In the
classical period two talents would
have been a huge sum (approximately
the cost of financing a trireme for
two months). But at 23.267–70 'two
gold talents' are offered as fourth
prize in the chariot race (worse than
an unused cauldron but better than
a two-handled jar). It seems likely
that the litigants have each deposited
a talent, and these are to be a reward
for the elder who proposes the most
reasonable solution.

508 τῷ ... ὅς to the one who
μετὰ τοῖσι among them
δίκη -ης, ἡ justice, judgement
ἰθύντατα most straightly, most fairly;
sup. adv. from ἰθύς (straight)
εἴποι: 3 s. opt. of εἶπον, aor. of λέγω (cf.
5), here indefinite

Τὴν δ᾽ ἑτέρην πόλιν ἀμφὶ δύω στρατοὶ ἥατο λαῶν
τεύχεσι λαμπόμενοι· δίχα δέ σφισιν ἥνδανε βουλή,   510
ἠὲ διαπραθέειν ἢ ἄνδιχα πάντα δάσασθαι,
κτῆσιν ὅσην πτολίεθρον ἐπήρατον ἐντὸς ἔεργεν·
οἱ δ᾽ οὔ πω πείθοντο, λόχῳ δ᾽ ὑπεθωρήσσοντο.
τεῖχος μέν ῥ᾽ ἄλοχοί τε φίλαι καὶ νήπια τέκνα
ῥύατ᾽ ἐφεσταότες, μετὰ δ᾽ ἀνέρες οὓς ἔχε γῆρας·   515
οἱ δ᾽ ἴσαν· ἦρχε δ᾽ ἄρά σφιν Ἄρης καὶ Παλλὰς Ἀθήνη,
ἄμφω χρυσείω, χρύσεια δὲ εἵματα ἕσθην,
καλὼ καὶ μεγάλω σὺν τεύχεσιν, ὥς τε θεώ περ
ἀμφὶς ἀριζήλω· λαοὶ δ᾽ ὑπολίζονες ἦσαν.
οἱ δ᾽ ὅτε δή ῥ᾽ ἵκανον ὅθι σφίσιν εἶκε λοχῆσαι,   520
ἐν ποταμῷ, ὅθι τ᾽ ἀρδμὸς ἔην πάντεσσι βοτοῖσιν,
ἔνθ᾽ ἄρα τοί γ᾽ ἵζοντ᾽ εἰλυμένοι αἴθοπι χαλκῷ.
τοῖσι δ᾽ ἔπειτ᾽ ἀπάνευθε δύω σκοποὶ ἥατο λαῶν,
δέγμενοι ὁππότε μῆλα ἰδοίατο καὶ ἕλικας βοῦς.
οἱ δὲ τάχα προγένοντο, δύω δ᾽ ἅμ᾽ ἕποντο νομῆες   525
τερπόμενοι σύριγξι· δόλον δ᾽ οὔ τι προνόησαν.
οἱ μὲν τὰ προϊδόντες ἐπέδραμον, ὦκα δ᾽ ἔπειτα

509–40: Scenes on the shield (3) A city at war. We might expect the contrast between the two cities to be straightforward, one showing the blessings of peace (new life in prospect through marriage, disputes settled amicably), the other showing the horrors of war. In fact in this brief description with its unexpected twists we see the drama and pathos as well as the horror of war. Several scenes are described. In the first there is a suggestion of Troy, with the old men upon the wall as in Book 3. In the following ambush we are reminded of Achilles' raids on Trojan and allied cities.

509–24: A raiding party sallies out of the besieged city.

509 ἥατο (here) were encamped (cf. 36 and 504)

510 δίχα (adv.) in two ways, at variance
ἁνδάνω I please, am acceptable to (+ dat.); ἥνδανε is 3 s. impf. The divided counsel of the attackers perhaps reflects the depiction of the town as assailed by forces on both sides.

511 ἠέ = ἤ
διαπέρθω I sack, destroy; διαπραθέειν is aor. inf.
ἄνδιχα (adv.) in two equal parts
δάσασθαι: aor. inf. of δατέομαι (cf. 264). The division envisaged is that half the wealth of the city should be handed over to buy off the besiegers.

512 κτῆσις -ιος, ἡ property
πτολίεθρον -ου, τό city, town
ἐπήρατος -ον lovely
ἐντός (adv.) within
ἐέργω I shut in, contain (= Att. εἴργω)

513 οἱ δ(έ) but they, i.e. the besieged citizens
οὔ πω (cf. 378): with the hint that the time will come, as it will for Troy
λόχος -ου, ὁ ambush; dat. here 'for an ambush'
ὑποθωρήσσομαι I arm myself; ὑπο- suggests 'in secret' (cf. on 319). We initially assume this ambush will be directed at the besieging forces themselves.

514 νήπιος -η -ον (here) young

515 ῥύομαι I guard; ῥύατ(ο) is 3 pl. impf.
    ἐφίσταμαι I stand on; ἐφεσταότες is perf.
        part. (m. nom. pl.) with pres. sense
        (despite f. and n. subjects, m. for the
        whole group, including old men about
        to be mentioned)
    μετά (as adv.) (here) along with them
516 οἱ δ(έ) but they, i.e. the raiding party
    ἴσαν: 3 pl. impf. of εἶμι (I go) 'were on
        their way'
    ἄρχω I lead, am commander of (+ dat.);
        ἦρχε is 3 s. impf. with the first of two
        subjects, but understood with both
        (cf. 28)
    σφίν: dat. of σφεῖς (cf. 66). Ares perhaps
        represents the fighters' determination
        to do battle, Athena the cunning of
        their plan. In the fighting of the *Iliad*
        they would never be on the same side
        (cf. 21.391–433).
517 χρυσείω: m. nom. dual of χρύσειος (cf.
        206). Occasional mention of materials
        brings us back from the world depict-
        ed to the fabric of the shield itself.
    εἷμα -ατος τό garment, pl. clothing
    ἕννυμι I clothe (someone), mid. I wear;
        ἕσθην is 3 dual plup. mid. (with impf.
        sense)
518 καλώ, μεγάλω, θεώ (and ἀριζήλω in
        519): all m. nom. dual
    ὥς τε as befits (the τε is generalising)
519 ἀρίζηλος -ον (here) clear to see, conspic-
        uous (cf. 219)
    ὑπολίζων -ονος (m. comp. adj.) on a
        smaller scale
520 οἱ δ(έ): i.e. the men

ὅθι (rel. adv.) where
εἶκε: 3 s. impf. of ἔοικα (cf. 418) as imper-
    sonal 'it seemed good'
λοχάω I lie in ambush; λοχῆσαι is aor.
    inf.
521 ποταμός -οῦ/οῖο, ὁ river
    ἀρδμός -οῦ, ὁ watering place
    πάντεσσι: Homeric n. dat. pl. of πᾶς (cf.
        30)
    βοτά -ῶν, τά flocks, herds
522 τοί = οἱ (cf. on 67)
    ἵζοντο: 3 pl. impf. mid. of ἵζω
        (cf. 422)
    εἰλύω I envelop; εἰλυμένοι is perf. pass.
        part. (m. nom. pl.)
    αἴθοψ -οπος (m. adj.) gleaming; a for-
        mulaic epithet for bronze but hardly
        appropriate for an ambush. The poet
        is concentrating on the fabric of the
        shield (cf. on 517), or perhaps just
        saying that the men were in armour.
523 τοῖσι for them
    ἀπάνευθε (here as adv.) at a distance
    σκοπός -οῦ, ὁ watchman, lookout
    ἧατο (here) took up position (cf. 504)
524 δέγμενοι: Homeric pres. part. (m. nom.
        pl.) of δέχομαι (cf. 115) 'waiting'
    ὁππότε (+ opt.) (here) for when they
        might
    μῆλα -ων, τά flocks
    ἰδοίατο: 3 pl. aor. opt. mid. of ὁράω (for
        the -ατο ending cf. on 504)
    ἕλιξ -ικος (m./f. adj.) with twisted
        horns
    βοῦς βοός, ὁ/ἡ ox/cow

525–9: The party attacks the besiegers' flocks and herds.

525 οἱ δέ and they, i.e. the flocks and herds
    τάχα (adv.) quickly, soon
    προγίγνομαι I advance, approach; προ-
        γένοντο is 3 pl. aor.
    ἕποντο: 3 pl. impf. of ἕπομαι (cf. 234)
    νομεύς -ῆος, ὁ herdsman
526 τέρπομαι I take pleasure in (+ dat.)
    σῦριγξ -ιγγος, ἡ pipe, Pan-pipe
    δόλος -ου, ὁ trick

προνοέω I foresee, suspect; προνόησαν is
    3 pl. aor.
527 οἱ μέν: i.e. the ambushers; μέν reminds us
        that their enemies are not far away
    τά them, i.e. the flocks and herds
    προεῖδον (aor.) I looked forward, caught
        sight of; προϊδόντες is part. (m. nom. pl.)
    ἐπιτρέχω I run up; ἐπέδραμον is 3 pl. aor.
    ὦκα quickly; adv. of ὠκύς (cf. 78)

τάμνοντ᾽ ἀμφὶ βοῶν ἀγέλας καὶ πώεα καλὰ
ἀργεννέων ὀΐων, κτεῖνον δ᾽ ἐπὶ μηλοβοτῆρας.
οἱ δ᾽ ὡς οὖν ἐπύθοντο πολὺν κέλαδον παρὰ βουσὶν   530
εἰράων προπάροιθε καθήμενοι, αὐτίκ᾽ ἐφ᾽ ἵππων
βάντες ἀερσιπόδων μετεκίαθον, αἶψα δ᾽ ἵκοντο.
στησάμενοι δ᾽ ἐμάχοντο μάχην ποταμοῖο παρ᾽ ὄχθας,
βάλλον δ᾽ ἀλλήλους χαλκήρεσιν ἐγχείῃσιν.
ἐν δ᾽ Ἔρις ἐν δὲ Κυδοιμὸς ὁμίλεον, ἐν δ᾽ ὀλοὴ Κήρ,   535
ἄλλον ζωὸν ἔχουσα νεούτατον, ἄλλον ἄουτον,
ἄλλον τεθνηῶτα κατὰ μόθον ἕλκε ποδοῖιν·
εἷμα δ᾽ ἔχ᾽ ἀμφ᾽ ὤμοισι δαφοινεὸν αἵματι φωτῶν.
ὡμίλευν δ᾽ ὥς τε ζωοὶ βροτοὶ ἠδ᾽ ἐμάχοντο,
νεκρούς τ᾽ ἀλλήλων ἔρυον κατατεθνηῶτας.   540
    Ἐν δ᾽ ἐτίθει νειὸν μαλακήν, πίειραν ἄρουραν,
εὐρεῖαν τρίπολον· πολλοὶ δ᾽ ἀροτῆρες ἐν αὐτῇ
ζεύγεα δινεύοντες ἐλάστρεον ἔνθα καὶ ἔνθα.
οἱ δ᾽ ὁπότε στρέψαντες ἱκοίατο τέλσον ἀρούρης,
τοῖσι δ᾽ ἔπειτ᾽ ἐν χερσὶ δέπας μελιηδέος οἴνου   545
δόσκεν ἀνὴρ ἐπιών· τοὶ δὲ στρέψασκον ἀν᾽ ὄγμους,
ἱέμενοι νειοῖο βαθείης τέλσον ἱκέσθαι.
ἡ δὲ μελαίνετ᾽ ὄπισθεν, ἀρηρομένῃ δὲ ἐῴκει,
χρυσείη περ ἐοῦσα· τὸ δὴ περὶ θαῦμα τέτυκτο.
    Ἐν δ᾽ ἐτίθει τέμενος βασιλήϊον· ἔνθα δ᾽ ἔριθοι   550

---

528 τάμνοντ(ο): 3 pl. impf. of τάμνω (cf. 177); with ἀμφί in an unusual form of tmesis 'they were intercepting and cutting off'
ἀγέλη -ης, ἡ herd

πῶυ -εος, τό flock
529 ἀργεννός -ή όν white
ὄϊς ὄϊος/οἰός, ὁ/ἡ sheep
ἐπί (as adv.) in addition
μηλοβοτήρ -ῆρος, ὁ shepherd

530–40: The besiegers join battle with the raiding party.

530 οἱ δ(έ) but they, i.e. the besiegers
ἐπύθοντο: 3 pl. aor. of πυνθάνομαι (cf. 19)
κέλαδος -ου, ὁ clamour, commotion
531 εἴρη -ης, ἡ speaking-place (probable meaning); εἰράων is gen. pl. The besiegers are still engaged in debate (as at 510–12); προπάροιθε (cf. 3) envisages the troops gathered in front of a group of speakers.
κάθημαι I sit; καθήμενοι is pres. part. (m. nom. pl.)

532 βάντες: aor. part. (m. nom. pl.) of βαίνω (cf. 416), here (with ἐφ᾽ (531) = ἐπί + gen.) 'mounting (chariots) behind'
ἀερσίπους -ποδος (m. adj.) high-stepping
μετακιάθω I go after, go in pursuit of
αἶψα (adv.) at once, immediately
533 στησάμενοι: aor. mid. part. (m. nom. pl.) of ἵστημι (cf. 344) here 'having got into line'
ὄχθη -ης, ἡ bank (of a river)

534 βάλλω (here) I pelt
χαλκήρης -ες bronze-tipped
ἐγχείη -ης, ἡ spear
535 Ἔρις -ιδος, ἡ Discord (personified)
Κυδοιμός -οῦ, ὁ Tumult (personified)
ὁμίλεον: 3 pl. impf. of ὁμιλέω (cf. 194)
ὀλοός -ή -όν deadly, destructive
Κήρ Κηρός, ἡ Death-spirit (personified)
536 νεούτατος -ον recently wounded
ἄουτος -ον unwounded
537 τεθνηῶτα: perf. part. (m. acc. s.) of θνήσκω (cf. 12)

ποδοῖιν: dat. dual of πούς (cf. 2)
538 δαφοινεός -όν red, gory
αἷμα -ατος, τό blood
539 ὡμίλευν: 3 pl. impf. of ὁμιλέω (cf. 194).
'They took part like living mortals'
might refer to the personified spirits,
but more probably refers to the human participants (the poet drawing
attention to the realistic nature of
Hephaestus' sculpture).
540 καταθνήσκω I die; κατατεθνηῶτας is
perf. part. (m. acc. pl.)

541–9: Scenes on the shield (4) Tilled lands.

541 ἐτίθει: 3 s. impf. of τίθημι (cf. 352)
νειός -οῦ/οῖο, ἡ fallow land
μαλακός -ή -όν soft
ἄρουρα -ης, ἡ (here) field (cf. 104)
542 τρίπολος -ον three times ploughed;
an epithet of fertile soil (repeated
ploughing in autumn makes it more
receptive of winter moisture)
ἀροτήρ -ῆρος, ὁ ploughman
543 ζεῦγος -εος, τό yoke, pl. team (of oxen)
δινεύω I turn (something) round repeatedly
ἐλαστρέω I drive
ἔνθα καὶ ἔνθα back and forth
544 ὁπότε (+ opt.) whenever
στρέψαντες: aor. part. (m. nom. pl.) of
στρέφω (cf. 139); understand 'the
team' as object
ἱκοίατο: 3 pl. aor. opt. of ἵκω (cf. 292)
τέλσον -ου, τό turning point, end
545 δέπας -αος, τό cup
μελιηδής -ές honey-sweet
οἶνος -ου, ὁ wine
546 δόσκεν: 3 s. aor. iterative of δίδωμι (cf. 84)

ἔπειμι I come up to, approach; ἐπιών is
pres. part. (m. nom. s.)
στρέψασκον: 3 pl. aor. iterative of στρέφω
(cf. 139)
ὄγμος -ου, ὁ furrow
547 ἱέμενοι: mid. part. (m. nom. pl.) of ἵημι
(cf. 182 and 501) 'hurrying eagerly'
βαθύς -εῖα -ύ deep
548 μελαίνομαι I become dark, grow black
ὄπισθε(ν) (adv.) behind
ἀρόω I plough; ἀρηρομένη is perf. pass.
part. (f. dat. s.)
ἐῴκει: 3 s. past of ἔοικα (cf. 418)
549 ἐοῦσα: pres. part. (f. nom. s.) of εἰμί (=
Att. οὖσα)
περί (as adv.) outstandingly
τέτυκτο: 3 s. plup. mid./pass. of τεύχω
(cf. 120). Between 541 ἐτίθει and 548
ἐῴκει there is nothing to remind us
that this is a static work of art. Eight
verbs describe motion. The most
complicated and miraculous feature
occurs in 548–9, just where we get the
reminder.

550–60: Scenes on the shield (5) The corn harvest.

550 τέμενος -εος, τό private estate (granted to
a lord, or dedicated to a god)

βασιλήιος -η -ον royal
ἔριθος -ου, ὁ hired labourer, harvester

ἥμων ὀξείας δρεπάνας ἐν χερσὶν ἔχοντες.
δράγματα δ᾽ ἄλλα μετ᾽ ὄγμον ἐπήτριμα πῖπτον ἔραζε,
ἄλλα δ᾽ ἀμαλλοδετῆρες ἐν ἐλλεδανοῖσι δέοντο.
τρεῖς δ᾽ ἄρ᾽ ἀμαλλοδετῆρες ἐφέστασαν· αὐτὰρ ὄπισθε
παῖδες δραγμεύοντες, ἐν ἀγκαλίδεσσι φέροντες,   555
ἀσπερχὲς πάρεχον· βασιλεὺς δ᾽ ἐν τοῖσι σιωπῇ
σκῆπτρον ἔχων ἑστήκει ἐπ᾽ ὄγμου γηθόσυνος κῆρ.
κήρυκες δ᾽ ἀπάνευθεν ὑπὸ δρυῒ δαῖτα πένοντο,
βοῦν δ᾽ ἱερεύσαντες μέγαν ἄμφεπον· αἱ δὲ γυναῖκες
δεῖπνον ἐρίθοισιν λεύκ᾽ ἄλφιτα πολλὰ πάλυνον.   560
    Ἐν δὲ τίθει σταφυλῇσι μέγα βρίθουσαν ἀλωὴν
καλὴν χρυσείην· μέλανες δ᾽ ἀνὰ βότρυες ἦσαν,
ἑστήκει δὲ κάμαξι διαμπερὲς ἀργυρέῃσιν.
ἀμφὶ δὲ κυανέην κάπετον, περὶ δ᾽ ἕρκος ἔλασσε
κασσιτέρου· μία δ᾽ οἴη ἀταρπιτὸς ἦεν ἐπ᾽ αὐτήν,   565
τῇ νίσοντο φορῆες, ὅτε τρυγόῳεν ἀλωήν.
παρθενικαὶ δὲ καὶ ἠΐθεοι ἀταλὰ φρονέοντες
πλεκτοῖς ἐν ταλάροισι φέρον μελιηδέα καρπόν.
τοῖσιν δ᾽ ἐν μέσσοισι πάϊς φόρμιγγι λιγείῃ
ἱμερόεν κιθάριζε, λίνον δ᾽ ὑπὸ καλὸν ἄειδε   570
λεπταλέῃ φωνῇ· τοὶ δὲ ῥήσσοντες ἁμαρτῇ
μολπῇ τ᾽ ἰυγμῷ τε ποσὶ σκαίροντες ἕποντο.
    Ἐν δ᾽ ἀγέλην ποίησε βοῶν ὀρθοκραιράων·
αἱ δὲ βόες χρυσοῖο τετεύχατο κασσιτέρου τε,
μυκηθμῷ δ᾽ ἀπὸ κόπρου ἐπεσσεύοντο νομόνδε   575
πὰρ ποταμὸν κελάδοντα, παρὰ ῥοδανὸν δονακῆα.

551 ἀμάω I reap; ἥμων is 3 pl. impf.
    δρεπάνη -ης, ἡ sickle
552 δράγμα -ατος, τό handful (of stalks of
    grain)
    ἄλλος … ἄλλος one … another, pl. some
        … others
    μετ(ά) (+ acc.) (here) along
    ἔραζε to the ground
553 ἀμαλλοδετήρ -ῆρος, ὁ sheaf-binder
    ἐλλεδανός -οῦ, ὁ cord (for binding
        sheaves)
    δέομαι (here) I bind, fasten
554 τρεῖς three
    ἐφίσταμαι I stand close by; ἐφέστασαν is
        3 pl. plup.
555 παῖδες (cf. 71): the boys must logically be
        just behind the harvesters, not behind
        the binders; the poet apparently adds
        this subsidiary detail out of sequence

δραγμεύω I gather handfuls
ἀγκαλίς -ίδος, ἡ arm; ἀγκαλίδεσσι is dat.
    pl.
556 ἀσπερχές (adv.) unceasingly
    παρέχω I give
    βασιλεύς -ῆος, ὁ king; but often to be
        understood as a local lord or
        chieftain
    σιωπή -ῆς, ἡ silence; σιωπῇ silently, in
        silence
557 ἑστήκει: 3 s. plup. of ἵσταμαι (cf. 160)
        with impf. sense 'was standing'
    γηθόσυνος -η -ον glad
558 δρῦς -υός, ἡ oak
    δαίς δαιτός, ἡ feast, meal
    πένομαι I prepare
559 ἱερεύω I sacrifice, slaughter; ἱερεύσαντες
        is aor. part. (m. nom. pl.)
    ἀμφέπω I am busy with (+ acc.)

560 δεῖπνον -ου, τό meal
   ἄλφιτον -ου, τό barley
   παλύνω I sprinkle. If the δεῖπνον is a
    separate economy-class dinner for the
    workers (only the lord and heralds

feasting on the ox), this refers to
sprinkling barley into water to make a
broth. If it is the same meal for all, the
women are sprinkling barley over the
meat, as at *Odyssey* 14.77.

561–72: Scenes on the shield (6) A vineyard.

561 σταφυλή -ῆς, ἡ bunch of grapes
   βρίθω I am weighed down
   ἀλωή -ῆς, ἡ (here) vineyard
    (cf. 57)
562 ἀνά (as adv.) all over it
   βότρυς -υος, ὁ cluster of grapes
563 ἑστήκει (cf. 557): understand 'the vine-
    yard' as subject. This line gives a good
    idea of the rows of head-high grape
    clusters, as seen now in Southern Italy.
   κάμαξ -ακος, ἡ vine pole, vine prop
   διαμπερές (adv.) throughout
564 ἀμφί (as adv.) around (the vineyard)
   κυάνεος -ον bluish black (made from
    κύανος, an enamel of this colour)
   κάπετος -ου, ἡ ditch
   ἕρκος -εος, τό fence, boundary wall
   ἐλαύνω (here) I draw out, extend; ἔλασσε
    is 3 s. aor.
565 εἷς μία ἕν (ἑνός) one
   ἀταρπιτός -ου, ἡ path
566 τῇ by which
   νίσομαι I go, come; νίσοντο is 3 pl. impf.
   φορεύς -ῆος, ὁ carrier (of grapes), vin-
    tager
   τρυγάω I gather harvest from; τρυγόωεν
    is 3 pl. opt. giving indefinite sense
    'whenever'
567 παρθενική -ῆς, ἡ maiden, unmarried girl
   ἠΐθεος -ου, ὁ unmarried young man (=
    Att. ἤθεος)

   ἀταλός -η -ον delicate, youthful; ἀταλά
    φρονέοντες (cf. 4) 'light-hearted'
568 πλεκτός -ή -όν woven, wicker
   τάλαρος -οῦ, ὁ basket
   καρπός -οῦ, ὁ fruit
569 λιγύς -εῖα -ύ clear, piercing
570 ἱμερόεις -εσσα -εν (-εντος) charming,
    lovely; n. here as adv.
   κιθαρίζω I play the cithara/lyre. Classi-
    fiers of Greek musical instruments
    distinguish the φόρμιγξ (cf. 495) and
    the κιθάρα by number of strings, but
    the distinction seems not to matter to
    the poet here.
   λίνος -ου, ὁ Linus song. It is odd to find
    this traditional lament for the death
    of the minstrel Linus (a shadowy
    figure) sung on a happy occasion, but
    he was perhaps in origin a vegetation
    god, and the harvest takes place when
    vegetation dies back.
   ὑπό (as adv.) (here) in accompaniment
    (i.e. to the harvesting)
   καλόν: n. as adv.; with ἄειδε
   ἀείδω I sing (= Att. ᾄδω)
571 λεπταλέος -η -ον fine, delicate
   ῥήσσω I stamp my feet
   ἁμαρτῇ (adv.) together, at once
572 μολπή -ῆς, ἡ singing and dancing
   ἰυγμός -οῦ, ὁ joyful cry
   σκαίρω I skip

573–86: Scenes on the shield (7) Cattle-herding.

573 ὀρθόκραιρος -η -ον with upright horns
    (cf. 3)
574 χρυσοῖο ... κασσιτέρου τε: ancient
    commentators saw 'gold and tin' as
    referring to the two colours of the
    hides of the cattle
   τετεύχατο: 3 pl. plup. pass. of τεύχω (cf.
    120)

575 μυκηθμός -οῦ, ὁ lowing, bellowing
   κόπρος -ου, ἡ lit. dung, (here) farmyard,
    byre (where dung accumulates)
   ἐπισσεύομαι I hurry
   νομός -οῦ, ὁ pasture; νομόνδε to pasture
576 πάρ = πάρα
   κελάδων -οντος (m. adj.) sounding
   ῥοδανός -ή -όν waving, swaying
   δονακεύς -ῆος, ὁ thicket of reeds

χρύσειοι δὲ νομῆες ἅμ᾽ ἐστιχόωντο βόεσσι
τέσσαρες, ἐννέα δέ σφι κύνες πόδας ἀργοὶ ἕποντο.
σμερδαλέω δὲ λέοντε δύ᾽ ἐν πρώτῃσι βόεσσι
ταῦρον ἐρύγμηλον ἐχέτην· ὁ δὲ μακρὰ μεμυκὼς   580
ἕλκετο· τὸν δὲ κύνες μετεκίαθον ἠδ᾽ αἰζηοί.
τὼ μὲν ἀναρρήξαντε βοὸς μεγάλοιο βοείην
ἔγκατα καὶ μέλαν αἷμα λαφύσσετον· οἱ δὲ νομῆες
αὕτως ἐνδίεσαν ταχέας κύνας ὀτρύνοντες.
οἱ δ᾽ ἤτοι δακέειν μὲν ἀπετρωπῶντο λεόντων,   585
ἱστάμενοι δὲ μάλ᾽ ἐγγὺς ὑλάκτεον ἔκ τ᾽ ἀλέοντο.
    Ἐν δὲ νομὸν ποίησε περικλυτὸς ἀμφιγυήεις
ἐν καλῇ βήσσῃ μέγαν οἰῶν ἀργεννάων,
σταθμούς τε κλισίας τε κατηρεφέας ἰδὲ σηκούς.
    Ἐν δὲ χορὸν ποίκιλλε περικλυτὸς ἀμφιγυήεις,   590
τῷ ἴκελον οἷόν ποτ᾽ ἐνὶ Κνωσῷ εὐρείῃ
Δαίδαλος ἤσκησεν καλλιπλοκάμῳ Ἀριάδνῃ.
ἔνθα μὲν ἠΐθεοι καὶ παρθένοι ἀλφεσίβοιαι
ὠρχεῦντ᾽, ἀλλήλων ἐπὶ καρπῷ χεῖρας ἔχοντες.
τῶν δ᾽ αἱ μὲν λεπτὰς ὀθόνας ἔχον, οἱ δὲ χιτῶνας   595
εἵατ᾽ ἐϋννήτους, ἦκα στίλβοντας ἐλαίῳ·
καί ῥ᾽ αἱ μὲν καλὰς στεφάνας ἔχον, οἱ δὲ μαχαίρας
εἶχον χρυσείας ἐξ ἀργυρέων τελαμώνων.
οἱ δ᾽ ὁτὲ μὲν θρέξασκον ἐπισταμένοισι πόδεσσι
ῥεῖα μάλ᾽, ὡς ὅτε τις τροχὸν ἄρμενον ἐν παλάμῃσιν   600

---

577 στιχάομαι I walk; ἐστιχόωντο is 3 pl. impf.

578 τέσσαρες four
   ἐννέα nine
   πόδας: acc. of resp.
   ἀργοί: cf. 283

579 σμερδαλέος -έα -έον fearful, terrible;
      σμερδαλέω is m. nom. dual
   λέοντε (cf. 161): m. nom. dual

580 ταῦρος -οῦ, ὁ bull
   ἐρύγμηλος -η -ον bellowing
   ἐχέτην: 3 dual impf. of ἔχω (cf. 21)
   μακρά (adv.) (audible) afar, i.e. loudly
   μυκάομαι I low, bellow; μεμυκώς is perf.
      part. (m. nom. s.)

581 ἕλκετο: 3 s. impf. pass. of ἕλκω (cf. 156)
   αἰζηός -οῦ, ὁ vigorous young man

582 τώ the two of them (i.e. the lions); m.
      nom. dual of article as personal pron.
   ἀναρρήγνυμι I burst (something) open;
      ἀναρρήξαντε is aor. part. (m. nom. dual)

βοείη -ης, ἡ hide

583 ἔγκατα, τά entrails
   λαφύσσω I gulp down; λαφύσσετον is 3
      dual impf.

584 αὕτως in vain
   ἐνδίημι I send in; ἐνδίεσαν is 3 pl. impf.
   ὀτρύνω I urge on

585 ἤτοι and yet
   δάκνω I bite; δακέειν is aor. inf.
   ἀποτρωπάομαι I shrink from (+ inf. and
      gen.)

586 ἱστάμενοι: part. (m. nom. pl.) of ἵσταμαι
      (cf. 160)
   ἐγγύς (adv.) near
   ὑλακτέω I bark
   ἐξαλέομαι I keep away; ἐκ ... ἀλέοντο
      is tmesis of 3 pl. impf. The simile
      at 17.61–7 is identical in narrative
      content to this scene on the shield, but
      with different emphasis.

587–9: Scenes on the shield (8) Shepherding.

588 βῆσσα -ης, ἡ glen, wooded valley
μέγαν: with νομόν (587)

589 σταθμός -οῦ, ὁ farmyard
κλισίη -ης, ἡ hut (= Att. κλισία -ας)
κατηρεφής -ές covered over, roofed
ἰδέ = ἠδέ and

σηκός -οῦ, ὁ pen, fold. The shepherding scene is much the shortest on the shield, with no human participants. It forms a peaceful interlude between the violence of the lion-attack and the cheerful vigour of the dance.

590–606: Scenes on the shield (9) A dancing-floor.

590 χόρος -ου/οῖο, ὁ dancing-floor
ποικίλλω I make with skill (used only here in Homer). The close similarity of 587 and 590 is remarkable.

591 τῷ ... οἷον (= rel. pron. ὅν) that one which
ἴκελος -η -ον like (+ dat.)
Κνωσός -οῦ, ἡ Cnossus, ancient chief city of Crete. Cretans were famous for dancing (cf. Aeneas' taunt – 'dancer that you are' – to the Cretan Meriones at 16.617).

592 Δαίδαλος -ου, ὁ Daedalus (legendary craftsman and inventor). This is the only reference to him building a dancing-floor. He is perhaps mentioned here because in his ingenious art he resembles both Hephaestus and the poet himself.
ἀσκέω I shape by art, create; ἤσκησεν is 3 s. aor.
Ἀριάδνη -ης, ἡ Ariadne, daughter of Minos (the king of Cnossus). There is no explicit reference here to the story of her helping Theseus through the Labyrinth (built by Daedalus to house the Minotaur), though the Crane Dance with which she was associated was a celebration of the escape of Theseus and his companions from Crete. Human characters from myth appear only in this comparison; there are none on the shield itself.

593 παρθένος -ου, ἡ maiden, unmarried girl
ἀλφεσίβοιος -η -ον earning cattle (as a gift from the suitor to the bride's parents), i.e. marriageable

594 ὀρχέομαι I dance; ὠρχεῦντ(ο) is 3 pl. impf.
καρπός -οῦ, ὁ wrist. Tr. phrase 'keeping each other's hands on their wrists'.

595 τῶν of these
αἱ μέν ... οἱ δέ the girls ... and the youths
λεπτός -ή -όν fine, delicate
ὀθόνη -ης, ἡ linen garment. Helen wore one at 3.141 when she went to join the old men of Troy on the city walls. Representations of dancing usu. show women wearing ankle-length dresses (there is a delightful example on the sixth-century BCE François Vase).

596 εἴατ(ο): 3 pl. plup. mid. of ἕννυμι (cf. 517), with impf. sense
ἐΰννητος -ον finely spun
ἦκα (adv.) gently
στίλβω I gleam. Treating clothes with olive oil gave them a sheen and also made them more long-lasting.

597 στεφάνη -ης, ἡ headband
μάχαιρα -ης, ἡ knife, dagger. It seems to have the same function as the sgian-dubh, the ceremonial dagger of formal Scottish Highland dress. Note the nearly identical pattern of expression in 595–6 and 597–8.

598 τελαμών -ῶνος, ὁ (here) sword belt (cf. 480)

599 ὁτέ (distinguish from ὅτε) μέν at one time; answered by ἄλλοτε δ(έ) (602)
τρέχω I run; θρέξασκον is 3 pl. aor. iterative (cf. on 159)
ἐπίσταμαι I know; part. (m. dat. pl.) ἐπισταμένοισι here 'skilled'

600 ῥεῖα (adv.) easily, lightly
τροχός -οῦ, ὁ wheel
ἄρμενον: aor. mid. part. (m. acc. s.) of ἀραρίσκω (cf. 275) here 'fitting'
παλάμη -ης, ἡ palm, hand

ἑζόμενος κεραμεὺς πειρήσεται, αἴ κε θέῃσιν·
ἄλλοτε δ᾽ αὖ θρέξασκον ἐπὶ στίχας ἀλλήλοισι.
πολλὸς δ᾽ ἱμερόεντα χορὸν περιίσταθ᾽ ὅμιλος
τερπόμενοι· δοιὼ δὲ κυβιστητῆρε κατ᾽ αὐτοὺς   604/5
μολπῆς ἐξάρχοντες ἐδίνευον κατὰ μέσσους.

    Ἐν δὲ τίθει ποταμοῖο μέγα σθένος Ὠκεανοῖο
ἄντυγα πὰρ πυμάτην σάκεος πύκα ποιητοῖο.

    Αὐτὰρ ἐπεὶ δὴ τεῦξε σάκος μέγα τε στιβαρόν τε,
τεῦξ᾽ ἄρα οἱ θώρηκα φαεινότερον πυρὸς αὐγῆς,   610
τεῦξε δέ οἱ κόρυθα βριαρὴν κροτάφοις ἀραρυῖαν,
καλὴν δαιδαλέην, ἐπὶ δὲ χρύσεον λόφον ἧκε,
τεῦξε δέ οἱ κνημῖδας ἑανοῦ κασσιτέροιο.

    Αὐτὰρ ἐπεὶ πάνθ᾽ ὅπλα κάμε κλυτὸς ἀμφιγυήεις,
μητρὸς Ἀχιλλῆος θῆκε προπάροιθεν ἀείρας.   615
ἡ δ᾽ ἴρηξ ὣς ἆλτο κατ᾽ Οὐλύμπου νιφόεντος,
τεύχεα μαρμαίροντα παρ᾽ Ἡφαίστοιο φέρουσα.

12. Marble portrait bust of Homer. Roman
copy of Hellenistic original, second century
BCE. British Museum.

601 κεραμεύς -ῆος, ὁ potter

πειράομαι I test; πειρήσεται is 3 s.
aor. subj. (indefinite 'whenever'
but, as oft. in Homer, without
ἄν/κε)

αἴ κε (+ subj.) (here) to see if

θέησι(ν): 3 s. subj. of θέω (cf. 167)

602 ἄλλοτε δ(έ) at another time

αὖ (adv.) again

στίχες -ων, αἱ rows. Tr. phrase 'in rows to
meet each other'.

603 πολλός = πολύς (cf. 103)

χορός: here not the dancing-floor but the
people dancing (cf. 590)

περιίσταμαι I stand around; περίσταθ' (=
περίστατο) is 3 s. impf.

ὅμιλος -ου, ὁ crowd, throng

604 τερπόμενοι: part. (m. nom. pl.) of τέρπομαι (cf. 526), pl. (with s. ὅμιλος (603))
for the sense

604–5: The abnormal line numbering at 604–5
results from deletion of a line (the rest
of 604 after τερπόμενοι and the start
of another) 'and among them a divine
singer was singing and playing the
lyre'. Though printed in some texts,
this is found in no manuscript or
papyrus of the *Iliad* and was probably
inserted by an ancient scholar from a
similar passage at *Odyssey* 4.17–18.

605 δοιώ (m. nom. dual) a pair of, two

κυβιστητήρ -ῆρος, ὁ acrobat; κυβιστητῆρε is nom. dual

κατ(ά) (+ acc.) (here) among

*607–8: Scenes on the shield (10) Oceanus. The mighty river Oceanus surrounds the
shield in Hephaestus' representation as it does on Homer's flat world-disc. A triple rim
(ἄντυξ) has previously been mentioned in 479–80; if it consists of three ridges of metal,
the outermost and middle ridge may have the band representing Oceanus between them.*

608 πύματος -η -ον last, outermost

πύκα (adv.) strongly

ποιητός -ή -όν made

609–13: The rest of the armour.

609 τεῦξε: 3 s. aor. of τεύχω (cf. 120); the
second half of this line repeats 478,
thereby winding up the shield passage
(ring composition)

610 φαεινότερον: comp. (m. acc. s.) of φαεινός
(cf. 422), here + gen. of comparison
'than'

611 κόρυς -υθος, ἡ helmet

βριαρός -ή -όν strong

κρόταφος -ου, ὁ temple (of the head)

ἀραρυῖαν: perf. part. (f. acc. s.) of ἀραρίσκω (cf. 275)

612 ἐφίημι (here) I place on; ἐπὶ ... ἧκε is
tmesis of 3 s. aor.

χρύσεον (cf. 206): has to be scanned as
two long syllables (cf. on 493)

λόφος -ου, ὁ crest; but presumably here
only the base into which the (horse-
hair) crest is fixed

613 ἑανός -ή -όν (here) fine, beaten out thin
(cf. 352). Tin is one of the precious
metals (cf. 474), no doubt because
difficult to source in the Mediterra-
nean area, and evidently used here
for decorative more than functional
qualities.

614–17: Hephaestus hands the armour to Thetis.

614 ὅπλα -ων, τά arms, armour

κάμε: 3 s. aor. of κάμνω (cf. 341)

615 μητρὸς Ἀχιλλῆος: Thetis is deliberately
described in this way to carry us over
to the scene (19.1–39) where she
brings the armour to Achilles

θῆκε: 3 s. aor. of τίθημι (cf. 352)

ἀείρω I lift, pick up (= Att. αἴρω); ἀείρας
is aor. part. (m. nom. s.)

616 ἴρηξ -ηκος, ὁ hawk

ἅλλομαι I leap, spring; ἆλτο is 3 s. aor.

νιφόεις -εσσα -εν (-εντος) snowy

Vocabulary

A

ἆ ah!

ἄαπτος -ον unapproachable, invincible

ἀάω (aor. pass. ἀάσθην) I mislead, delude

ἀγαθός -ή -όν good, brave

ἀγακλεής -ές very famous, highly renowned

Ἀγακλεής -ῆος, ὁ Agacles (a Myrmidon, father of Epeigeus)

ἀγακλειτός -ή -όν very famous, highly renowned

ἀγάλλομαι I take delight in (+ dat. or part.)

Ἀγαμέμνων -ονος, ὁ Agamemnon

ἀγάννιφος -ον snow-capped

Ἀγαύη -ης, ἡ Agauë (a Nereid)

ἀγαυός -ή -όν illustrious, noble, lordly

ἀγγελίη -ης, ἡ message, news (= Att. ἀγγελία -ας)

ἄγγελος -ου, ὁ messenger

ἄγγος -εος, τό bucket

ἄγε, pl. ἄγετε come! (before another imper. or jussive subj.)

ἀγείρω (aor. pass. ἠγέρθην) I gather

ἀγέλη -ης, ἡ herd

ἀγεληδόν in a pack, in herds

ἀγέρωχος -ον lordly, proud

Ἀγήνωρ -ορος, ὁ Agenor (a Trojan)

ἀγινέω I lead, conduct

ἀγκαλίς -ίδος, ἡ arm

ἄγκεα -ων, τά valleys, gorges

ἀγκυλομήτης -αο/εω of crooked counsel, wily

ἀγκυλοχείλης -αο/εω with crooked beak

ἀγκών -ῶνος, ὁ elbow; corner (of wall)

ἀγλαός -ή -όν splendid, shining

ἄγνυμι (aor. part. ἄξας) I break

ἀγοράομαι I speak in assembly

ἀγορεύω I speak, say, declare

ἀγορή -ῆς, ἡ assembly, meeting-place (= Att. ἀγορά -ᾶς)

ἀγός -οῦ, ὁ leader

ἄγραυλος -ον living in open country

ἄγυρις -ιος, ἡ crowd, heap

ἀγχέμαχος -ον fighting hand-to-hand

ἄγχι/ἀγχίμολον/ἀγχοῦ near

ἄγω (fut. ἄξω, aor. ἤγαγον) I lead, carry off; mid. ἄγομαι I take with me, take as wife, marry

ἀγών -ῶνος, ὁ assembly place; contest

ἁδινός -ή -όν dense, repeated, beating; (n. as adv.) repeatedly, abundantly

Ἄδρηστος -ου, ὁ Adrastus (a Trojan)

ἄεθλος -ου, ὁ contest, competition (= Att. ἆθλος)

ἀείδω I sing (= Att. ᾄδω)

ἀεικής -ές unseemly, disgraceful

ἀεικίζω (aor. ἀείκισσα) I disfigure, abuse

ἀείρω (aor. ἄειρα) I lift, pick up (= Att. αἴρω)

ἀεκήλιος -ον unwelcome

ἀέκων -ουσα -ον (-οντος) unwilling(ly), reluctant(ly), unintentional(ly) (= Att. ἄκων)

ἀέλλη -ης, ἡ whirlwind, wind storm, whirl of dust (= Att. ἄελλα)

ἀέξομαι I grow, increase (= Att. αὔξομαι)

ἀερσίπους -ποδος high-stepping

ἅζομαι I stand in awe of (+ gen.)

ἀήρ ἠέρος, ἡ air, mist (= Att. ἀήρ ἀέρος)

ἀθάνατος -η -ον immortal

Ἀθηναίη/Ἀθήνη -ης, ἡ Athena (= Att. Ἀθηνᾶ -ᾶς)

ἀθρόοι -αι -α all together, in crowds

αἰ if (= Att. εἰ); αἲ γάρ would that, I wish; αἲ κε if, to see if, in the hope that (= Att. ἐάν)

αἶα = γαῖα

Αἰακίδης -αο/εω, ὁ son or descendant of Aeacus

Αἴας -αντος, ὁ Ajax; Αἴαντε (nom. or acc. dual) the two Ajaxes

αἰγανέη -ης, ἡ javelin

αἰγίλιψ -ιπος steep, sheer, deserted by goats

αἰγίς -ίδος, ἡ aegis

αἰγυπιός -οῦ, ὁ vulture

Ἀΐδης -αο/εω (dat. Ἀΐδι), ὁ Hades, god of the Underworld (= Att. Ἅιδης -ου); Ἀϊδόσδε to Hades

αἰδοῖος -η -ον honoured

αἰδώς -όος, ἡ shame

αἰεί/αἰέν always, ever (= Att. ἀεί)

αἰειγενέτης -αο/εω immortal (= Att. ἀειγενέτης -ου)

αἰζηός -οῦ, ὁ active, vigorous; (as m. noun) vigorous young man

ἄητος -ον gasping, panting

αἰθαλόεις -εσσα -εν (-εντος) smoky, grimy

αἴθε would that, if only … (introducing a wish) (= Att. εἴθε)

αἰθήρ -έρος ἡ upper air, sky

αἴθοψ -οπος gleaming, sparkling

αἴθω I set ablaze; pass. αἴθομαι I burn, blaze

αἴθων -ωνος glittering, fiery; (of animals) tawny

αἷμα -ατος, τό blood

αἱματόεις -εσσα -εν (-εντος) bloody

αἰναρέτης -αο/εω of harmful valour

Αἰνείας -αο/εω, ὁ Aeneas (a Trojan)

αἰνός -ή -όν dreadful, terrible; adv. αἰνῶς terribly

αἰολοθώρηξ -ηκος of the glittering breastplate

αἰόλος -η -ον glittering, gleaming, flashing

αἰπύς -εῖα -ύ sheer, utter

αἱρέω (aor. εἷλον/ἕλον) I take, seize, kill; mid. αἱρέομαι I take for myself, choose

αἶσα -ης, ἡ share, portion; fate, fate of death

ἀΐσθω I breathe out

ἀΐσσω I move swiftly, dart

αἰσχύνω (perf. pass. part. ᾐσχυμμένος) I disfigure, defile; pass. αἰσχύνομαι I am ashamed

αἰτιάομαι I accuse

αἰχμή -ῆς, ἡ spear-point, spear

αἰχμητής -αο/εω, ὁ spearman, warrior

αἶψα at once, immediately

ἀΐω I hear (+ acc. or gen.)

αἰών -ῶνος, ὁ life, life force

ἀκάκητα -αο/εω, ὁ deliverer (epithet of Hermes)

ἀκάμας -αντος untiring

Ἀκάμας -αντος, ὁ Acamas

ἀκάματος -ον untiring, inexhaustible

ἀκαχίζω (aor. ἤκαχον) I bring grief to

ἀκέομαι I heal

ἀκμής -ῆτος untiring

ἀκμόθετον -ου/οιο, τό anvil block

ἄκμων -ονος, ὁ anvil

ἄκοιτις -ιος, ἡ wife

ἀκοντίζω I hurl (a javelin), let fly

ἀκοντιστής -ᾶο/έω, ὁ javelin-thrower

ἀκουή -ῆς, ἡ hearing, sound

ἀκούω I hear (+ gen. of person)

ἄκρος -η -ον top part of, end part of

Ἀκταίη -ης, ἡ Actaea (a Nereid)

ἀκτή -ῆς, ἡ shore

Ἀκτορίδης -αο/εω, ὁ son of Actor

Ἄκτωρ -ορος, ὁ Actor (father of Menoetius)

ἀκωκή -ῆς, ἡ point

ἄκων -οντος, ὁ javelin, spear

ἀλαλητός -οῦ, ὁ cry, war cry, yell

ἀλγίον more painful, worse

ἄλγος -εος, τό pain, sorrow, pl. troubles

ἀλεγεινός -ή -όν painful

ἀλέγω I heed, care about

ἀλεείνω I shun, avoid

ἀλείς -εῖσα -έν (aor. pass. part. of εἴλω) cooped up; rolled up, crouching

ἄλειφαρ -ατος, τό ointment, unguent

ἀλείφω I anoint

ἀλέξω (aor. ἄλαλκον) I ward off X (acc.) from Y (dat.); I defend (+ dat.)

ἀλέομαι/ἀλεύομαι I avoid, flee

ἀλῆναι/ἀλήμεναι (aor. pass. inf. of εἴλω) to throng together, assemble

ἀλίαστος -ον unabating, unceasing

Ἁλίη -ης, ἡ Halië (a Nereid)

ἅλιος -η -ον (1) of the sea; (as f. pl. noun) sea-goddesses

ἅλιος -η -ον (2) fruitless, unprofitable; (n. as adv.) in vain

ἁλιόω I make fruitless, throw in vain

ἀλκή -ῆς, ἡ fighting spirit

Ἀλκιμέδων -οντος, ὁ Alcimedon (a Myrmidon leader)

ἄλκιμος -ον (of men) brave; (of weapons) strong, stout

ἀλκτήρ -ῆρος, ὁ defender against, protector from (+ gen.)

ἀλλά but; ἀλλ᾽ εἰ (+ 1 pl. opt.) come on, let's …!

ἀλλήλους -ας -α (no nom.) each other, one another

ἀλλοδαπός -ή -όν foreign

ἅλλομαι (3 s. aor. ἆλτο) I leap

ἄλλος -η -ο other

ἄλλοτε at another time

ἄλοχος -ου, ἡ wife

ἅλς ἁλός, ἡ sea

ἀλφεσίβοιος -η -ον earning cattle (i.e. as a dowry)

ἄλφιτον -ου, τό barley

ἀλωή -ῆς, ἡ orchard; vineyard

ἄμ = ἀνά

ἅμα at the same time; along with (+ dat.)

Ἀμάθεια -ας, ἡ Amatheia (a Nereid)

ἀμαιμάκετος -η -ον huge, enormous

ἀμαλλοδετήρ -ῆρος, ὁ sheaf-binder

Ἄμαξα -ης, ἡ the Wagon, another name for Great Bear (constellation)

ἁμαρτάνω (aor. ἥμαρτον/ἥμβροτον) I miss (+ gen.)

ἁμαρτῇ together, at once

ἀμάω (impf. ἤμων) I reap

ἀμβροσίη -ης, ἡ ambrosia (food of the gods, also an ointment) (= Att. ἀμβροσία -ας)

ἀμβρόσιος -η -ον divine

ἄμβροτος -ον immortal, divine

ἀμείβομαι I answer, reply to

ἀμείνων -ον better

ἀμέρδω I deprive, rob

ἀμήχανος -ον helpless, impossible (to deal with)

Ἀμισώδαρος -ου, ὁ Amisodarus (a Lycian)

ἀμιτροχίτωνες -ων wearing unbelted tunics

ἄμμορος -ον without a share in (+ gen.)

ἀμοιβηδίς in turn

ἀμός -ή -όν our (= Att. ἡμέτερος -α -ον)

Ἀμυδών -ῶνος, ὁ Amydon (city in Macedonia)

ἀμύμων -ον blameless, excellent

ἀμύνω I ward off X (acc.) from Y (dat.), defend (+ dat.), protect (+ gen.); mid. ἀμύνομαι I defend (+ gen.), put up a defence

ἀμφαγαπάζω I love dearly

ἀμφαγείρομαι I gather around

ἀμφέπω I am busy with; I envelop

ἀμφί (+ acc.) around, at; (+ gen.) about, concerning; (+ dat.) around, over, on, about, concerning, entangled in; (as adv.) on both sides, all around, round about, everywhere

ἀμφιβαίνω I surround, bestride

ἀμφιγυήεις -εντος bow-legged (probable sense; epithet of Hephaestus)

ἀμφίγυος -ον double-edged

ἀμφιέλισσα -ης curved

ἀμφιέπω I move around, envelop

ἀμφιζάνω I settle on (+ dat.)

Ἀμφιθόη -ης, ἡ Amphithoë (a Nereid)

ἀμφικαλύπτω I cover, hide

Ἄμφικλος -ου, ὁ Amphiclus (a Trojan)

ἀμφιμάχομαι I fight around (+ acc.); I fight for, fight over (+ gen.)

ἀμφινέμομαι I live around

Ἀμφινόμη -ης, ἡ Amphinome (a Nereid)

ἀμφιπένομαι I am busied about, take care of

ἀμφίπολος -ου, ἡ female servant

ἀμφίς on both sides

ἀμφίσταμαι I stand around

ἀμφότεροι -αι -α both

ἀμφότερον in both respects

Ἀμφότερος -ου, ὁ Amphoterus (a Lycian)

ἀμφοτέρωθεν from both sides, on both sides

ἄμφω both

ἄν (particle indicating a possibility or condition)

ἀνά (+ acc.) up, up to, up through, in, in through, along, towards, among, throughout, all round; (+ dat.) on; (as adv.) all over it

ἀναβαίνω I go up

ἀναγκαῖος -η -ον necessary, inevitable

ἀνάγκη -ης, ἡ necessity

ἀναίνομαι I refuse; I deny

ἀναιρέομαι I pick up, take in my arms

ἀνακυμβαλιάζω I turn upside down

ἄναλκις -ιδος cowardly

ἀναμίμνω I wait, remain, stand fast

ἀνανεύω I refuse; I deny

ἄναξ -ακτος (voc. ἄνα), ὁ lord, master

ἀνάπνευσις -εως, ἡ respite in, rest from (+ gen.)

ἀναπνέω I breathe again, rest myself

ἀναρπάζω I snatch up

ἀναρρήγνυμι I burst (something) open

ἀνάσσω I rule, am lord

ἀναστενάχω I groan aloud for

ἀνατρέχω (aor. ἀνέδραμον) I run back; I shoot up

ἀναφανδόν openly, publicly

ἀναχάζομαι I withdraw, draw back

ἀνδάνω I please, am acceptable to (+ dat.)

ἄνδιχα in two

ἀνδροτής -ῆτος, ἡ manhood, manliness

ἀνδροφόνος -ον man-slaying

ἄνειμι I go up, rise

ἄνεμος -ου, ὁ wind

ἀνεμοσκεπής -ές to keep the wind out

ἄνευθεν apart, apart from (+ gen.)

ἀνέχω (aor. ἄνεσχον) I hold up

ἀνεψιός -οῦ, ὁ cousin

ἀνηκουστέω I fail to listen to, am disobedient to (+ gen.)

ἀνήρ ἀνδρός/ἀνέρος, ὁ man

ἀνθίσταμαι I stand against, withstand, resist

ἄνθρωπος -ου, ὁ man, person

ἀνιάζω I am burdened with (+ dat.)

ἀνίημι (aor. ἀνῆκα) I send forth, make spring up

ἀνιπτόπους -ουν (-ποδος) with unwashed feet

ἀνίστημι I rouse, arouse; mid. ἀνίσταμαι I stand up, rise up

ἀνοίγω (impf. ἀνέῳγον) I open

ἄντα (+ gen.) opposite, against, face to face with; (as adv.) opposite, straight ahead

ἀντάω I meet (+ gen.)

ἄντην opposite, in front

ἀντιβολέω I encounter, come in the way of

ἀντίθεος -ον godlike

ἀντικρύ straight through, completely

Ἀντίλοχος -ου, ὁ Antilochus (son of Nestor)

ἀντίον in reply

ἄντομαι I meet (+ dat.)

ἄντυξ -υγος, ἡ rail (of chariot), rim (of shield)

ἄνω I finish

ἄνωγα (perf. with pres. sense) I order, urge

Ἀξιός -οῦ, ὁ Axius (river in Macedonia)

ἄξων -ονος, ὁ axle

ἀολλής -ές all together, in a mass

ἄορ ἄορος, ὁ sword

ἄουτος -ον unwounded

ἀπάγω I lead away, bring away

ἁπαλός -ή -όν tender

ἀπαμάω I cut

ἀπαμείβομαι I answer, reply to

ἀπαμύνω I ward off

ἀπάνευθε(ν) (+ gen.) away from, (as adv.) at a distance

ἀπαράσσω I strike off

ἅπας ἅπασα ἅπαν (-αντος) all (together)

ἀπάτερθε apart, away from

ἀπαυράω (impf. ἀπηύρων; aor. part. ἀπούρας) I rob, deprive

ἀπειλέω I threaten

ἀπειλή -ῆς, ἡ threat

ἀπερείσιος -ον unlimited, boundless

ἀπερωέω I withdraw from (+ gen.)

ἀπέχομαι I hold off from (+ gen.)

ἀπήμβροτον (aor. of ἀφαμαρτάνω)

ἀπηνής -ές unfeeling, harsh

ἀπιθέω I disobey

ἀπό from, away from (+ gen.)

ἀποβαίνω I go away

ἀποδειροτομέω I cut the throat of, slaughter

ἀποδίδωμι I pay, deliver up

ἀποδύω I strip off

ἀποθρῴσκω (aor. ἀπέθορον) I leap from (+ gen.)

ἀποκόπτω I cut off, cut loose

ἀποκρύπτω I hide (someone/something) away

ἀπόλλυμι I lose, destroy; mid. ἀπόλλυμαι I perish

Ἀπόλλων -ωνος, ὁ Apollo

ἀπολούω I wash X (acc.) off Y (also acc.)

ἀπομόργνυμι I wipe clean

ἀποναίω (aor. ἀπένασσα) I remove, send away, send back

ἀπονέομαι I return

ἀποπαύω I hold in check; mid. ἀποπαύομαι I cease from, desist from (+ gen.)

ἀποπέτομαι (aor. ἀπεπτάμην) I fly away

ἀποπρό away from

ἀπορρίπτω I throw away, throw off, cast aside

ἀποστυφελίζω I shove back, knock back

ἀποτίθημι I put away

ἀποτίνυμαι I exact X (acc.) from Y (gen.)

ἀποτίνω (aor. ἀπέτεισα) I pay back

ἀποτμήγω I cut through, furrow

ἀποτρωπάομαι I shrink from (+ inf. and gen.)

ἀπούρας (aor. part. of ἀπαυράω)

ἀποφθίμενος -η -ον dead, killed

ἀποφθινύθω I waste away

ἀποφθίομαι I perish, die

ἅπτομαι I touch, take hold of, cling to (+ gen.); I strike home, hit my target

ἀπωθέω (aor. ἀπέωσα/ἄπωσα) I push away, drive away

ἄρ = ἄρα

ἄρα then, in that case, as it turns out, as is well known, indeed (oft. hard to translate, but typically expresses consequence)

ἀραιός -ή -όν slender, stunted

ἀραρίσκω (aor. ἤραρον/ἄραρον) I fit

ἀραρυῖα -ης fitted with (+ dat.)

ἀργαλέος -η -ον difficult, painful

Ἀργεάδης -αο/εω, ὁ son of Argeas

Ἀργεῖοι -ων, οἱ Argives (i.e. Greeks)

Ἀργειφόντης -αο/εω, ὁ Argeiphontes (title of Hermes oft. tr. 'killer of Argus')

ἀργεννός -ή -όν white

ἀργός -ή -όν swift

ἀργύρεος -η -ον (made of) silver (= Att. ἀργυροῦς -ᾶ -οῦν)

ἀργυρόηλος -ον silver-studded

ἀργυρόπεζα -ης silver-footed

ἄργυρος -ου, ὁ silver

ἀργύφεος -η -ον white, glittering

ἀρδμός -οῦ, ὁ watering place

ἀρείων -ον better, superior

ἀρή -ῆς, ἡ prayer, curse; ruin, destruction

ἀρήγω I aid, support (+ dat.)

Ἀρηΐλυκος -ου, ὁ Areilycus (a Trojan)

ἀρήϊος -ον warlike (= Att. ἄρειος)

ἀρηΐφιλος -ον dear to Ares

ἀρημένος -η -ον overcome, worn out

Ἄρης -ηος, ὁ Ares; warfare

Ἀριάδνη -ης, ἡ Ariadne

ἀρίζηλος -ον clear to see, conspicuous; piercing

ἀριστερός -ή -όν left, on the left

ἀριστεύω I am best

ἄριστος -η -ον best

Ἄρκτος -ου, ἡ the Great Bear (constellation)

ἅρμα -ατος, τό chariot

ἄρμενος -η -ον fitting

ἄρνα (no nom. s.), τόν/τήν lamb, sheep

ἀρνευτήρ -ῆρος, ὁ diver

ἄρνυμαι (aor. ἀρόμην) I win, earn

ἀροτήρ -ῆρος, ὁ ploughman

ἄρουρα -ης, ἡ earth; field

ἀρόω I plough

ἁρπάζω I snatch, seize

Ἅρπυια -ας, ἡ Harpy

Ἄρτεμις -ιδος, ἡ Artemis

ἀρτύ(ν)ω I make ready

ἄρχω I begin; I am commander of (+ gen. or dat.)

ἀρωγός -οῦ, ὁ supporter

ἄσβεστος -ον inextinguishable

ἄσθμα -ατος, τό panting

ἀσθμαίνω I pant

Ἄσιος -ου, ὁ Asius (a Phrygian, uncle of Hector)

ἀσκέω I shape by art, create

ἀσκηθής -ές unscathed

ἀσπασίως happily

ἀσπερχές unceasingly

ἄσπετος -ον immense, beyond description

ἀσπιδιώτης -αο/εω shield-bearing

ἀσπίς -ίδος, ἡ shield

ἀσπιστής -άο/έω, ὁ shield-bearer, warrior

ἀστερόεις -εσσα -εν (-εντος) shining like a star

ἄστυ -εος, τό city, town; ἄστυδε to the city

ἄσχετος -ον irresistible, overwhelming

ἀτάλαντος -ον like, equal to (+ dat.)

ἀταλός -ή -όν delicate, youthful

ἀτάρ but; and in turn

ἀταρπιτός -οῦ, ἡ path

ἀτειρής -ές that does not wear out

ἄτη -ης, ἡ folly, delusion

ἀτίμητος -ον dishonoured, without rights

ἄτιμος -ον dishonoured

ἀτιτάλλω I rear, cherish

Ἀτρείδης -αο/εω, ὁ son of Atreus

ἄτρομος -ον fearless

ἀτυζόμενοι (part. only) running wildly

Ἀτύμνιος -ου, ὁ Atymnius (a Lycian)

αὖ again, in turn

αὐγή -ῆς, ἡ beam, brightness

αὐδάω (impf. ηὔδων) I speak, tell, shout

αὐδή -ῆς, ἡ voice

αὖθι (right) there, just there, on the spot

αὐλός -οῦ, ὁ pipe, flute

αὐλῶπις -ιδος with a tube to hold the plume,
    i.e. plumed

αὔριον tomorrow

αὐτάρ but, however

αὖτε on the other hand, again, too; in the
    future

ἀυτή -ῆς, ἡ battle cry, battle

αὐτῆμαρ on the same day

αὐτίκα at once, straightaway

αὖτις again, once again, back again, afresh

ἀϋτμή -ῆς, ἡ breath, blast

αὐτόθι there, right there, on the spot

αὐτοκασίγνητος -ου, ὁ own brother

αὐτόματος -η -ον self-moving

Αὐτομέδων -οντος, ὁ Automedon (charioteer
    of Achilles)

Αὐτόνοος -ου, ὁ Autonous (a Trojan)

αὐτός -ή -ό self, oneself, by oneself; (not
    nom.) him, her, it, them

αὐτοσχεδά near at hand, in close combat

αὐτοῦ there, right there, on the spot, in the
    same place

αὔτως like this; just as it is/was, just as you
    are; in vain

αὐχήν -ένος, ὁ neck

ἀΰω (aor. ἤϋσα) I shout, cry out

ἀφαιρέω I take away

ἀφαμαρτάνω (aor. ἀφήμαρτον/ἀπήμβροτον) I
    miss (+ gen.)

ἄφαρ at once

ἄφθιτος -ον imperishable

ἀφίημι I send away, let fly

ἀφικνέομαι I arrive at, reach

ἀφραδία -ας, ἡ folly

ἄφρος -ου, ὁ foam

ἄφρων -ον foolish, deluded

ἀφύσσω I draw off (liquid)

Ἀχαιοί -ῶν, οἱ Achaeans (i.e. Greeks)

ἀχερωΐς -ΐδος, ἡ white poplar

ἀχεύω I grieve

ἀχέω I grieve about (+ gen.); pass. ἀχέομαι I
    am distressed

ἄχθος -εος, τό burden

Ἀχιλ(λ)εύς -ῆος, ὁ Achilles

ἀχλύς -ύος, ἡ mist, darkness

ἄχνυμαι/ἄχομαι I am distressed

ἄχος -εος, τό grief

ἄχρι(ς) utterly

ἄψ back, back again

Ἀψευδής -έος, ἡ Apseudes (a Nereid)

ἄψορρον back again

ἀψόρροος -ον back-flowing

ἄω (aor. ἄσα) I give X (acc.) a fill of Y (gen.)

B

βάζω I say

Βαθυκλῆς -ῆος, ὁ Bathycles (a Myrmidon)

βαθύκολπος -ον deep-bosomed

βαθύς -εῖα -ύ deep

βαίνω I go

Βαλίος -ου, ὁ Balius ('Dapple', a horse of
    Achilles)

βάλλω I throw, shoot, hit, strike

βαρύθω I am heavy, am paralysed

βαρύς -εῖα, -ύ heavy; (n. as adv.) heavily

βασιλεύς -ῆος, ὁ king

βασιλήιος -η -ον royal

βέλος -εος, τό missile

βέλτερος -η -ον better

βένθος -εος, τό depth (= Att. βάθος -ους)

βέομαι I shall live

βῆσσα -ης, ἡ glen, wooded valley

βιάζω I press hard, overpower (also mid.
    βιάζομαι with same sense)

βιάω (perf. βεβίηκα) = βιάζω

βιβάσθω I stride

βίη -ης, ἡ force, might, violence, pl. blasts (=
    Att. βία -ας); βίηφιν (= βίη) by force

βίοτος -ου/οιο, ὁ life

βλάπτω (perf. pass. βέβλαμμαι) I harm,
    wound, entangle

βλωθρός -ή -όν tall

βοείη -ης, ἡ hide (of ox)

βοή -ῆς, ἡ shout, loud sound

βομβέω I clang

βόσκομαι I feed, graze

βοτά -ῶν, τά flocks, herds

βότρυς -υος, ἡ cluster of grapes

Βούδειον -ου, τό Budeum (town in Phthia)

βουλή -ῆς, ἡ council; counsel, plan

βούλομαι I want, wish, wish for

βουλυτόνδε towards evening

βουλυτός -οῦ, ὁ time for unyoking oxen (from
    the plough), evening

βοῦς βοός, ὁ/ἡ ox, cow; (f. also) oxhide, shield
    (of oxhide)

βοῶπις -ιδος ox-eyed

βράχε (3 s. of ἔβραχον)

βραχίων -ονος, ὁ arm

βριαρός -ή -όν strong

βριθύς -εῖα -ύ heavy

βρίθω I am weighed down

βρομέω I buzz

βροτός -οῦ, ὁ mortal

βρότος -ου, ὁ gore, clotted blood

βρυχάομαι I roar, bellow

Βῶρος -ου, ὁ Borus (husband of Polydora)

Γ

γαῖα -ης, ἡ earth, land, ground (= Att. γῆ γῆς)

Γαλάτεια -ας, ἡ Galateia (a Nereid)

γάμος -ου, ὁ marriage, wedding

γαμφηλαί -ῶν, αἱ jaws

γαμψῶνυξ -υχος with crooked claws

γάρ for, because

γαστήρ -έρος, ἡ belly

γάστρη -ης, ἡ belly (of cauldron)

γε at least, at any rate

γενεή -ῆς, ἡ birth (= Att. γενεά -ᾶς)

γέντο (3 s. aor. only) he took, grasped

γέρας -αος, τό prize, gift of honour, privilege

γέρων -οντος, ὁ old man, pl. elders

γηθέω I rejoice, am glad

γηθόσυνος -η -ον glad

γῆρας -αος, τό old age

γίγνομαι (aor. ἐγενόμην) I become, happen,
    prove to be

γιγνώσκω I get to know, know, realise

γλάγος -εος, τό milk

Γλαύκη -ης, ἡ Glauce (a Nereid)

γλαυκός -ή -όν grey

Γλαῦκος -ου, ὁ Glaucus (a Lycian leader)

γλαυκῶπις -ιδος gleaming-eyed

γλαφυρός -ή -όν hollow

γλυκύς -εῖα -ύ sweet

γλῶσσα -ης, ἡ tongue

γναθμός -οῦ/οῖο, ὁ jaw

γναμπτός -ή -όν curved

γοάω I wail, lament

γόνυ γόνατος/γούνατος, τό knee

γόος -ου/οιο, ὁ lamentation

γουνός -οῦ, ὁ fruitful land

γυῖον -ου, τό limb

γυμνός -ή -όν naked, unarmed

γυμνόω I strip, leave unarmed

γυνή γυναικός, ἡ woman, wife

γύψ γυπός, ὁ vulture

Δ

δαιδάλεος -η -ον skilfully made, skilfully
    decorated

δαιδάλλω I decorate

δαίδαλον -ου, τό skilfully made ornament

Δαίδαλος -ου, ὁ Daedalus (legendary
    craftsman of Crete)

δαΐζω I tear, slash, cut to shreds

δαίμων -ονος, ὁ god, divine power

δαΐς -ΐδος, ἡ torch

δαίς δαιτός, ἡ feast, meal

δαΐφρων -ον fiery-hearted

δαίω I set ablaze

δάκνω I bite

δάκρυ (no gen. s.), τό tear

δακρυόεις -εσσα -εν (-εντος) weeping, in tears

δάκρυον -ου, τό tear

δακρύω I weep, cry (perf. pass. δεδάκρυμαι I
    am bathed in tears)

δαμάζω (aor. pass. ἐδαμάσθην/ἐδάμην) I
    subdue, overcome; I subject X (acc.) as wife
    to Y (dat.)

Δαμαστορίδης -αο/εω, ὁ son of Damastor

δαμνάω = δαμάζω

Δαναοί -ῶν, οἱ Danaans (i.e. Greeks)

δάπτω I tear apart, devour

Δαρδανίς -ίδος, ἡ Dardanian woman

Δάρδανος -ου Dardanian, Trojan

δατέομαι (aor. inf. δάσασθαι) I divide, share out

δαφοινεός -όν red, gory

δάω I learn

δέ and, but

δέγμενος -η -ον (Homeric pres. part. of δέχομαι) waiting

δείδια/δείδοικα (perf. with pres. sense) I fear, am afraid

δειδίσσομαι I scare away

δειλός -ή -όν wretched, miserable

δεινός -ή -όν terrible, terrifying, awe-inspiring; (n. as adv.) terribly, terrifyingly

δεῖπνον -ου, τό meal

δειρή -ῆς, ἡ neck (= Att. δέρη)

δέμας like, in form of (+ gen.)

Δεξαμένη -ης, ἡ Dexamene (a Nereid)

δεξιός -ή -όν right, on the right

δεξιτερός -ή -όν right, on the right

δέομαι I bind, fasten

δέπας -αος, τό cup

δέρμα -ατος, τό skin

δεσμός -οῖο, ὁ fastening, rivet

δεῦρο (to) here

δεύτερος -ή -όν second, next; n. as adv. with same sense

δεύω I wet, fill (with liquid)

δέχομαι I receive, accept

δέω I need, have need of (+ gen.)

δή indeed, in fact

δήϊος (-η) -ον hostile, (of fire) destructive (= Att. δάϊος); (as m. pl. noun) enemies

δηϊοτής -ῆτος, ἡ combat

δῆμος -ου/οιο, ὁ country, people, community

δήν long, for a long time

δηόω/δηϊόω I cut down, kill

δηριάομαι/δηρίομαι (3 dual aor. pass. δηρινθήτην) I fight

δηρόν long, for a long time

διά through (+ gen.)

διαμπερές continually, throughout, once and for all

διαπέρθω (aor. διέπραθον) I sack, destroy

διαπρό right through

διαρπάζω I carry off as plunder, snatch

διασχίζω I tear apart

διατμήγω (aor. pass. διετμάγην) I scatter

διαφράζω (aor. διεπέφραδον) I tell clearly

διδάσκω I teach; pass. διδάσκομαι I learn about (+ gen.)

διδυμάονες -ων, οἱ twins

δίδωμι I give, grant

διελαύνω I drive through (+ gen.)

δίζω I am in doubt, at a loss

διπετής -ές fallen from Zeus, fed by rain from Zeus

διίσταμαι I stand apart

διίφιλος -ον dear to Zeus

δικάζω I give judgement

δίκη -ης, ἡ justice, judgement

δινέω/δινεύω I turn (something) round repeatedly; I whirl, turn (myself) round and round

διογενής -ές Zeus-born

δίομαι I drive away

Διομήδης -εος, ὁ Diomedes

δῖος -α -ον bright, clear, noble, glorious, godlike

διφάω I dive after

δίφρος -ου/οιο, ὁ chariot

δίχα/διχθά in two, in two ways, at variance

διώκω I chase, pursue

δμωή -ῆς, ἡ female slave

δνοφερός -ή -όν dark, murky

δοάσσατο it seemed (= Att. ἔδοξε)

δοιώ (m. nom. dual) two, a pair of

δοκεύω I watch closely

δολιχόσκιος -ον long-shadowed

δόλος -ου, ὁ trick

δόμονδε homeward, to home

δόμος -ου/οιο, ὁ house, home

δονακεύς -ῆος, ὁ thicket of reeds

δόρπον -ου/οιο, τό evening meal, supper

δόρυ δόρατος/δούρατος/δουρός, τό spear

δουπέω I thud

δοῦπος -ου, ὁ thud, thudding

δουρικλυτός -ή -όν famed for the spear

δράγμα -ατος, τό handful (of stalks)

δραγμεύω I gather handfuls

δράσσομαι (perf. part. δεδραγμένος) I clutch at

δρεπάνη -ης, ἡ sickle
δριμύς -εῖα -ύ sharp
δρόμος ου, ὁ running
δρύπτω I tear
δρῦς δρυός, ἡ oak
δρυτόμος -ον wood-cutting
Δύμας -αντος, ὁ Dymas (a Phrygian, father of
    Hecuba)
δύναμαι I am able
Δυναμένη -ης, ἡ Dynamene (a Nereid)
δύ(ν)ω (aor. ἔδυν) I put on (clothes); I enter,
    make my way into, plunge into, go deep
    (also mid. δύ(ν)ομαι with same sense)
δύο two
δυσαριστοτόκεια (nom. only) unhappy
    mother of an excellent son
δυσηχής -ές evil-sounding, hateful
δυσκέλαδος -ον harsh-sounding
δυσμενής -ές hostile; (as m. noun) enemy
δυσπέμφελος -ον (of the sea) rough, stormy
δυσχείμερος -ον wintry
δύω (1) = δύο
δύω (2) = δύνω
δ(υ)ώδεκα twelve
δῶ = δῶμα
Δωδωναῖος -η -ον of Dodona (epithet of Zeus)
Δωδώνη -ης, ἡ Dodona
δῶμα -ατος, τό house, home, palace
Δωρίς -ίδος, ἡ Doris (a Nereid)
δῶρον -ου, τό gift
Δωτώ -οῦς, ἡ Doto (a Nereid)

E

ἕ/ἑ (acc.) him, her, it
ἑανός/εἱανός -οῦ, ὁ dress
ἑᾱνός -ή -όν fine, soft
ἐάω I allow, leave (something) be
ἔβραχον (aor.) I roared, shrieked
ἐγγύθεν/ἐγγύθι/ἐγγύς near, near at hand
ἐγείρω I wake (someone) up, stir up; mid.
    ἐγείρομαι I wake up
ἔγκατα ων, τά entrails
ἐγκέφαλος -ου, ὁ brain
ἐγχείη -ης, ἡ spear
ἐγχέω I pour in
ἔγχος -εος, τό spear

ἐγώ(ν) I
ἔγωγε = ἐγώ + γε
ἕδνα -ων, τά bridal gifts
ἔδυν (aor. of δύ(ν)ω)
ἔδω (fut. ἔδομαι) I eat, devour (= Att. ἐσθίω)
ἐείκοσι(ν) twenty (= Att. εἴκοσι(ν))
ἐέλδομαι/ἔλδομαι I desire, long for
ἐέλδωρ/ἔλδωρ (nom. and acc. s. only),
    τό desire, wish
ἐέργω I shut in, contain (= Att. εἴργω)
ἕζομαι I sit down
ἔθειραι -ῶν, αἱ horse-hair plume
ἐθέλω I wish, want, am willing
ἔθνος -εος, τό company, people
ἔθων -οντος (m. part.) (doing something)
    habitually, typically
εἰ if; εἰ καί even if; εἰ μή if not; εἴ … περ if
    really
εἰ δ᾽ ἄγε but come!
εἰανός = ἑανός
εἰαρινός -ή -όν of spring (= Att. ἐαρινός)
εἴδομαι (aor. εἰσάμην) I look like, take the
    form of (+ dat.)
εἴκελος -η -ον like (+ dat.)
εἰλαπίνη -ης, ἡ feast, banquet
Εἰλείθυια -ας, ἡ Eilithyia (goddess of
    childbirth)
εἰλέω/εἴλω I confine, hem in; pass. εἰλέομαι/
    εἴλομαι I crowd together, am hunched
εἰλίπους -ποδος of rolling gait, shambling
εἰλύω I envelop
εἷμα -τος, τό garment, pl. clothing
εἰμί I am
εἶμι I go, come
εἰνάετες for nine years
εἵνεκα/ἕνεκα for the sake of, because of (+
    gen.)
εἰνόδιος -η -ον by the roadside
εἶπον (aor.) I said
εἴρη -ης, ἡ speaking place
εἰς/ἐς into, to (+ acc.)
εἷς μία ἕν (ἑνός) one
εἰσάλλομαι (aor. εἰσηλάμην) I leap into, leap at,
    leap inside
εἰσαναβαίνω I go up on to
εἰσανεῖδον (aor.) I looked up into

εἰσέρχομαι I go into
εἰσοράω I look at
εἴσω (postposition + acc.) to, into; (as adv.) inside
ἐκ/ἐξ out of, from, from among, out of range of (+ gen.)
Ἑκάβη -ης, ἡ Hecuba (wife of Priam, mother of Hector)
ἐκάεργος -ον far-working, far-shooting (epithet of Apollo)
ἔκαθεν from far away
ἑκάς far
ἕκαστος -η -ον each
ἑκατηβόλος -ον far-shooting (epithet of Apollo)
ἐκβάλλω I throw out, let fall
ἐκδύ(ν)ω I get out from, escape
ἐκεῖνος/κεῖνος -η -ο that (one); he, she, it
ἑκηβόλος -ον far-shooting (epithet of Apollo)
ἐκθρῴσκω (aor. ἐξέθορον/ἔκθορον) I leap out of
ἐκλανθάνομαι I forget completely
ἔκπαγλος -ον terrifying; extraordinary
ἐκπεράω I pass through
ἐκπέρθω I sack, destroy
ἐκπλήσσω (aor. pass. ἐξεπλάγην) I terrify
ἐκτάμνω (aor. ἐξέταμον) I fell, cut down
ἐκτελέω I fulfil, accomplish
ἐκτινάσσω I shake out
ἐκτρέχω (aor. ἐξέδραμον) I run out
Ἕκτωρ -ορος, ὁ Hector
ἐκφαίνω I reveal, bring to light; mid. ἐκφαίνομαι I appear, show myself
ἐκφέρω I carry out
ἐκφεύγω I escape from, fly from
ἐκχέω I pour out
ἔλαιον -ου, τό olive oil
Ἔλασος -ου, ὁ Elasus (a Trojan)
ἐλαστρέω I drive
ἐλαύνω (aor. ἤλασα/ἔλασα/ἔλασσα) I drive, ride, strike at; I draw out, extend
ἐλαφηβόλος -ου, ὁ deer hunter
ἔλαφος -ου/οιο, ὁ/ἡ deer, stag; hind (female deer)
ἐλαφρός -ή -όν light, nimble
ἔλδομαι I desire

ἐλεέω I pity
ἐλεύθερος -η -ον free
ἕλικες -ων, αἱ armbands
ἑλίκωψ -ωπος darting-eyed
ἕλιξ -ικος with twisted horns
ἑλίσσομαι I bustle about
ἕλκος -εος, τό wound
ἕλκω I drag
Ἑλλάς -άδος, ἡ Hellas
ἑλλεδανός -οῦ, ὁ cord
Ἑλλήσποντος -ου, ὁ Hellespont
ἔλπομαι I hope, expect, think, suppose
ἔλωρ, τό prey, spoil; pl. penalty for killing, blood price of (+ gen.)
ἐμβαίνω I step into, enter
ἐμβάλλω I throw/put X (acc.) on/in Y (dat.)
ἐμός -ή -όν my
ἐμπάζομαι I care about (+ gen.)
ἔμπεδον firmly
ἔμπεδος -ον firm, steady, unshaken
ἐμπί(μ)πλημι (aor. ἐνεπλήσθην) I fill X (acc.) with Y (gen.)
ἐμπίμπρημι I burn
ἐμπίπτω (aor. ἐνέπεσον) I fall upon
ἐμφύω I grow into; aor. ἐνέφυν I clasped (+ dat.)
ἐν/ἐνί/εἰν (+ dat.) in, among; (as adv.) on it
ἐναίρω I kill (in battle) (also mid. ἐναίρομαι with same sense)
ἐναρίζω I strip (of armour), kill
ἔναυλος -ου, ὁ watercourse, channel
ἐνδίημι I send in
ἔνδοθι within (+ gen.)
ἔνδον within, in the house
ἔνειμι I am in
ἕνεκα/εἵνεκα because of (+ preceding gen.)
ἐνέπω I tell, relate
ἔνθα then, so then, thereupon, there, where; ἔνθα καὶ ἔνθα back and forth
ἐνθάδε here
ἐνί = ἐν
ἐνίημι I cause, implant X (acc.) in Y (dat.)
ἐνίπτω (aor. ἠνίπαπον/ἐνένιπον) I rebuke, reproach
ἐνισκίμπτω I stick X (acc.) in Y (dat.)
ἐννέα nine

ἐννέωρος -ον nine years old

ἕννυμι (aor. ἕσσα) I clothe (someone), mid.
   ἕννυμαι I wear

ἐνοπή -ῆς, ἡ din of battle

ἐνόρνυμι I arouse X (acc.) in/among Y (dat.)

ἐνορούω I rush upon, leap upon (+ dat.)

ἔντεα -ων, τά armour

ἐντός within

Ἐνυάλιος -ου, ὁ Enyalius (a title of Ares)

ἐξάγω I lead out, bring out

ἐξαιρέω I take out, pick out, select, choose,
   take away, remove

ἐξαλέομαι I keep away

ἐξαναλύω I set free

ἐξανίημι I emit

ἐξαπίνης suddenly

ἐξαπόλλυμαι I perish, vanish

ἐξάρχω I begin, lead (+ gen.)

ἐξαυδάω I speak out

ἐξαῦτις again, once again

ἔξειμι I go out

ἐξελαύνω I drive out

ἐξεναρίζω I strip of armour, kill

ἐξερύω I pull out

ἐξευρίσκω I find, come upon

ἐξονομάζω I address

ἐξόπιθεν behind

ἔξοχος -ον prominent among (+ gen.)

ἔοικα I am like, resemble (+ dat.)

ἔοργε (3 s. perf. of ἔρδω)

ἑός -ή -όν his (own), her (own)

ἐπαγάλλομαι I exult in (+ dat.)

ἐπαγλαΐζομαι I glory in

ἐπαινέω I praise, approve; I assent to, give
   approval to (+ dat.)

ἐπαΐσσω I dart forth, attack

ἐπακούω I listen to, hear

Ἐπάλτης -αο/εω, ὁ Epaltes (a Lycian)

ἐπαμύνω I bring help to (+ dat.)

ἐπασσύτεροι -αι -α close together, one after
   another, in quick succession

ἐπαυρίσκω (aor. inf. ἐπαυρέμεν) I enjoy, have
   the benefit of

ἐπεί when, after, since, because

Ἐπειγεύς -ῆος, ὁ Epeigeus (a Myrmidon)

ἔπειμι I come up to, approach

ἔπειτα then, next, so then

ἐπέρχομαι I pass through

ἐπεύχομαι I boast over, exult

ἔπεφνον (aor. only) I killed

ἐπήν when, whenever (= ἐπεί + ἄν)

ἐπηπύω I applaud

ἐπήρατος -ον lovely

ἐπήτριμος -ον thick, numerous

ἐπί (+ acc.) to; (+ gen.) on, on board, at; (+
   dat.) on, at, by, beside, over, towards, on to;
   (as adv.) thereupon, in addition, above

ἐπιβαίνω I come out against, set foot on,
   climb on to

ἐπιδεύομαι I am in need of (+ gen.)

ἐπιεικτός -ή -όν yielding, ceasing

ἐπιέννυμι I clothe (someone), mid.
   ἐπιέννυμαι I wear, with perf. part.
   ἐπιειμένος clothed in

ἐπιθύω I am eager

ἐπικάρ headlong

ἐπικείρω I mow down, cut off

ἐπικερτομέω I mock

ἐπίκλησις -εως, ἡ name, extra name; (acc. as
   adv.) in name, nominally

ἐπίκουρος -ον helping; (as m. pl. noun) allies

ἐπικραίνω (aor. imper. ἐπικρήηνον) I fulfil,
   accomplish

ἐπικρατέως mightily, victoriously

ἐπιπείθομαι I am convinced

ἐπιπροίημι I send out X (acc.) with Y (dat.)

ἐπισ(σ)εύομαι I hurry, rush against, charge at

ἐπίσταμαι I know, know how to (+ inf.)

Ἐπίστωρ -ορος, ὁ Epistor (a Trojan)

ἐπισφύριον -ου, τό ankle-protector

ἐπισχερώ one after another

ἐπιτανύω I spread X (acc.) over Y (dat.)

ἐπιτέλλω I lay (an instruction) upon, give
   instructions to

ἐπιτίθημι I lay X (acc.) on Y (dat.)

ἐπιτρέχω (aor. ἐπέδραμον) I run up

ἐπιχέω I pour in/on, pour over

ἐπιχράω (aor. ἐπέχραον) I attack

ἔπλευ (2 s. aor. of πέλομαι)

ἐποίχομαι I go to and fro

ἕπομαι (aor. ἑσπόμην) I follow

ἔπορον (aor. only) I gave, provided

ἐπορούω I rush at

ἔπος -εος, τό word

ἐποτρύνω I stir up, urge on

ἔπτατο (3 s. aor. of πέτομαι)

ἔραζε to the ground

ἐράομαι (aor. ἠρασάμην) I love, fall in love with (+ gen.)

ἐρατεινός -ή -όν lovely

ἐργάζομαι I work

ἔργον -ου, τό work, deed, skill, pl. treatment

ἔργω (= ἐέργω/εἴργω) I shut in, hem in, confine

ἔρδω (perf. ἔοργα) I do, work

Ἔρεβος -εος, τό Erebus (a dark region in the Underworld)

ἐρείδω I press hard, hit repeatedly, bump into; mid. ἐρείδομαι (aor. part. ἐρεισάμενος) I lean on, brace myself

ἐρείπω I tear down; pass. ἐρείπομαι (with aor. act. ἤριπον) I fall down

ἐρεύγομαι I belch forth, bellow

ἐρεύθω I make (something) red

ἐρευνάω I trace, track

ἐρητύω I hold back, restrain

ἐριαύχην -ενος high-necked

ἐριβῶλαξ -ακος/ἐρίβωλος -ον fertile, fruitful

ἐρίγδουπος -ον loud-thundering

ἐριδαίνω I compete with (+ dat.)

ἐριδμαίνω I irritate

ἐρίηρος -ον (m. pl. ἐρίηρες, -ων) trusty

ἔριθος -ου, ὁ hired labourer, harvester

ἔρις -ιδος, ἡ strife, discord; Ἔρις Discord (personified)

ἔριφος -ου ὁ/ἡ kid, young goat

ἕρκος -εος, τό fence, boundary wall; enclosure, courtyard

ἕρμα -ατος, τό support, bulwark

Ἑρμείας -αο/εω, ὁ Hermes (= Att. Ἑρμῆς -οῦ)

ἔρνος -εος, τό shoot, young tree

ἔρρω I move with difficulty

ἐρύγμηλος -η -ον bellowing

ἐρύκω I hold back X (acc.) from Y (gen.)

Ἐρύλαος -ου, ὁ Erylaus (a Trojan)

Ἐρύμας -αντος, ὁ Erymas (1) a Trojan killed by Idomeneus; (2) a Lycian killed by Patroclus

ἐρυσάρματος -ον (m. pl. ἐρυσάρματες -ων) chariot-drawing

ἐρύω I draw up, drag; mid. ἐρύομαι I protect, guard

ἔρχομαι (aor. ἦλθον/ἤλυθον) I go, come

ἐρωή -ῆς, ἡ rest, relief from

ἔσβεσα (aor. of σβέννυμι)

ἐσθλός -ή -όν good, brave

ἔσπετε (2 pl. aor. imper. of ἐνέπω) tell, relate

ἑταῖρος/ἕταρος -ου, ὁ companion, comrade

ἐτεόν truly

ἑτεραλκής -ές inclining to the other side

ἕτερος -η -ον the other (of two); ἕτερος … ἕτερος one … the other

ἑτέρωθεν from/on the other side

ἔτης -αο/εω, ὁ kinsman

ἐτήτυμος -ον true

ἔτι still, yet, any longer

ἑτοῖμος -η -ον ready, at hand

ἐτώσιος -ον fruitless, useless

εὖ/ἐΰ well

ἐΰδμητος -ον well-built

Εὔδωρος -ου, ὁ Eudorus (a Myrmidon leader)

εὐεργής -ές well-made

Εὔιππος -ου, ὁ Euippus (a Lycian)

ἐϋκνήμις -ιδος well-greaved

εὐνάομαι I sleep with (+ dat.)

εὐνή -ῆς, ἡ bed

ἐΰννητος/εὔνητος -ον finely spun

εὔξεστος (ἐΰ-) -η -ον well-polished

ἐϋπλόκαμος -ον with beautiful hair

εὐποίητος -ον well-made

εὐπρηστος -ον strong-blowing

εὔπωλος -ον with fine horses

εὑρίσκω I find

Εὖρος -ου, ὁ Eurus (the east wind)

Εὐρυνόμη -ης, ἡ Eurynome (mother of the Graces)

εὐρυόδεια -ης with broad ways (epithet of the earth)

εὐρύοπα (= εὐρυόπης) -αο/εω far-seeing (epithet of Zeus)

Εὐρύπυλος -ου, ὁ Eurypylus (leader of the Thessalians)

εὐρύς -εῖα -ύ wide, broad; (n. as adv.) widely

ἐΰς ἐΰ/εὐς εὖ/ἠΰς ἠΰ good, noble, brave

ἐΰσσελμος -ον well-decked

ἐΰσταθής -ές well-built

εὖτε when

εὐτειχής -ές well-walled

εὔτυκτος -ον well-made

Εὔφορβος -ου, ὁ Euphorbus (a Trojan)

ἐϋφρονέων -ουσα -ον (-οντος) with good
    intent

εὔχομαι I pray, boast; I declare

εὖχος -εος, τό vow, boast, glory

ἐφέπω I drive on, urge on

ἐφετμή -ῆς, ἡ command

ἐφίημι I incite, cause, place on, let X (acc.) fly
    against Y (dat.)

ἐφίσταμαι I stand close by, stand on

ἐφορμάομαι I make an attack

Ἐχεκλῆς -ῆος, ὁ Echecles (a Myrmidon)

Ἔχεκλος -ου, ὁ Echeclus (a Trojan)

ἐχθρός -ή -όν hateful, hostile

Ἐχίος -ου, ὁ Echius (a Lycian)

ἔχω I have, hold, hold back, make (a sound),
    am able to (+ inf.); mid. ἔχομαι I hold on,
    hold my ground

ἔωσα (aor. of ὠθέω)

Z

ζεύγνυμι I yoke together, join

ζεῦγος -εος, τό yoke, pl. team (of oxen)

Ζεύς Διός/Ζηνός, ὁ Zeus

Ζέφυρος -ου, ὁ Zephyrus (the west wind)

ζέω I boil

ζυγόν -οῦ, τό yoke

ζώάγρια -ων, τά reward for saving life

ζωός -ή -όν alive, living

ζώς = ζωός

ζώω I live (= Att. ζάω)

H

ἤ/ἠέ or; than; ἤ ... ἤ whether ... or

ἦ (1) indeed; ἦ μάλα for sure; ἦ μέν indeed; ἦ
    που doubtless, I presume; ἦ τε and yet ...
    certainly

ἦ (2) he/she said, spoke (3 s. impf. of ἠμί)

ᾗ where (dat. f. of ὅς as adv.)

ἥβη -ης, ἡ youth

ἡγεμονεύω I am leader

ἡγεμών -όνος, ὁ leader, commander

ἡγέομαι I lead, guide (+ dat.)

ἡγήτωρ -ορος, ὁ leader

ἠδέ and

ἤδη now, already

ἦδος -εος, τό enjoyment

ἠέλιος -ου/οιο, ὁ sun (= Att. ἥλιος)

ἠερόφωνος -όν loud-voiced

Ἠετίων -ωνος, ὁ Eëtion (king of Thebe, father
    of Andromache)

ἠΐθεος -ου, ὁ unmarried young man (= Att.
    ἤθεος)

ἠΐχθην (aor. pass. of ἀΐσσω)

ἦκα gently

ἠλασκάζω I wander about

ἠλίβατος -ον lofty, sheer, precipitous

ἡλικίη -ης, ἡ age, prime of life; those of the
    same age, contemporaries (= Att. ἡλικία
    -ας)

ἧμαι I sit

ἦμαρ -ατος, τό day (= Att. ἡμέρα -ας, ἡ); ἦμαρ
    ἀναγκαῖον day of necessity (i.e. slavery)

ἤμβροτον (aor. of ἁμαρτάνω, = Att. ἥμαρτον)

ἡμεῖς -ῶν we

ἠμέν ... ἠδέ both ... and, just as ... so

ἡμέτερος -η -ον our

ἠμί (= φημί) I speak; 3 s. impf. ἦ (= ἔφη)

ἡμιδαής -ές half-burnt

ἦμος when

ἤν if (= Att. ἐάν)

ἠνεμόεις -εσσα -εν (-εντος) windy

ἡνία -ων, τά reins

ἡνιοχεύς -ῆος, ὁ charioteer

ἡνίοχος -ου, ὁ charioteer

ἦνοψ -οπος gleaming

Ἦνοψ -οπος, ὁ Enops (father of Thestor)

ἧος while (= Att. ἕως)

ἤπιος -η -ον kind, mild, gentle

Ἡρακλέης -ῆος, ὁ Heracles (= Att. Ἡρακλῆς
    -έους)

Ἥρη -ης, ἡ Hera (= Att. Ἥρα -ας)

ἤριπον (aor. of ἐρείπω)

ἥρως -ωος, ὁ hero, warrior

ἥσσων -ον inferior

ἤτοι indeed, though to be sure, and yet; ἤτοι ὁ
    μέν then he

ἦτορ -ορος, τό heart

ἠϋγένειος -ον with fine beard and/or mane (= Att. εὐγένειος)

ἠΰκομος -ον with beautiful hair (= Att. εὔκομος)

ἠΰς = ἐΰς

ἠΰτε like, as when

Ἥφαιστος -ου/οιο, ὁ Hephaestus (the smith god)

ἠχή -ῆς, ἡ noise

ἠῶθεν in the morning (= Att. ἔωθεν)

ἠώς ἠοῦς, ἡ dawn, morning (= Att. ἕως ἕω)

Θ

θ᾽ = τε (before vowel with rough breathing)

θάλαμος -ου, ὁ bedroom

θάλασσα -ης, ἡ sea

Θάλεια -ας, ἡ Thaleia (a Nereid)

θάμα often

θαμέες -ειαί (pl.) crowded together

θαμίζω I come/go frequently

θανατόνδε to death

θάνατος -ου/οιο, ὁ death; Θάνατος Death (personified)

θαρσαλέος -η -ον bold, courageous (= Att. θαρραλέος)

θαρσέω I take courage, cheer up (= Att. θαρρέω)

θάρσυνος -ον confident, full of confidence

θαρσύνω I encourage, cheer, make bold (= Att. θαρρύνω)

θάσσων -ον (comp. of ταχύς) faster; n. as adv. with same sense

θαῦμα -ατος, τό wonder, marvel

θαυμάζω I wonder, wonder at, admire

θεά -ᾶς, ἡ goddess

θέειον -ου, τό sulphur (= Att. θεῖον -ου)

θείνω I strike, slash

θεῖος -η -ον divine, godlike, of the gods

θείω = θέω

θέμις -ιστος, ἡ judgement; what is right, permitted

θεοπροπίη -ης, ἡ prophecy, divine pronoucement (= Att. θεοπροπία -ας)

θεός -οῦ/οῖο, ὁ/ἡ god, goddess

θεράπων -οντος, ὁ aide, battle companion

θερμός -ή -όν warm, hot

θέρμω I warm, heat

θεσπέσιος -η -ον tremendous, awful

Θέστωρ -ορος, ὁ Thestor (a Trojan)

Θέτις -ιδος, ἡ Thetis (mother of Achilles)

θέω I run

θήν surely, certainly

θνήσκω (aor. ἔθανον, perf. τέθνηκα) I die; perf. I am dead

θνητός -ή -όν mortal

Θόας -αντος, ὁ Thoas (a Trojan)

Θόη -ης, ἡ Thoë (a Nereid)

θοός -ή -όν swift, fast

θοῦρις -ιδος impetuous

θοῶς swiftly

Θρασυμήδης -εος, ὁ Thrasymedes (son of Nestor)

Θρασύμηλος -ου, ὁ Thrasymelus (charioteer of Sarpedon)

θρασύς -εῖα -ύ bold, daring

θρῆνυς -υος, ὁ footstool

θρόνος -ου, ὁ armchair

θυγάτηρ -τέρος/τρός, ἡ daughter

θυμοβόρος -ον heart-devouring

θυμοραϊστής -ᾶο/έω life-destroying

θυμός -οῦ, ὁ heart, mind, soul; life

θύραζε to the door, out, outside

θυσσανόεις -εσσα -εν (-εντος) tasselled

θύω I rage, storm

θώρηξ -ηκος, ὁ breastplate, corselet (= Att. θώραξ -ακος)

θωρήσσω I arm (with a breastplate); mid./pass. θωρήσσομαι I arm myself, ready myself

Ι

Ἴαιρα -ας, ἡ Iaera (a Nereid)

Ἰάνασσα -ης, ἡ Ianassa (a Nereid)

Ἰάνειρα -ας, ἡ Ianeira (a Nereid)

ἰαύω I lie, sleep

ἰαχή -ῆς, ἡ cry, shout, shriek

ἰάχω I cry, scream

Ἰδαῖος -η -ον of Mount Ida, Idaean

Ἰδομενεύς -ῆος, ὁ Idomeneus (Cretan leader)

ἰδρείη -ης, ἡ skill (= Att. ἰδρεία -ας)

ἰδρόω I sweat

ἱδρώς -ῶτος, ὁ sweat

ἱερεύω I sacrifice, slaughter

ἱερός -ή -όν holy, sacred; spirited, vigorous

ἵζω I sit down

ἵημι I send, throw; mid. ἵεμαι I am eager, press on, long (to)

ἱῆς = μιᾶς (f. gen. of εἷς)

ἱητρός -οῦ, ὁ doctor (= Att. ἰατρός)

Ἰθαιμένης -εος, ὁ Ithaemenes (a Lycian)

ἰθύντατα most straightly, most fairly

ἰθύνω I straighten (= Att. εὐθύνω)

ἰθύς -εῖα -ύ straight (= Att. εὐθύς); (m. or n. as adv. or prep. + gen.) straight for, straight at, straight ahead

ἰθύω I go straight forward

ἱκάνω I come to, arrive, come upon

ἴκελος -η -ον like, resembling (+ dat.)

ἱκετεύω I supplicate, approach as suppliant

ἱκνέομαι I arrive at, reach, come over

ἵκω I come to, reach

Ἴλιος -ου, ἡ/Ἴλιον -ου, τό Ilium, another name for Troy

ἱμερόεις -εσσα -εν (-εντος) charming, lovely; (n. as adv.) charmingly

ἵνα so that, in order that

ἰός -οῦ, ὁ arrow

ἰότης -ητος, ἡ will, wish

ἱππεύς -ῆος, ὁ horseman, charioteer

ἱππηλάτα -εω, ὁ horseman, charioteer

ἱππόδαμος -ον horse-taming

ἱπποκέλευθος -ον chariot-driving, driver of horses; (as m. noun) charioteer

ἱππόκομος -ον with horse-hair crest

ἱπποκορυστής -ᾱο/έω, ὁ chariot-fighter

ἵππος -ου, ὁ horse, pl. chariots

ἱπποσύνη -ης, ἡ horsemanship

ἱππότα -εω, ὁ horseman, charioteer

ἵππουρις -ιδος with horse-hair crest

ἵπτομαι (aor. ἰψάμην) I strike, chastise

ἱρεύς -ῆος, ὁ priest (= Att. ἱερεύς -έως)

ἴρηξ -ηκος, ὁ hawk

Ἶρις -ιδος, ἡ Iris (the messenger goddess)

ἱρός = ἱερός

ἴσκω I liken X (acc.) to Y (dat.), take X for Y

ἰσόθεος -ον godlike

ἴσος -η -ον like, equal to (+ dat.)

ἵστημι I make to stand, set up, set in order, mid. ἵσταμαι (with aor. act. ἔστην) I stand

ἵστωρ -ορος, ὁ judge

ἰυγμός -οῦ, ὁ joyful cry

Ἰφεύς -ῆος, ὁ Ipheus (a Lycian)

ἴφθιμος -η -ον strong

ἶφι with force

ἰχθυόεις -εσσα -εν (-εντος) full of fish

ἰχθύς -ύος, ὁ fish

ἴχνια -ων, τά footprints

ἰωή -ῆς, ἡ blaze

Κ

κάδ = κατά

καθαίρω I clean, cleanse

καθάπτομαι I chide, reprimand

κάθημαι I sit

καθίζω I sit (someone) down

καθοράω I look down on

καθύπερθε(ν) above, from above, on top

καί and, also, even, even though; καὶ ὧς even so

καί ... πέρ even though, although

καίνυμαι (perf. with pres. sense κέκασμαι) I surpass, excel

κάκ = κατά

κάκιστος -η -ον (sup. of κακός) worst

κακός -ή -όν bad, evil, cruel

καλέω I call

Καλλιάνασσα -ης, ἡ Callianassa (a Nereid)

Καλλιάνειρα -ας, ἡ Callianeira (a Nereid)

καλλίθριξ -τριχος with beautiful mane

καλλιπλόκαμος -ον with beautiful hair

καλός -ή -όν beautiful, fine

κάλυξ -υκος, ἡ earring

καλύπτω I cover, hide

κάμαξ -ακος (ὁ) ἡ vine pole, vine prop

κάμνω I work hard at; I grow tired; mid. κάμνομαι I win by effort

καναχή -ῆς, ἡ ringing sound

κάπ = κατά

κάπετος -ου, ὁ ditch

καπνός -οῦ, ὁ smoke

κάρη κρατός, τό head

καρπάλιμος -ον swift

καρπός -οῦ, ὁ (1) fruit

καρπός -οῦ, ὁ (2) wrist

καρτερός = κρατερός

καρτύνω I strengthen

κασιγνήτη -ης, ἡ sister

κασίγνητος -ου/οιο, ὁ brother

κασσίτερος -ου/οιο, ὁ tin

κατά (+ acc.) through, down, down through, around, in, among, all over; (+ gen.) down, down from, down over; (as adv.) down, utterly

καταδημοβορέω I consume in common

καταδύω I go down into, enter, sink, (of the sun) set

καταθνῄσκω I die; perf. I am dead

κατακαλύπτω I cover up, come down over

κατακτείνω I kill

κατακύπτω I bend down

καταλείβω I pour down; pass. καταλείβομαι I run down, trickle down

καταμάρπτω I overtake, catch up with

καταπαύω I put an end to, stop

καταπίπτω I fall down

καταπρηνής -ές downturned, with the flat of (the hand)

καταρρέω I flow down

κατασβέννυμι I extinguish

κατατίθημι I lay/set (something) down

καταχέω/καταχεύω I pour over, shower down

κατείβω I shed

κατερύκω I hold back, hinder

κατέχω I hold down, cover; I fill X (acc.) with Y (dat.)

κατηρεφής -ές covered over, roofed

κατηφείη -ης, ἡ disgrace, shame

κατωθέω I thrust down

καυλός -οῦ, ὁ spear shaft, sword hilt; socket

κε(ν) (particle indicating a possibility or condition; = Att. ἄν)

κεάζω I split

Κεβριόνης -αο/εω, ὁ Cebriones (son of Priam, charioteer of Hector)

κεδάννυμι (aor. ἐκεδάσθην) I scatter, spread

κεῖμαι I lie, am placed, lie idle, lie dead

κειμήλιον -ου, τό treasure

κεῖνος = ἐκεῖνος

κεκμηώς -ῶτος/ότος (perf. part. of κάμνω)

κεκορυθμένος (perf. pass. part. of κορύσσω)

κελαδεινός -ή -όν sounding, echoing

κελαδέω I shout in applause

κέλαδος -ου, ὁ clamour, commotion

κελάδων -οντος sounding

κελαινεφής -ές dark

κελαινός -ή -όν dark, black

κελεύω I order, give orders to, urge (+ acc. or dat.)

κέλομαι I order, urge on, call out to (+ acc. or dat.)

κενεών -ῶνος, ὁ belly

κεραΐζω I lay waste, ravage

κεραμεύς -ῆος, ὁ potter

κεραός -οῦ horned

κερδίων -ον more profitable, more advantageous

κερτομέω I torment, provoke

κεύθω I hide, cover

κεφαλή -ῆς, ἡ head

κεχηνώς (perf. part. of χαίνω)

κέχυτο (3 s. plup. pass. of χέω)

κήδομαι I am in distress

κῆδος -εος, τό care, trouble, distress, torment

κήλεος -ον blazing

κήρ κηρός, ἡ death, fate; Κήρ Death-spirit (personified)

κῆρ κῆρος, τό heart

κῆρυξ -υκος, ὁ herald

κιθαρίζω I play the lyre

κινέω I move, stir, disturb

κίον (aor. only) I went

κιχάνω (aor. part. κιχείς) I catch up with

κλάζω I shriek, scream

κλαίω I weep, cry

κλειτός -ή -όν famous, renowned

Κλεόβουλος -ου, ὁ Cleobulus (a Trojan)

κλέος (nom. and acc. only), τό glory

κληΐς -ῖδος, ἡ oar lock (= Att. κλεῖς)

κλίνω I lean (something)

κλισίη -ης, ἡ hut (= Att. κλισία -ας)

κλιτύς -ύος, ἡ hillside

κλονέω I drive in confusion; pass. κλονέομαι I rush about in confusion

κλόνος -ου, ὁ turmoil, confusion

Κλυμένη -ης, ἡ Clymene (a Nereid)

κλυτόπωλος -ον with famous horses

κλυτός -η -ον famous, glorious

κλυτοτέχνης -αο/εω renowned for
craftsmanship

κλύω I hear, listen

κνήμη -ης, ἡ shin

κνημίς -ῑδος, ἡ greave, shin guard

Κνωσός -οῦ, ἡ Cnossus

κοῖλος -η -ον hollow

κοιμάω I put to rest, soothe

κολοιός -οῦ, ὁ jackdaw

κόλος -ον broken off, without its point

κόλπος -ου, ὁ bosom

κομάω (m. pl. part. κομόωντες) I have long
hair

κόμη -ης, ἡ hair

κοναβέω I resound

κονίη -ης, ἡ dust (= Att. κονία -ας)

κόνις -ιος, ἡ dust

κόπρος -ου, ὁ dung; farmyard, byre

κόπτω I strike, smite, cut; I forge

κορέννυμι (aor. ἐκόρεσα) I satisfy, satisfy the
hunger of

κορυθαίολος -ον with shining helmet

κόρυς -υθος, ἡ helmet

κορύσσω I arm (with a helmet)

κορυστής -ᾱο/έω helmeted, armed; (as m.
noun) warrior

κορυφή -ῆς, ἡ summit

κορωνίς -ίδος curved

κοτέομαι I am angry with (+ dat.)

κότος -ου, ὁ resentment

κούρη -ης, ἡ girl, young woman (= Att. κόρη)

κοῦρος -ου, ὁ boy, youth (= Att. κόρος)

κραδαίνομαι I quiver

κραδίη -ης, ἡ heart (= Att. καρδία -ας)

κραιπνός -ή -όν swift

κράνεια -ης, ἡ cornelian cherry (tree)

κραταιός -ή -όν mighty, resistless

κρατερός/καρτερός -ή -όν strong, mighty

κρατερῶνυξ -υχος strong-hoofed

κρατερῶς mightily

κρατέω I have power, rule

κράτος -εος, τό strength, power

κρατύς (m. nom. s.) = κρατερός

κρείσσων -ον stronger, better

κρείων -οντος, ὁ lord, ruler

κρήδεμνον -ου, τό headband, pl. battlements
(of city)

κρῆθεν from the head; κατὰ κρῆθεν from top
to bottom, completely

κρήνη -ης, ἡ spring

κρίζω (aor. ἔκρικον) I creak

κρίνω I divide, organise; I decide, give
(judgement); mid. κρίνομαι I contend

Κρονίδης -αο/εω, ὁ son of Cronus (i.e. Zeus)

Κρονίων -ονος/ωνος, ὁ son of Cronus (i.e.
Zeus)

Κρόνος -ου, ὁ Cronus (father of Zeus)

κρόταφος -ου, ὁ temple (of the head)

κρύβδα in secret from, without the knowledge
of (+ gen.)

κρύπτω I hide

κτεάτεσσιν (dat. pl. only), τοῖς
(n.) possessions

κτεατίζω I obtain

κτείνω (aor. ἔκτεινα/ἔκτανον) I kill

κτερίζω I bury with solemn honours

κτῆμα -ατος, τό possession, pl. property,
treasures

κτῆσις -ιος, ἡ property

κυάνεος -α -ον dark, bluish black

κυβιστάω I turn somersaults

κυβιστητήρ -ῆρος, ὁ acrobat

κυδάλιμος -ον noble, glorious

κυδοιμός -οῦ, ὁ uproar, confusion;
Κυδοιμός Tumult (personified)

κῦδος -εος, τό glory

κυδρός -ή -όν venerable, honoured

κυκάω I stir up, throw into confusion

κύκλος -ου, ὁ (pl. κύκλοι or κύκλα, τά) circle,
wheel

κυλίνδομαι I roll along

κυλλοποδίων -ονος club-footed, lame

κῦμα -ατος, τό wave

Κυμοδόκη -ης, ἡ Cymodoce (a Nereid)

Κυμοθόη -ης, ἡ Cymothoë (a Nereid)

κυνέη -ης, ἡ helmet, cap (= Att. κυνῆ)

κυνῶπις -ιδος dog-faced, shameless

κύων -νός, ὁ/ἡ dog

κωκύω I wail

κωπήεις -εσσα -εν (-εντος) hilted

Λ

λᾶας -ος, ὁ stone

λάβρος -ον furious, blustering

λαγχάνω (aor. ἔλαχον) I obtain by lot, receive

Λαέρκης -εος, ὁ Laerces (a Myrmidon)

λάζομαι I take

λάθρη secretly (= Att. λάθρα)

λαῖλαψ -απος, ἡ storm, tempest

λαιμός -οῦ, ὁ throat

λαμβάνω I take, take hold of

λαμπρός -ή -όν bright, gleaming

λάμπω I shine (also mid. λάμπομαι with same sense)

λανθάνω (aor. ἔλαθον) I escape notice of (+ acc.); mid. λανθάνομαι I forget (+ gen.)

λάξ with the heel

Λαόγονος -ου, ὁ Laogonus (a Trojan)

λαός -οῦ, ὁ people, army (usu. pl.) (= Att. λεώς -ώ)

λαπάρη -ης, ἡ flank, loins (= Att. λαπάρα -ας)

λάπτω I lap up, drink

λάρναξ -ακος, ἡ chest, box

λάσιος -η -ον shaggy, stout

λαφύσσω I gulp down

λαχνήεις -εσσα -εν (-εντος) hairy, shaggy

λέγω (fut. ἐρέω, aor. εἶπον) I say

λείβω I pour, shed

λειμών -ῶνος, ὁ meadow

λείπω (aor. ἔλιπον) I leave

λελίημαι (perf. only) I am eager

λεπταλέος -η -ον fine, delicate

λεπτός -ή -όν fine, delicate

λευκός -ή -όν white

λεύσσω I see

λέχος -εος, τό litter, bier

λέων -οντος, ὁ lion

ληΐζομαι I carry off as booty (= Att. λήζομαι)

ληΐς -ΐδος, ἡ booty (= Att. λεία -ας)

Λητώ -οῦς, ἡ Leto (mother of Apollo and Artemis)

λιγύς -εῖα -ύ clear, piercing

λίθος -ου, ὁ stone, rock

λιλαίομαι I desire, am eager

Λιμνώρεια -ας, ἡ Limnoreia (a Nereid)

λίνον -ου, τό string, line

λίνος -ου, ὁ Linus song

λίπα richly

λιπαροκρήδεμνος -ον with shining veil

λίς (acc. λῖν), ὁ lion

λίσσομαι (aor. ἐλιτόμην) I beg, beseech, pray (for)

λιτί (dat. only), τῷ linen

λοετρόν -οῦ, τό bath (= Att. λουτρόν)

λοετροχόος -ον holding water for washing (= Att. λουτροχόος)

λοιγός -οῦ, ὁ ruin, destruction, death

λούω I wash, bathe

λόφος -ου, ὁ crest, plume

λοχάω I lie in ambush

λόχος -ου, ὁ ambush

λυγρός -ή -όν sad, dreadful

Λυκίη -ης, ἡ Lycia (= Att. Λυκία -ας)

Λύκιοι -ων, οἱ Lycians

λύκος -ου, ὁ wolf

Λύκων -ωνος, ὁ Lycon (a Trojan)

λύω I loose, loosen, undo

λώβη -ης, ἡ disgrace

M

Μαιμαλίδης -αο/εω, ὁ son of Maemalus

μαίνομαι I am mad, rage, rave

Μαῖρα -ης, ἡ Maera (a Nereid)

μακρός -ή -όν long, high; (n. pl. as adv.) loudly

μάλα very, very much, hard, seriously

μαλακός -ή -όν soft

μάλιστα (sup. of μάλα) most, especially

μᾶλλον (comp. of μάλα) more

μάν indeed; but, yet (= Att. μήν)

μαντεύομαι I prophesy, predict

Μάρις -ιος, ὁ Maris (a Lycian)

μαρμαίρω I sparkle, gleam

μαρμάρεος -η -ον flashing, glittering

μάρμαρος -ον sparkling

μάρναμαι I fight

ματάω I linger, delay; I am unsuccessful

μάχαιρα -ης, ἡ knife, dagger

μάχη -ης, ἡ battle

μαχητής -ᾶο/έω, ὁ fighter, warrior

μάχομαι I fight

Μεγάδης -αο/εω, ὁ son of Megas

μεγάθυμος -ον great-hearted

μεγαλήτωρ -ορος great-hearted

μεγαλωστί greatly, stretched over a great space

μέγαρον -ου, τό hall, pl. house, palace

μέγας μεγάλη μέγα big, great; (n. s. or pl. as adv.) greatly, by far, loudly

μεδέων = μέδων

μέδομαι I think about (+ gen.)

μέδων -οντος, ὁ ruler, guardian

μεθίημι I let go

μείλινος -η -ον ashen, of ash wood (= Att. μέλινος)

μελαίνομαι I grow black, become dark

Μελάνιππος -ου, ὁ Melanippus (a Trojan)

μελάνυδρος -ον of dark water

μέλας μέλαινα μέλαν black, dark

μέλεον in vain

μέλι -ιτος, τό honey

μελίη -ης, ἡ ash spear (= Att. μελία -ας)

μελιηδής -ές honey-sweet

Μελίτη -ης, ἡ Melite (a Nereid)

μέλλω I intend to, am about to, going to, fated to

μέλος -εος, τό limb

μέλπηθρα -ων, τά plaything

μέλπομαι I celebrate with song and dance

μέλω I am an object of care to (+ dat.)

μέμαα (perf. with pres. sense) I am eager

μέμονα (perf. with pres. sense) I rage, strive

μέν (1) certainly, in fact; (2) (sets up a contrast, usu. answered by δέ)

μενεαίνω I am eager; I struggle, rage

Μενέλαος -ου, ὁ Menelaus

Μενέσθιος -ου, ὁ Menesthius (a Myrmidon leader)

Μενοιτιάδης -αο/εω, ὁ son of Menoetius (i.e. Patroclus)

Μενοίτιος -ου, ὁ Menoetius (father of Patroclus)

μένος -εος, τό might, fighting spirit

μένω I wait, wait for, remain, stay, hold my ground

μερμηρίζω I ponder

μέροπες -ων mortal

μεσ(σ)ηγύ(ς) in the middle, in the space between

μέσ(σ)ος -η -ον middle (part of), in the middle, between (+ gen.)

μετά (+ acc.) after, to, in pursuit of, into the midst of, among, along; (+ dat.) among, in, with; (as adv.) along with them

μεταΐσσω I attack, rush on

μετακιάθω I go after, go in pursuit of

μετανάστης -αο/εω, ὁ migrant, refugee

μετανίσσομαι I pass over, move over

μεταπρεπής -ές conspicuous among (+ dat.)

μεταπρέπω I am conspicuous among (+ dat.)

μεταυδάω I speak among (+ dat.)

μετάφρενον -ου, τό upper back

μεταφωνέω I speak among (+ dat.)

μέτειμι I am among (+ dat.)

μετεῖπον (aor.) I spoke among, spoke to (+ dat.)

μετέρχομαι I come/go among (+ dat.)

μετόπισθε behind, from behind

μετώπιον -ου, τό forehead

μέτωπον -ου, τό forehead, brow, front (of helmet)

μή not, don't, may … not, so that … not, lest, in case, for fear that

μηδέ and not, and don't

μῆδος -εος, τό plan, counsel

μηκάομαι (aor. part. μακών) I shriek, cry

μηκέτι no longer

μηλοβοτήρ -ῆρος, ὁ shepherd

μῆλον -ου, τό sheep, goat; pl. flocks, herds

μήν indeed

μηνιθμός -οῦ, ὁ wrath

μῆνις -ιος, ἡ wrath

μηνίω I am angry at (+ dat.)

Μηονίη -ης, ἡ Maeonia (= Att. Μαιονία -ας)

Μηριόνης -αο/εω, ὁ Meriones

μηρός -οῦ, ὁ thigh

μήστωρ -ωρος, ὁ leader

μήτε and not; μήτε … μήτε neither … nor

μήτηρ μητρός, ἡ mother

μητιάω I plan, devise

μητίετα (nom. and voc. only), ὁ counsellor

μήτρως -ωος, ὁ maternal uncle

μιαίνω I stain, befoul

μίγνυμι I mix, mingle

μιμνήσκω I remind; mid. μιμνήσκομαι I remember, turn my thoughts to (+ gen.)

μίμνω = μένω

μιν (personal pron. acc. s.) him, her, it (= Att. αὐτόν -ήν -ό)

μινύθω I am destroyed

μίσγω I mix, mingle

μνάομαι I turn my thoughts to (+ gen.)

μογοστόκος -ον producer of labour pains

μόθος -ου, ὁ fray

μοῖρα -ης, ἡ portion, space; fate, destiny; κατὰ μοῖραν in an orderly way

μολπή -ῆς, ἡ singing and dancing

μορμύρω I roar

μόρος -ου, ὁ fate, doom

Μούλιος -ου, ὁ Mulius (a Trojan)

μοῦσα -ης, ἡ Muse (goddess of poetic inspiration)

μυθέομαι I speak of as, call

μῦθος -ου, ὁ word, speech, instructions

μυῖα -ας, ἡ fly

μυκάομαι (perf. part. μεμυκώς) I low, bellow

μυκηθμός -οῦ, ὁ lowing, bellowing

μυρίος -η -ον measureless, pl. countless, numberless

Μυρμιδόνες -ων, οἱ Myrmidons

μύρομαι I weep

μυών -ῶνος, ὁ muscle

μῶλος -ου, ὁ toil, struggle

μώνυχες -ων single-hoofed, with uncloven hoof

N

ναί yes

ναίω I live, dwell

νάπη -ης, ἡ glen

νεηκής -ές newly sharpened, whetted

νεῆνις -ιδος, ἡ young girl (= Att. νεᾶνις)

νείαιρα -ης lower (part of)

νείατος -η -ον lowest (part of) (= Att. νέατος)

νεικέω I quarrel

νεῖκος -εος, τό dispute, quarrel

νειός -οῦ/οῖο, ὁ fallow land

νεκρός -οῦ, ὁ corpse, dead body

νεκτάρεος -η -ον nectar-like, fragrant

νέκυς -υος, ὁ dead body

νεμεσ(σ)άω I am angry; mid./pass. νεμεσ(σ)άομαι I am ashamed

νέομαι I go

νεούτατος -ον recently wounded

νέρθεν under, beneath, down below

Νεστορίδης -αο/εω, ὁ son of Nestor

Νέστωρ -ορος, ὁ Nestor

νευρή -ῆς, ἡ bowstring

νεῦρον -ου, τό tendon, sinew

νεύω I nod, move my head, hang down

νεφέλη -ης, ἡ cloud

νεφεληγερέτα -αο/εω, ὁ cloud-gatherer (epithet of Zeus)

νέφος -εος, τό cloud

νήδυμος -ον sweet

νήϊος -η -ον for ships; (as n. noun) ship's timber

νηλεής -ές pitiless

Νημερτής (nom. only), ἡ Nemertes (a Nereid)

νηπίαχος = νήπιος

νήπιος -η -ον young, childish, helpless, foolish

Νηρηΐδες -ων, αἱ Nereids, daughters of Nereus (sea-nymphs)

Νησαίη -ης, ἡ Nesaea (a Nereid)

νῆσος -ου, ἡ island

νηῦς νηός, ἡ ship (= Att. ναῦς νεώς)

νίζω (aor. ἔνιψα) I wash

νικάω I defeat, am superior

νίκη -ης, ἡ victory

νίσομαι I go, come

νιφόεις -εσσα -εν (-εντος) snowy

νοέω I notice, observe

νόημα -ατος, τό thought, idea

νόθος -η -ον illegitimate, bastard

νομεύς -ῆος, ὁ herdsman

νομός -οῦ, ὁ pasture; νομόνδε to pasture

νόος -ου, ὁ mind, thought, intelligence

νοστέω I return home

νόστος -ου, ὁ homecoming

νόσφιν far away from (+ gen.)

Νότος -ου, ὁ Notus (the south wind)

νύ(ν) now then, well then, I suppose (enclitic particle)

νύμφη -ης, ἡ bride

νῦν now; νῦν δέ but as things are

νύξ -κτός, ἡ night, darkness

νύσσω I strike, stab, pierce

νῶϊν (nom. dual.) we two (= Att. νῷν)

νῶροψ -οπος gleaming, shining

Ξ

Ξάνθος -ου, ὁ Xanthus ('Bay', a horse of Achilles)

ξείνιον/ξεινήϊον -ου, τό gift of hospitality (= Att. ξένιον)

ξεστός -ή -όν smoothed, polished

ξίφος -εος, τό sword

ξύλον -ου, τό (piece of) wood, pl. wood, firewood

ξύν = σύν

ξυνός -ή -όν common, shared, even-handed (= Att. κοινός)

O

ὁ ἡ τό (definite article 'the', mainly used in Homer as personal, demonstrative or rel. pron.)

ὄβριμος -ον heavy, mighty

ὄγμος -ου, ὁ furrow

ὅδε ἥδε τόδε this

ὁδίτης -αο/εω, ὁ traveller

ὁδός -οῦ, ἡ road, path

ὁδούς -όντος, ὁ tooth

ὀδύνη -ης, ἡ pain

ὀδύρομαι I lament

Ὀδυσ(σ)εύς -ῆος, ὁ Odysseus

ὀδύσσομαι I hate

ὄζος -ου, ὁ branch

ὅθι where

ὀθόνη -ης, ἡ linen garment

οἷ/οἱ (dat. of ἕ/ἑ)

οἷα as, how

οἶδα (perf. with pres. sense) I know

οἴκαδε home, homewards

οἰκία -ων, τά dwellings

οἰκτείρω I pity

Ὀϊλιάδης -αο/εω, ὁ son of Oileus

οἶμα -ατος, τό rush, spring

οἰμώζω I cry, groan

οἶνος -ου, ὁ wine

οἶος -η -ον alone

οἷος -η -ον as, such, such as, of the sort which

ὄϊς ὄιος/οἰός, ὁ/ἡ sheep

ὀϊστός -οῦ, ὁ arrow

οἴχομαι I go, depart

ὀκριόεις -εσσα -εν (-εντος) jagged

ὄλβος -ου, ὁ happiness, prosperity

ὄλεθρος -ου, ὁ destruction, ruin, death

ὀλέκω I destroy; mid. ὀλέκομαι I perish

ὀλετήρ -ῆρος, ὁ destroyer

ὀλιγοδρανέων (m. part.) failing in strength

ὀλίγος -η -ον little, small, pl. few

ὄλλυμι (aor. ὤλεσα) I destroy; mid. ὄλλυμαι (aor. ὠλόμην) I am killed, perish

ὀλοός -ή -όν deadly, destructive

ὀλοφύρομαι I lament, mourn, feel sympathy for

Ὀλύμπιος -ον Olympian, on Mount Olympus; (as m. noun) the Olympian (i.e. Zeus)

Ὄλυμπος -ου/οιο, ὁ Mount Olympus (home of the gods)

ὄμαδος -ου, ὁ din, noise

ὁμιλέω I gather, throng; I join battle

ὅμιλος -ου, ὁ crowd, throng

ὁμοΐιος = ὁμοῖος

ὁμοῖος -η -ον like, the same, similar, equal, equally balanced

ὁμοκλάω/ὁμοκλέω I urge on with a shout (+ acc. or dat.)

ὁμοκλή -ῆς, ἡ call

ὀμόργνυμι I wipe X (acc.) from Y (gen.)

ὀμφαλόεις -εσσα -εν (-εντος) bossed, with a central boss

ὀνείδειος -ον reproachful

ὄνειδος -εος, τό reproach, matter of reproach

Ὀνήτωρ -ορος, ὁ Onetor (a Trojan)

ὀνίνημι I benefit (someone); mid. ὀνίναμαι (fut. ὀνήσομαι) I derive benefit from (+ gen.)

ὀνομάζω I name

ὀνομαίνω I call by name

ὀξυόεις -εσσα -εν (-εντος) sharp-pointed

ὀξύς -εῖα -ύ sharp

ὀπάζω I give, grant, provide as follower(s)

ὅπη where, by which way

ὀπίζομαι I respect, heed

ὄπις -ιδος, ἡ gaze, avenging eye

ὄπι(σ)θε(ν) behind, from behind (+ gen. or as adv.)

ὀπίσ(σ)ω backwards

ὅπλον -ου, τό tool, implement; pl. arms, armour

Ὀπόεις -εντος, ὁ Opus (city in Locris)

ὁπ(π)ότε when, whenever; for when … might (+ opt.)

ὅπ(π)ως how, as, according to how

ὀπυίω I have as my wife, am married to

ὀπωρινός -ή -όν of autumn

ὁράω I see

ὀρέγω I stretch, strain; mid. ὀρέγομαι I lunge at, strike

ὀρθόκραιρος -η -ον (of oxen) with upright
    horns, (of ships) with upright beaks
ὀρθός -ή -όν upright
ὀρίνω I throw into confusion
ὀρμαίνω I turn over, ponder
ὀρμάομαι I rush, charge out
ὅρμος -ου, ὁ necklace
ὄρνυμι I arouse; mid. ὄρνυμαι (with perf. act.
    ὄρωρα) I rise, get up
ὄρος -εος (dat. pl. οὔρεσι), τό mountain
ὀρούω I rush forth, dart forward
ὀρυκτός -ή -όν dug, dug out
ὀρυμαγδός -οῦ, ὁ noise, din
ὀρχέομαι I dance
ὀρχηστήρ -ῆρος, ὁ dancer
ὀρχηστής -ᾶο/έω, ὁ dancer
ὅς ἥ ὅ (rel. pron.) who, which; ὅς κε whoever
ὅς ἥ ὅν (possessive pron., = ἑός) his (own), her
    (own)
ὅσον ... τόσον as much as ... so much
ὅσ(σ)ος -η -ον how much, as much as, as big
    as; pl. how many; as many as, all those
    who
ὄσσε, τώ the (two) eyes
ὄσσομαι I foresee
ὀστέον -ου, τό bone
ὅστις ἥτις ὅ τι who(ever), which(ever)
ὅτε/ὅ τε when, since
ὁτὲ μέν ... ἄλλοτε δέ at one time ... at another
    time
ὅτε μή except
ὅτ(τ)ι that, because
ὀτρύνω I rouse, urge on
οὕ/οὗ (gen. of ἕ/ἑ)
οὐ/οὐκ/οὐχ not
οὖδας -εος, τό ground
οὐδέ and not, nor, not even
οὐδείς οὐδεμία οὐδέν (-ένος) no one, nothing;
    (n. as adv.) not at all
οὐκέτι no longer
οὖλος -η -ον woolly
Οὔλυμπος = Ὄλυμπος; Οὐλυμπόνδε to
    Olympus
οὖν therefore, and so, then; well then
οὕνεκα because
οὔπω/οὔ πω not yet

οὐρανός -οῦ, ὁ sky, heaven; οὐρανόθεν from
    heaven
οὐρίαχος -ου, ὁ butt end (of spear)
οὖρος = ὄρος
οὖς οὔατος, τό ear; handle
οὐτάω I stab, wound
οὔτε ... οὔτε neither ... nor
οὔ τι not at all
οὗτος αὕτη τοῦτο this
ὀφέλλω (1) (aor. ὄφελον) I owe, ought (= Att.
    ὀφείλω)
ὀφέλλω (2) I increase, multiply
ὀφθαλμός -οῦ, ὁ eye
ὄφρα while, so long as, until; that, so that, in
    order that
ὀφρύς -ύος, ἡ brow
ὄχεα -ων, τά chariot(s)
ὀχθέω I am disturbed, upset, angered
ὄχθη -ης, ἡ bank (of river)
ὄψ ὀπός, ἡ voice
ὀψίγονος -ον born in a later age, of a future
    generation

Π

πάγχυ entirely (= Att. πάνυ)
Παίονες -ων, οἱ Paeonians
παῖς/πάϊς παιδός, ὁ boy, son
πάλαι long ago
παλάμη -ης, ἡ palm, hand
παλιμπετές back, backwards
πάλιν back; away from (+ gen.)
Παλλάς -άδος, ἡ Pallas (epithet of Athena)
πάλλω (aor. ἔπηλα) I brandish, shake
παλύνω I sprinkle
πάμπαν altogether; (with negative) not at all
παμφανόων -όωσα -όν (-ωντος) shining
    brightly
πανημέριος -η -ον all day long
Πανθοΐδης -αο/εω, ὁ son of Panthus
παννύχιος -η -ον all night long
Πανόπη -ης, ἡ Panope (a Nereid)
πάντη on all sides, everywhere
πάντοθεν from every side, on every side, all
    around
παντοῖος -η -ον of every kind; from all
    directions

πάντοσε in every direction, from everywhere, all over
παπταίνω I look about
παρά/πάρ (+ acc.) to the side of, along, by, close by; (+ gen.) from; (+ dat.) beside, with, by; (as adv.) beside
παραείρομαι (aor. παρηέρθην) I hang to one side
παράκοιτις -ιος, ἡ wife
παραλέγομαι I lie with
παρατίθημι I put X (acc.) beside/before Y (dat.)
παρειαί -ῶν, αἱ cheeks
πάρειμι I am present, at hand
παρέχω I give
παρήϊον -ου, τό cheek, jaw
παρηορίαι -ῶν, αἱ side-traces
παρήορος -ου, ὁ trace-horse
παρθενική -ῆς, ἡ maiden, unmarried young woman
παρθένιος -ου, ὁ son of an unmarried mother
παρθένος -ου, ἡ maiden, unmarried young woman
παρίσταμαι I stand beside, come up to (+ dat.)
πάροιθε in front of (+ gen.)
πάρος (as adv.) before, formerly, (as conj.) before (+ inf.)
πᾶς πᾶσα πᾶν (παντός) all, each, every
πάσχω (aor. ἔπαθον) I suffer
πάταγος -ου, ὁ crashing, din
πατήρ πατρός, ὁ father
πάτρη -ης, ἡ native land (= Att. πάτρα or πατρίς)
πατρίς -ίδος of one's fathers, native
Πάτροκλος -ου/οιο (or Πατροκλῆς -ῆος), ὁ Patroclus
παύω I stop
πάχιστος -η -ον thickest, very thick
παχύς -εῖα -ύ thick, sturdy
πεδίον -ου/οιο, τό plain
πείθω I persuade; mid. πείθομαι I listen (to), trust, obey (+ dat.)
πεινάω I am hungry
πειράομαι I try, test, try my strength
πεῖραρ -ατος, τό decision, judgement

πείρω I pierce
Πείσανδρος -ου, ὁ Pisander (a Myrmidon leader)
πελάζω I bring X (acc.) near to Y (dat.)
Πελασγικός -ή -όν Pelasgian
πέλεκυς -εος, ὁ axe
πελεμίζω I shake
πέλλα -ης, ἡ milking-pail
πέλομαι I am, become
πέλωρ (nom. only), τό monstrous figure
πελώριος -η -ον huge
πέμπτος -η -ον fifth
πέμπω I send
πένθος -εος, τό grief
πένομαι I prepare
πέντε five
πεντήκοντα fifty
πεπνυμένος -η -ον prudent
πέποιθα (perf. with pres. sense) I trust in
πέπον (voc.) my friend, dear
πεπρωμένος -η -ον destined, doomed
πέπρωται (3 s. perf. pass.) it is destined, fated
περ (particle emphasising preceding word, oft. suggesting 'even' or 'although')
περάω I cross over
πέρθω (aor. ἔπερσα/ἔπραθον) I sack, plunder, lay waste
περί (+ acc.) about, around; (+ gen.) about, around, for the sake of, over, above, more than; (+ dat.) around, in; (as adv., also πέρι) all around, exceedingly
περιάγνυμι I break around; pass. περιάγνυμαι I reverberate all around
περιβάλλω I place around
περιγλαγής -ές filled with milk
περιέννυμι I put (clothing or armour, acc.) on (someone, also acc.)
Περιήρης -εος, ὁ Perieres (father of Borus)
περιίσταμαι I stand around
περικαλλής -ές very beautiful
περικαλύπτω I envelop
περικλυτός -ή -όν highly renowned, famous
περικτίονες -ων, οἱ those who live nearby
Πέριμος -ου, ὁ Perimus (a Trojan)
περιπλόμενος -η -ον moving round, circling
περιπρό around and in front

περιστένω I cram full; pass. περιστένομαι I am stuffed full

πέρνημι I sell

πέτομαι (aor. ἐπτόμην/ἐπτάμην) I fly

πέτρη -ης, ἡ rock, cliff (= Att. πέτρα)

πέτρος -ου, ὁ stone

πη anywhere, in any way

πήγνυμι I fix, plant firmly

Πήδασος -ου, ὁ Pedasus (a horse of Achilles)

Πηλεΐδης -αο/εω, ὁ son of Peleus (i.e. Achilles)

Πηλεΐων -ωνος, ὁ son of Peleus

Πηλεύς -ῆος/έος, ὁ Peleus (father of Achilles)

Πηληϊάδης -αο/εω, ὁ son of Peleus

Πηλήϊος -η -ον of Peleus

πήληξ -ηκος, ἡ helmet

Πηλιάς -άδος Pelian, of/from Mount Pelion

Πήλιον -ου, τό Pelion (mountain in Thessaly)

Πηνέλεως -ω, ὁ Peneleos (leader of the Boeotians)

πῖδαξ -ακος, ἡ spring (of water)

πιέζω I press, squeeze

πίειρα -ας fertile, rich

πίμπλημι (aor. ἔπλησα) I fill X (acc.) with Y (gen.)

πίνω (aor. ἔπιον) I drink

πίπτω (aor. ἔπεσον) I fall

πιστός -ή -όν trusty, faithful

πίτυς -υος, ἡ pine

πιφαύσκω I declare, make known

πίων -ονος rich, fertile

πλεῖστος -η -ον (sup. of πολύς) most

πλεκτός -ή -όν woven, wicker

πλέων -ον (comp. of πολύς) more, greater

πληγή -ῆς, ἡ blow

πλήθω I am full, am in flood

Πληϊάδες -ων, αἱ Pleiades (constellation)

πλησίον nearby

πλήσσω I strike

πλοῦτος -ου, ὁ wealth, riches

πνοιή -ῆς, ἡ breath, blast of wind (= Att. πνοή)

Ποδάργη -ης, ἡ Podarge (a harpy)

ποδάρκης -ες swift-footed

ποδήνεμος -ον wind-footed

ποδώκης -ες swift-footed

ποθεν somewhere, from somewhere

ποιέω I make; mid. ποιέομαι I appoint

ποιητός -ή -όν made

ποικίλλω I make with skill

ποικίλος -η -ον skilfully made, elaborate

ποιμήν -ένος, ὁ shepherd

ποινή -ῆς, ἡ vengeance, retribution, blood price, compensation

ποῖος -η -ον what sort of? what a …!

ποιπνύω I bustle about

πολεμίζω I make war against (+ dat.), fight

πολεμιστής -ᾶο/έω, ὁ warrior

πόλεμος -ου/οιο, ὁ war, warfare, battle

πόλις -ιος/ηος, ἡ city

Πολυδώρη -ης, ἡ Polydora (daughter of Peleus)

Πολυμήλη -ης, ἡ Polymele (daughter of Phylas)

Πολύμηλος -ου, ὁ Polymelus (a Lycian)

πολύς πολλή πολύ much, pl. many

πολυφάρμακος -ον skilled in many drugs

πολύφρων -ονος very thoughtful

πολύχαλκος -ον rich in bronze

πολύχρυσος -ον rich in gold

πομπός -οῦ, ὁ escort

πονέομαι I am busy, work, toil at

πόνος -ου, ὁ toil, labour

ποντοπόρος -ον seafaring

πόντος -ου/οιο, ὁ sea

πόποι (always with ὤ/ὦ) well, now! (expressing grief and/or disagreeable surprise)

πόρπη -ης, ἡ brooch

πορφύρεος -η -ον purple, dark

πόρωσι (3 pl. subj. of ἔπορον)

πόσε to where? (= Att. ποῖ)

πόσις -ιος, ὁ husband

ποταμός -οῦ/οῖο, ὁ river

ποτε once, ever; οὐδέ ποτε never

ποτί = πρός

ποτιδέρκομαι I look upon (= Att. προσδέρκομαι)

πότμος -ου, ὁ fate, death

πότνια (nom. and voc. only), ἡ lady

που somewhere, perhaps, probably, no doubt

πουλυβότειρα -ης much-nourishing

Πουλυδάμας -αντος, ὁ Polydamas (a Trojan)

πούς ποδός, ὁ foot

πραπίδες -ων, αἱ mind

πρήθω I blow, spurt

πρηνής -ές headlong, on the face

πρήσσω I do, accomplish (= Att. πράσσω)

Πριαμίδης -αο/εω, ὁ son of Priam

Πρίαμος -ου/οιο, ὁ Priam (king of Troy)

πρίν (as adv.) before, formerly, sooner; (as conj.) until (+ subj.)

πρό (+ gen.) in front of; (as adv.) forward

προβαίνω I go forward, am superior

προβλής -ῆτος projecting, jutting out

προβλώσκω (aor. προὔμολον) I come forward

προγίγνομαι I advance, approach

προεῖδον (aor.) I looked forward, caught sight of

πρόθυρον -ου, τό front porch, doorway

προΐημι I send out, send forth

πρόμαχος -ου, ὁ foremost fighter

προνοέω I foresee, suspect

Πρόνοος -ου, ὁ Pronous (a Trojan)

προπάροιθε (+ gen.) in front of; (as adv.) forwards

πρός/προτί (+ acc.) to, towards; (+ gen.) from; (as adv.) in addition

προσαμύνω I protect, aid

προσαυδάω I speak to, address

προσβαίνω I go to, step on

προσεῖπον/προσέειπον (aor.) I spoke to, addressed

πρόσθε(ν) in front of (+ gen.)

πρόσκειμαι I am attached

πρόσ(σ)ω forward, ahead

πρόσφημι I speak to, address

πρόσωπον -ου, τό face

πρότερος -η -ον first of two

προτέρω onward, forward

προτεύχω I make/do beforehand; perf. inf. pass. προτετύχθαι to be over and done with

προτί = πρός

προτροπάδην in headlong flight

πρυμνή -ῆς, ἡ stern

πρυμνός -ή -όν end part of, top part of, stern of

πρῶϊ early, in the morning (= Att. πρῷ)

πρών πρώονος, ὁ headland

Πρωτεσίλαος -ου, ὁ Protesilaus

πρώτιστος -η -ον first of all (also n. pl. as adv. with same sense)

πρῶτον/πρῶτα first, at first

πρῶτος -η -ον first

Πρωτώ -οῦς, ἡ Proto (a Nereid)

πτερόεις -εσσα -εν (-εντος) winged

πτόλεμος = πόλεμος

πτολίεθρον -ου, τό city, town

πτόλις = πόλις

πτύξ -υχός, ἡ fold, layer

πυθμήν -ένος, ὁ base, bottom

πύκα strongly

πυκ(ι)νός -ή -όν close, thick, close-packed, close-set; shrewd; (n. as adv.) repeatedly

Πυλάρτης -ου, ὁ Pylartes (a Trojan)

πύλη -ης, ἡ gate, gatepost

πύματος -η -ον last, outermost

πυνθάνομαι (fut. πεύσομαι, aor. (ἐ)πυθόμην) I learn, hear

πῦρ πυρός, τό fire

πυράγρη -ης, ἡ fire tongs

Πυραίχμης -αο/εω, ὁ Pyraechmes (a Paeonian)

πύργος -ου, ὁ tower

πυρή -ῆς, ἡ pyre (= Att. πυρά -ᾶς)

Πύρις -ιος, ὁ Pyris (a Lycian)

πυρσός -οῦ, ὁ beacon, fire signal

πω yet, ever

πῶμα -ατος, τό lid, cover

πῶς how?

πως somehow; οὐ … πως in no way

πῶυ -εος, τό flock

Ρ

ῥα = ἄρα

ῥαιστήρ -ῆρος, ὁ hammer

ῥαίω (aor. pass. ἐρραίσθην) I break, shatter

ῥάπτω I stitch up, devise

ῥέθος -εος, τό limb

ῥέζω (aor. ἔρ(ρ)εξα) I do, work

ῥεῖα easily, lightly

ῥέω I flow

ῥηγμίς -ῖνος, ἡ shore

ῥήγνυμι (aor. ἔρρηξα) I break

ῥηΐδιος -η -ον easy (= Att. ῥᾴδιος)

ῥηϊδίως easily (= Att. ῥᾳδίως)

ῥηΐτερος -η -ον (comp. of ῥηΐδιος) easier (= Att. ῥᾴων)

ῥηξήνωρ -ορος breaking through ranks

ῥήσσω I stamp my feet

ῥιγέω I shudder (at)

ῥινός -οῦ, ὁ hide, skin

ῥιπή -ῆς, ἡ flight, throw

ῥίς ῥινός, ἡ nose, pl. nostrils

ῥοδανός -ή -όν waving, swaying

ῥοή -ῆς, ἡ stream

ῥοῖζος -ου, ὁ whistling, whirring

ῥόος -ου, ὁ flow, stream

ῥυμός -οῦ, ὁ pole (of chariot)

ῥύομαι I protect, save, guard

ῥυτήρ -ῆρος, ὁ rein

ῥώομαι I move quickly, rush forth

Σ

Σαγγάριος -ου, ὁ Sangarius (river in Asia Minor)

σάκος -εος, τό shield

σάλπιγξ -ιγγος, ἡ trumpet

σανίς -ίδος board, pl. door

σαόω I save (= Att. σῴζω)

Σαρπηδών -όνος, ὁ Sarpedon (Lycian leader)

σβέννυμι (aor. ἔσβεσα) I quench, extinguish

σέβας, τό awe, reverence, respect, sense of shame

σέθεν = σοῦ (gen. of σύ)

σέλας -αος, τό gleam

σελήνη -ης, ἡ moon

Σελλοί -ῶν, οἱ Selli (priests of Zeus at Dodona)

σεῦ = σοῦ (gen. of σύ)

σεύομαι I hurry, am in a hurry

σηκός -οῦ, ὁ pen, fold

σημαίνω I command, give orders

Σθενέλαος -ου, ὁ Sthenelaus (a Lycian)

σθένος -εος, τό strength, forces

σίδηρος -ου, ὁ iron, iron weapon

σίντης -αο/εω ravening, predatory

σιωπή -ῆς, ἡ silence

Σκαιαί -ῶν, αἱ the Scaean Gate (of Troy)

σκαιός -ή -όν on the left; (as f. noun) left hand

σκαίρω I skip

σκέλος -εος, τό leg

σκέπτομαι I watch out for, am on the alert for

σκῆπτρον -ου, τό staff

σκίδναμαι I spread out

σκολιός -ή -όν crooked

σκόλοψ -οπος, ὁ stake

σκοπιή -ῆς, ἡ lookout; mountain peak (= Att. σκοπιά -ᾶς)

σκοπός -οῦ, ὁ watchman, lookout

σκότος -ου, ὁ darkness

σκύμνος -ου, ὁ cub

σμερδαλέος -η -ον fearful, terrible; (n. s. or pl. as adv.) terribly

σόος -η -ον safe (= Att. σῶς/σῶος)

σός σή σόν your, of you (s.)

σπάω I draw, draw out

Σπειώ -όος, ἡ Speio (a Nereid)

σπένδω (aor. ἔσπεισα) I pour a libation

σπέος -είους, τό cave

Σπερχειός -οῦ, ὁ Spercheius (river in Thessaly)

σπεύδω I hasten

σπόγγος -ου, ὁ sponge

σταθμός -οῦ, ὁ farmyard

σταφυλή -ῆς, ἡ bunch of grapes

στείχω (aor. ἔστιχον) I march, march out

στενάχω I sigh, groan, roar

στένω I sigh, groan

στέρνον -ου, τό chest

στεροπηγερέτα -αο/εω, ὁ gatherer of lightning

στεῦμαι I undertake, promise

στεφάνη -ης, ἡ headband

στεφανόω I put around as a crown

στέφω I put as a crown

στῆ he/she stood

στῆθος -εος, τό breast, chest

στήλη -ης, ἡ pillar, gravestone

στηρίζω I set firmly

στιβαρός -ή -όν firm, strong

στίλβω I gleam

στιχάομαι I walk

στιχός, τῆς (s. gen. only; pl. στίχες -ων, αἱ) line of ships; row, rank, company

στόμα -ατος, τό mouth; face

στοναχέω I lament

στρατός -οῦ, ὁ army, camp

στρεφεδινέω I whirl (something) round

στρέφω I turn, twist; mid. στρέφομαι I turn round

στροφάλιγξ -ιγγος, ἡ eddy, whirl

στυγερός -ή -όν hateful

στυγερῶς hatefully, with horrible consequences

στυφελίζω I strike, strike against, knock about

σύ σοῦ/σέο/σεῦ/σέθεν you (s.)

συγχέω I pour together, entangle with

συλάω I strip off, plunder

συλλέγω I collect, gather up

συμβάλλω I throw together; I join (battle)

σύν with (+ dat.)

συνάγω I bring together; I join (battle)

συναιρέω I crush, destroy

σύνειμι I come together, meet

συντρέχω (aor. συνέδραμον) I rush together

σῦριγξ -ιγγος, ἡ pipe, Pan-pipe

σῦς συός, ὁ/ἡ pig, wild boar

σφεδανόν eagerly

σφεῖς σφῶν/σφέων they, them, themselves

σφέτερος -η -ον their

σφήξ σφηκός, ὁ wasp

σφός -ή -όν their, their own

σφῶϊ/σφώ σφῶϊν (dual of σύ) you two

σχεδόθεν near at hand, close by

σχεδόν near

σχέτλιος -η -ον cruel, hard, stubborn

σῶμα -ατος, τό body

T

τ᾽ = τε (before vowel with smooth breathing)

ταί = αἱ

τάλαντον -ου, τό talent (unit of weight); pl. pair of scales

τάλαρος -ου, ὁ basket

τάμνω (aor. ἔταμον) I cut (= Att. τέμνω)

ταναός -όν long

τανυήκης -ες long-bladed, slender-pointed

τανύπεπλος -ον with trailing robes

τανύφλοιος -ον with smooth bark

τανύω I stretch, stretch out, strain

ταπής -ῆτος, ὁ rug

ταρχύω I inter, bury solemnly

ταύρειος -η -ον of bull's hide

ταῦρος -ου, ὁ bull

τάφρος -ου, ἡ ditch, trench

ταφών -οῦσα -όν in a daze, as if paralysed

τάχα quickly, soon

τάχιστα very quickly

ταχύς -εῖα -ύ quick, swift

τε and; ('generalising', implying 'as usually happens'); τε … καί/τε … τε both … and

τέθνηκα (perf. of θνήσκω) I am dead

τείνω I spread out

τείρεα -ων, τά constellations (Homeric pl. of τέρας -ατος, τό sign, portent)

τείρω I wear out, exhaust

τεῖχος -εος, τό wall

τέκμωρ (nom./acc. only), τό end, goal, solution (= Att. τέκμαρ)

τέκνον -ου, τό child

τέκος -εος, τό child, young animal

τέκτων -ονος, ὁ maker, carpenter

τελαμών -ῶνος, ὁ sword belt, shield strap

Τελαμωνιάδης -αο/εω, ὁ son of Telamon (i.e. Ajax the Great)

Τελαμώνιος -ον of Telamon

τελευτάω I fulfil

τελευτή -ῆς, ἡ end

τελέω I fulfil, accomplish

τέλος -εος, τό end, purpose, outcome, fulfilment, finish, completeness; unit, company

τέλσον -ου, τό turning point, end

τέμενος -εος, τό private estate

τένων -οντος, ὁ sinew, tendon

τεός -ή -όν = σός

τέρην -εινα -εν tender, soft

τερμιόεις -εσσα -εν (-εντος) fringed, tasselled

τερπικέραυνος -ον delighting in thunder

τέρπομαι I take pleasure in (+ dat.)

τερσαίνω (aor. τέρσηνα) I dry, dry up

τέσσαρες -α four

τέταρτος -η -ον fourth

Τεῦκρος -ου, ὁ Teucer (a Greek archer)

τεύχεα -ων, τά arms, armour

τεύχω I make, prepare

τέφρη -ης, ἡ ashes (= Att. τέφρα -ας)

τῆθος -εος, τό oyster

τῆλε far, a long way, far away

τηλόθεν from far away

τηλόθι (+ gen.) far away from; (as adv.) far
away

τι (as adv.) in some way, in any way, at all

τί what? why?

τίθημι I put, place; I make

τίκτω (aor. ἔτεκον) I give birth to

τιμάω I honour

τιμή -ῆς, ἡ honour

τιμήεις -εσσα -εν (-εντος) precious

τίνω I pay

τίπτε why ever?

τίς τί (τίνος) who? what? which?

τις τι (τινός) someone/anyone, something/
anything; some, any, a certain

τίω (aor. ἔτισα) I honour, value

τλάω (aor. ἔτλην) I dare, have the courage,
endure

Τληπόλεμος -ου, ὁ Tlepolemus (a Lycian)

τμήγω (aor. pass. ἐτμάγην) I cut, divide, break

τοί (1) = οἱ (pl. of ὁ)

τοί (2) = σοί (dat. of σύ)

τοι (1) = σοι (dat. of σύ, enclitic)

τοι (2) (particle) therefore, accordingly, in
truth, I tell you

τοῖος -η -ον such, of such a kind

τοιοῦτος -αύτη -οῦτο(ν) such, of such a kind

τοῖχος -ου, ὁ wall

τόσ(σ)ος -η -ον so big, so great, so much

τοσ(σ)όσδε = τόσ(σ)ος

τότε then

τοὔνεκα (= τοῦ ἕνεκα) therefore

τόφρα so long, in the meantime

τρεῖς τρία three

τρέπω (aor. ἔτρεψα/ἔτραπον) I turn; mid.
τρέπομαι I turn myself

τρέφω (aor. ἔθρεψα) I bring up, rear

τρέχω (aor. ἔδραμον) I run

τρίπλαξ -ακος with three layers

τρίπολος -ον three times ploughed

τρίπους -οδος, ὁ tripod (three-legged
cauldron)

τρίς three times

τρίτος -η -ον third

Τροίη -ης, ἡ Troy (= Att. Τροία -ας)

τρόμος -ου, ὁ trembling

τροπέω I turn (something) round

τροχός -οῦ, ὁ wheel

τρυγάω I gather harvest from

τρυφάλεια -ας, ἡ helmet

Τρῶες -ων, οἱ Trojans

Τρωϊάς -άδος, ἡ Trojan woman (= Att.
Τρῳάς)

Τρωϊκός -ή -όν Trojan

Τρῳός -ή -όν Trojan; (f. pl. as noun) Trojan
women

τρωπάω I turn, change; mid. τρωπάομαι I
turn myself

τυγχάνω (fut. τεύξομαι, aor. ἔτυχον) I hit,
chance on

Τυδεΐδης -αο/εω, ὁ son of Tydeus (i.e.
Diomedes)

τύμβος -ου, ὁ grave-mound

τύνη = σύ

τύπτω (aor. pass. ἐτύπην) I strike, hit

τυτθός -όν little, small

τῶ/τώ therefore, so

Υ

Ὑάδες -ων, αἱ Hyades (constellation)

ὕδωρ -ατος, τό water, rain

υἱός -οῦ/έος, ὁ son

ὑλακτέω I bark

ὕλη -ης, ἡ wood, forest

ὑμεῖς -ῶν you (pl.)

ὑμέναιος -ου, ὁ wedding song

ὑπάγω I lead under, yoke

ὑπαί = ὑπό

ὕπαιθα in support of (+ gen.)

ὑπασπίδια under cover of a shield

ὕπειμι I am under (+ dat.)

ὑπέκ out of, from among, out from under (+
gen.)

ὑπεκφεύγω I escape

ὑπέρ (+ acc.) over, beyond; (+ gen.) over

ὑπερβασίη -ης, ἡ presumptuousness (= Att.
ὑπερβασία -ας)

ὑπέρβιος -ον over-violent

ὑπερθρῴσκω (aor. ὑπερέθορον) I leap over

ὑπερφιάλως excessively

ὑπερῷον -ου, τό upper room
ὑπηοῖος -η -ον at dawn
Ὕπνος -ου, ὁ Sleep (personified)
ὑπό (+ acc.) through, throughout, below; (+
    gen.) by, because of, at the hands of, to the
    accompaniment of, under; (+ dat.) under,
    by, by the agency of; (as adv.) underneath,
    in accompaniment
ὑποδείδω I come to fear
ὑποδέχομαι I receive, welcome
ὑπόδρα sternly, with a frown
ὑποδύω I plunge beneath
ὑποείκω I withdraw
ὑποθερμαίνω I warm (something); pass.
    ὑποθερμαίνομαι I grow warm
ὑποθωρήσσω I arm; mid. ὑποθωρήσσομαι I
    arm myself
ὑπολίζων -ονος (comp. of ὀλίγος) on a smaller
    scale
ὑπολύω I loose, undo
ὑπομένω (aor. ὑπέμεινα) I await, withstand
ὑπορρήγνυμαι (aor. ὑπερράγην) I break out,
    burst through
ὑποτίθημι I fix X (acc.) under Y (dat.)
ὑποφήτης -αο/εω, ὁ interpreter
ὑποχωρέω I retreat, give ground
ὕπτιος -η -ον on the back, backwards
ὑσμίνη -ης, ἡ battle
ὕστατος -η -ον last
ὕστερος -η -ον later, too late, next, in turn
ὑφαρπάζω I snatch away
ὑψηλός -ή -όν high
ὑψί on high
ὑψιβρεμέτης -αο/εω high-thundering
ὑψίζυγος -ον high-throned
ὑψίπυλος -ον high-gated
ὑψόσε upward

Φ

φαεινός -ή -όν bright, shining
φαίδιμος (-η) -ον glorious, illustrious
φαίνω I reveal, put forward; mid. φαίνομαι
    (aor. ἐφάνην) I appear, show myself
φάλαγξ -αγγος, ἡ battle line, column
φάλαρα -ων, τά metal plates

φάλος -ου, ὁ metal plate
φάος -εος, τό light, light of deliverance (= Att.
    φῶς φωτός)
φᾶρος -εος, τό robe, shroud
φάσγανον -ου, τό sword
Φέρουσα -ης, ἡ Pherusa (a Nereid)
φέρτατος -η -ον strongest, mightiest
φέρτερος -η -ον better, braver
φέρτρον -ου, τό litter, bier
φέρω I carry, bring; mid. φέρομαι I win
    (something)
φεύγω I run away, flee, escape from
φηγός -οῦ, ἡ oak
φημί I say, speak, think
φθάνω (aor. ἔφθασα/ἔφθην) I anticipate, get
    in first
φθέγγομαι I call out
Φθίη -ης, ἡ Phthia (= Att. Φθία -ας)
φθίμενος -η -ον dead, killed
φθίνω I cause to perish, kill; mid. φθίνομαι I
    perish
φθίω I waste away
φθογγή -ῆς, ἡ voice
φιλέω I love
φιλοπτόλεμος -ον war-loving (= Att.
    φιλοπόλεμος)
φίλος -η -ον dear, pleasing, one's own; (as m.
    noun) friend
φιλότης -ητος, ἡ friendship
φλεγέθω I blaze, flare up
φλόξ φλογός, ἡ flame, blaze
φοβέω I put to flight; mid./pass. φοβέομαι I
    flee, take flight
φόβος -ου/οιο, ὁ flight, panic, fear
Φοῖβος -ου, ὁ Phoebus (epithet or alternative
    name of Apollo)
Φοῖνιξ -ικος, ὁ Phoenix (tutor of Achilles)
φοινός -ή -όν red
φονεύς -έως/ῆος, ὁ killer, murderer
φόνος -ου, ὁ violent death, slaughter, means of
    slaughter; gore, clotted blood
φορεύς -ῆος, ὁ carrier, vintager
φορέω I carry, bear, wear
φόρμιγξ -ιγγος, ἡ lyre
φόως = φάος; φόωσδε to the light

φράδμων -ον observant, shrewd

φράζω (aor. ἔφρασα/ἐπεφραδον) I tell, declare; mid. φράζομαι I consider, think, devise

φρήν φρενός, ἡ mind, heart, soul; pl. (with same sense or) midriff

φρονέω I think, consider, intend

Φρυγίη -ης, ἡ Phrygia (= Att. Φρυγία -ας)

φύγαδε to flight

φυκτά -ῶν, τά means of escape

φυλάκη -ης, ἡ watch, guard

Φύλας -αντος, ὁ Phylas

φυλάσσω I guard, harbour, cherish, observe

Φυλεΐδης -αο/εω, ὁ son of Phyleus

φύλοπις -ιδος, ἡ combat

φῦσαι -ῶν, αἱ (pair of) bellows

φυσάω I blow

φυσιάω I pant, snort

φυτόν -οῦ, τό plant

φωνέω I speak

φωνή -ῆς, ἡ voice

φώς φωτός, ὁ man

X

χάζομαι I draw back, give way

χαίνω (aor. ἔχανον, perf. κέχηνα) I gape

χαίρω I rejoice, enjoy

χαλεπαίνω I rage, am angry, am harsh

χαλεπός -ή -όν hard, difficult

χάλκειος -η -ον (made of) bronze

χάλκεος -ον (made of) bronze, bronze-armoured

χαλκεύω I fashion in metal

χαλκήρης -ες bronze-tipped

χαλκοκορυστής -ᾱο/έω bronze-helmeted, bronze-armoured

χαλκός -οῦ, ὁ bronze; copper

χαλκοχίτων -ωνος bronze-clad

Χάλκων -ωνος, ὁ Chalcon (a Myrmidon)

χαμάδις/χαμᾶζε to the ground

χαμαί on the ground, to the ground

χαμαιευνής -αο/εω sleeping on the ground

χαράδρη -ης, ἡ mountain torrent (= Att. χαράδρα -ας)

χαρίεις -εσσα -εν (-εντος) pleasing, handsome

Χάρις -ιτος, ἡ Charis (Grace)

χάρμη -ης, ἡ battle, joy of battle

χατίζω I have need of (+ gen.)

χείρ χειρός/χερός, ἡ hand

Χείρων -ωνος, ὁ Chiron (a centaur)

χερμάδιον -ου, τό stone

χέω I pour, shed

χηλός -οῦ/οῖο, ὁ chest, box

χθών χθονός, ἡ earth, ground

Χίμαιρα -ας, ἡ the Chimaera (a monster)

χιτών -ῶνος, ὁ tunic

χλαῖνα -ης, ἡ cloak

χόανος -ου, ὁ melting-pit

χόλος -ου, ὁ anger, wrath, bile

χολόω I enrage, anger; mid./pass. χολόομαι I am angry (about, + gen.)

χορός -οῦ, ὁ dance, dancing-floor

χραισμέω I am useful to, help (+ dat.)

χρεώ -όος, ἡ need

χρή it is necessary

χρίω I anoint

χρύσε(ι)ος -η -ον golden, made of gold

χρυσηλάκατος -ον of the golden arrow (or distaff)

χρυσός -οῦ/οῖο, ὁ gold

χρώς -ωτός/οός, ὁ skin, flesh, body

χωλεύω I limp

χωλός -ή -όν lame

χώομαι I am angered about (+ gen.)

χωρέω I give way, withdraw (from, + gen.)

χώρη -ης, ἡ space, place, land (= Att. χώρα -ας)

Ψ

ψαύω I touch

ψήρ ψηρός, ὁ starling

ψιάς -άδος, ἡ raindrop

ψυχή -ῆς, ἡ breath, spirit

Ω

ὦ O (+ voc.)

ὤ μοι (ἐγώ) alas! ah me!

ὧδε so, (in) this way

ὠθέω (aor. ἔωσα/ὦσα) I push, thrust

ὦκα quickly

Ὠκεανός -οῦ/οῖο, ὁ Oceanus

ὠκύμορος -ον short-lived, doomed to an early death

ὠκύπους -ποδος swift-footed

ὠκύς -εῖα/έα -ύ swift

ὦμος -ου, ὁ shoulder

ὠμοφάγος -ον eating raw flesh

Ὠρείθυια -ης, ἡ Oreithyia (a Nereid)

ὥρη -ης, ἡ season, time (= Att. ὥρα -ας)

Ὠρίων -ωνος, ὁ Orion (constellation)

ὥς so, thus (= Att. οὕτως)

ὡς as, like, that, so that, in order that, when; I wish that, how …!

ὠτειλή -ῆς, ἡ wound

Grammar Index

References are to the notes on the lines indicated.